Symbols of Eternity

The Art of Landscape Painting in China

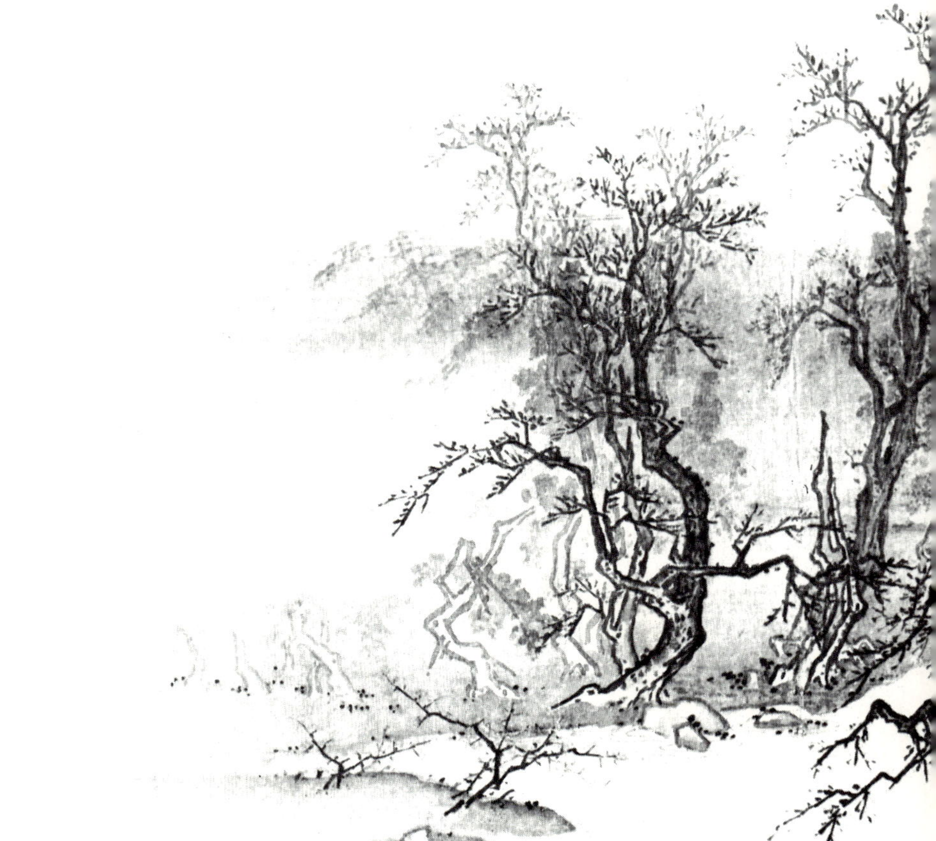

MICHAEL SULLIVAN

Symbols of Eternity

THE ART OF LANDSCAPE PAINTING IN CHINA

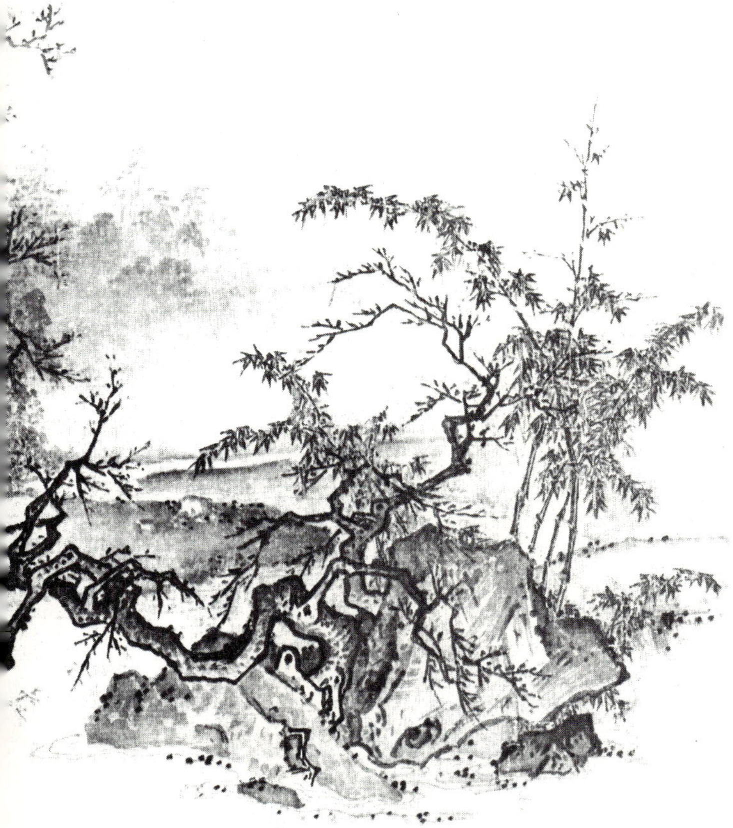

CLARENDON PRESS · OXFORD
1979

Oxford University Press, Walton Street, Oxford OX2 6DP

OXFORD LONDON GLASGOW
NEW YORK TORONTO MELBOURNE WELLINGTON
KUALA LUMPUR SINGAPORE JAKARTA HONG KONG TOKYO
DELHI BOMBAY CALCUTTA MADRAS KARACHI
NAIROBI DAR ES SALAAM CAPE TOWN

ISBN 0 19 817351 2

Printed in the United States of America

Contents

Plates

Preface

This book has grown out of the Slade Lectures, given at Oxford in the spring of 1974. It was written for my patient and sympathetic audience at the Playhouse Theatre, and for anyone who loves art but knows little about Chinese painting, and would like to approach a little closer to one of the great artistic traditions of the world. So it is not a book for specialists, nor is it a history of Chinese landscape painting, but rather an attempt to interpret its history.

I have tried to suggest something of the richness of Chinese landscape painting, its vitality, its depth and its range. But there came a difficulty. One can write about European landscape painting with little regard to politics, philosophy, or the social position of the artist. The reader already has enough history for his purpose, while it is little help in understanding the art of Turner, say, or of Cézanne, to know just where they stood in society, and whether or not they had read Aristotle or Descartes. That is not true of China. The Chinese landscape painter, generally a member of the very small educated élite, was deeply affected by politics and the rise and fall of dynasties, very much aware of his own position in society, steeped in history and philosophy. Even his choice of style often had political, philosophical, and social implications. We need to know something about these things if we are to understand why he painted as he did, for they are not just the "background" to his art, but a part of his total experience in the world. I hope that I have not burdened the reader with too much history and philosophy, however, and that the pictures will speak for themselves, for it is not in the artist's learning, but in his dialogue with the medium, that the mystery and the beauty lie.

This book, which differs a good deal from the lectures as they were given, was written at Oxford under the happiest circumstances while I held a Visiting Fellowship at St. Antony's College, and received generous support from the National Endowment for the Humanities in Washington, D.C. I should like to express my gratitude to them, and to our friends and colleagues who made our sojourn at Oxford so conducive to thinking and writing. I should also like to thank the staff of the Ashmolean Museum and the Oriental Institute for their hospitality, and David Piper particularly for reading the manuscript and making some valuable suggestions. To the collectors and museums that have supplied me with illustrations and allowed their reproduction I should like also to express my thanks.

Once again Allen and Carmen Christensen have given their generous support to our work, and I am grateful, as ever, to them.

My wife Khoan has been with me in this enterprise ever since the theme came to me climbing the hills above Lake Como one summer afternoon, as the nightingales sang in the woods of San Martino, with Nibby, Alan, and Khoan. This book is dedicated to them.

M.S.

A Note on the Pronunciation of Chinese Names

Chinese names often present the Western reader with a problem, especially as there is no really satisfactory way of romanising them. I have used the Wade-Giles system in this book because it is the most widely known, and a little less confusing than the new Chinese *pin-yin* system.

The important thing to remember is that hard consonants are aspirated, while soft consonants use the same initial letter or letters without the aspirate. For example the dynasties are T'ang and Ch'ing, not Tang (which would be pronounced Dang) and Ching (pronounced Jing). Likewise we have Ch'u and Chu (pronounced Ju), Ch'ou and Chou (pronounced Jou), K'ai and Kai (Gai), P'ei and Pei (Bei), and so on. So the name of the painter Ku K'ai-chih is pronounced Gu Kai-je, that of Tung Ch'i-ch'ang pronounced Dung Chi-chang. The Chinese also distinguish the Umlaut, as in Chu and Chü, Ch'uan and Ch'üan, and have an aspirated initial sound *hs*, as in *hsi*, *hsün*, *hsiao*, etc.

For well-known place names I have followed the customary Chinese Post Office spelling, e.g. Peking (which in Wade-Giles would be Pei-ching) and Kiangsi (Wade-Giles, Chiang-hsi).

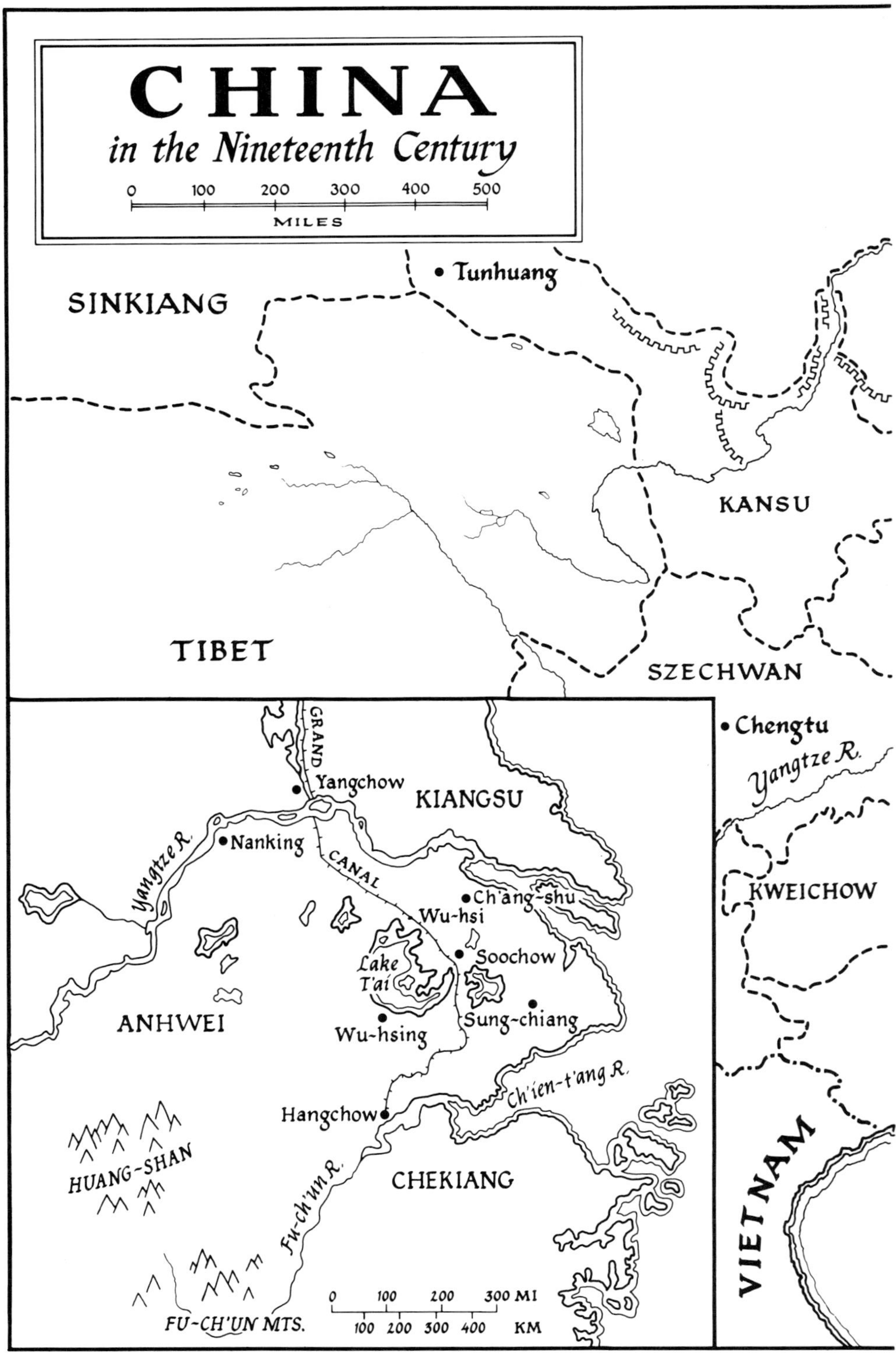

China, with an inset showing the centres of art and scholarship in the Yüan and Ming dynasties

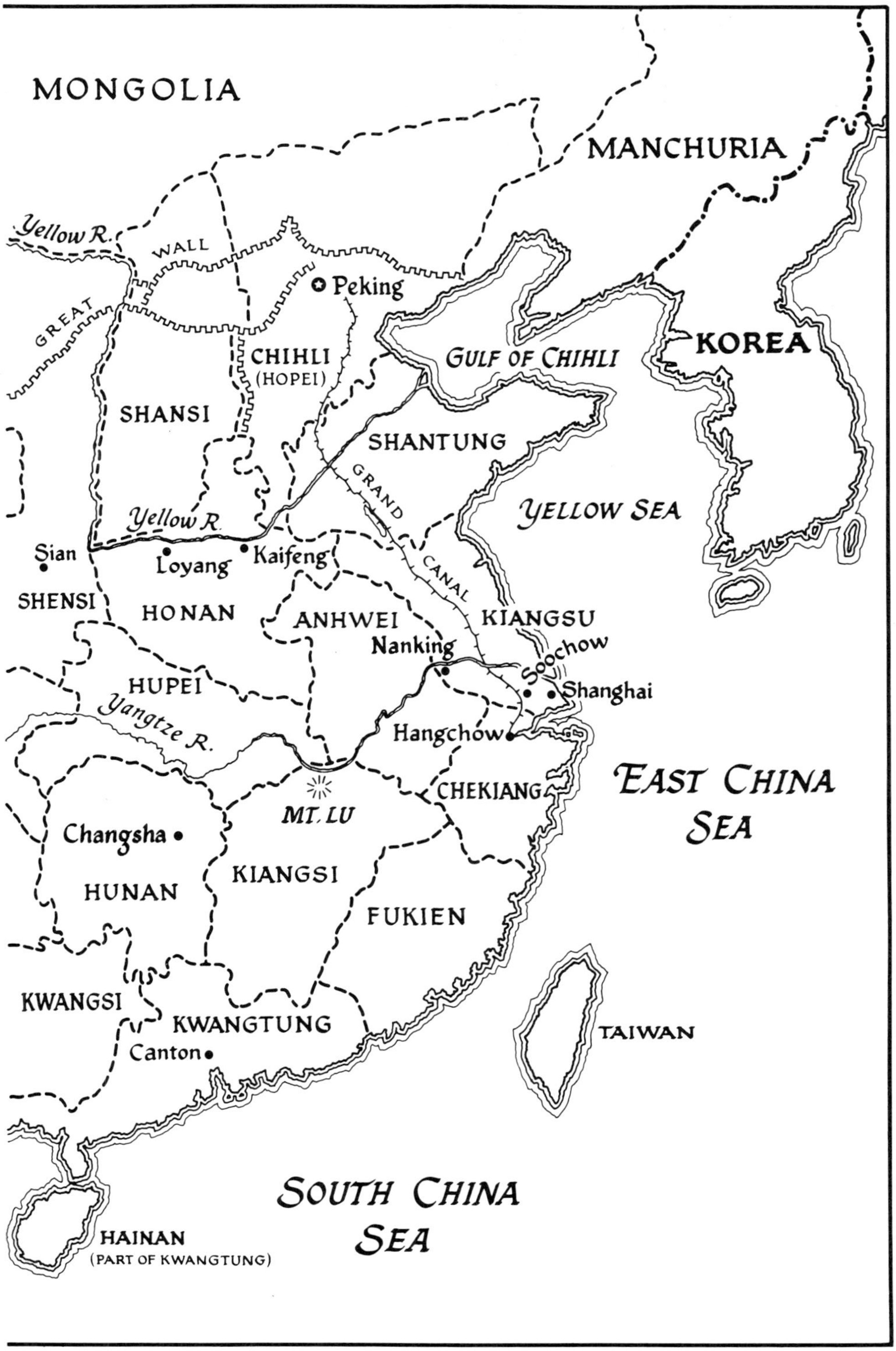
MONGOLIA
MANCHURIA
Yellow R.
WALL
GREAT
Peking
CHIHLI
(HOPEI)
GULF OF CHIHLI
KOREA
SHANSI
SHANTUNG
GRAND
CANAL
YELLOW SEA
Yellow R.
Sian
Loyang
Kaifeng
SHENSI
HONAN
ANHWEI
KIANGSU
Nanking
Soochow
Shanghai
HUPEI
Yangtze R.
Hangchow
EAST CHINA
SEA
CHEKIANG
MT. LU
Changsha
HUNAN
KIANGSI
FUKIEN
KWANGSI
KWANGTUNG
TAIWAN
Canton
SOUTH CHINA
SEA
HAINAN
(PART OF KWANGTUNG)

Symbols of Eternity

The Art of Landscape Painting in China

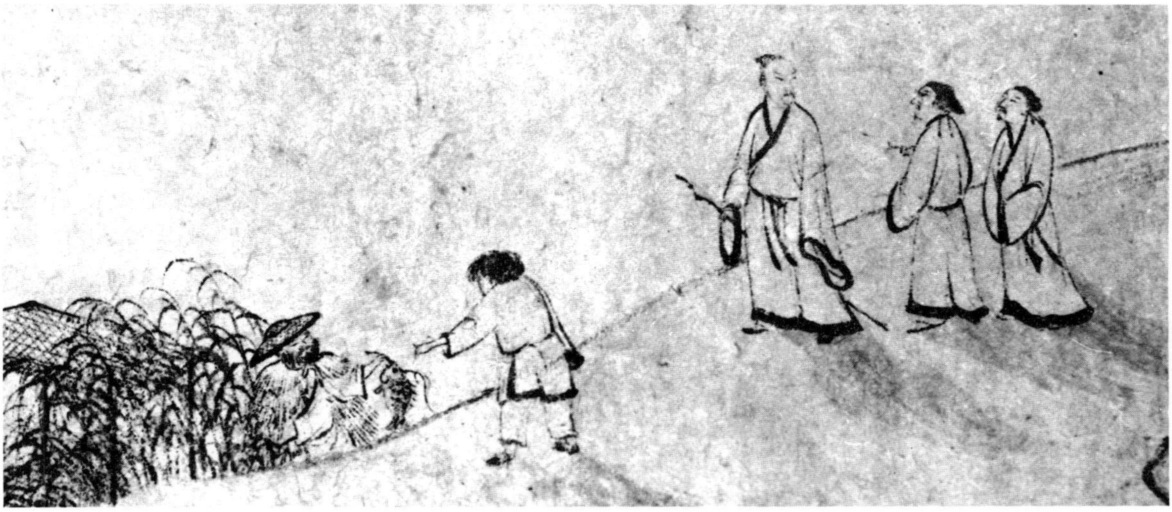

Introduction

Detail of Plate 1 (p. 9), "The Poet and His Friends on the Riverbank Under the Full Moon."

The first impression the reader will almost certainly get on leafing through the pictures in this book is that they are very agreeable to look at. He might not have got quite the same feeling from looking at reproductions of Indian sculpture, or of Flemish paintings of the seventeenth century. The Chinese landscapes have an air of living nature, of harmony and peace, that is not always to be found in the art of other civilizations. After a while the reader may find himself wondering why the same subjects occur over and over again—the same misty mountains, the same scholars gazing at waterfalls or pretending to fish. But if ever, not knowing what the pictures are really about, he begins to feel a little bored by them, never will he be disconcerted or shocked. Never will he find himself asking, "Why on earth did the artist paint a subject like *that*?"—a question that often occurs to the Oriental, and particularly to the cultivated Chinese, when confronted with the battles, martyrdoms, and dead game that seem to him to take up so many acres in our Western picture galleries.

To suggest that the beauty of a painting could lie even partly in its subject matter is to modern Western thinking shockingly philistine. But there is a sense in which this is true of Chinese and indeed of much Oriental art, for to the Chinese the theme of a painting is inseparable from its form, and both are the expression of an all-embracing philosophical attitude toward the visible world. He could never accept a work that was not elevating to the spirit, cleansing and refreshing to the mind, or at least charming and agreeable; and he is quite unable to see how the West can separate form and subject matter, can find, for example, Rubens's *Rape of the Daughters of Leucippus* a satisfying work because it is beautiful in a purely formal sense. To him that is not enough. If he found the rape offensive, as he certainly would, he would not be able to admire the picture, however much he admired the artist's skill. Indeed, the more beautifully it was painted the more objectionable it would be. Mao Tse-tung, speaking of "reactionary" art, said that the higher its artistic quality the more poisonous it is. A traditional Chinese critic would not have put it quite that way, of course, but he too would have insisted on the unity of form and content, for he saw things whole.

We can enjoy a Chinese landscape painting as a pure aesthetic experience, much in the way we enjoy music. The atmosphere and tone of the painting; the rhythmic movement of the calligraphic line; the touch of the artist in the brushwork; and, in the landscape handscrolls we unroll little by little as we move through them, the dimension of time—all evoke some of the same kinds of response that music does. Indeed, we could pursue the analogy a little further, because in listening to music we are, for the most part, listening to familiar works, and this does not trouble us at all. In the hands of a master interpreter each familiar work is born again, and much of our pleasure comes from the performer's understanding of the theme, from subtle nuances of his interpretation and, above all, from his touch. In Chinese painting, too—particularly from the fourteenth century on—what matters is not the novelty of the theme (which might be a very hackneyed one) but the artist's interpretation of it, and the quality of his touch.

Yet while our response to the "music" of Chinese painting is fundamental to our enjoyment of it, we will never get very far if we stop at the merely visual pleasure that it gives us; this is where the analogy with music breaks down. Beethoven's late quartets have their place in history, but knowing precisely where they belong is not really necessary for a complete enjoyment of them, for they speak for themselves, outside time. This is not quite so true of Chinese painting, because the Chinese painter was also a scholar very much aware of the sources of his technique—or techniques, for he might be master of many—drawing sustenance from the work of earlier masters as he ranged back and forth over the centuries. Many of the paintings I have chosen for this book, and particularly the later ones, are full of stylistic allusions: Huang Kung-wang, for instance, paints deliberately in the manner of Chü-jan; Wen Cheng-ming, in that of Huang Kung-wang. Missing the references would be like failing to catch an apt quotation in the conversation of a friend; we would miss half the point, and half the pleasure, that the picture had to offer.

It is because the Chinese painter is himself so steeped in history that it is difficult to write of Chinese painting effectively except from a historical point of view. For to him the history of his art became, in the course of time, as rich a source of inspiration as nature itself—in the eighteenth and nineteenth centuries, alas, an even richer source. We often think of China as ageless and unchanging. But Chinese history was turbulent and wavelike, with long periods of stability destroyed by violent convulsions and shifts of cultural gear. The drama of Chinese history is reflected in the arts. Not only did style in painting develop and change in very obvious ways, but the position of the artist in society, his attitude to his art, and the very philosophy of art itself all underwent changes every bit as radical as those that have marked the history of European art from classical times to the present day.

It has taken a long time—four centuries, in fact—for the West to arrive at even the beginning of an understanding of Chinese painting. After a promising start in the seventeenth century, the history of European reactions to it is one of indifference, condescension, or mere amusement. The great Jesuit missionary Matteo Ricci (1552–1610) mentioned it only in passing in his encyclopedic account of China, but a Portuguese scholar, Alvarez de Semedo, writing in 1635, was a little more perceptive, for he noted that though weak in figure painting, the Chinese artist excelled in depicting nature: "In *Painting,*" he wrote, "they have more curiositie, than perfection. They know not how to make use either of *Oyles* or of *shadowing* in this art; and do therefore paint the figures of men without any grace at all: but trees, flowers, birds, and such things, they paint very much to the life. But at present there are some of them, who have been taught by us, that use *Oyles*, and are come to make perfect pictures."*

Joachim von Sandrart, in the first attempt at a world history of art, published in Amsterdam in 1675, described a group of paintings he claimed he had obtained from the Chinese themselves (he probably saw them in the Jesuit College in Rome), although he rather spoils his account by reproducing as "the greatest Chinese painter" an engraving of a cheerful African named Higiemondo. Writers of the eighteenth century took

**The History of that Great and Renowned Monarchy of China, lately written in Italian [sic] by F. Alvarez Semedo, a Portughese* (London, 1655).

even less note of Chinese painting than did those of the seventeenth, for by now Europe was flooded with porcelains and screens, and they no doubt felt they had the measure of this exotic and purely decorative art, the essential frivolity of which was finally summed up in Charles Lamb's famous essay on "that world before perspective," the painting on a Chinese teacup.

Lamb's gentle sally was almost the last flutter of *chinoiserie,* after which amusement at the quaintness of the arts and crafts of China was chilled by the aggressive eastward expansion of the European powers. In the nineteenth century the door to mutual understanding, instead of opening wider, slammed shut, and we can only speculate about what sensitive Western critics might have thought if they had been confronted with some of the great works reproduced in this book. Would they have found them more than merely charming? Could they have grasped even a fraction of what the artist was driving at? It seems doubtful. Nineteenth-century Europe and America, whose view of the benighted Chinese was largely formed by the missionaries, would have thought this unredeemed race quite incapable of the higher levels of art.

What would Ruskin have thought? Might he have found in the great Fan K'uan (Plate 37) something of what he found in Turner—the grandeur, the depth of feeling, the truth to nature? It is pertinent to ask this question, because in some ways Ruskin's attitude toward art, and particularly toward landscape painting, was very Chinese. But he never saw any Chinese paintings, and we will never know. We only know that in 1863, when Sino-European relations were at their lowest ebb, he was touched, very lightly and briefly, by the craze for *japonaiserie* that was sweeping Paris and London. In that year William Michael Rosetti sent him from Paris an album of Japanese landscape prints, and he wrote back, "The book is delightful. . . . I should like to go and live in Japan. . . . I return Japan by book post. The seas and clouds are delicious, the mountains very good."* Seven years later, when Ruskin gave the first of his Slade Lectures at Oxford, Japan was forgotten; and so far as I know he never mentioned Oriental art again.

This is a pity, for though the young Ruskin was perhaps too obsessed with Turner to have eyes for anything as exotic as Chinese painting, Ruskin the mature moralist would have understood it as have few Western writers before the mid-twentieth century. He would have thoroughly approved of the Confucian elements in the outlook of the Chinese scholar-painter, the emphasis on intense study, on the uplifting function

***Rossetti Papers: A Compilation by William Michael Rossetti* (New York, 1903), pp. 25–26.

of art, and on the literatus's obligation to cultivate himself and establish a standard for the whole of society. Yet the socialist in Ruskin would have roundly condemned the social and intellectual snobbery of the literati, and would have shared Mao Tse-tung's conviction that the artist must serve society, and that before we can talk about the freedom of the artist the people whom he serves must be educated, prosperous, and secure. And surely the man who could write "Mountain terrain affords the greatest grandeur in all nature[;] if any element of landscape could breed *virtue*, it was the mountains" would have found himself completely at home in the company of such a man as Huang Kung-wang. How many modern Western critics, one wonders, are equipped to approach Far Eastern painting from so many directions?

Though in the last decades of the nineteenth century growing numbers of Western critics and connoisseurs were writing enthusiastically about Japanese art, none gave so much as a glance in the direction of China. The curtain lifted very suddenly when, within a space of eight years (1905 to 1912), Lionel Giles, Friedrich Hirth, Laurence Binyon, and Ernest Fenollosa all published books on Chinese painting. There were at this time hardly any Chinese pictures of quality in Western collections. Giles and Hirth went to the Chinese texts, Binyon and Fenollosa to the Japanese ones, for the Japanese had been collecting Chinese paintings for 1,200 years. The great Arthur Waley suffered from the same handicaps—he saw very few Chinese paintings of any quality—but his knowledge of Chinese literature and poetry was deep, and we can read his brilliant *Introduction to the Study of Chinese Painting* (1923) for the sheer pleasure of contact with his penetrating mind and his limpid literary style. It was Osvald Sirén—travelling tirelessly through the East, Europe, and America, photographing, cataloguing, describing—who laid the foundations for a systematic study of Chinese painting in a series of volumes published between 1934 and 1958. Since Sirén, the monographs have begun to be written, one by one, and it might be said that now the study of Chinese painting stands about where the study of Italian painting stood at the turn of the century. It is thanks to these many scholars, chiefly in China, Japan, and America, that we no longer need look on Chinese painting, as Binyon and Fenollosa did, as redolent of a vague poetic "mood"; nor need we feel, as Bernard Berenson did, that while exotic, it was ultimately wearisome because it lacked the "tactile values" he considered essential to all good art.

If today we understand Chinese painting a little better, it is not simply because of the labours of the scholars, or because our collections have become so rich, but because we ourselves have changed. Not only the art, but the philosophy and the religion of the Far East have become intelligible to us to a degree that would have been unthinkable a century ago. For we have arrived, chiefly through the physical sciences, at a view of the nature of reality that in certain fundamental respects is strikingly similar to the view that the East arrived at, through intuition and reflection, over 2,000 years ago. The East has expressed this view in metaphysics, poetry, and the visual arts, while the West formulates it in scientific or mathematical terms—although now, in expressing concepts that lie on the outer frontiers of science, Western scientists are reaching out toward Oriental thought. Einstein once said that "if there is any religion that would cope with modern needs, it would be Buddhism"; and Maurice Percheron has written "We see physics joining Buddhism in its theory of universal flux, of the lack of substance inherent in matter, of impermanence, of fundamental error attaching to the testimony of the senses and consequent doubt regarding the validity of the mind's speculations."

Western art, since Kandinsky, has found in such movements as Abstract Expressionism, Kinetic Art, and Environmental Art ways of expressing thoughts and feelings about the natural world as we are beginning to apprehend it that are, in some ways, very close to those of the East. Much of modern Western art is concerned not with solid objects in space but with space itself; with the world beyond the telescope and the microscope; with movement, energy, rhythm, and the mysterious forces that animate matter—concepts expressed in such terms as the Hindu *atman* and *prāna*, the Buddhist *samsāra*, the Chinese *ch'i-yün*. We cannot say that Chinese and Western art now speak the same language: that would be to deny history. But having arrived at this point—the one through meditation and intuition, the other through the sciences—they have at least begun a dialogue, and can say to each other "I think I see what you mean."

Next to the supremely difficult art of calligraphy, the Chinese have for centuries looked on landscape painting as the highest form of visual art. Unlike bamboo, flower, or figure painting, with which the painter can take few liberties, landscape painting in China is a language of extraordinary richness and breadth, able to embody the strongest emotional and poetic feelings and the profoundest philosophical and metaphysical ideas. What of Zen painting, we might ask? Surely that is a tradition that goes straight to the heart of the matter? It does indeed, but in doing so it goes beyond ideas, beyond even forms. Zen (or Ch'an) art denies history, tradition, the intellect, poetry, literature, even style itself, for to the extent to which a painting concerns itself with these things it ceases to be Zen. In essence, Zen painting is an act, not a thing. Zen art stands outside place and history in a timeless, existential present. To speak of the history of Zen painting is a contradiction in terms.*

To convey so much, Chinese landscape painting must be much more than the painting of a landscape. When the European masters went beyond the world of their own experience, it was generally into the realm of myth and legend. We think of Claude Lorraine, inspired by Ovid and Vergil, painting his ideal landscapes that conjure up a Golden Age. But as Kenneth Clark pointed out in *Landscape into Art*, the history of the ideal landscape was brief: people simply ceased to believe in it.† The ideals that illuminate Chinese landscape painting are of a much more enduring kind. For its forms, often as generalised as those of Claude or Poussin, are far more richly charged with symbolic content. Critics of poetry sometimes said that the poem should go "beyond the image," *hsiang-wai*, carrying the reader into realms of thought and feeling that are only hinted at in the poem itself. In the same way, the landscape painter carries us "beyond the image," on the wings of what Wordsworth in *The Prelude* called the "symbols of Eternity." I am not thinking, any more than Wordsworth was, of specific symbols, such as the pine tree standing for endurance in adversity, or the bamboo for the pliant yet unbreakable spirit of the scholar-official; I am thinking rather of something much vaguer and more all-embracing. The mountains and rocks, trees and water, the very style of the picture *mean* something. But to discover what they mean, we should ideally have seen a great many Chinese paintings, steeped ourselves in the *Classics* and *Histories*, studied Buddhist, Taoist, and Neo-Confucian philosophy, and committed to memory a vast amount of poetry: for that is the kind of equipment that the Chinese amateur would bring to his appreciation of landscape painting. Beyond that, we should not worry too much about symbolism, for it is diffused throughout the painting. Rather, we should remember what Suzanne Langer so aptly said on the subject of the symbolic function of art. "The import of an art symbol," she wrote, "cannot be built up like the meaning of a

*This is taking a somewhat theoretical view of Zen art (being a Chinese school of meditative Buddhism, we should properly use the less familiar Chinese term Ch'an, but I have kept the Japanese "Zen" as it has almost become an English word). While the pure Zen experience is evanescent and inexpressible in the permanent forms of art, Zen painting itself does draw upon techniques and conventions that have their place in history; the landscapes of Mu-ch'i, for example, derive their style and technique ultimately from those of the Southern Sung Academy. But the Zen artist, unlike the scholar-painter and the academician, is not in the least concerned with the sources of his style or his place in the tradition. In this sense Zen painting is, in Chinese terms, uniquely antihistorical.

†*Landscape into Art* (London, 1976), pp. 143–45.

discourse, but must be seen *in toto* first: that is, understanding of a work of art begins with an intuition of the whole presented feeling." If one feels, as I do, that Chinese landscape painting is uniquely consistent in the "wholeness" of its presented feeling, that is perhaps because the Chinese artist's attitude, both to nature and to the art of painting itself, is a philosophical one.

How was it, we might ask, that the Chinese painter managed to convey so much without the aid of those pictorial devices that Western art through much of its history regarded as so essential? For the typical Chinese painting makes no use of scientific perspective, shading, or plastic three-dimensional modelling, and uses colour very sparingly or not at all. I have only found one instance of the use of cast shadows in the whole history of Chinese landscape painting. It occurs on a scroll illustrating Su Tung-p'o's *Second Red Cliff Ode*, where the poet describes how he and his friends stood one night on the river bank while the full moon threw their shadows on the ground behind them (Plate 1). All the artist can manage is a few smudges. But this is not pictorial realism as we understand it so much as a rather crude attempt to translate a vivid poetic image into a pictorial one. As we can see, it was not a success, and among the many later illustrations of this famous poem it never, so far as I can discover, occurs again; painters must have known instinctively that it was "wrong."

The answer appears to be that after experimenting with these devices the Chinese painter—at least if he was in the mainstream of the scholarly tradition—deliberately rejected them because, in one way or another, they actually defeated his purpose. For unlike the Western artist, the Chinese is not trying to create the illusion that he is standing at a particular spot, at a particular moment in the day, and looking at a particular view with the sunlight slanting, shall we say, from the upper right corner of the picture—effects that can only be got by the use of these typically Western skills. Such an approach to his art he would find much too limiting. Rather is he making a general statement about nature. The title of the painting might be *Spring in the South*, or *Fisherman on a Wintry Lake*, but beyond suggesting the scenery of a particular part of China and of a season of the year, the artist does not actually *tell* us very much. His picture was not, in any case, painted out-of-doors; it is a distillation of years of wandering amid "mountains and water" (the literal translation of *shan shui*, the Chinese term for landscape), and a presentation not so much of a unique experience as of an accumulation of experiences recollected in tranquility. He did often sketch *sur le motif*. The tenth-century master Ching Hao, for example, noted how one day he discovered a grove

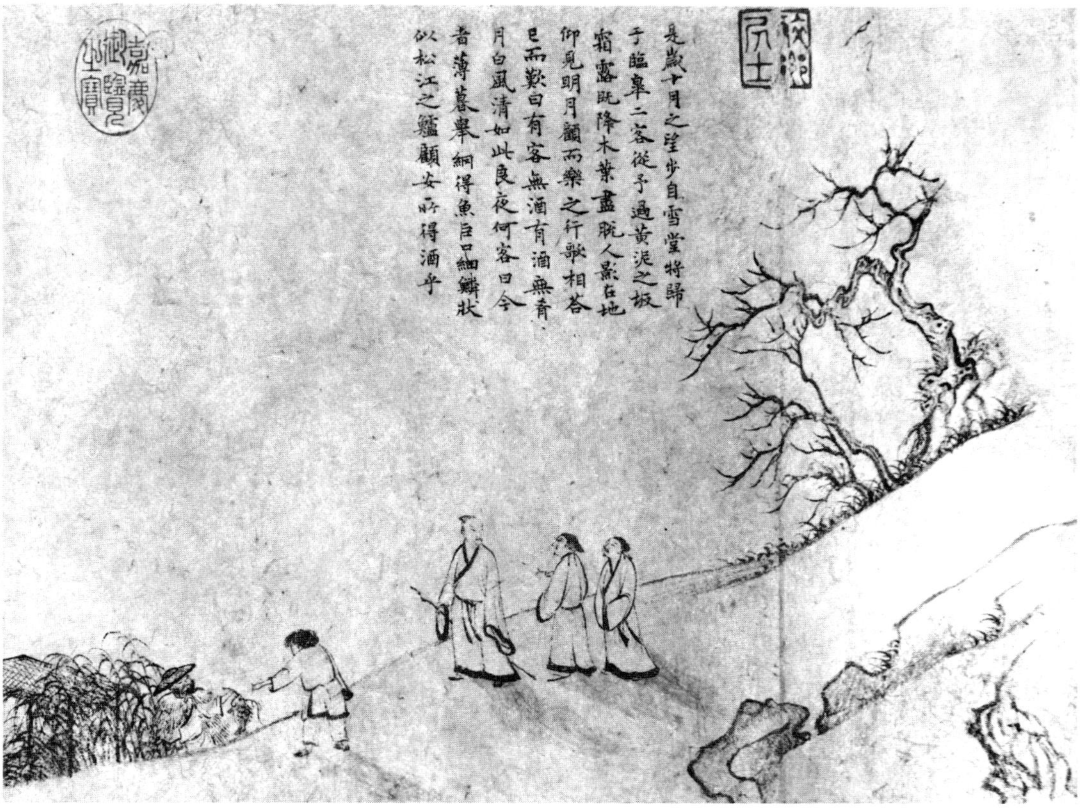

1. Attributed to Ch'iao Chung-ch'ang (early twelfth century): Part of an illustration to the "Second Red Cliff Ode" by the Sung poet Su Tung-p'o: "The Poet and His Friends on the Riverbank Under the Full Moon." Detail of a handscroll; ink on paper. Ht. 29.5 cm. Sung Dynasty. John M. Crawford Collection, New York.

of fantastically contorted pine trees in a hidden valley, and how he went out day after day to sketch them, until after he had drawn "some ten thousand of them" his drawings came to look like the real thing. But these were studies, working material for pictures painted in the studio. If the artist did not throw them away, his children did; for the Chinese never had the notion that any scrap from the hand of a painter was valuable, however hasty, careless, or incomplete. This was particularly so because the "finished" work, unlike the Western oil painting, was—or was supposed to be—just as free and spontaneous in its execution as the slightest sketch. Only the inspired or considered statement mattered; the rest, like the daily exercises of a pianist, was merely a means to that end.

This is a pity, because we learn so much about a painter from his studies and sketches. The page illustrated here (Plate 2)

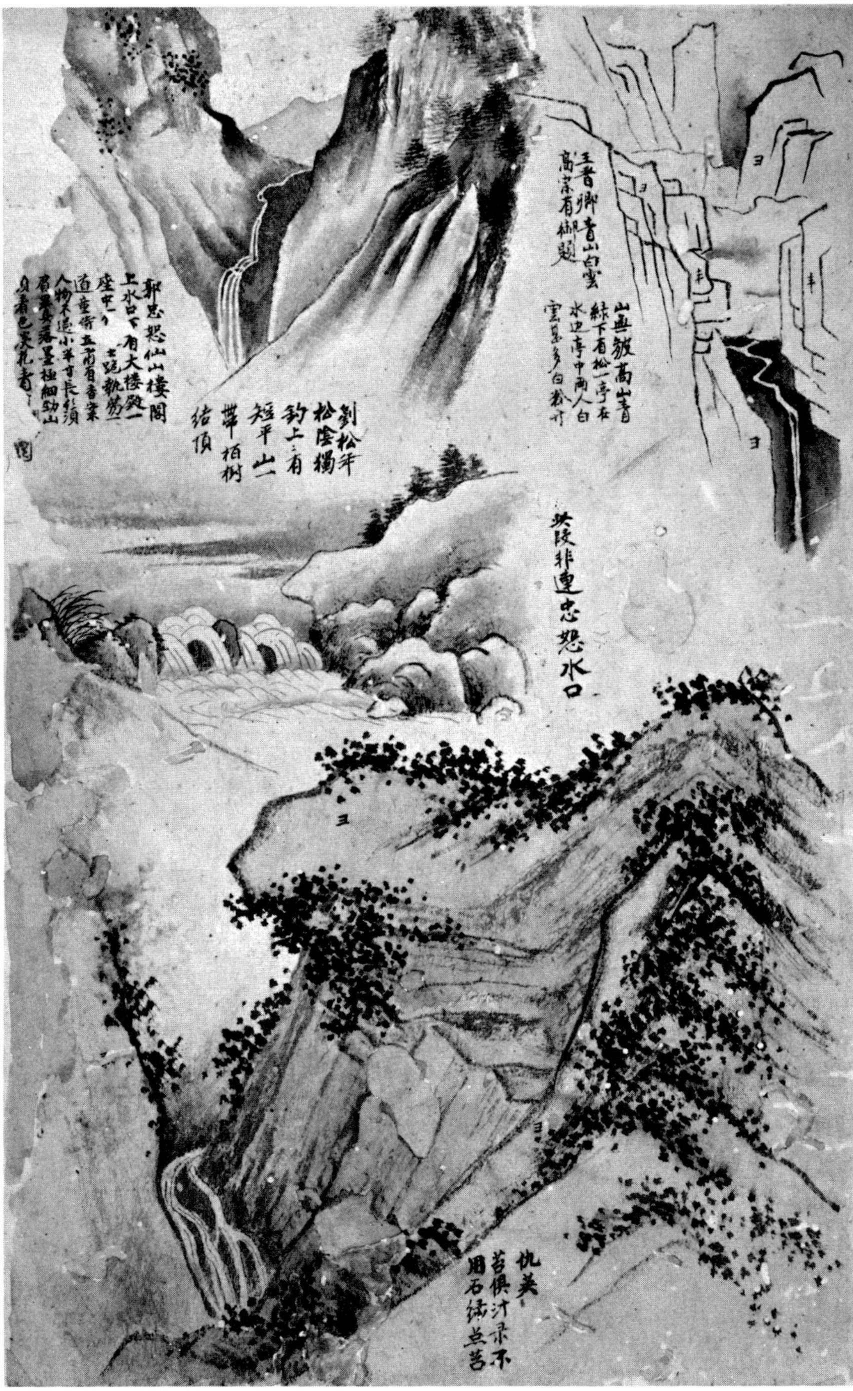

2. *Ku Chien-lung (1606–after 1686): Page of details copied from paintings in the Imperial collection. Album-leaf; ink on paper. Ht. 36.9 cm. Ch'ing Dynasty. Nelson-Atkins Gallery of Art, Kansas City, Mo.*

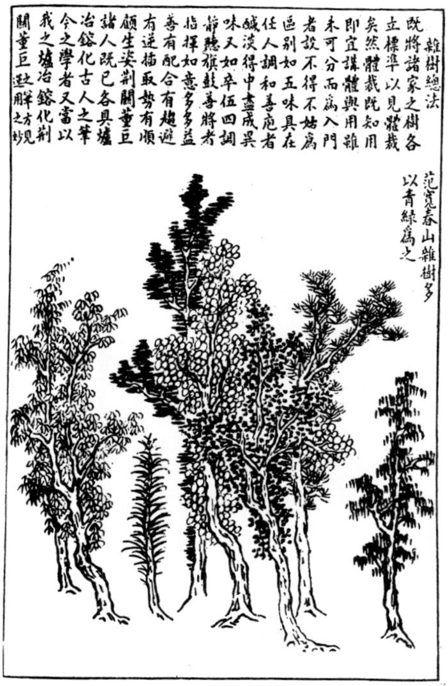

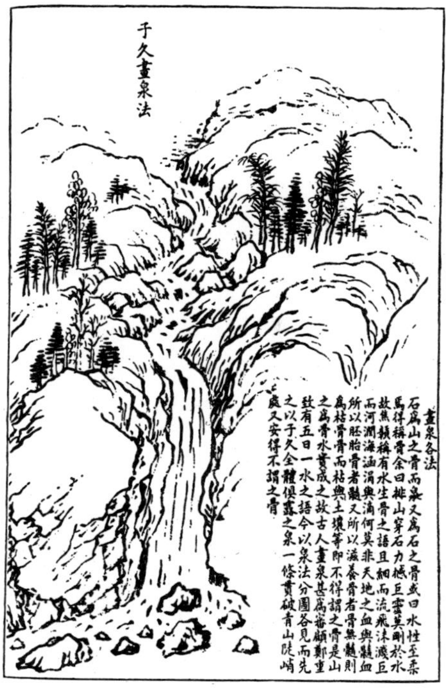

3. Left. How to paint trees in the manner of Fan K'uan. A page from "The Painting Manual of the Mustard Seed Garden" ("Chieh-tzu-yüan hua-chuan"), 1679. Modern photographic reprint. Ch'ing Dynasty.

4. Right. How to paint a waterfall in the manner of Huang Kung-wang. Another page from "The Painting Manual of the Mustard Seed Garden."

is from one of the very few sets of study sheets that have survived. They were done by a minor seventeenth-century court painter who had access to the Imperial collection. His notes tell that they are details copied from paintings by the Sung master Kuo Chung-shu and by the Ming professional artist Ch'iu Ying, whose works—although not the ones these are taken from—are illustrated in Plates 39 and 67. But though the sketches and studies have almost all gone, every Chinese painter for the last 300 years has learned from one of the handbooks of style and technique, such as the famous *Painting Manual of the Mustard Seed Garden*, from which the illustrations showing how to do trees in the manner of Fan K'uan and waterfalls in the manner of Huang Kung-wang are reproduced (Plates 3 and 4). Similar "how to do it" books, though chiefly devoted to the human figure, were very popular in eighteenth-century Europe.

The educated Chinese painter was, unlike his European counterpart, never just a painter. He was something of a philosopher, too; and being a philosopher, his vision did not fade with the passing of his youth, but strengthened and deepened as he grew older. The Chinese have little sympathy for immaturity, or for a romantic view that sees nature as a projection of the artist's own emotion. They would find incomprehensible Wordsworth's poignant "Whither is fled the visionary gleam?," and would mark the irony in the fact that the lament for the decay of the

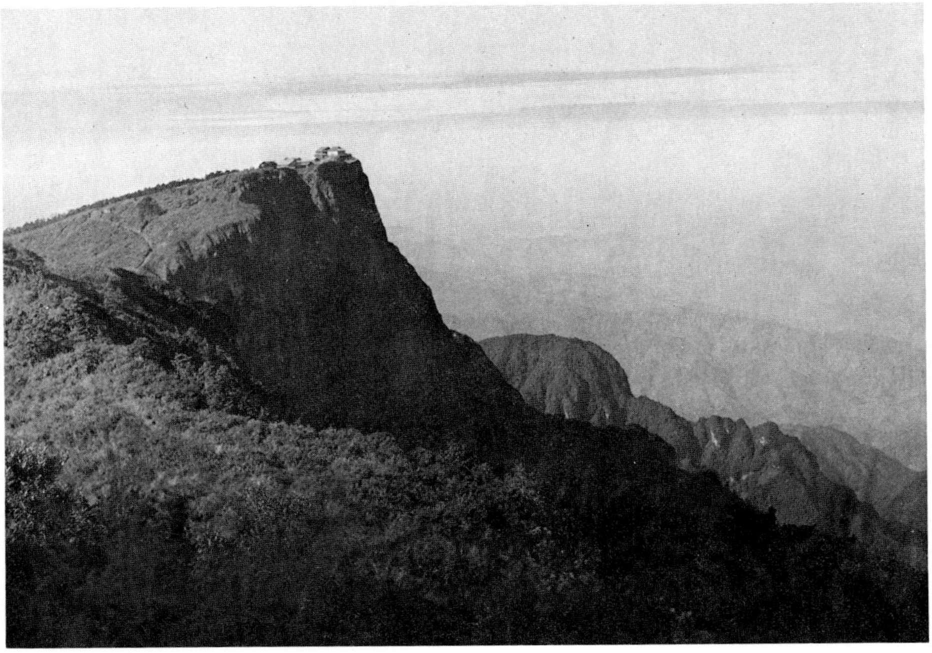

5. Mount Omei in Szechwan.
A view of the temple on the summit.

artist's power to respond to nature in which that famous line occurs is one of the finest poems in the English language. For "the years that bring the philosophic mind" meant to Wordsworth not, as they did to the Chinese philosopher Chuang-tzu, a joyous acceptance of nature, life, and mortality, but a sad resignation, fortified at the end by "the faith that looks through death."* The older the Chinese painter grew, the deeper grew his understanding, the richer his art. The electrifying moments of discovery of the young Chinese wandering in the mountains were not forgotten, but became part of the artistic and philosophical equipment of the mature artist. When Shen Chou wandered from temple to temple on the slopes of Mount Lu and Shih-t'ao scaled the terrifying crags of Huangshan, they must have experienced scores of such moments that remained indelibly printed on their minds; and when later they took up the brush, they drew upon this store of visions and images, distilling from them landscapes that are not so much deliberate exaggerations or distortions—for the photographs in Plates 5 and 6 show how close to reality they are—as attempts to express what is quintessential in the landscape experience.

*At the end of *Intimations of Immortality*, Wordsworth indeed asserts that the love of landscape is with him still, though it has become a reflection of his own melancholy awareness of the transience of human existence (a view more Japanese than Chinese): ". . . The Clouds that gather round the setting sun/ Do take a sober colouring from an eye/ That hath kept watch o'er man's mortality. . . ."

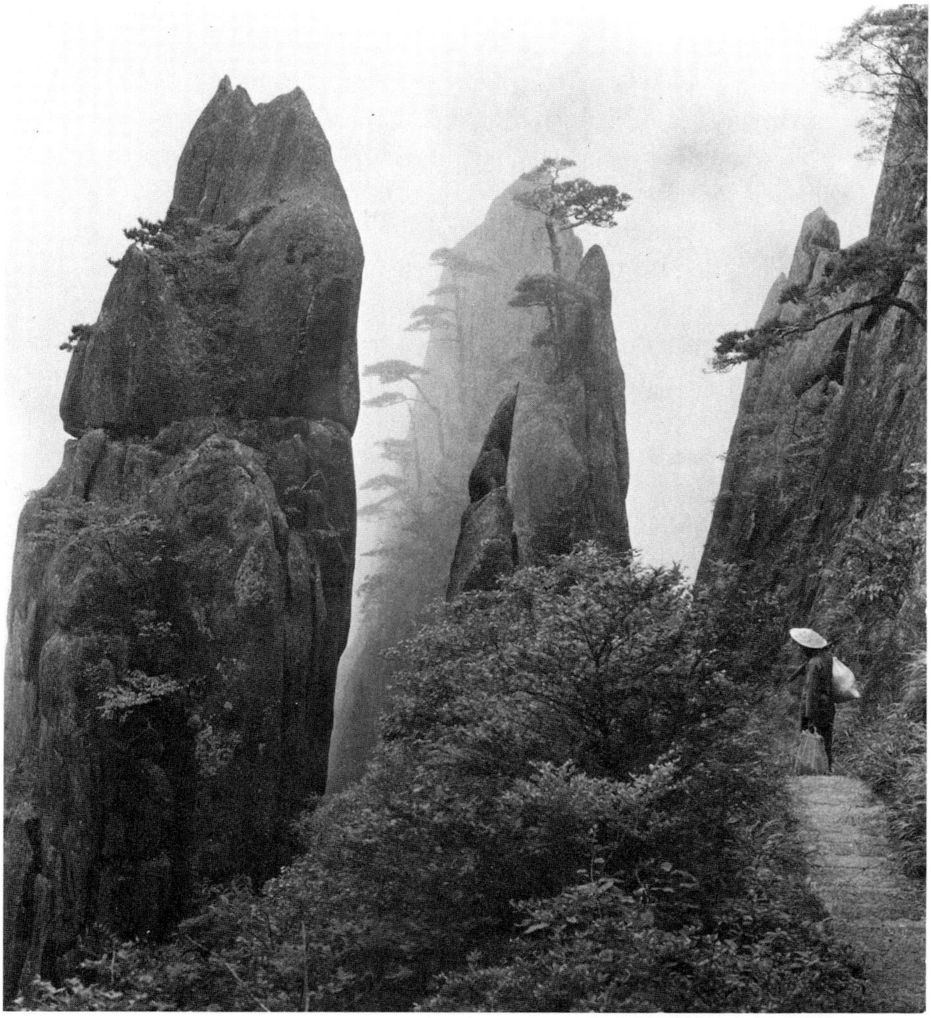

6. Huang-shan in the rain; Anhwei Province. Photograph by Fan Chi-ko.

Some painters, particularly those who lived comfortably amid the lush fields and streams of the Chiang-nan, the region "south of the River," were stay-at-homes who never ventured very far into the interior of the country. Yet their landscape sense was fed by the poems and travel diaries of more adventurous spirits: men like the T'ang poets Tu Fu and Li Po; like Lu Yu, who wrote a vivid account of his journey up the Yangtze in 1170; or like Hsü Hsia-k'o (1580–1641), the greatest traveller of them all. Hsü explored, and described in encyclopedic detail, beauty spots and famous mountains all over China, including those in Fukien and Yunnan in the far south and west, remote tribal country that no gentleman before his time had dared to penetrate, and that few did after him. Many a painter must have had Hsü Hsia-k'o's diary in his library, and must have come to feel that he knew the Hsiao and Hsiang rivers, and the strange landscape of The Nine Easily Confused Peaks in Fukien, as well as if he had been there himself.

With so much experience of nature behind and before them, why, we might ask, do Chinese painters not actually paint what they see? This is a question that has implications far beyond painting, for it applies to the whole realm of artistic expression in China. The Chinese poet, too, likes to generalise. He may, like the painter, use a succession of images that are quite clear and unambiguous in themselves, but that he leaves hovering, as it were, in some unspecified time and space, so that we are often not even sure who or what is the subject of his verse. Take, for instance, these lines by the Sung poet Ch'in Kuan, translated literally, word by word: *

Mist dusk wine-banner slant
Only lean railing exhaust-eye

Here the translator must provide not only tense and number, but subject and sometimes verb as well, to produce a readable paraphrase:

A tavern's banner aslant in the misty dusk
I can only lean on the railings and gaze afar

The translator of these lines, who would no doubt agree that a more poetic rendering of them would not be impossible, writes of this vagueness in Chinese poetry:

> This is at once a source of strength and weakness, for on the one hand it enables the writer to concentrate on essentials and be as concise as possible, while on the other hand it leads easily to ambiguity. In other words, what Chinese poetry gains in conciseness, it loses in preciseness. As far as poetry is concerned, the gain is on the whole greater than the loss, for, as Aristotle observed, the poet is concerned with the universal rather than the particular, and the Chinese poet especially is often concerned with presenting the essence of a mood or a scene. . . . Moreover, the absence of "tense" in Chinese enables the poet to present the scene not from the point of view of any specific time but almost "*sub specie aeternitatis.*"

The Chinese painter's aim is no different from this. He, too, is concerned with the eternal, the essential, and the whole aim of his evolving technique down the centuries has been to achieve this universal quality.

*James J. Y. Liu, *Major Lyricists of the Northern Sung* (Princeton, N.J., 1974), p. 107.

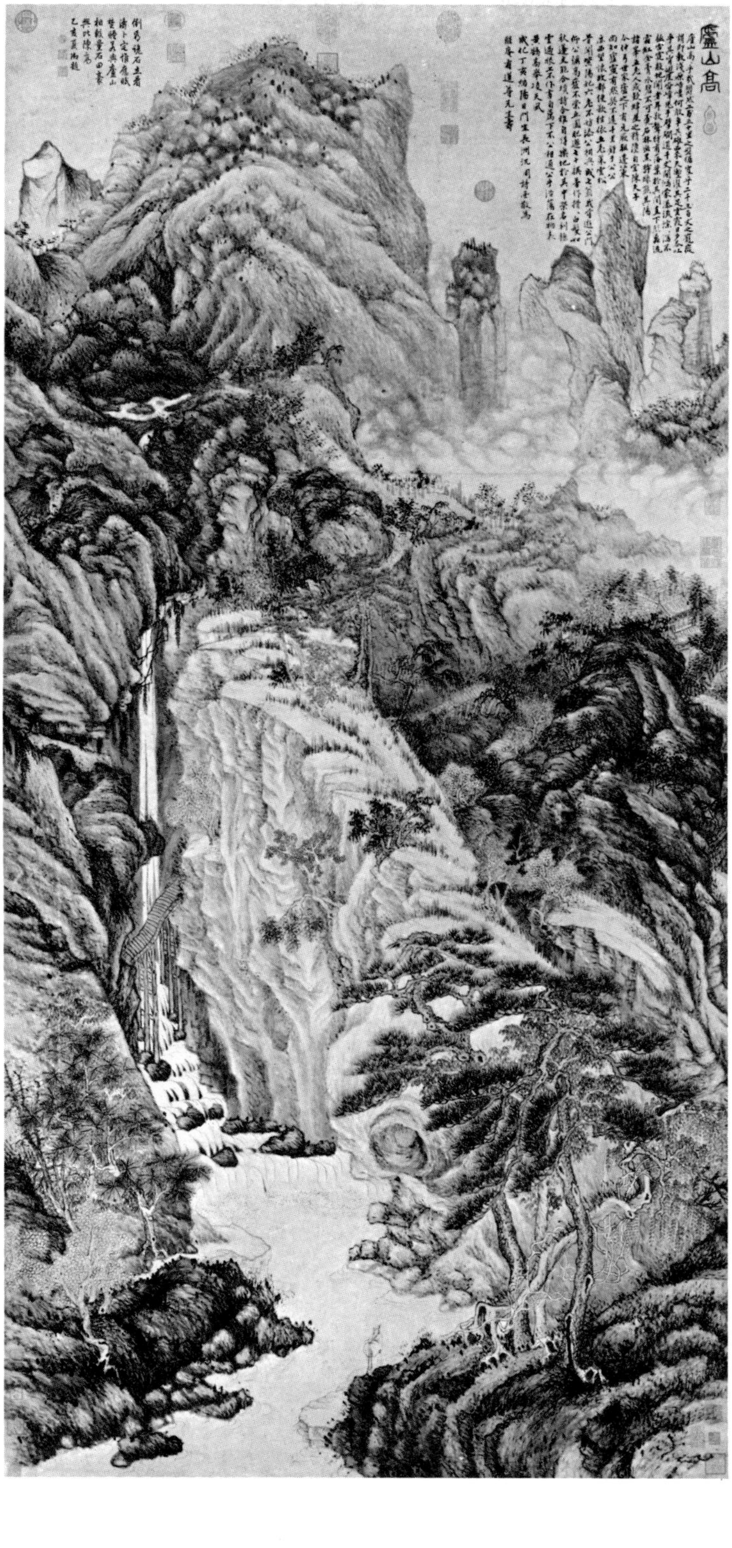

7. Shen Chou (1427–1509): "Towering Mount Lu." Painted for Shen Chou's teacher Ch'en K'uan in 1467. Hanging scroll; ink and colour on paper. Ht. 193.8 cm. Ming Dynasty. National Palace Museum, Taipei.

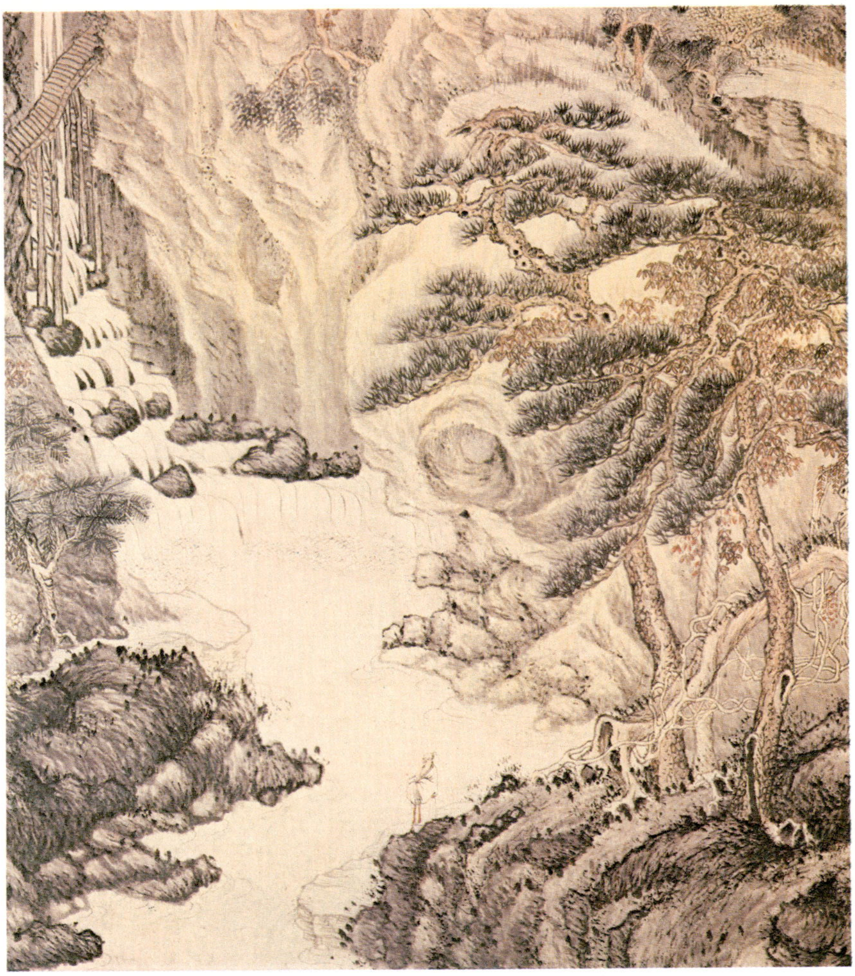

8. Detail of Shen Chou, "Towering Mount Lu."

But general statements, whether in poetry or painting, however lofty and true, sooner or later become boring. It is here that the artist's inscription, and those of his friends and others who saw the painting, often help to fix the artist's purpose and source of inspiration, to establish the occasion when the picture was painted, and so to hold our interest after the charm of the first encounter with the picture's beauty has faded.

The message of the painting, therefore, is carried not merely by the artist's skill in representing nature accurately—although, almost in spite of himself, he may be very skilful indeed—but by the theme, by the animating power of his brushwork, by his choice of style, and, increasingly in later centuries, by his inscription. A typical example of this synthesis of painting, poetry, and calligraphy is the very richly conceived landscape by the Ming Dynasty artist Shen Chou (1427–1509), *Towering Mount Lu,* illustrated here (Plates 7 and 8). The subject—ostensibly—is a famous mountain in central China much frequented by Taoists, poets, and painters. The artist chose it not merely because of its associations, however, but because it suggested the noble character of his teacher, Ch'en K'uan. Shen Chou's poem at the top, after describing the wonders of the mountain, pays a graceful compliment to Ch'en:

> I was one who listened about his door
> Looking up at his lofty eminence
> Mount Lu is no longer high . . .

As for the style, Shen Chou has deliberately chosen—the fact that he *could* choose is a feature of later Chinese painting that will concern us very much in this book—that of the fourteenth-century master Wang Meng, one of the great figures of the Yüan Dynasty whom many later painters sought to emulate. So we may interpret this picture in at least three ways: as an evocation of the spectacular scenery of Mount Lu, with its famous flying bridge rather awkwardly obvious in the centre; as the artist's tribute to a revered teacher; and as a form of homage to Wang Meng, and so to the tradition itself.

This, of course, is only one kind of Chinese landscape painting, and there are many. It would be illuminating to compare, for example, the landscapes in Plates 83 and 91, both painted in the last years of the seventeenth century, to see whether we could find in the landscape painting of Western Europe in the same period any two pictures so different in style, technique, feeling, and *intention*. I very much doubt it. Moreover, not only were these quite different kinds of landscape painted at the same time, but the aims and methods of the Chinese painter have changed profoundly during the last thousand years. It could be said that Western landscape painting, almost to the end of the nineteenth century, moved toward an ever-greater truth to nature as observed by the eye of the artist. In China, by contrast, the painter's purpose shifted many centuries ago from representation to expression, or to the creative reworking of the tradition itself.

If what I have written makes Chinese painting seem repetitive, excessively literary, or absorbed in itself, I would remind the reader of what I said at the beginning about music; for Chinese painting is not only an expressive art but an interpretive one as well, and the beauty, when all's said and done, is in the artist's touch, which is his brushwork. Not only must the way in which he plies his brush fix the essential character of trees, rocks, and mountains, but the brushwork must itself be alive—it must dance on the paper or silk, for only thus can the artist animate what would otherwise be a set of lifeless conventions. Like the touch of the pianist, the vitality of the brushwork (a quality that painting shares with its twin, calligraphy) not only brings form to life, but reveals the personality of the painter himself—transmitting a kind of excitement, an élan, that is often lost in the labouriously finished Western oil painting. If the brushwork, in the eyes of traditional critics, has this animating quality, the painting is admirable; if not, however skilfully painted, it is a dead thing.

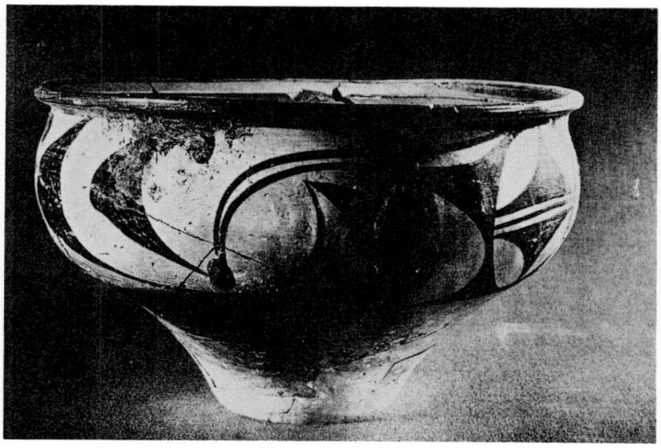 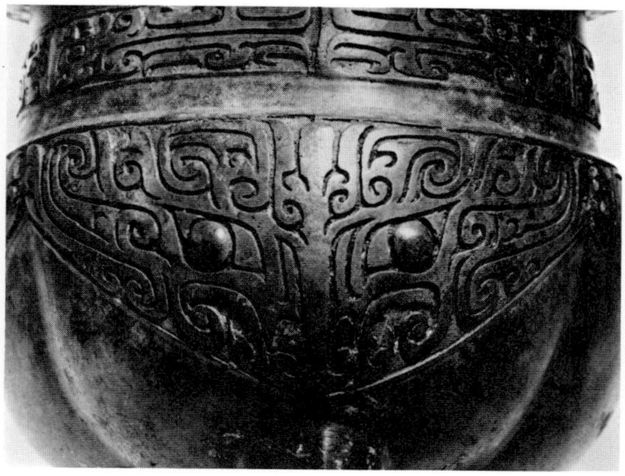

1 Art into Landscape
Painting Before A.D. 600

The vital rhythms that are fundamental to Chinese painting were present in Chinese art long before the first landscape was ever painted. They enliven the volutes that decorate the painted pottery of the late Stone Age (Plate 9); they animate the extraordinary collection of creatures, real and imaginary, that crawl over the surface of the sacrificial bronzes of the Shang Dynasty (Plate 10); they govern the sweeping coils of the jade dragons of the Chou, and the painted lacquer, mirrors, and textiles of the Han (Plate 11). In all we find a line that is alive because it follows the natural movement of the craftsman's arm and hand: you only have to try copying these designs to find that to do it successfully you must let your hand and arm swing quite freely, and never let your pencil come to a complete stop. We find this line, too, in the contour of a Chinese ceramic jar (Plate 12), which preserves in clay forever the life that flowed through the potter's fingers. We find it even governing so intractable a medium as stone sculpture (Plate 13), because sculpture was not a fine art in its own right but always subservient to painting. When landscape painting eventually appeared, it too was animated by the feeling for linear rhythm transmitted down the arm of the painter, through his fingers, to the tip of his brush.

9. Left. Painted pottery vessel from P'ei-hsien, Kiangsu. Diam. 18 cm. Neolithic period.

10. Right. Detail of the decoration of a ritual bronze vessel, li-ting, of the late Shang period (ca. 1200–1000 B.C.). Ashmolean Museum, Oxford.

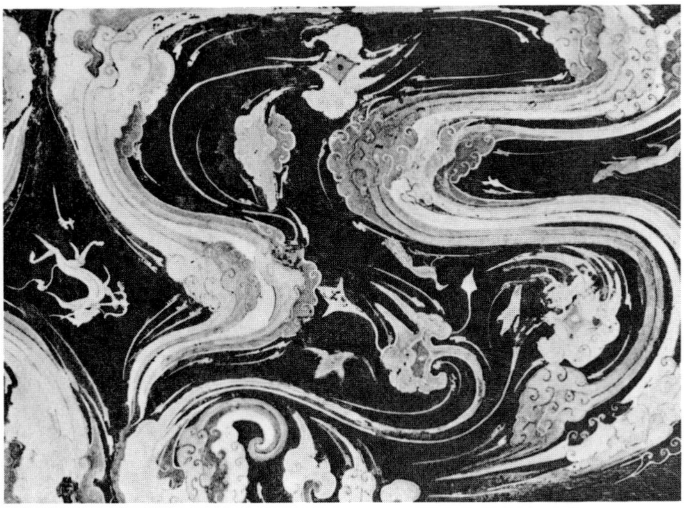

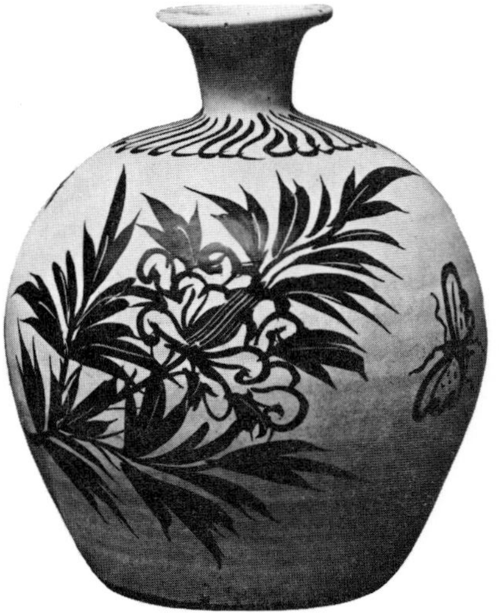

11. *Left. Fairy mountains, clouds, and fabulous beings. Detail of lacquer decoration on the wooden coffin from Tomb No. 1 at Ma-wang-tui, Changsha, Hunan. Western Han Dynasty (second century B.C.). Hunan Provincial Museum, Changsha.*

12. *Right. Jar; stoneware with floral sprays painted under the glaze. Ht. 20 cm. Sung Dynasty. Victoria and Albert Museum, London.*

Landscape painting is a late development in the art of any society, and China is no exception. Indeed, China came late on the scene. We are apt to think Chinese things far older than their Western counterparts, but what survives from the Han Dynasty—roughly the period of early Imperial Rome—chiefly in the form of badly damaged wall paintings in tombs, suggests that the art was much less developed than it was at Pompeii and Herculaneum. Like the Roman frescoes, the earliest Chinese landscapes were no more than settings for some story or legend. The main job of the artisans in the palace workshops was to paint imaginary portraits of Confucian worthies, loyal ministers, filial sons, and virtuous concubines (and their opposites) as an example and a warning to the heir apparent and members of the court. Here landscape played little or no part; nor could it have been much in evidence in the wall paintings of divinities and immortals in the palaces and ancestral shrines, which are all lost. They survive today only in the probably highly fanciful descriptions of them in the rhapsodic prose-poems, called *fu*, of the Han period. Here is a fragment of one of these *fu* describing a fresco cycle in an ancient palace that was already half ruined when the Han poet Wang Yen-shou stumbled upon it: *

*Arthur Waley, *Introduction to the Study of Chinese Painting* (London, 1923), pp. 30–31. I am using the term "fresco" loosely: Chinese wall paintings were always done on dry plaster.

Upon the great walls
Flickering in dim semblance glint and hover
The Spirits of the Dead.
And here all Heaven and Earth is painted, all living things
After their tribes, and all marryings
Of sort with sort: strange spirits of the sea,
Gods of the hills. To all their thousand guises
Had the painter formed
His reds and blues, and all the wonders of life
Had he shaped truthfully and coloured after their kind . . .

Note that in this poem it is not the hills and seas that are painted on the palace walls—the time for that has not yet come—but the spirits that inhabit them. The idea that the landscape could be interesting or significant simply for itself would never have occurred to the Han poet, still less to the Han painter.

To ask how truthfully the painter depicted "all the wonders of life" would be like asking how accurately Fra Angelico painted angels. The miscellany *Han Fei Tzu* tells the story of a painter of feudal times (i.e. before the Han) chatting with the King of Ch'i while doing a painting for him, and remarking that dogs and horses are more difficult to draw than ghosts and spirits. The king asks him why, and he explains that

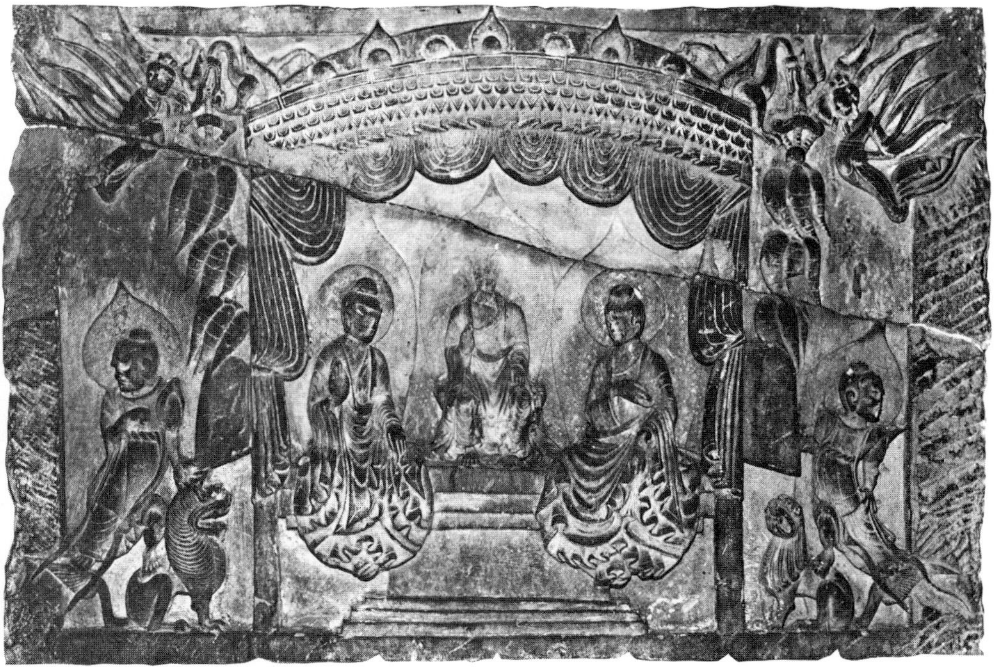

13. Buddha group; detail from a stone stele in Cave 133 at Maichishan, Kansu. Sixth century. Photograph by Dominique Darbois.

everyone has seen dogs and horses but no one has ever seen ghosts or spirits, so no one can tell how skilful the painter is. If this was so, then the delightful tale of the astronomer Chang Heng (78–139) is certainly apocryphal. It seems that Chang Heng went into the mountains to sketch a curious pig-bodied, man-headed creature that lived in the water. It was very shy, and as soon as it saw Chang Heng it plunged down out of sight. Chang sat down patiently to wait, quite still, with his arms conspicuously folded. The beast, reassured, came out of the water and began to sun itself on a rock, whereupon Chang stealthily picked up his brush between his toes and sketched it from life. Did artists *really* sketch from life in the Han? We would give much to know.

These are by no means the only Han stories about painting, but all such stories have to do with figures or animals, or with depicting the "myriad things," or with the products of the Nine Regions. None has to do with landscape, which suggests that people had not yet begun to consider landscape painting as an art in its own right. This does not mean that it did not exist in any form at all. For in one sense the basic formal language out of which landscape painting was to emerge was already there, in the undulating, wavelike sweep of the line that we find at its purest, perhaps, in lacquer painting (Plate 11 above), where the brush must drip its oily pigment in a continuous movement of the hand, producing scrolls and volutes that need only the addition of such accessories as fishes, birds, or bounding deer to turn them into waves, clouds, or hills. Because Chinese landscape painting grew out of this language of waves and volutes, and not, like Hellenistic and Roman painting, from an attempt to produce *illusionistic* effects through the use of perspective, highlights, and shadows, it acquired from the very beginning an abstract quality that it never lost, and that ensured that, at the highest levels of art at least, the quality of the line came to be regarded as more important than likeness to the object.

Until quite recently it was thought that Han landscape painting could never be reconstructed except by inference, as it were, from such crafts as lacquer and inlaid bronze, and from a few objects on which these wavelike hills appear. But the discoveries made in China since 1949 have raised our hopes that real landscape painting on silk may one day come to light. Already, from the waterlogged tombs at Ma-wang-tui near Chang-sha have come funerary banners dating back to the second century B.C., pictorial maps, and figure paintings on silk. Moreover, some much-damaged wall paintings in tombs have been published. Most of these depict ritual or feasting, but here and there we find simple natural settings, such as the landscape from the wall of a first-century tomb in P'ing-lu-hsien, Shansi (Plate 14). Even allowing for the freedom of the copyist, this panel seems to anticipate, in its piling up of hills, the feeling for space and depth that we will find in the landscape painting of much later times. It is from such crude daubs by some unknown artisan in provincial Shansi that we must try to imagine what the wall paintings and standing screens in the houses of the rich must have been like.

If painters were not yet looking at the mountains and streams as subjects for their brush, that was partly because, in the Han at least, and in North China certainly, people did not like to stray too far from home. The winters were harsh and cold, Huang-shan and the T'ai-hang Mountains the haunt of immortals possibly, but much more likely of bandits and tigers. No Buddhist monasteries, no Taoist retreats yet beckoned the wanderer into their hidden valleys, and only dire political necessity forced the educated man to take the desperate step of becoming a recluse. Liu An, Prince of Huai-an, who died in 12 B.C., wrote a summons to a gentleman who had thus withdrawn that ends with the words "O prince, return!/ In the mountains you cannot stay long." Besides, to a Confucian gentleman in the Han Dynasty, aware of his responsibilities, opting out was not acceptable conduct; and the passionate nature poetry of the period just before the Han had been the product not of the bleak north but of the much more hospitable lakes and rivers of the Yangtze Valley. If the northern poets describe the landscape at all, it is not nature as directly experienced by the wanderer in the mountains, but the huge artificially created hunting parks and gardens of the Han emperors: the more fanciful and exaggerated the poems, the more they were admired and the less likely it was that painters, still struggling with the most elementary problems of form and space, could adequately illustrate them; while in any case extravagant imagery was precisely

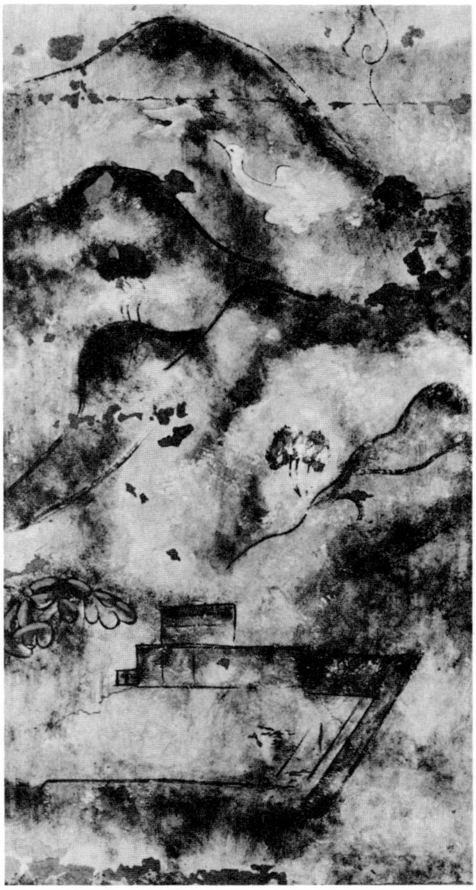

14. Fortified house in a landscape. Detail of a wall-painting (copy) in a tomb in Ts'ao-yüan-ts'un, P'ing-lu-hsien, Shansi. Ht. 88 cm. Han Dynasty.

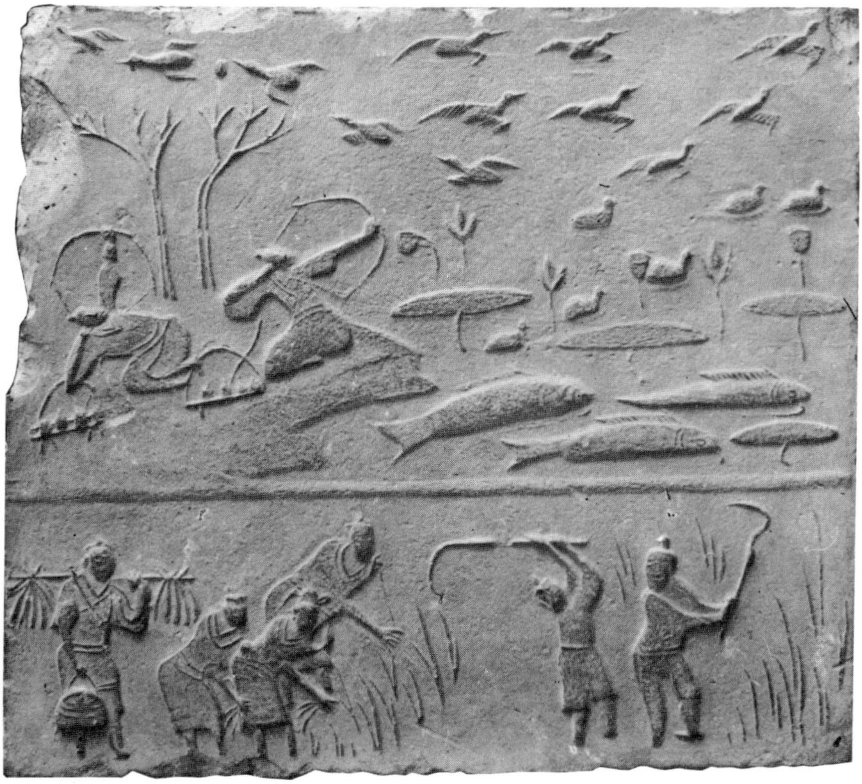

15. Shooting birds by a lake shore, and a harvesting scene. Molded pottery tile from the wall of a tomb. Ht. 42 cm. From Kuang-han, Szechwan. Later Han Dynasty (first or second century A.D.). Szechwan Provincial Museum, Chengtu.

what the *fu* poets were striving for. It may be—although on so little evidence this is no more than a guess—that the farther away we get from the heartland of traditional Chinese culture the more natural does the rendering of nature become. One of the most convincing of Han landscapes is not a painting at all, but a molded tile taken from the wall of a tomb in Szechwan that shows men shooting birds beside a lake filled to the brim with fishes and lotuses (Plate 15). The sense of space that the craftsman has achieved in this unpromising medium is little short of miraculous.

By the last century of the Han, painters were presumably beginning to master the problems of form and space; but if so their efforts must have been frustrated by the chaos into which the dynasty was so swiftly sinking. A succession of rebellions culminated in the sack of Loyang in A.D. 220, an event vividly evoked in this short poem by Ts'ao Chih, son of the great warlord Ts'ao Ts'ao: *

*Arthur Waley, *Chinese Poems* (London, 1948), pp. 79–80.

I climb to the ridge of the Pei-mang Hills
And look down on the city of Loyang.
In Loyang how still it is!
Palaces and houses all burnt to ashes,
Walls and fences all broken and gaping,
Thorns and brambles shooting up to the sky.
I do not see the old old-men;
I see only the new young men.
I turn aside, for the straight road is lost;
The fields are overgrown and will never be ploughed again.
I have been away such a long time
That I do not know which path is which.
How sad and ugly the empty moors are;
A thousand miles without the smoke of a chimney.
I think of our life together all those years;
My heart is tied with sorrow and I cannot speak.

Even greater desolation was to follow, for soon North China was again engulfed in civil war, leaving her prostrate and bleeding before the hordes of nomads pouring across the Great Wall. By 317 they had devastated both Ch'ang-an and Loyang, and this time the north did not recover.

After another century of utter chaos, the north came under the control of the Toba Turks, to remain under barbarian rule for over 250 years. All who could escape fled south over the mountains to the safety of the Yangtze Valley, and with this vast migration a profound change took place in Chinese society and art. The old order crumbled; Confucianism, the mainstay of the Han, was discredited; traditional attitudes and standards of behaviour were undermined. It was every man for himself. In the north the dark ages had arrived, and such fitful light as falls on the earlier decades of the long Occupation is shed chiefly by Buddhism. Embraced by the barbarian rulers for political reasons and by the masses for consolation in troubled times, the new faith inspired devotional image-making on a prodigious scale. But it was no inspiration to the landscapist, so it is not very surprising that landscape painting in the north seems to have just faded away. In the first Chinese histories of painting, written in the ninth century, not a single northern landscape painter is recorded in the 200 years between the middle of the fourth century and the middle of the sixth.

Now begins the flowering of the south, and the great north-south dialectic that was to enliven Chinese culture for centuries to come. Some of the emperors of the Southern Dynasties, ruling from Nanking between 317 and 589, were highly cultivated men and patrons of the arts; but their courts were riddled with corruption, and court life could be hazardous. As a contemporary poet put it:*

> Contentment with poverty is fortune's best gift
> Riches and honour are handmaids to disaster.

Scholars kept their heads down, and may have called to mind Chuang-tzu's remark in equally perilous times that he would rather be a little pigling than a sacrificial ox. The thoughtful man tended to withdraw to a country mansion or a thatched hut on a hillside, with results disastrous for government but of enormous benefit to art. This was the age of the literary picnic, when gentlemen would spend days at a time in the hills, or in a bamboo grove beside a stream, writing verses, getting mildly drunk, and indulging in the pleasure of *ch'ing-t'an,* "pure conversation," in which the talk ranged over a wealth of subjects, serious and frivolous, philosophical and moral, personal and critical. What was chiefly required of the participants in this sort of Senior Common Room exchange was the epigram, the paradox, the apt characterisation. It was fashionable, for example, to grade public figures in three classes, or nine, according to their merits—a rather crude technique that was to be borrowed by the critics of poetry, and eventually of painting. If one's contribution to this "pure talk" sounded a little artificial or forced, that was no defect so long as it was elegantly expressed. We will find the same qualities of a lively, slightly precious elegance in the newly evolving art of landscape painting, too.

Now, as Buddhism began to come to terms with Chinese philosophy, Buddhists and Taoists found common ground in their search for beautiful spots for their temples and retreats and in their desire to cleanse the mind of worldly thoughts and cravings through communion with nature. We find none of our European religious exclusiveness here: the message of the nature poets of these restless years is both Buddhist and Taoist. Their belief that the truth was to be sought in the mountains inspired many poets and painters to go wandering. The landscape poet Hsieh Ling-yün (385–433) had a special pair of climbing boots fitted with adjustable studs (on the heel for going up, on the toe for going down) in which he would clamber up the hills of his beloved Kuei-chi, not only to gather herbs to make a drug that he hoped might keep him forever young, but to experience the sheer joy of climbing in the hills. Hsieh's expeditions took place nearly a thousand years before the time of Petrarch, who,

*Fu Hsüan (217–78), "A Gentle Wind," translated in Arthur Waley, *Chinese Poems* (London, 1948), p. 84.

as Kenneth Clark said in the first of his Slade Lectures, was probably the first man in the West "to express the emotion on which the existence of landscape painting so largely depends; the desire to escape from the turmoil of the cities into the peace of the countryside." "Would that you could know," Petrarch wrote to a friend, "with what joy I wander free and alone among the mountains and streams." Yet even as he drank in the view from a hill top, his eyes fell upon a passage in St. Augustine's *Confessions* (which he had with him—a Chinese wanderer would surely have carried a book of poetry) that reminded him of the impropriety of feasting his eyes on nature when they should be turned inward upon his own soul. "And from that time," Petrarch noted, "not a syllable fell from my lips till I reached the bottom again." As Kenneth Clark observed, nature, to medieval man, "opens the mind to dangerous thoughts." No such doubts could conceivably have assailed Hsieh Ling-yün, or indeed any of his contemporaries, dedicated Confucians and pious Buddhists though many of them undoubtedly were. From now on, no Chinese gentleman would feel that climbing mountains was anything but enjoyable, proper, and good for the soul; for, as Hsieh Ling-yün most pertinently asked, "if enjoyment of nature should end, who would understand what all this means?"

The landscape was not just a symbol of the Tao, it was the very substance of the Tao itself. As the fourth-century poet Sun Ch'o put it in his *fu* "Wandering on Mount T'ien-t'ai":*

> The Great Void, vast and wide, that knows no boundary
> Sets in cycle the mysterious Being, So-of-itself;
> Melting, it forms the rivers and waterways,
> Thickening, it turns into mountains and hills . . .

And, we might add, vaporising, it becomes mists and clouds, the visible *ch'i*, or breath of living nature. The Buddhists shared all these Taoist feelings. Like Hsieh Ling-yün, the Buddhist monk Chih Tun collected herbs on the hillsides to concoct an elixir of immortality—a thoroughly Taoist activity. Sun Ch'o's fourth-century contemporary, the Buddhist poet and painter Tsung Ping, says in a brief essay on landscape painting that he has spent so much time in the mountains that he forgot he was getting old; that he had tried Taoist techniques of breath control in vain (he admitted he was not very good at them) and had failed as a responsible Confucian gentleman; so he took to landscape painting, which he suggests is every bit as effective a path to understanding as meditating upon the Tao.

*Burton Watson, *Chinese Rhyme-prose: Poems in the Fu Form from the Han and Six Dynasties Periods* (New York, 1971), p. 81.

Sun Ch'o confessed that he lacked the nerve and the faith actually to seek out the immortals himself. The sacred mountains were formidable: the T'ang scholar Han Yü became so paralysed with fear on the ridges of Hua-shan that he wrote a farewell letter and had to be helped down. It was safer, and for an artist perhaps just as satisfying, to make the journey with his brush on paper or silk. We cannot help wondering how many Chinese mountain landscapes owe their awe-inspiring precipitousness to the timidity of the artist!

The "landscape experience" was closely bound up with the sudden discovery of himself as a creative being that burst upon artist and poet in the turbulent period that followed the collapse of the Han. The most profound and passionate expression of this new awareness of what happens when a work of art is born is a rhapsodic prose-poem on the art of letters, the *Wen fu*, written by the young poet and adventurer Lu Chi shortly before his death in A.D. 300. From it let me cite these lines: *

Writing is itself a joy
Yet saints and sages have long since held it in awe
For it is Being created by tasking the great void,
And 'tis sound wrung out of profound silence.
In a sheet of paper is contained the Infinite,
And, evoked from an inch-size heart, an endless panorama.
The words as they expand, become all evocative,
The thoughts, still further pursued, will run the deeper.
Till flowers in full bloom exhale an all-pervading fragrance
And tender boughs, their saps running, grow to a whole jungle of splendor.
Bright winds spread their luminous wings, quick breezes soar from the earth,
And, nimbus-like amidst all these, rises the glory of the literary world.

Two lines, the fifth and sixth, express Lu Chi's sense of wonder that the poet can compress all the vastness of the cosmos within the confines of his verse. Early scroll painters, too, will speak with amazement of their newly discovered power to, as they put it, "bring down a panorama of ten thousand *li* into a scant foot of silk." Already, the landscape painting was not just a picture; there was, it was felt, something almost miraculous about it.

This new attitude to what man can do with nature also helped to bring about the birth of garden designing as a fine art, long before the Japanese ever thought of it. At the beginning of the Six Dynasties (that is, in the early fourth century) gardens as we know them seem not yet to have existed in China. Royal parks were landscaped on a huge scale to

*Ch'en Shih-hsiang, trans., *Literature as Light against Darkness* (Portland, Maine, 1952).

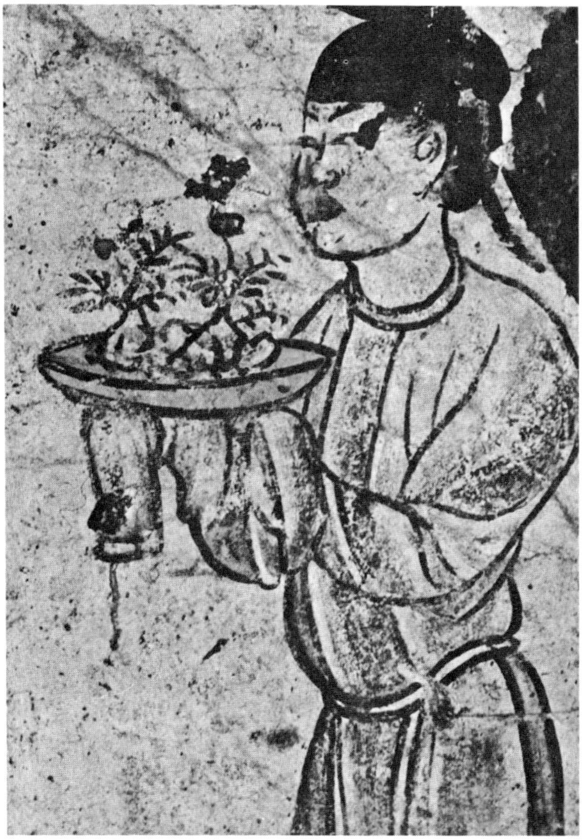

16. "Tray scenery" (p'an-ching) carried by a servant. Detail of a wall-painting in the tomb of Prince I-te (706), near Sian, Shensi. T'ang Dynasty.

suggest Mount K'un-lun to the West, the Eastern Sea, the blessed isle P'eng-lai, and haunts of nature deities, fairies, and immortals. But now, in and around Nanking, gentlemen were beginning to design gardens for their villas that were more intimate in scale, and still a microcosm of the world of nature. By the T'ang Dynasty, miniaturisation had been carried even further, for we find in tomb frescoes of about A.D. 700 pictures of servants bearing dishes on which are arranged little fancy rocks and plants (Plate 16). A gentleman would have these *p'an-ching* ("tray scenery" as they were called) as objects of pleasurable contemplation on his desk. The *p'an-ching* is, of course, the origin of the Japanese *bonsai*.

The notion that the picture was not an object in a frame, to be looked at and admired for its form and colour, but rather a mysterious thing that, like the miniature garden, contained the essence of the world of nature, now gives Chinese landscape painting, however primitive in technique, a special concentration of meaning and content for which I

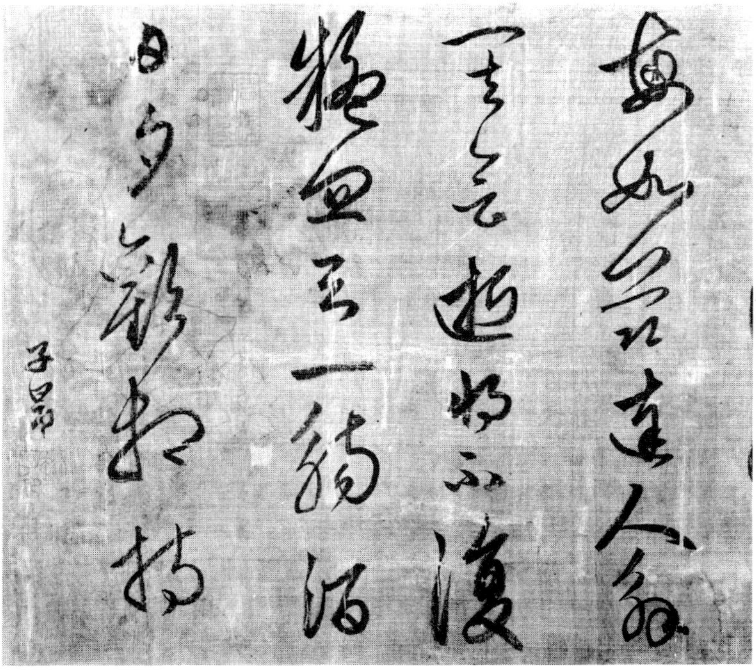

17. Chao Meng-fu (1254–1322): Part of a poem by T'ao Ch'ien (365–427) written in ts'ao-shu (draft or cursive script). National Palace Museum, Taipei.

can think of no parallel in Western art. No wonder Tsung Ping wrote that painting landscapes was just as good a path to the Tao as meditation itself.

The literati of the fifth and sixth centuries, who would probably have called themselves good Confucians still, no longer held quite so firmly to the doctrine, implicit in Confucianism, that art must serve the social order. Instead, they developed a truly revolutionary aesthetic that verges on "art for art's sake": I say verges, because even when the style of their paintings is most precious and mannered, the subject matter is generally of a didactic or improving kind. But the standards by which it is judged are now no longer purely ethical. Lu Chi had written in the *Wen fu* that what the poet delights in is "nothing less than the perfection of Beauty's form and matter," an idea that would have profoundly shocked a Han Confucian. The theorists of painting were later to take up this theme. Long before they appeared on the scene, however, the calligraphers had established the aesthetic foundations of their difficult art, and their theories were to have an enormous influence on painting.

The third century had seen a sudden flowering of the swift cursive style called *ts'ao-shu*, "draft script" (Plate 17), which had been invented for practical reasons in the Han Dynasty or even earlier but had now become, like the Italian Chancery hand today, something of a fashion among the literati, and especially among those with Taoist leanings. Almost the first we hear of it is an attack on the cult written by a disgruntled Confucian at the end of the Han, who complained that its devotees "wear out a brush in ten days, and in one month use several cakes of ink. Their collars and sleeves are black and so are their lips and teeth. Even when they are in company they don't relax and chat, but draw lines with their fingers on the floor." Writing as the dynasty was in its death throes, he clearly saw the craze for the *ts'ao-shu* as a symptom of the rot that was setting in all around him and that had to be stopped.

Calligraphy was judged by the vitality of the line, the balance and structural strength of the character, and the composition of the page. But not until the middle of the sixth century, so far as we know, were such standards applied to painting. It was an obscure portrait painter in Nanking named Hsieh Ho who set them down, in the preface to his *Ku hua p'in lu*, or *Classified Record of Ancient Painters*. In a few brief paragraphs he set out the famous Six Laws which were to become the cornerstone of Chinese æsthetics: spirit consonance and life movement; the "bone method" (structural strength) in the use of the brush; fidelity to the object; correct colour; proper placing and disposition; and the transmission of ancient masters by copying. These principles, which it will be noted are *purely* æsthetic (Hsieh Ho says nothing about ethics or subject matter), have been examined, discussed, translated, and retranslated until students of Chinese painting have become heartily sick of them; but we cannot ignore them, because they contain the essence of the Chinese philosophy of art—especially the first two, which may be summarised very simply as "vitality" and "structure." *

When we turn from the sophisticated æsthetics of the Six Dynasties to the landscape painting itself, we cannot but wonder at how naive it was, and at how poorly equipped painters still were not only to depict faithfully what they saw before their eyes, but still more to convey a sense of what they felt lay "beyond the image." Perhaps we would get a

*Any educated Chinese will tell you that he knows what *ch'i-yün* means, although he might have difficulty in putting it into English. There is some question whether Hsieh Ho sees the *ch'i* as the spirit of nature, to which man must attune himself (the literal meaning of *yün* is "consonance" or "rhythm"), or whether it is something personal to the artist that has a tone (*yün*) or *timbre* unique to him. But even if, as Richard Lynn has suggested, the painter "endows his subject with a sense of life through the expression of his own spirit (*ch'i*)," a Taoist would probably say that his *ch'i* partakes of the universal *ch'i*, so it is the same thing in the end. Although it would be wrong to say that *ch'i-yün* can mean whatever we want it to mean, it is, as much as anything, its suggestive vagueness that has ensured its enduring place in Chinese aesthetics.

different picture if any original works had survived from the hand of Ku K'ai-chih, Tsung Ping, or Chang Seng-yu, who seem to have forged a landscape style out of the old conventions. But all their work was lost in the rise and fall of a succession of short-lived dynasties, when the palace was repeatedly destroyed, and with it the masterpieces that greedy emperors had successively creamed off from what was left (chiefly in private hands) from the previous coup d'état. One southern emperor, when his dynasty was collapsing, heaped the whole of the Imperial library, including the paintings, in the palace courtyard and set fire to it, exclaiming "Culture shall not survive this night!" Today not even bad copies of the landscape scrolls of such masters as Tsung Ping and Chang Seng-yu survive. Like the work of Apelles, they exist only in books and in the tradition that has grown up about them.

But all is not lost, for several ancient pictures survive that are associated with the name of Ku K'ai-chih (ca. 344–406), eccentric, courtier, Taoist, and poet, who is said to have protected himself from the hazards of court life at Nanking by acting the fool. Ku K'ai-chih was perhaps the first to combine the old art of portraiture with the new art of landscape painting: he once painted a picture of a famous Taoist eccentric in a setting of crags and gorges because, he said, the Taoist understood the mountains so well. Ku K'ai-chih wrote a very high-pitched *fu* on thunder and lightning, and an essay attributed to him describes in detail how he would go about painting—or perhaps how he actually did paint—a panorama of the Yün-t'ai-shan, the Cloud Terrace Mountain, on which a Han Taoist and magician was said to have tested the faith and powers of his disciples. Ku K'ai-chih's illustration to the romantic *fu* of the "Fairy of the Lo River" by Tso Ssu survives in what is probably a copy of about the twelfth century (Plate 18). The story moves from right to left as we follow the young scholar through his encounter with the water fairy, her vain attempt, like Ondine's, to lure him beneath the waves, and her sad departure, which left him, full of regrets at his timidity, alone on the river bank. The artist clearly has not mastered the fifth principle of Hsieh Ho, placing and composition; and he seems unable to distinguish foreground rocks and bushes from distant mountains and trees, using the same conventions for both, although he arranges them in a charming way to both separate and link together the successive incidents in the story. The figures are much too big, the mountains much too small —or perhaps we should say that they still reflect an old order of priorities, for soon we shall see the figures shrinking to their proper size. About the artist's handling of atmosphere and depth we can say nothing useful, for

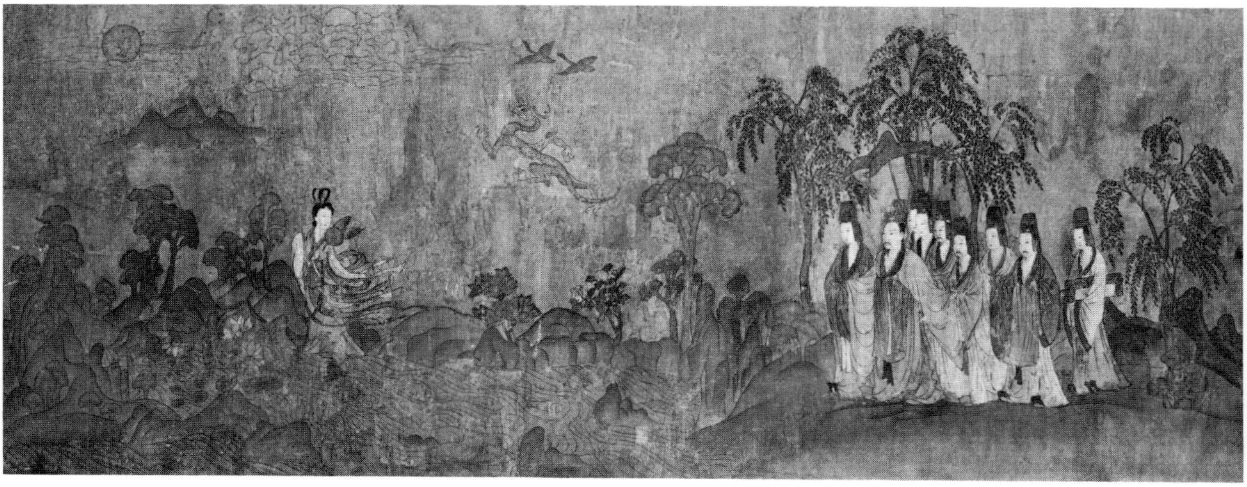

18. Ku K'ai-chih (ca. 344–406): "The Fairy of the Lo River." Detail of a handscroll illustrating the "fu" of the same name by Ts'ao Chih; ink and slight colour on silk. Ht. 24 cm. Probably a copy of the Sung Dynasty. Freer Gallery of Art, Washington, D.C.

this is a Sung copy, or a copy of a copy, and while copyists would generally be very careful to preserve the antique style of the figures, they often allowed themselves some liberties with the landscape.

Roughly contemporary with Ku K'ai-chih are the brick decorations that have been discovered in several fourth- and fifth-century tombs near Nanking (Plate 19). They depict the Seven Sages of the Bamboo Grove, a group of famous and much-envied eccentrics and recluses of the third century (an eighth has been added, presumably for symmetry: a hermit of the time of Confucius). Each sits beneath a tree with his attribute—a guitar, a fly whisk, a wine cup, and so on—and his name is written beside him. The arrangement is very old-fashioned, but the trees, among which we can distinguish the pine, the weeping willow, the acacia, and the ginko, are reproduced in an unusual medium (raised thread relief) with a skill and understanding we have not encountered before. Probably these panels preserve the design of a long-lost, but at the time widely admired, wall painting, screen, or handscroll, possibly even by Ku K'ai-chih himself. Although very much the sedulous courtier, Ku K'ai-chih cultivated all the attitudes and eccentricities of a recluse, and this was a theme after his own heart.

The message of the Seven Sages panels, that in times of bad government the virtuous man simply opts out, was balanced by the Confucian doctrine that the worse the government the greater

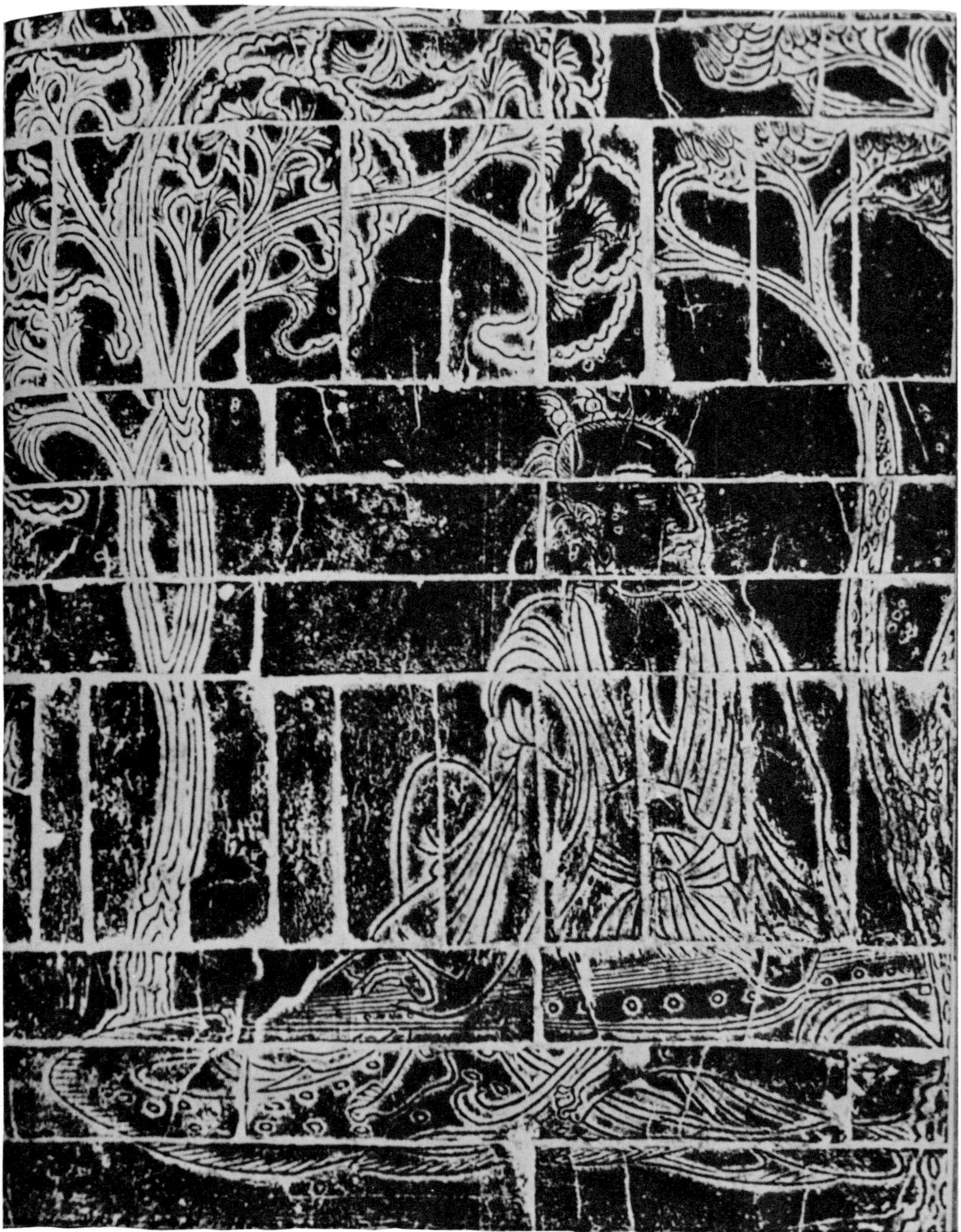

19. The poet and lutanist Hsi K'ang under a ginko tree. Rubbing of a brick relief in a tomb near Nanking. Fourth or fifth century.

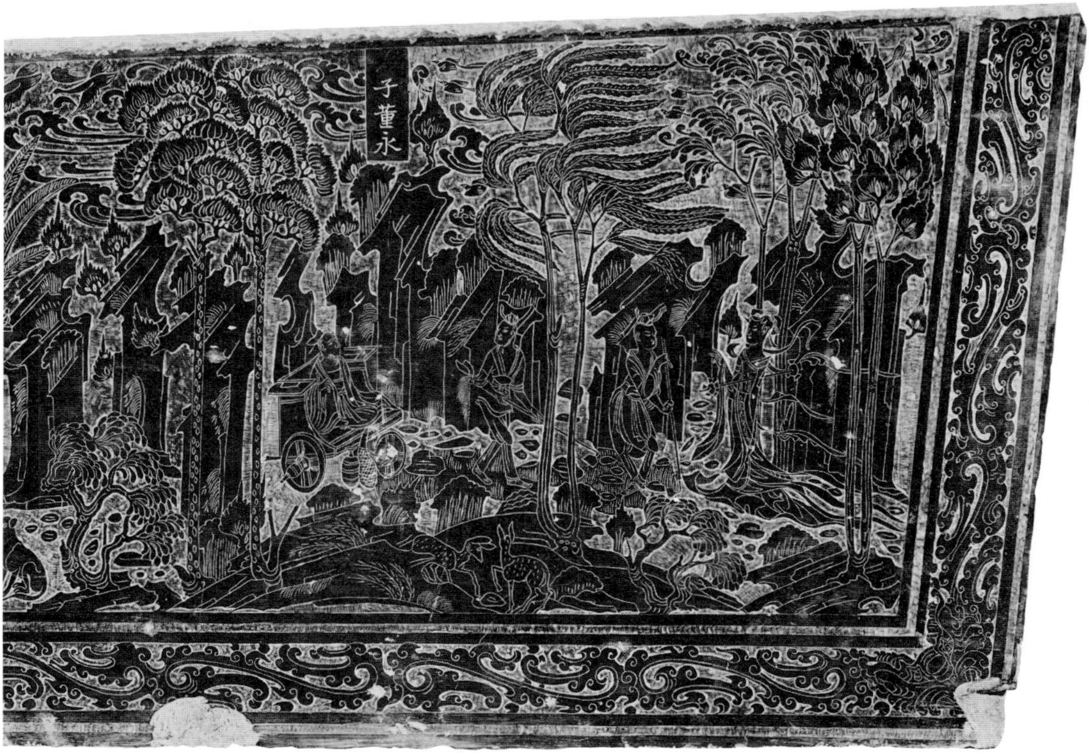

20. *The story of the filial son Tung Yung. Rubbing of the side of an engraved stone coffin. Ht. 61 cm. Ca. 520–40. Nelson-Atkins Gallery of Art, Kansas City, Mo.*

one's obligation to improve it; hence the theme of these reliefs is somewhat equivocal, and typically Taoist. Quite unambiguous —as regards subject matter at least—are the paragons of filial piety whose unselfish deeds are engraved on the sides of a sixth-century stone coffin in the Nelson Gallery in Kansas City (Plate 20). Here, although the theme is respectably Confucian, the treatment of the natural setting is very Taoist in feeling. We see the filial Tung Yung working for the creditor who had lent him the money for his father's funeral, and we see the good fairy who helped him pay the debt and then flew up into heaven. The mountains are arranged like the wings of a toy theatre to isolate the story from its neighbours, and they are still absurdly out of scale. But the landscape is beginning to come to life and assert itself: a wind rushing through the trees tosses the branches, sends the clouds and birds hurtling across the sky, and flutters the robes and scarves of the "fairy godmother." This is a delightful way of suggesting that while man may be earthbound, fairies, trees, and clouds are redolent of the *ch'i*, the breath of life. The

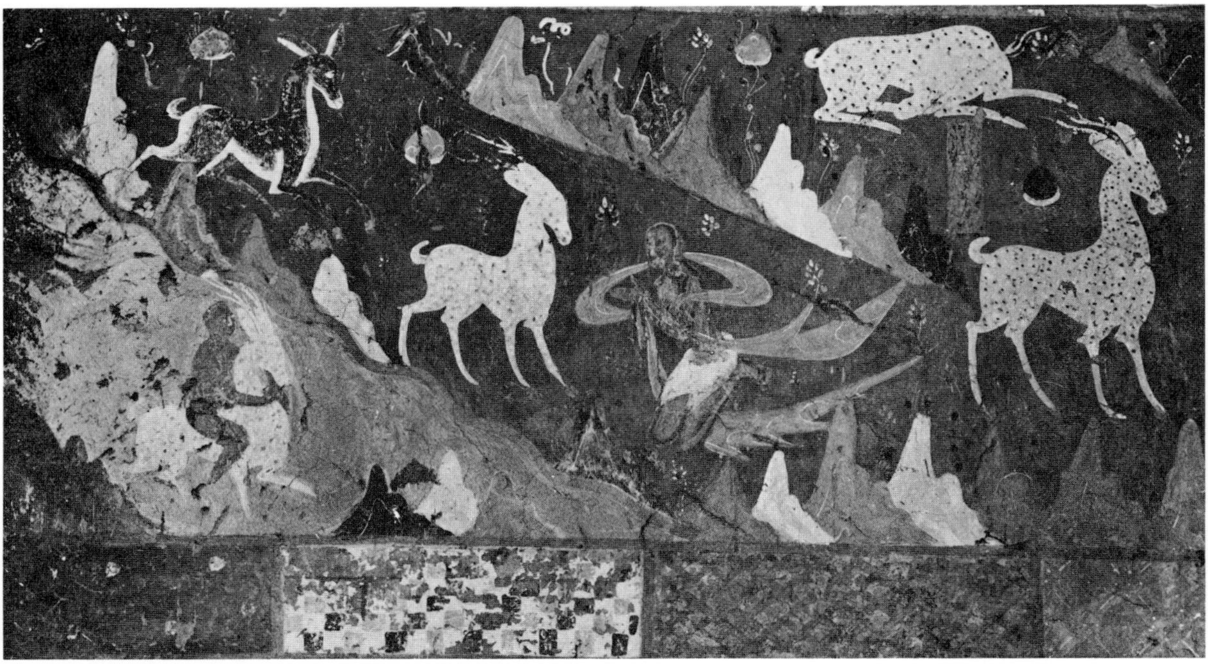

21. The story of the Buddha incarnate as a Golden Deer ("the Rūrū Jātaka"). Painting on the wall of Cave 257 at Tunhuang, Kansu. Northern Wei Dynasty; fifth century. Photograph by Dominique Darbois.

same sweeping rhythms, derived ultimately from Han decorative art, enliven the cloud-scrolls that run around the border.

While the painters of Nanking and Loyang were enjoying the pleasures of enlightened, if unpredictable, court patronage, far out on the northwest frontier Buddhist monks, lay brothers, and journeyman painters were decorating the walls of the cave-shrines at Tunhuang with frescoes as votive offerings from the travellers and pilgrims who had made, or were about to make, the long and dangerous journey across Central Asia to India and the sacred places of Buddhism. These crude, lively paintings, actually done on dry plaster, consist chiefly of scenes from the life of the Buddha and from his many previous incarnations (the *Jātaka* tales), and scenes of the disasters from which the bodhisattva Avalokiteśvara, or Kuan-yin, protects the faithful—the latter a popular subject with patrons who knew only too well the dangers from storms and drought, wild animals and robbers that faced them on their pilgrimage. Some of the earliest of these paintings are strangely un-Chinese in the mechanical repetition of their camel-hump-like mountains painted in contrasting colours and laid out in strips, as though the painter had cut up a handscroll and pasted it on the wall (Plate 21). There are no trees, only little flowering plants scattered prettily over the red ground in the Persian fashion. But gradually, as we look at the paintings in the sixth-century caves, we see the landscape becoming more natural. The red background gives way to white; hills and figures are painted with a lively line; tree trunks and branches, drawn with a continuous upward sweep of the brush, often sway in the wind; and there is a clear lateral movement across the panel from right to left, as though we were "reading" a handscroll (Plate 22). Storytelling rather than landscape painting is still, of course, the painter's aim; but being Chinese, or under the growing influence of Chinese art, he cannot help emphasising the landscape more and more.

By the end of the sixth century, the wall painting at Tunhuang has broken through these superimposed scroll-like layers of painting, and for a brief moment all is chaos; but by very early in the seventh century, the craftsmen have learned how to decorate a whole wall with one big composition harbouring a number of separate incidents in a series of linked, womblike "space cells," which we see superbly handled in Cave 217 at Tunhuang (Plate 23). While mineral colour is still used in a decorative way,

22. Landscape with animals and celestial beings. Painting on the ceiling of Cave 249 at Tunhuang. Northern Wei Dynasty; early sixth century. Photograph by Dominique Darbois.

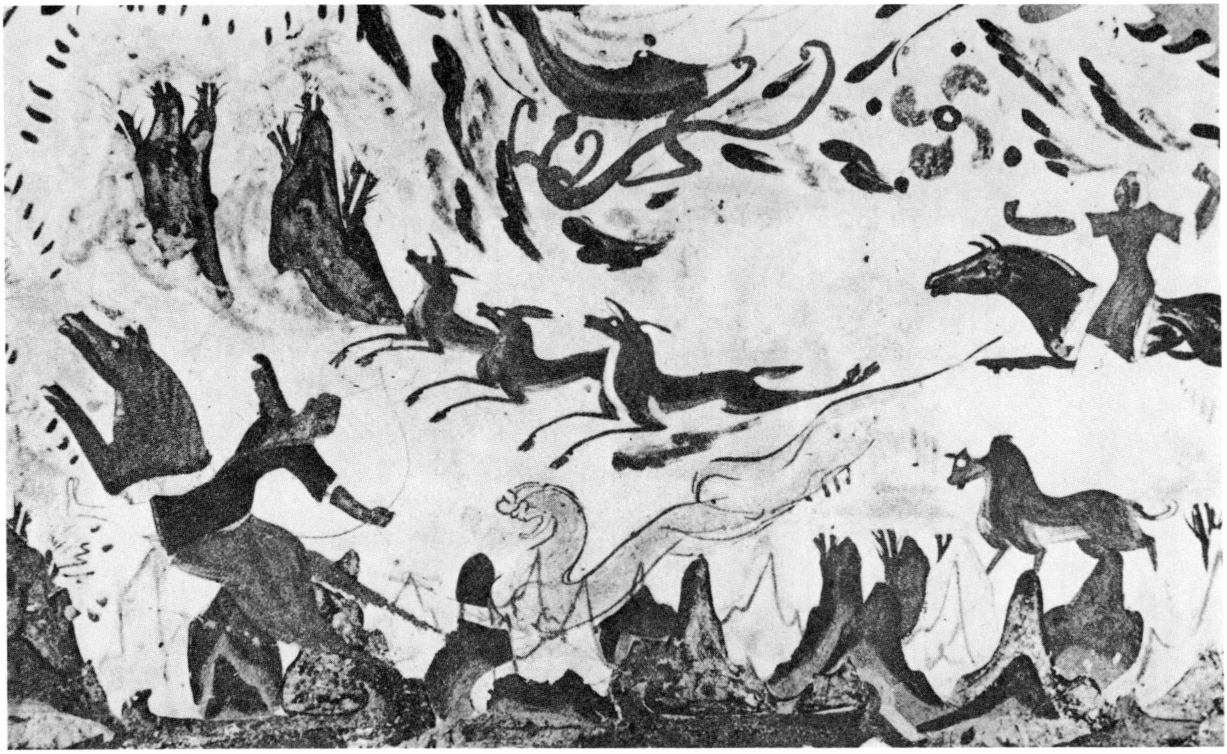

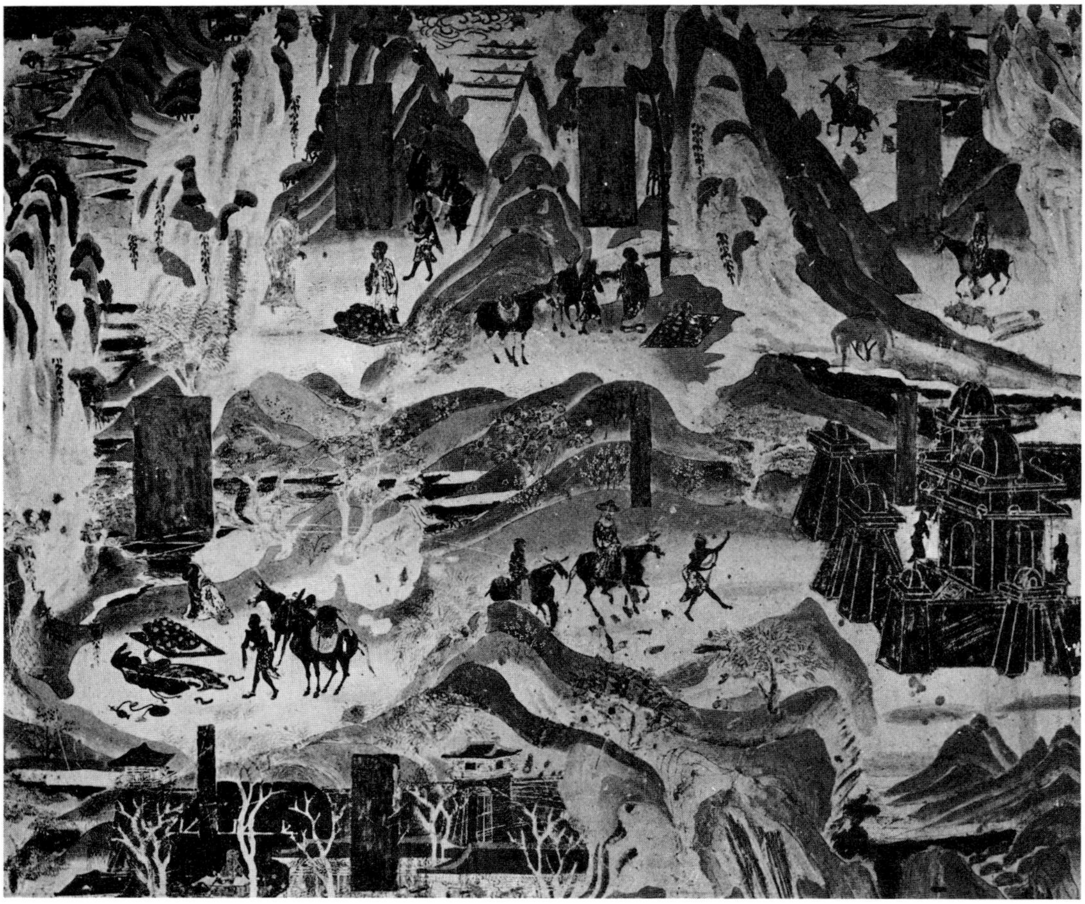

23. Landscape with Travellers. Painting on the south wall of Cave 217 at Tunhuang. T'ang Dynasty; eighth century. Photograph by Dominique Darbois.

the Near Eastern influence has, in the usual Chinese fashion, been absorbed. Provincial and unrepresentative as these Tunhuang paintings undoubtedly are, they give us a hint of what the frescoes in the Buddhist temples of sixth-century Loyang might have been like. In South China there was no Tunhuang, and to what sort of landscapes such great sixth-century masters as Chang Seng-yu painted we have no guide at all, except for the brief descriptions of their style in the writings of later art historians. It seems unlikely, however, that the Near Eastern influence we saw at Tunhuang could have penetrated as far south as Nanking.

Some literary critics in the T'ang Dynasty condemned the elegant poetry and "parallel prose" of the Six Dynasties as artificial and self-conscious. The ninth-century art historian Chang Yen-yüan likewise had nothing but contempt for the absurdities of the landscape painting of former times, in which (he said) the fantastic crowded peaks were like the teeth of a "pearl-inlaid rhinoceros-horn comb," the water left no room to float a ship, and people were drawn larger than mountains, which looked like "the ax-blade edges of melting ice"—an apt description of the rocks on the Nelson Gallery sarcophagus (Plate 20). Chang Yen-yüan shows a healthy belief in the progress of art, but we need not take so severe a view. For these stern Confucian critics did not give the "primitive" artists the credit that was due them for setting painting free from the tradition of anonymous Han craftsmanship; for endowing it with the æsthetic of that most rarefied of arts, calligraphy; and for making it a fit occupation for a gentleman.

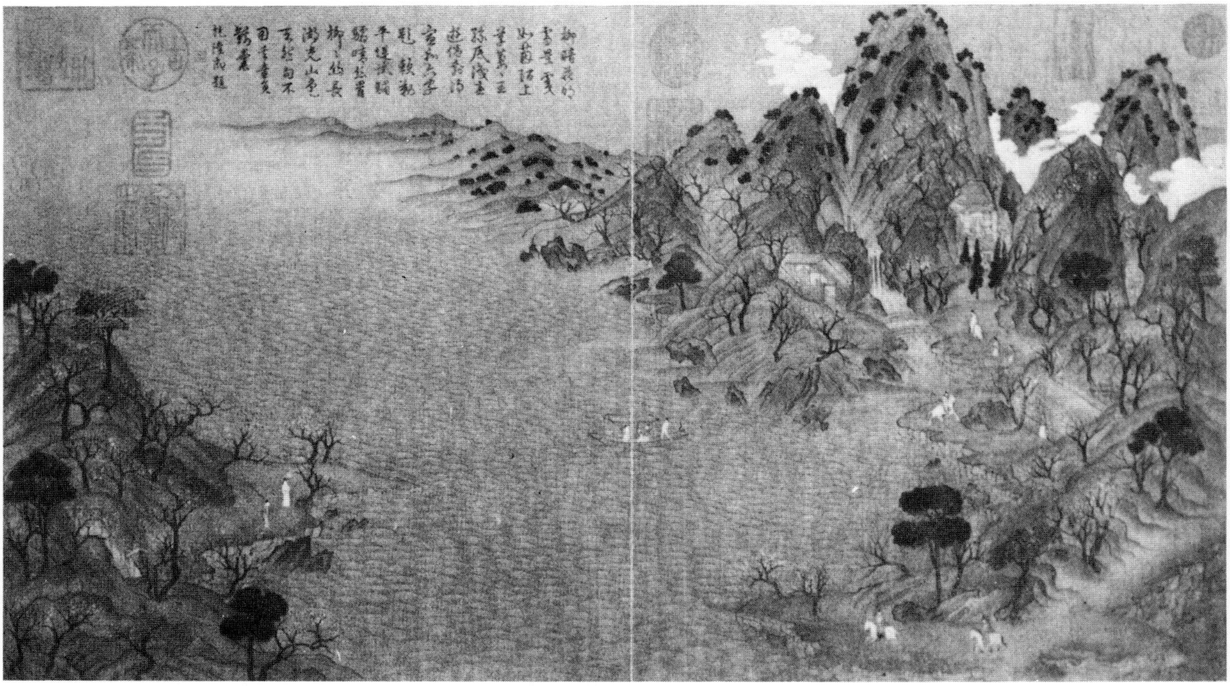

II The Language Takes Shape

The T'ang Dynasty, 618-906

24. Attributed to Chan Tzu-ch'ien (late sixth century): "Journey in Springtime." Detail of a handscroll; ink and slight colour on silk. Palace Museum, Peking.

There is something almost symphonic about T'ang history as it sweeps up to its great climax and slowly dies away to its miserable end. The seventh century was an age of reunification and expansion, when China stretched out her arms westward to embrace much of Central Asia, eastward to win the tribute of Korea, and southward to bring civilisation to the Cantonese. The Chinese were too busy expanding and consolidating their new empire, it seems, to devote much of their creative energy to the fine arts, and for some decades painting, like poetry, remained content with the charming artificiality of the sixth century. This period has been called by Chinese literary critics the springtime of T'ang poetry. As we shall see, it can be called the springtime of T'ang landscape painting, too.

T'ang culture came to its full flowering in the first half of the eighth century, especially during the brilliant reign of the Emperor Hsüan-tsung (or Ming-huang, 713-56). This was the period of achievement, of enormous material prosperity. The court was enlightened, liberal, and extravagant. In the palace, Ming-huang had eight orchestras—two of them from Central Asia—and 400 horses who were trained first to dance at imperial banquets holding brimming winecups between their teeth and then to lay them at the feet of his guests, in the course of which, we are told, the horses got as "tipsy as wobbling mud." Ming-huang was also an enthusiastic collector and patron of the arts, although for a time the salons of his more cultivated brothers, the princes Chi and Ning, attracted an even more brilliant circle of artists and poets than did that of Ming-huang himself. This is a period of towering figures in art: of Wu Tao-tzu, the Michelangelo of T'ang China, who painted over 300 frescoes in the temples of Ch'ang-an and Loyang; of Chang Tsao, the greatest master of landscape painting in monochrome ink; and of Wang Wei, gentleman, poet, and landscape painter, who came, as we shall see, to occupy a unique position in the landscape tradition.

The poets of this high summer of T'ang culture still sing of the pleasures of life, of companionship, of drinking together, even when their own circumstances were hard, as in these lines of Li Po (701-62):*

> They sang to me and drummed, the boys of Yen and Chao,
> Lovely girls plucked the sounding string.
> Their painted cheeks shone like dazzling suns;
> The dancers' sleeves shook out like blossoming boughs . . .

And he ends, more prophetically than he knew:

> Let us make merry, get something in our own day
> To set against the pity of ages yet unborn.

For in 755, while the elderly Ming-huang dallied with his mistress Yang Kuei-fei, the dream was shattered. A provincial commander named An Lu-shan rebelled and marched on the capital. The emperor, with Yang Kuei-fei and a small escort, fled westward. At Ma-wei, the escort demanded Yang Kuei-fei as the price of their loyalty. The grieving emperor yielded. The soldiers killed her, wrapped her body in a mat, and left it in a ditch. The palace meantime was ransacked by the rebels; the orchestras, the dancing girls, and the dancing horses were scattered. The dynasty almost collapsed. But in the nick of time An Lu-shan died, and the T'ang struggled to its feet, to survive for another 150 years, a shadow of its former self. The 50 years after the rebellion were a period of partial restoration, of autumnal ripeness, when men increasingly lived on their memories. If in the early T'ang poets had shed tears, it was in thinking of home, of a girl encountered at a wayside inn, of heroes killed in the

*Translated by Arthur Waley, *The Poetry and Career of Li Po* (London, 1950), p. 26-27.

frontier wars. When, after 756, the poets lament, they are grieving for the ghost of Ma-wei, for the grass growing in the palace courtyards, for the dynasty itself.

Autumn turned to winter. China's boundaries shrank, and her heart with them. The economy collapsed, people became intolerant and anti-foreign, garrison commanders turned into local warlords, and the peasants were stirred into rebellion. The death of the dynasty was slow and painful. As the poets lost heart and lost contact with each other, poetry turned in on itself—as in these bitter lines by the ninth-century poet Han-shan, which are a good deal less obscure than much of the verse of this twilight period:*

Yesterday I saw the trees by the river's edge,
Wrecked and broken beyond belief.
Only two or three trunks left standing
Scarred by blades of a thousand axes.
Frost strips the yellowing leaves,
River waves pluck at withered roots.
This is the way the living must fare.
Why curse Heaven and Earth?

T'ang culture is very much all of a piece, and from the literature of Chinese painting we know that this dramatic rise to splendour and fall into chaos is true of T'ang landscape painting as well. But when we come to charting its course we run into problems that are all the more exasperating because this is a period of which we expect to have a very clear picture. Mention "T'ang" and all at once we have a vivid image of an unmistakable T'ang style, of splendour in the crafts, of prancing pottery horses, and of camels glazed yellow, brown, and green. But what visions do the words "T'ang landscape painting" conjure up? Where are the works of the masters? They are lost beyond recall. So the T'ang, a period of brilliant achievement in landscape painting, is the hardest for the historian to chronicle. Earlier, we were groping in the dark, and any inlaid bronze or fragment of engraved stone gave us a precious clue to what the painters might have been doing. Later, the great masterpieces will be ranged in their serried ranks before us. But for the T'ang, all we have are some texts and poems, some anonymous paintings (chiefly on the walls of shrines and tombs), and a handful of scrolls to which the name of some T'ang master has been attached, often with little reason, since few of these scrolls could conceivably have been painted in the T'ang Dynasty in any case.

*Translated by Burton Watson, *Cold Mountain, 100 Poems by the T'ang Poet Han-shan* (London, 1972), p. 53.

Yet we can at least be thankful for the fact that the ninth century was a period of acute nostalgia for lost glories, a period when men looked back to the great days of Ming-huang's reign and earlier. For it was in the ninth century that the first histories of Chinese painting were compiled—700 years before Vasari. Chang Yen-yüan's *Li tai ming hua chi, Record of Famous Painters of Successive Dynasties* (847), which is probably the first history of art ever written, treats of every aspect of painting, from the philosophical to the historical, the critical, the technical, and the purely anecdotal. He includes a sort of Baedeker's guide to the frescoes in the temples of Ch'ang-an and Loyang; he even has a chapter on forgeries and on the current market values of old masters. He describes the style of many painters whose work is now lost forever; he lavishes as much praise on his idol Wu Tao-tzu as did Vasari on Michelangelo; and he deplores the painting of his own day, which he feels has fallen into a sad state of indiscipline and anarchy.

From Chang's book, and from another written at about the same time by Chu Ching-hsüan, one striking fact emerges very clearly: that the north-south dialectic that I mentioned in the last chapter is dramatically evident in the landscape painting of the T'ang. In the first half of the dynasty we find that every painter of any importance at all either was a northerner by birth or worked in the north. After the disaster of 756, the twin capitals suddenly ceased to be the magnet that drew talent from all over the empire. From now on, almost all the painters that these authors mention, and certainly all the interesting ones, were southerners, living in that region of the lower Yangtze Valley, the Chiang-nan, that 500 years earlier had given birth to Ku K'ai-chih and Hsieh Ling-yün. Moreover, *all* the new developments in technique that we know of—and there were some astonishing ones—came at the hands of the southern individualists and eccentrics.

By the time these wild men appeared on the scene, however, painting had come a long way from the archaic efforts of the sixth and seventh centuries. No genuine works by the early T'ang masters survive, but perhaps we get a hint of their style from the delightful *Journey in Springtime* (Plate 24), attributed to Chan Tzu-ch'ien, who worked in North China under the Northern Chou and Sui dynasties, roughly between 580 and 620. The artist suggests depth by a device that we saw at Tunhuang (Plate 21), ranging his mountains back diagonally across the picture to open a sort of corridor into space—although he rather spoils the illusion by a sudden jump from the trees in the near half of the picture to the bushes farther back. The drawing is careful, the line thin and springy but rather weak, the colour quietly festive and now very faded. We have no

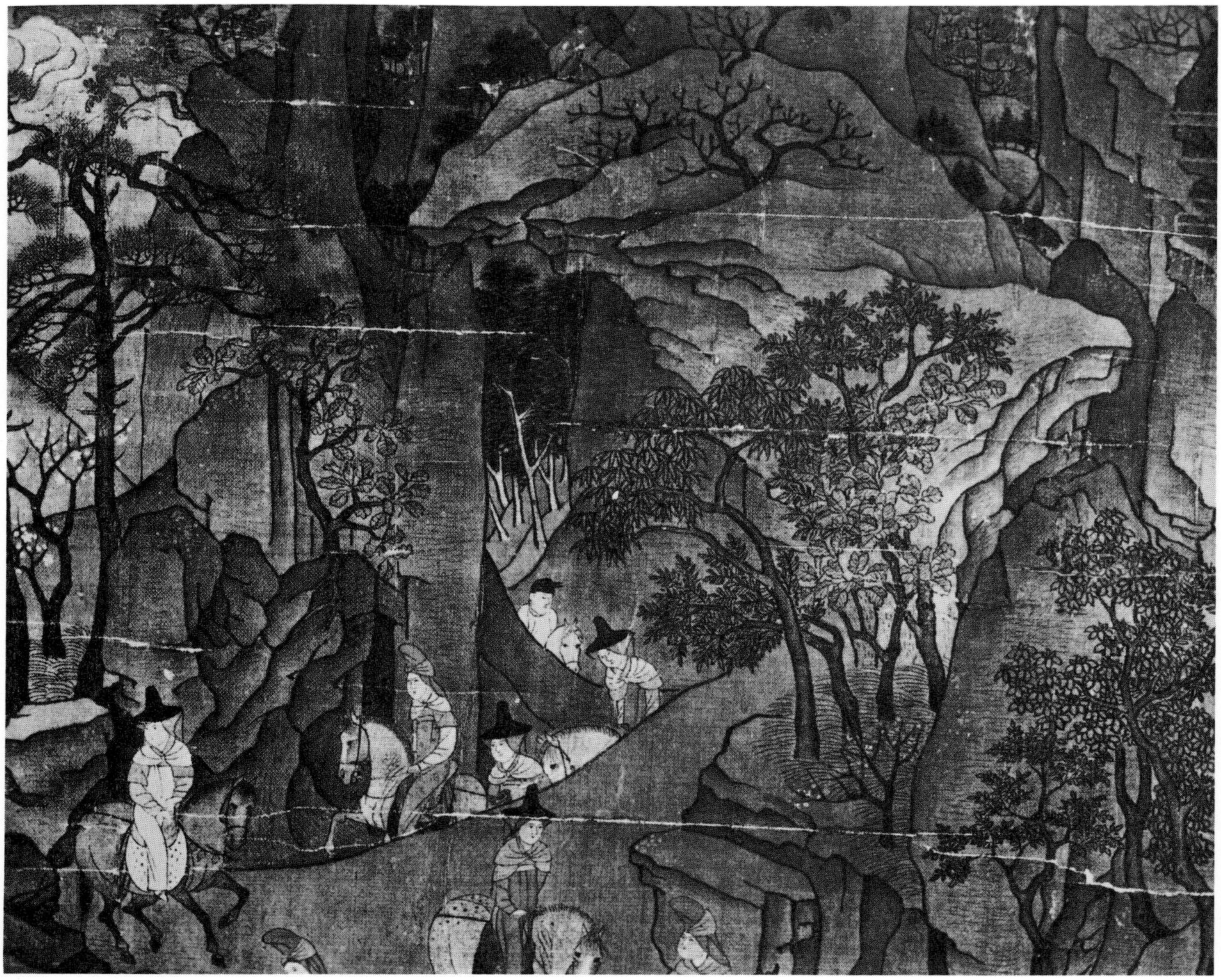

25. Anon: "The Emperor Ming-huang's Journey to Shu." Detail of a hanging scroll; ink and colour on silk. Ht. 55.9 cm. Possibly a Sung Dynasty painting in the T'ang courtly style. National Palace Museum, Taipei.

way of knowing just when this picture was painted, or even whether it has anything to do with Chan Tzu-ch'ien, whose name on the mounting is in the handwriting of a Sung emperor. All we can say for certain is that the style is archaic, and that the scroll has a vernal freshness that seems appropriate to the springtime of T'ang culture.

Chan Tzu-ch'ien's most famous successors in the first half of the T'ang were Big General Li (Li Ssu-hsün) and his son Li Chao-tao (called Little General Li by courtesy). Of Li Ssu-hsün, Chang Yen-yüan wrote "His brush style had an intense forcefulness. His rapids really did seem to be running water; his clouds and vapours added a hazy uncertainty. Sometimes when one looks at his paintings one senses all the mystery of cliffs and ranges." Would that something from his hand had survived! Chang Yen-yüan conjures up an evocative mastery of atmosphere and depth, a true landscape feeling, very different from the naive "Chan Tzu-ch'ien" and very different too from the carefully painted, colourful pictures that are traditionally associated with the two Li. The most interesting picture in what we might call the Li tradition is the well-known *Emperor Ming-huang's Journey to Shu* (Plate 25), which depicts in the technique of a miniaturist either an imperial excursion or (though this seems less likely) the emperor's flight from An Lu-shan in 756 transformed into a leisurely progress through the hills. Whenever this exquisite picture was painted—and it has been assigned a date anywhere from the eighth century to the fifteenth!—it seems to preserve, possibly in a very squeezed-up form, a composition of the T'ang Dynasty and a decorative palace style that one would associate with Li Chao-tao rather than with his father, for there is about it nothing of the forcefulness, hazy uncertainty, or mystery that the critic assigned to Li Ssu-hsün.

With Wang Wei (?699-?761) we would expect to be on more certain ground, for he is one of the truly great figures in Chinese intellectual and artistic history. From time to time an official in the upper ranks of the bureaucracy, Wang Wei was a courtier and a gentleman, a scholar and a poet, a devout Buddhist (particularly in later life), and an amateur painter of landscapes. He once wrote of himself: *

> In a past life I was mistakenly a poet
> In a former existence I must have been a painter
> Unable to throw off my remnant habits
> I find the world has come to know me for them . . .

What Wang Wei seems to be saying is "I know I'm a gifted painter, but forgive me—I can't help it." Although he half meant it as a joke, he might not have put it quite the way he did—he uses the term *hua shih*, "master painter," which carries derogatory connotations of professionalism—unless he had meant to make a distinction between the specialist and the kind of amateur poet-painter that he felt himself to be. This distinction, first articulated in the T'ang Dynasty, was to become sharper with time, and was to have a profound effect upon the future development of landscape painting in China. Indeed, Wang Wei's own later reputation was based not so much on his painting, about which there were conflicting accounts, as on what he stood for as the founding father of the school of amateur, "literary" landscape painting. Just how well he deserved that reputation is a fascinating question to which, in the absence of a single genuine work from his hand, we will never know the answer.

*Translated by B. W. Robinson, *Poems of Wang Wei* (Harmondsworth, Eng., 1973), p. 140.

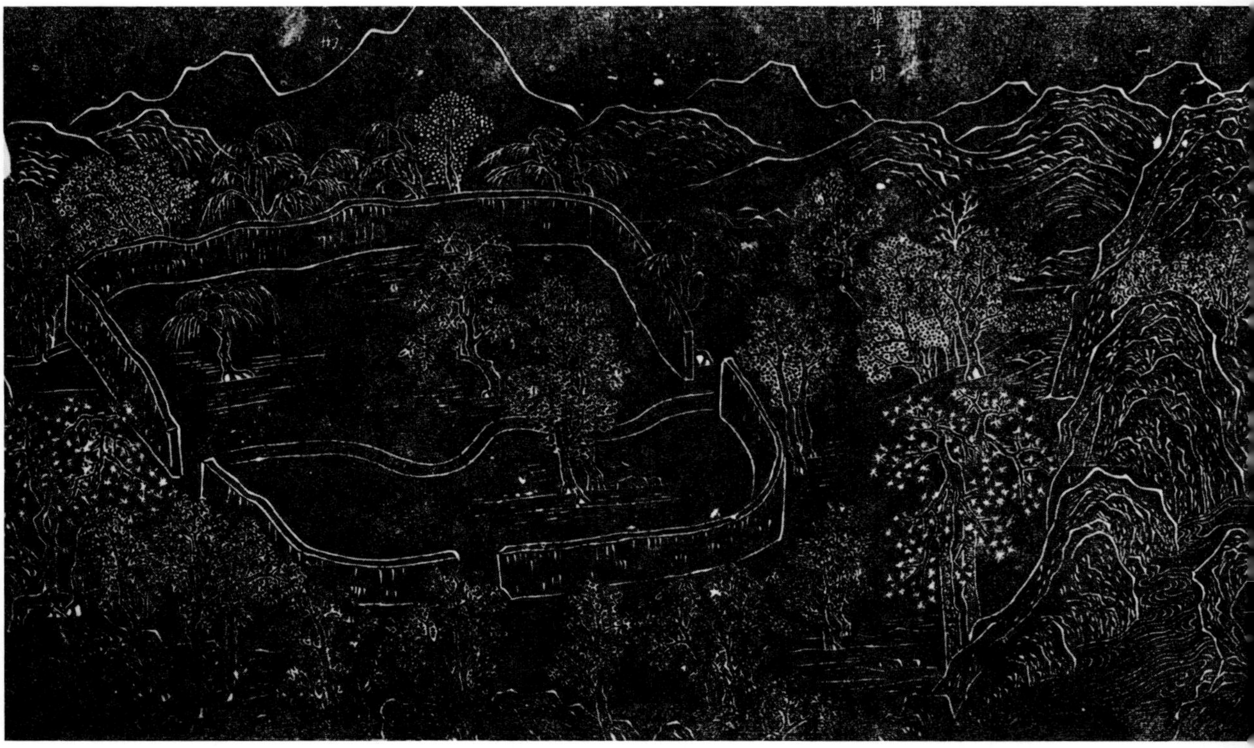

In middle life Wang Wei acquired a country estate on the Wang River, about 25 miles south of Ch'ang-an. There he spent his happiest days, overseeing the improvements, entertaining his literary companions, writing poetry, and doing a bit of painting. With a friend, P'ei Ti, he composed 24 short poems describing The Deer Enclosure, The Hollow of Ming's Wall, the Path of the Ash Trees, and other spots that became famous through his poems. Rather than repeat those oft-quoted lines, I give here a letter he wrote to P'ei Ti that evokes, far better than the poems, something of the flavour of the man himself; for he speaks from the heart, with none of the formal constraints that the regular five-character-to-a-line verse form imposes:

This twelfth month the weather has been bright and agreeable, and I could have come over the mountain, but I hesitated to disturb you, deep as you are in the Classics. So I went off for a walk in the hills. I rested at the Kan-p'ei Temple, where I had something to eat with the hill monks, before I left and went north over the Black Water. The clear moon lit up all the country. In the night I went up Hua-tzu Hill, and the waters of the Wang River were rippling up and down with the moon. Distant lights in the cold hills were coming and going beyond

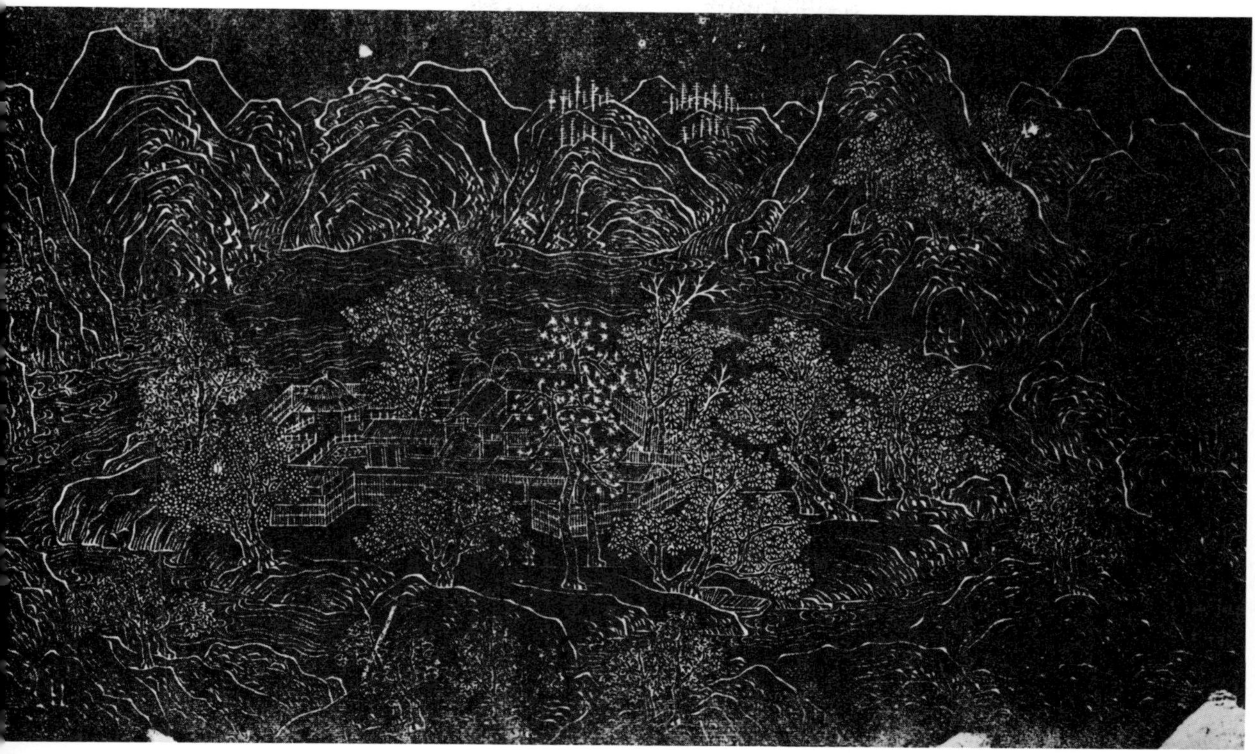

26. After Wang Wei (?699–?761): "The Wang-ch'uan Estate." Detail of rubbing from a stone relief made after a copy of Wang Wei's handscroll. Ming Dynasty; fifteenth century. Art Museum, Princeton University, Princeton, N.J.

the woods. The barking of the winter dogs in the deep lanes sounded like leopards. The pounding of grain in the village could be heard between the strokes of a distant bell. Now I am sitting by myself. The servants are asleep. I am thinking a lot about the old days, our composing poems as we walked arm in arm along steep paths beside clear streams.

We must wait for the spring, when all the grasses and trees will come out again and we can look at the spring hills. The light dace coming out of the water. The gulls soaring. Dew wetting the green banks. The morning call of the pheasants in the corn. All this is not far off, and then you can surely come and wander about with me? If it weren't for your natural genius, I would of course not impose anything so inessential on you. But it holds deep interest. No urgency. This goes to you by a hillman. No more now.

*From Wang Wei, man of the hills.**

Wang Wei is thought to have painted a panorama of his beloved Wang River estate several times—once on the walls of a building that he converted into a Buddhist temple after the death of his mother in 749 or 750. These paintings all disappeared centuries ago, but one of the versions was engraved on stone slabs hundreds of years later during the

*Translated by B. W. Robinson, *Poems of Wang Wei*, p. 141.

Ming Dynasty (Plate 26), and rubbings from these slabs have begotten still more versions, each one taking us further and further away from the original Wang Wei. It is sad to think that the rubbings are as close as we may ever get to him, for he is a figure of enormous importance in the history of Chinese landscape painting. For later critics claimed not only that he was the first to "break his ink," an expression I shall explain in a few moments, but also that he was the founder of the "Southern School" of gentlemen's landscape painting, in contrast to the "Northern School" founded by the court painters Li Ssu-hsün and Li Chao-tao and represented by such works as *Ming-huang's Journey to Shu*. We shall see, when we come to the Ming Dynasty, that the doctrine of the Northern and Southern schools was virtually invented by a sixteenth-century critic for reasons that had more to do with the politics of his own day than with art itself, and that his theory throws more light on Ming painting than it does on that of the T'ang. All we know for certain is that we do not know how Wang Wei painted, and that Chinese critics and historians became more and more certain that they *did* know the further the real Wang Wei receded from them into the mists of the past. The historical truth about Wang Wei's style, therefore, has become less important than the tradition about him, which helped to form in the minds of the scholar class the conviction that there was a special kind of landscape painting—free, relaxed, spontaneous, calligraphic, using "broken" ink on paper rather than fine line and colour on silk—that was appropriate for a scholar and a gentleman.

A much more exciting painter than Wang Wei must have been his younger contemporary Chang Tsao, a southerner by birth who spent some time in the capital, Ch'ang-an. A friend of Wang Wei's named Pi Hung saw him painting with worn-out brushes and smearing on the ink with his bare hand. He asked him where he had learned this technique, to which Chang Tsao replied, "Outwardly, nature has been my teacher, but inwardly I follow the springs of inspiration in my heart." At this, we are told, the modest Pi Hung "laid down his brush." We get a more informative picture of Chang Tsao's genius from a vivid (and apparently eyewitness) account of him at work written by a poet from Szechwan named Fu Tsai.* Fu Tsai tells of a wealthy man who invited Chang to paint in his house. "The Master," Fu relates, "spoiled with the gifts of Heaven, suddenly appeared, demanding fresh silk to display his extraordinary art." The host gave a shout, the 24 guests all stood up, and Chang Tsao

**Kuan Chang Yüan-wai hua sung-shih hsü*, reprinted in *Chung-kuo hua-lun lei-p'ien* (Shanghai, 1957), vol. 1, p. 20. Chang Tsao is the subject of my article "A Forgotten T'ang Master of Landscape Painting," *Burlington Magazine* (July 1975), pp. 484–87.

strode into the room, sat down on the floor with his legs spread out, took a deep breath, and then "His inspiration began to pour out. Those present were startled as if lightning were shooting across the heavens or a whirlwind sweeping up into the sky. Ravaging and pulling, spreading in all directions, the ink seemed to be spitting from his flying brush. He clapped his hands with a cracking sound. Dividing and drawing together, suddenly strange shapes were born. When he had finished, there stood pine trees, scaly and riven, crags steep and precipitous, clear water and turbulent clouds. He threw down his brush, got up, and looked about him in every direction. It seemed as if the sky had cleared after a storm, to reveal the true essence of the thousand things."

"When we contemplate Master Chang's art," Fu Tsai concludes, "it is not painting, it is the very Tao itself. Whenever he was engaged in painting, one already knew that he had left mere skill far behind. His ideas reach into the dark mystery of things, and for him, things lay not in the physical senses, but in the spiritual part of his mind. And thus he was able to grasp them in his heart, and make his hand accord with it." Fu Tsai's stress on the "spiritual" aspect of these performances suggests that people were so amazed at his sheer technical bravura that their critical faculties were, for the time being at least, suspended. It is hard to imagine that a scholar-painter like Wang Wei would not have thought the whole thing rather vulgar. Yet the fact that Chang Tsao could conjure up so vivid an impression of real nature shows that by the mid-eighth century, or a decade or two later, landscape painting had made enormous strides beyond the charming archaism we have encountered so far, and had become, at last, a fully expressive art.

Now, for the first time, we can begin to talk about technique. We can distinguish, for example, between the delicate linear style of *Ming-huang's Journey to Shu* and the broad sweeping washes of mineral colour of the paintings in Cave 217 at Tunhuang. The linear was a miniaturist's technique, suitable for scroll paintings and popular with court painters and professionals. The Tunhuang style, which the Chinese call "boneless" (*mo-ku hua*) because it has no outlines, was essentially a decorator's technique, suitable for covering a large wall. As such, it eventually died out in China; but it lived on in Japan where it was put to quite different uses. For, as the technique of the Yamato-e, "Japanese painting," it came to be regarded—and this is one of the nicer ironies of art history—as an essentially *Japanese* response to the overwhelming influence of T'ang painting.

All the primitive landscapists seem to have worked in colour, whether their mountains had outlines or not. The achievement of the

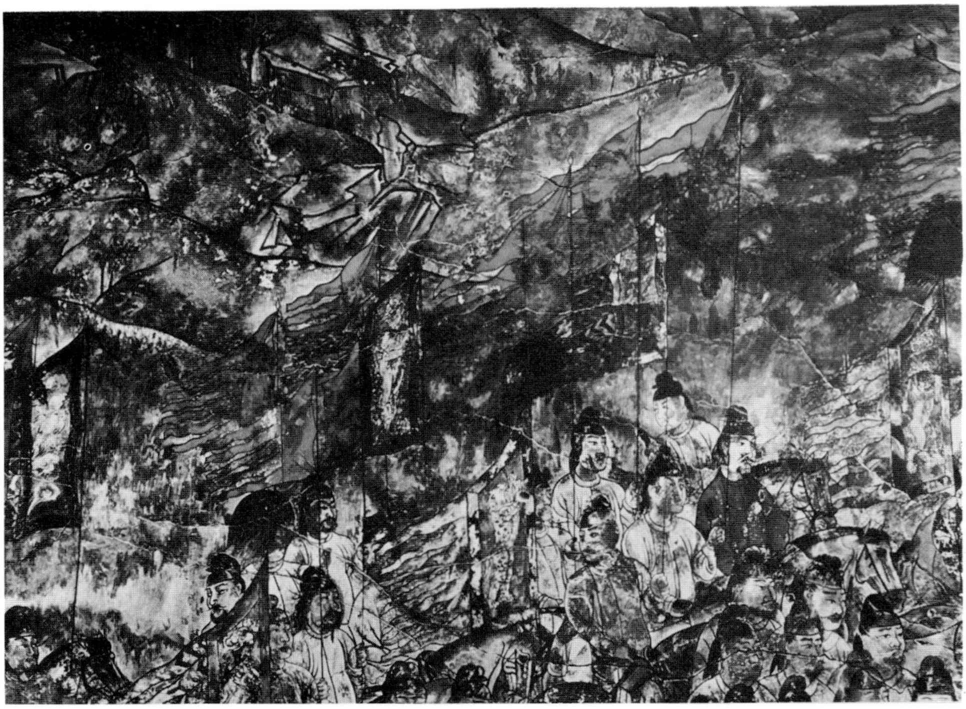

27. Anon: Processional scene, with landscape in the linear style. Detail of a wall-painting (copy) in the tomb of Prince I-te (706) near Sian, Shensi. T'ang Dynasty.

T'ang masters was not merely that they substituted ink wash for colour wash, as some recent writers have suggested—although they certainly did that—but that they carried the articulated, calligraphic line right through the whole picture, so that the broken interior washes that give form and character to the hills and rocks became one with the outlines in a new integration of texture. This technique, which for want of a better term I have called "painterly," will become the basic technique of almost all the great masters from the T'ang Dynasty to the present day. They applied colour more and more sparingly, for their aim was, as they put it, "to use ink as if it were the five colours." Colouristic effects, they felt, could be left to the craftsmen-painters.

Although the germs of this painterly style must have existed before the T'ang, the eighth century seems to have been the time when the calligraphic line and broken interior washes were first successfully brought together. T'ang critics first speak of the technique of "breaking the ink" (*p'o mò*) and ink wash (*shui mo*) in connection with Wang Wei and Chang Tsao. We see its beginnings in the way the outlines of the rocks in the paintings in the tomb of Prince I-te (706) are modulated and filled with ink washes suggesting form and texture (Plate 27). We see the tech-

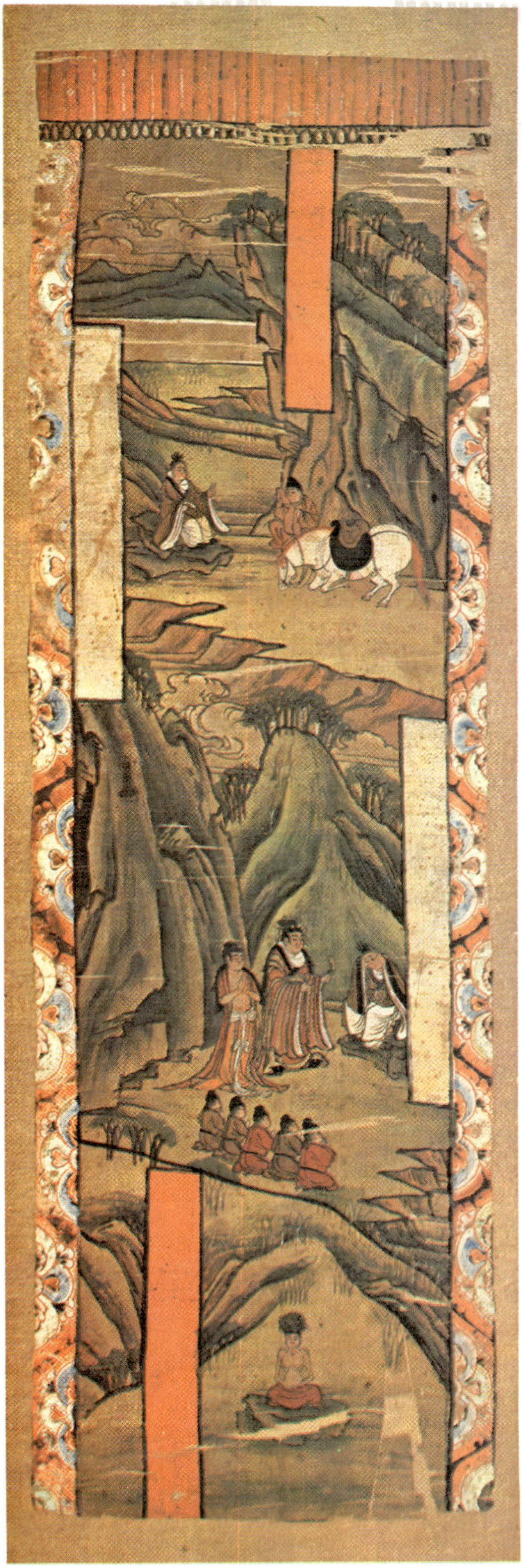

28. Anon: A panel showing the Buddha cutting off his hair, with the landscape in the painterly style. Detail of a banner from Tunhuang; ink and colour on silk. T'ang Dynasty, about eighth century. British Museum, London.

nique fully mature in the banner paintings on silk found by Sir Aurel Stein at Tunhuang. The panel (Plate 28) that illustrates incidents in the life of the Buddha when he cut off his hair, said farewell to his horse and groom, and prepared to embark upon the life of an ascetic is still arranged in the old way (the distant hills of one scene become the foreground rocks of the one above it), but the calligraphic line and broken ink washes are integrated with complete assurance: the artist is clearly master of a well-established technique.

For other early examples of the painterly style we must look beyond the confines of China, and particularly to Nara in Japan, where the treasures of the Emperor Shōmu were placed in the Shōsōin, the storehouse of the temple of Tōdaiji, after his death in 756. At this time the domination of T'ang art over Japan was almost total, and it matters little whether the lovely landscape on the leather plectrum-guard of a lute in the Shōsōin (Plate 29) was brought from China, or painted by a Japanese artist, or painted by a Korean immigrant, for in the eighth century T'ang art was virtually the international style of the Far East. It is an odd composition. The great white elephant with its band of Turkic musicians lurching toward us—we can almost hear the shrill trumpet, the clamour of the cymbals and drums—seems an intrusion into an otherwise peaceful landscape. The cliffs are painted in broken washes of ink and colour, opening up to reveal a deep valley, a line of cormorants alighting on a sandy spit, and the sun setting over distant mountains across the water.

Perhaps the most astonishing example of the painterly style surviving from the T'ang Dynasty is to be found on a tattered fragment of a Buddhist banner that was unearthed by Count Otani's expedition in East Turkestan before the First World War (Plate 30). The pine trunks and branches, painted with extraordinary power, could almost have come from the brush of Chang Tsao himself. They twist and coil like a dragon in convulsions, their clawlike extremities groping their way into the air like the tentacles of a living organism. If we examine carefully the interior drawing of the trunks and branches, we find that the artist's range of brushstrokes is in fact rather limited, which suggests an early date. But this is indeed a bravura performance, and we cannot help feeling that if such mastery of brush and ink is manifest in a fragment of a devotional, painting by some unknown artist found in the desert sands of Central Asia, how much more wonderful must have been the ink landscapes of the great T'ang masters.

Somewhere beyond the performances of Chang Tsao were those of the late T'ang eccentrics, who practised techniques every bit as outlandish

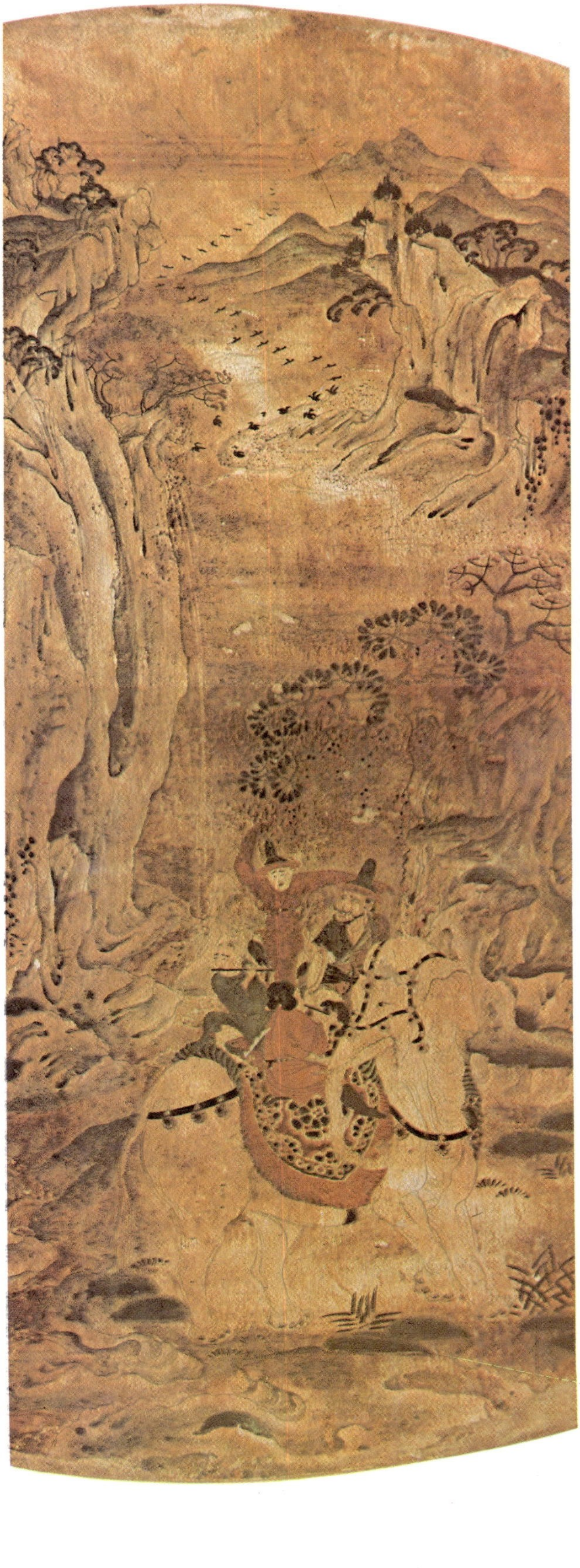

29. *Anon: Landscape with musicians on an elephant, painted on the leather plectrum-guard of a biwa (lute) in the Shōsōin Repository, Nara, Japan. Ht. 53 cm. First half of eighth century.*

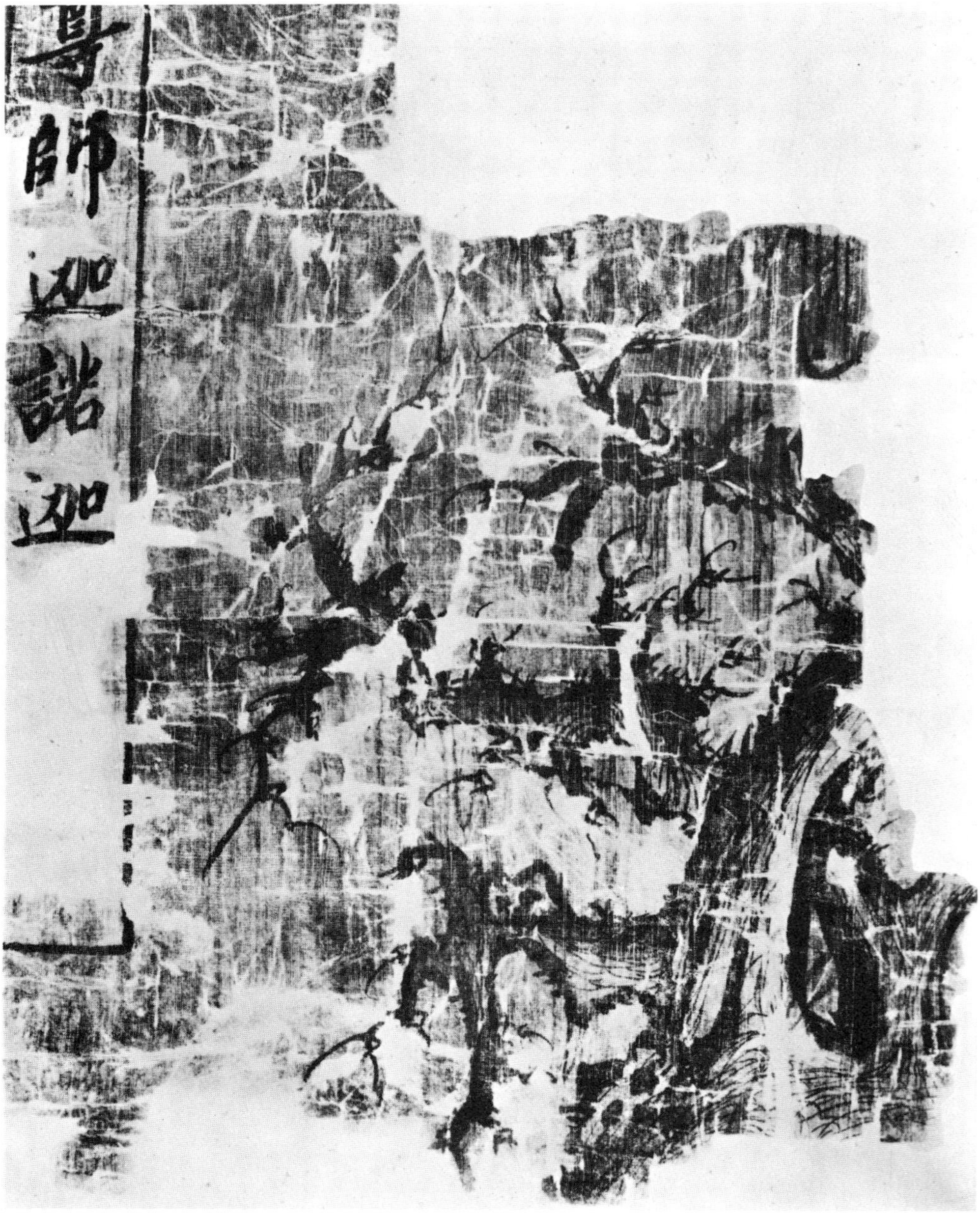

30. Anon: Pine tree. Fragment of a Buddhist banner found by the Otani expedition in Central Asia. Ink on silk. T'ang Dynasty, about eighth century.

as those of the New York Action Painters of the 1950's and 1960's. One man painted with his hair dipped in ink; another danced to music, like Mathieu, facing in one direction and wielding his brush in another. A T'ang text tells of Ink Wang, who would get drunk and then, laughing and singing, spatter ink onto the silk and stamp it with his feet and smear it with his hands. Another, like Jackson Pollock, poured ink and colour onto strips of silk that covered the floor, then had someone sit on a sheet, which he dragged round and round, making great swirls and swashes. But at this point the resemblance to the Action Painters stops. For these T'ang masters were not content with mere gestures with ink and colour. When they had done, they took up a brush and with a few deft strokes—a pine tree here, a boat there—converted their smears and blots into landscapes.

The T'ang critic Chu Ching-hsüan divided painters into three classes: competent, wonderful, and divine. But these "action painters," who so obviously flouted all the rules of painting, clearly could not be judged by them. For these men who were, so to speak, *hors concours*, he devised the term *i p'in*, the "unconfined" or "untrammeled" class. The term was revived from time to time by later critics, but it seems that never again was it applied to techniques quite as outrageous as those I have described.

Of course, none of the works of Ink Wang and his like have survived. They were in any case always considered freakish and not to be imitated: moreover, it is impossible to imagine a later student actually copying them. But the way these late T'ang expressionists went about their work showed the very limits of the art, and perhaps from time to time inspired individual Zen painters such as the mysterious thirteenth-century master Ying Yü-chien (Plate 52), who seems to have found the ink-flinging technique a perfect vehicle for the spontaneous expression of the sudden, irrational moment of awareness that comes to the Zen adept.

In a tradition that flourished on orthodoxy, these periodic breakings of the bounds of acceptable artistic behaviour come as a welcome relief. They are rare, and have more often than not been symptomatic of a general decay at the upper levels of Chinese society. Yet the periods of dynastic breakdown were often the periods of artistic breakthrough, and it was the wild antics of Ink Wang and his like, as much as the more orthodox experiments of such masters as Chang Tsao, that made it possible for Chinese landscape painting, once it had emerged from the darkness and fog of the ninth century, to achieve an expressive power not matched by the landscape art of any other civilisation.

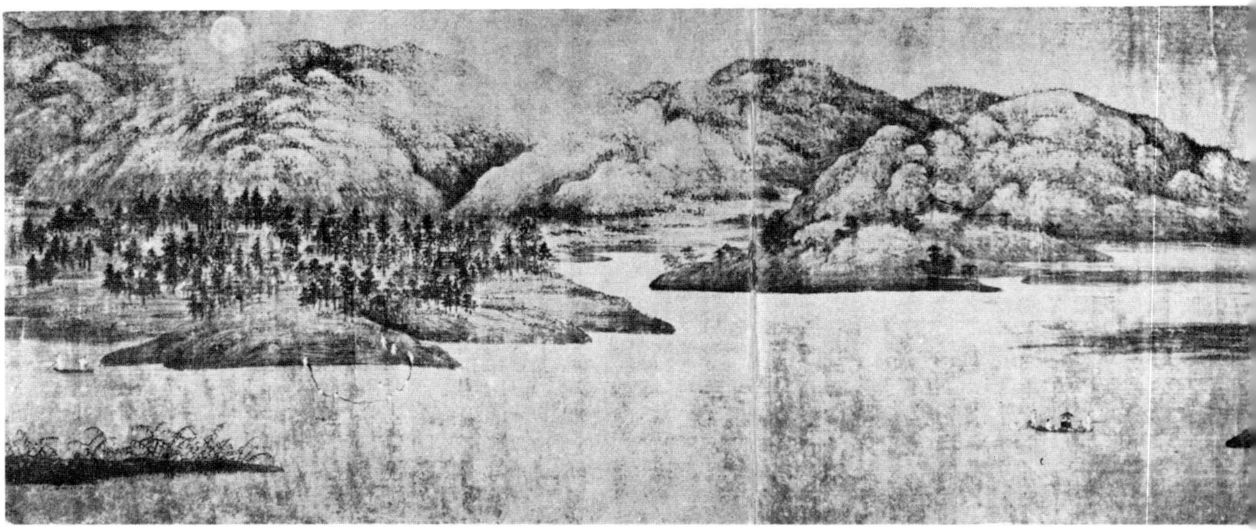

31. *Attributed to Tung Yüan (tenth century): River landscape. Part of a handscroll; ink and slight colour on silk. Early Sung Dynasty? Palace Museum, Peking.*

III Realism Achieved and Abandoned

The Sung Dynasty, 960-1279

We are coming to one of the great moments in the history of Chinese landscape painting. For all that we have seen so far—the discovery of nature and of the artist's creative power in the Six Dynasties, the mastery of space and of the expressive range of brush and ink in the T'ang—was now about to bear fruit in the work of a group of masters who were to become the classic models for later generations. The epoch of the Five Dynasties and Sung, covering the years from 906 to 1279, did not begin very well: when the T'ang finally collapsed, China once again was shattered into fragments. The northern Five Dynasties were in a state of such constant civil war that it is surprising that any painting was produced in the north at all. By comparison, the petty kingdoms of the south were peaceful, and the cities and courts of Nanking and Chengtu became havens of refuge for scholars, poets, and painters fleeing from the north, who brought with them the remnants of T'ang imperial culture. By 960 the founder of the Sung Dynasty had conquered the northern states and established his capital at Pien-ching (modern Kaifeng), but it was another fifteen years before he succeeded in mopping up the southern kingdoms and unifying the empire once more.

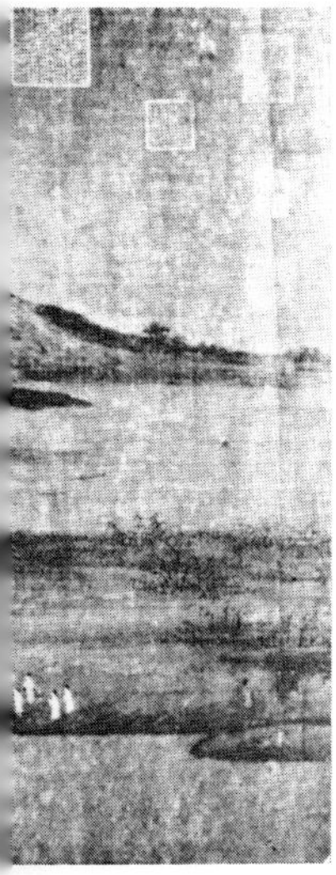

The last ruler of one of these petty southern kingdoms, the "Southern T'ang," was a *bon viveur*, a sensitive poet, and a connoisseur ill-suited to the cares of office, preferring the company of his poet and painter friends to that of his ministers and officials. In 975 he and a devoted band of equally cultivated men were carried off to Pien-ching to languish out their remaining years as harmless prisoners, dreaming sadly of the old days in Nanking. Among this company was a landscape painter named Chü-jan. The form of his name shows that he was a Buddhist monk, and how he became a member of the imperial entourage is a mystery. Little is known about Chü-jan except for the fact that in landscape painting he carried on the style of Tung Yüan, an equally obscure minor official in the department of imperial parks, who is not mentioned—at least in the surviving literature on painting—until more than a hundred years after his death in 962. But later critics endowed Tung Yüan and Chü-jan with extraordinary importance, so we need to know just what it was about them that was so special.

Tung Yüan, the Sung writers tell us, was chiefly famous for his landscapes in the old-fashioned coloured style and for his dragons. It was the scientist, archaeologist, and astronomer Shen Kua (1030–95) who was the first, so far as we know, to speak of a distinct southern ("Chiang-nan") style and to name Tung Yüan and Chü-jan as its founders. Shen Kua does not indulge in the vague generalities that we so often find in Chinese writings on painting; he does not simply say that Tung Yüan's painting is redolent of the *ch'i* and leave it at that. He says that Tung Yüan "did not paint strange peaks"—which could mean either the towering crags of the north or the fantastic distortions of the late T'ang expressionists—but painted "the real mountains of Chiang-nan." He also says that he "was particularly skilled in painting the mists of autumn and distant views." In a "Song about Painting" (*T'u-hua ko*), a poem in which he hits off the style of each of the major masters in a line or two, Shen Kua writes:*

> In Chiang-nan Tung Yüan and the priest Chü-jan
> With pale ink and light mists create a new style.

**Meng-ch'i pi-t'an*, quoted in *Chung-kuo hua-lun lei-p'ien* (Shanghai, 1957), vol. 1, p. 45.

He notes, too, that Chü-jan's paintings were roughly done and meant to be seen (like those of Monet) at a distance, and that (again like Monet) his brushwork got looser and more impressionistic as he grew older. Another early critic, the painter and eccentric Mi Fu (1050–1107), wrote that Tung Yüan's work was "natural" and *tan*. *Tan* literally means "bland" or "weak"; it is the word used for a weak green tea that yet has a subtle flavour. This quality of blandness, or unassertiveness, was to become an ever-sought and often elusive ideal for the later scholar-painter. Tung Yüan and Chü-jan got their effects by a sort of pointillist technique, with blobs and touches of wet ink that perfectly suggest the broad horizons, the soft contours, the hazy summer heat of the countryside around Nanking. Here we find none of the bravura effects, the "tricked-out ingenuities" as a Sung critic put it, of Chang Tsao or Ink Wang. Instead, all is calm, relaxed, and very close to nature. Neither Tung Yüan nor Chü-jan was noted for his poetry or scholarship, and their styles seem to have been anything but calligraphic. A critic might have said of Tung Yüan, as was said of one of his late T'ang predecessors, that "he obtained the secret of mysterious truth only in the use of ink, but in his brush there was no bone"—in other words, that he did not use the calligraphic line to express feeling and structure.

Only copies of Chü-jan's landscapes survive, but there are several long scrolls, or parts of scrolls, that bring us close to Tung Yüan. Just how close we shall never know, for there are almost no documents about early Chinese painters such as we find about the early Italian masters; no municipal archives; no accounts, or letters from patrons; and no scientific tests yet devised that will establish whether the ink and silk of a Chinese scroll were made in the tenth century or in the fourteenth. One of the most convincing works attributed to Tung Yüan is a broad panorama with foreshore, an expanse of water, a distant village half hidden among the trees, and low rounded hills beyond (Plate 31). There are a few figures on the shore, in a boat, and hauling in a fishing net. Just what the people in the foreground are doing is not clear. The Sung records speak of a painting by Tung Yüan called *Marriage of the Lord of the River*—an ancient sacrifice of a virgin to the spirit of the Yellow River. If, as has been ingeniously suggested, this is the picture, then the girl standing by herself is the fearful victim, the important figure in the boat the shaman come to perform the sacrifice. When we think how reluctant Chinese painters are to depict unedifying subject matter, this seems very improbable. But the history of the sacrifice has a happy ending, for one day a magistrate appeared who instead of giving the proceedings his sanction threw the shamans into the river and put an end to this barbaric rite. It is just conceivable that the figure in the boat is the magistrate arriving on his mission of mercy, but the total indifference of the fishermen to a spectacle that must have drawn crowds to the riverbank makes even this unlikely. Perhaps this is just a part of Tung Yüan's equally famous *Waiting for the Ferry at the Foot of Summer Mountains*. Whatever its subject—and iconographic problems of this sort are not very common in Chinese painting—this picture does seem to embody all those qualities that made Tung Yüan the idol of later landscape painters of the "Literary School." We note the unemphatic brushwork and feel the calm, relaxed atmosphere, the sense of nature softly breathing, the mood of a quiet evening by the waterside not only seen but felt in the artist's innermost being.

The contrast between Tung Yüan's still, horizontal world of lakes and rivers and the crags and precipices of the northern masters is very striking. The names of Ching Hao (ca.870–940) and Li Ch'eng (919–67) reverberate through the pages of Chinese art history with a more heroic note than do those of the tranquil southern landscapists. Ching Hao was a scholar and petty official who retired into the hills when the T'ang fell to devote himself to painting. His fame rests chiefly on his *Essay on Brush Methods* (*Pi fa chi*), in which he tells how he met an old Taoist sage in the mountains who taught him the secret of landscape painting. The Taoist gave him some practical hints, told him that Chang Tsao was the greatest landscape painter of former times, and impressed upon him the necessity of achieving absolute truth to nature. Ching Hao, through the mouth of his imaginary sage, was the first, it seems, to stress as one of the fundamentals of painting the notion of "thought." Just what he meant by "thought" is not clear, but I believe he may have been referring to the intense effort of painters at that time to distil their visual experience into a vocabularly of conventions for trees, rocks, and leaves often clumsily called "type-forms." The artist was actually creating a visual language, which demanded a close observation of natural forms to discover and fix their essential, eternal aspects. His realism therefore was not the relatively unselective realism of an artist such as Gustave Courbet, but a deep concentration of the mind on essentials. Once the "true" forms were felt to have been discovered and distilled, however, the seeds of the conventionalisation of landscape painting were sown, and the gradual retreat from realism would begin (Plate 32).

Like others before him, Ching Hao probably worked on a big scale. One day a monk sent him a poem requesting a landscape painting. The first line, "The six-board panel should be specially solidly built," shows that what the monk wanted was not a scroll, but a large standing screen six planks high, or rather a painting on silk that could be framed on such

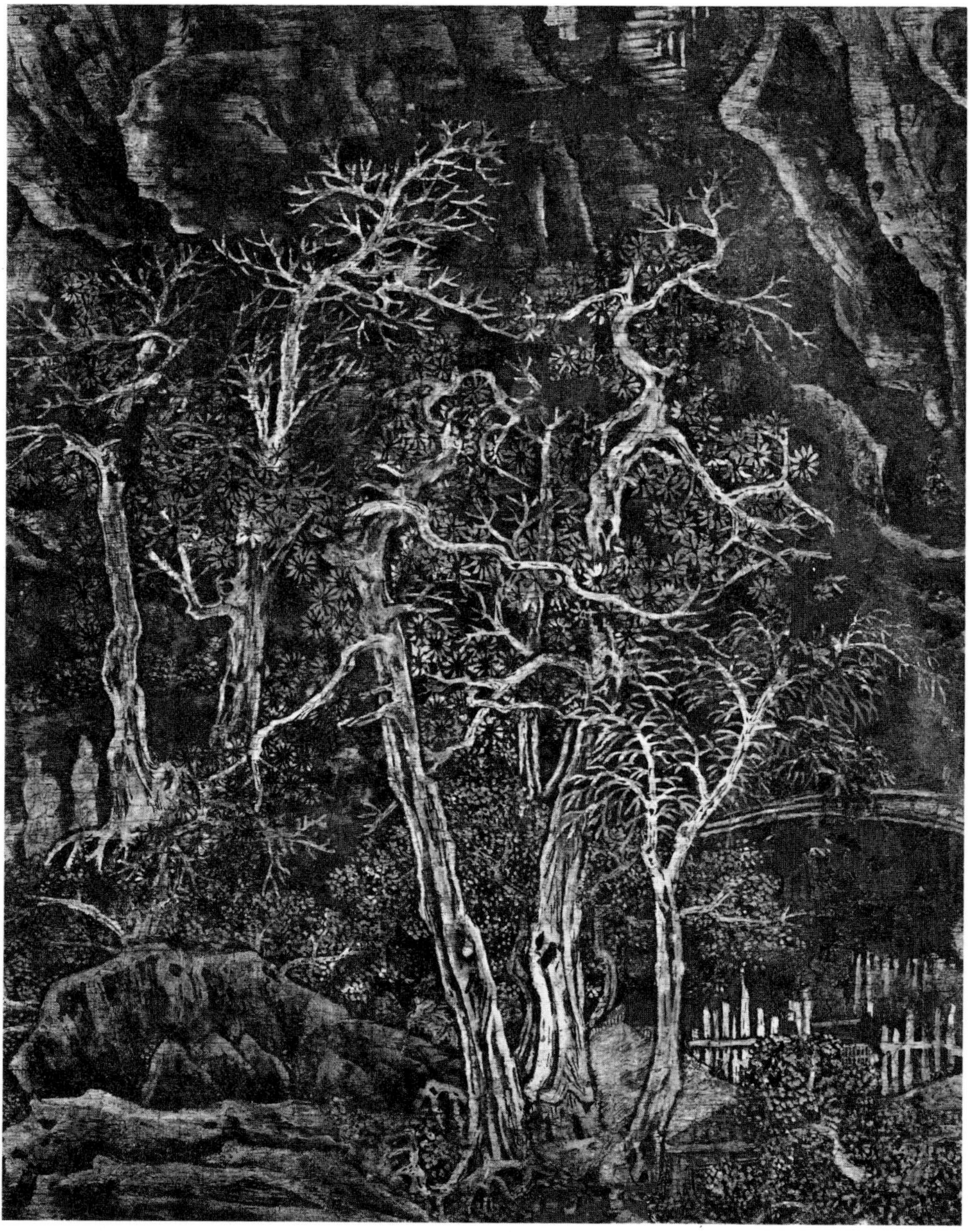

32. Anon: "Travellers in a Landscape." Detail of a hanging scroll excavated from a tomb and bearing the signature of Ching Hao (late ninth to early tenth century). Ink and slight colour on silk. Nelson-Atkins Gallery of Art, Kansas City, Mo.

a screen. These standing screen paintings, sometimes as large as the largest of Turner's canvases, challenged the painter to compose on a far grander scale than did the comparatively narrow hanging scrolls and handscrolls that we see today. They were treated as furniture and as room-dividers in the open-plan pavilions of the Chinese palace or mansion (Plate 33); they were even carried out into the garden to serve as protection from the wind. Not surprisingly, after a few years of this kind of treatment the paintings stretched on these screens became so stained or tattered that they were simply thrown away, or the parts that could be saved were cut up and mounted as scrolls. Today all these early standing screens have vanished, and with them what must have been some of the most marvellous works of the masters of classical landscape painting.

Of the great northern master Li Ch'eng (Plates 34 and 35) a Sung critic wrote: "Li Ch'eng painted landscapes and winter forests such as had never been seen before. His pictures were vibrant with unconstricted inspiration and his scenes of misty forests embraced unsullied reaches. The power of his brush came through in every stroke and his skill with ink was surprisingly fine. The wonder of his art is unique among artists of all time. Truly he may be a master of a hundred generations."* The catalogue of the Northern Sung imperial collection notes, "Anyone praising landscape painters considers Li Ch'eng the greatest of all time."

*Chiang Shao-yü, *Huang-ch'ao shih-shih lei-yüan* (1145). Tr. Wai-kam Ho, *Proceedings of the International Symposium on Chinese Painting* (Taipei, 1972), pp. 254–55.

33. Attributed to Ku Hung-chung (tenth century): "The Night Revels of Han Hsi-tsai." Detail of a handscroll showing an interior with landscapes and flower paintings on standing screens (in the background) and mounted on the bed-couches. Ht. 29 cm. Sung Dynasty. Palace Museum, Peking.

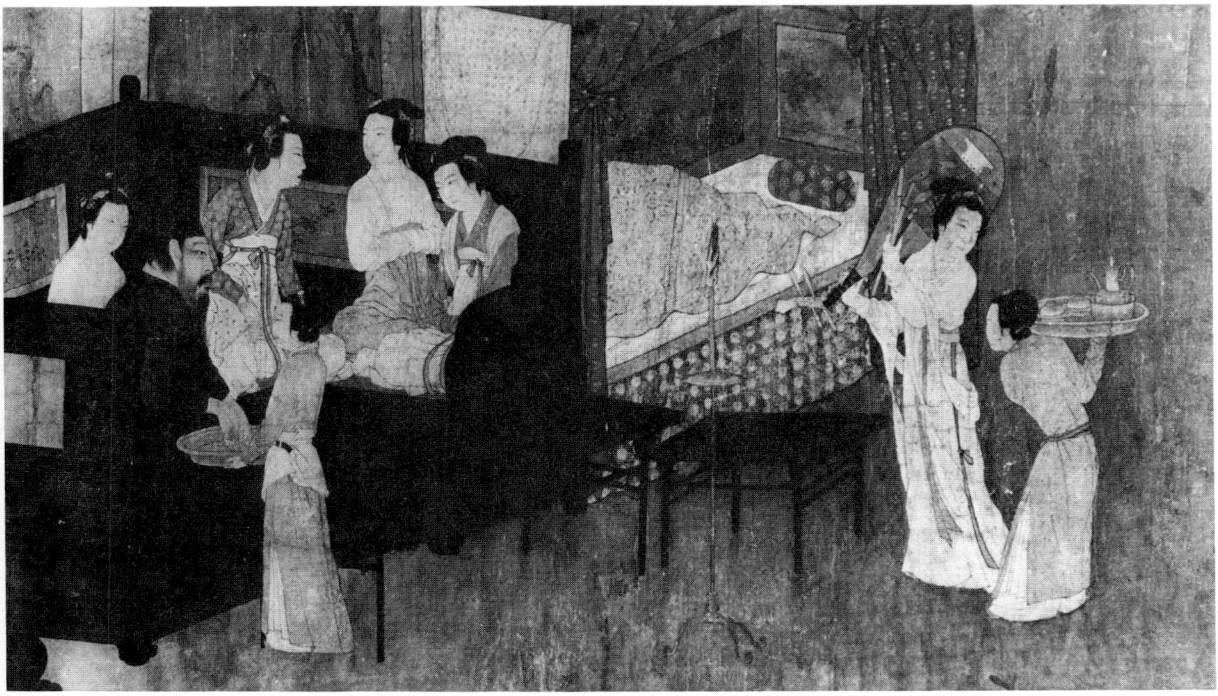

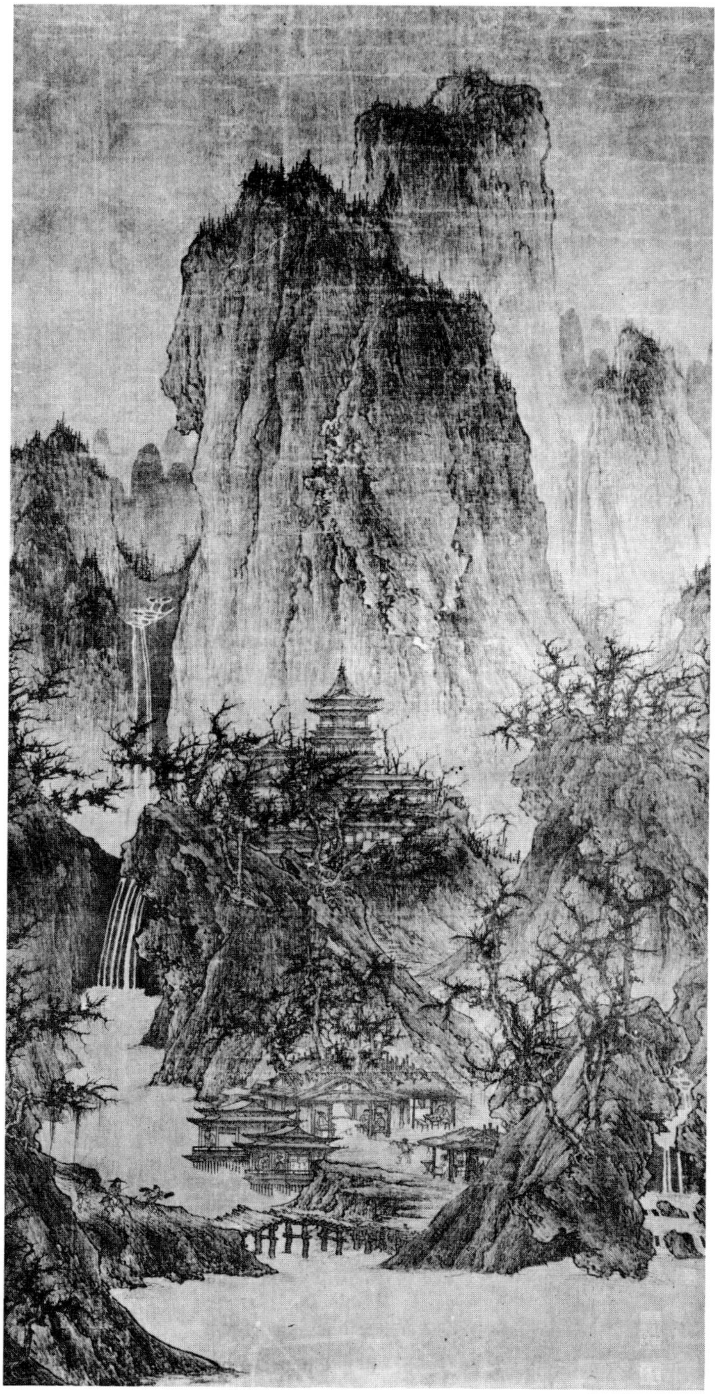

34. Attributed to Li Ch'eng (died 967): "Buddhist Temple in the Mountains After Rain." Hanging scroll; ink and slight colour on silk. Ht. 112 cm. Sung Dynasty. Nelson-Atkins Gallery of Art, Kansas City, Mo.

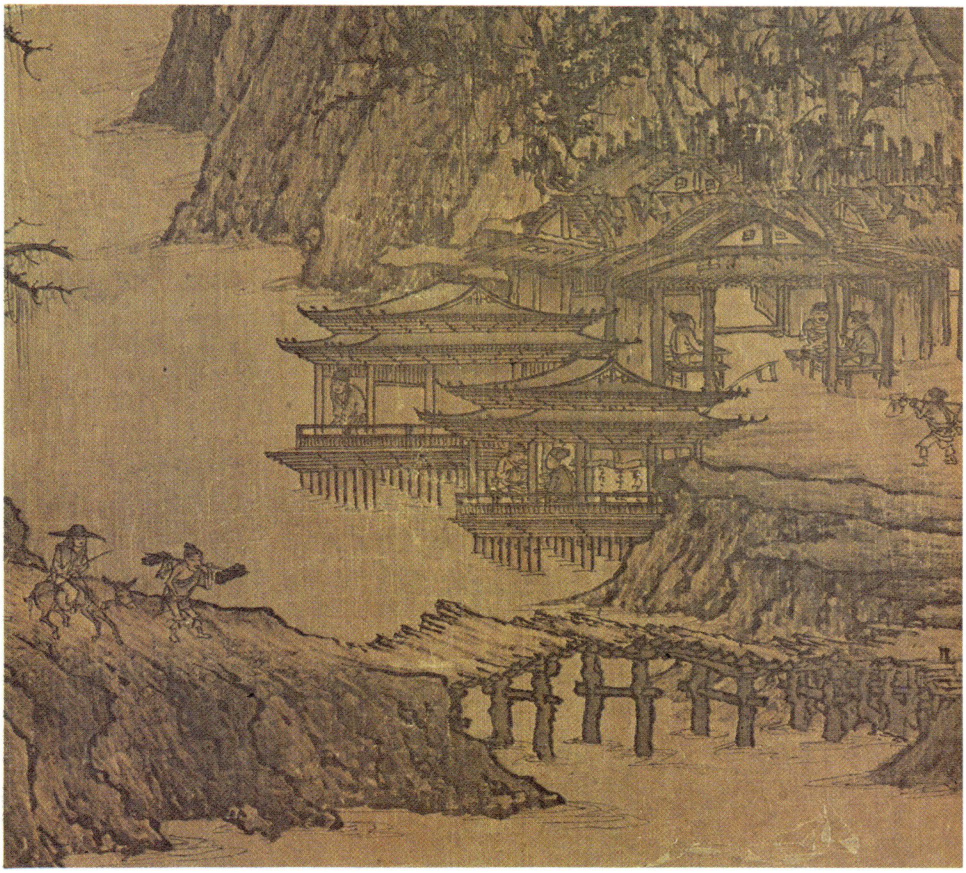

35. Detail of the landscape attributed to Li Ch'eng, "Buddhist Temple in the Mountains After Rain."

Li Ch'eng—unsuccessful aspirant to office, gentleman, poet, recluse—came of a family of Confucian scholars that had gone down in the world. One wonders what he lived on. To a persistent patron, owner of a fashionable restaurant in the capital, he is said to have written: "Since antiquity the four social classes have not mixed. I am a Confucian scholar, and although I paint, I do it only for my own pleasure. Why should I submit to being a retainer in a great household who grinds and licks his colours and is classed with the *hua shih* [i.e., men who hold office by virtue of their skill as painters] and other such riffraff?" Yet he had to live, and did not consider it beneath him to exhibit his paintings in that same restaurant, which the emperor himself patronised. Li Ch'eng's son and grandson were rather ashamed of him, for in spite of his disclaimer, he was a professional from necessity. This was a predicament that was to face more and more artists of the scholar class, and the most delicate and indirect ways had to be found to reward them for their work without causing them to lose face as amateurs and gentlemen.

The amateur might be forced into the position of a professional, but the professional could, up to a point, cultivate the tastes of an amateur. Li Ch'eng's follower Kuo Hsi (ca. 1020–80) worked his way up through the ranks of court painters as far as Scholar in Arts (*I-hsüeh*) in the 1070's. It is surprising that he never rose higher, to Painter in Waiting or even Painter in Attendance, for contemporary art historians wrote that he was the supreme figure of his generation, and that the Emperor Shen-tsung loved his work. Kuo Hsi's son collected his thoughts and sayings about the art of landscape painting in the *Lofty Message of the Forests and Streams,* which is not only a how-to-do-it book but shows that Kuo Hsi had had a classical education, and sought inspiration in the poets of the Six Dynasties and T'ang. The following verses—the first two lines by Ch'ien Wei-yen, the second two by Wei Ying-wu—are the sort he found particularly suggestive, presumably because of their intensely visual imagery.*

> Clouds wait brooding for snow and hang heavily over the earth;
> The wail of autumn is uninterrupted as the wild geese sweep over the sky.
> . . .
> Heavy with rain the spring flood rushes rapidly through the night;
> Not a soul on the bank; a solitary ferry lies aslant the water.

This is of course not the first time that poetry has been the inspiration for landscape painting, but the idea that a painter might have ready to hand a store of such verses to draw upon when he needed a subject suggests that the relationship between painting and poetry, which was later to become so typical a feature of the Chinese landscape tradition, was already beginning to become conventionalised.

Kuo Hsi, for all his literary tastes, seems to have carried still further the decorative bravura in the handling of ink wash that he had derived from Li Ch'eng, who had painted his mountains "as if they were clouds." We do not often think of chiaroscuro as an element in Chinese painting, but Kuo Hsi was a master of it. Besides painting huge screens and wall hangings, he would have plasterers roughen the surface of a wall so that in painting his mountains and chasms he could follow the bumps and hollows they had made and get an even more convincing effect of relief. His greatest surviving work, the *Early Spring* of 1072 in the National Palace Museum, Taipei (Plate 36), shows him as a master of monumental design, in which the realistic details of buildings, boats, and fishermen are totally subordinated to broad effects and dramatic contrasts of light and dark. Most Northern Sung paintings are meant to be examined

*Translated by S. Sakanishi, *An Essay on Landscape Painting by Kuo Hsi* (Wisdom of the East Series, London, 1936), p. 52.

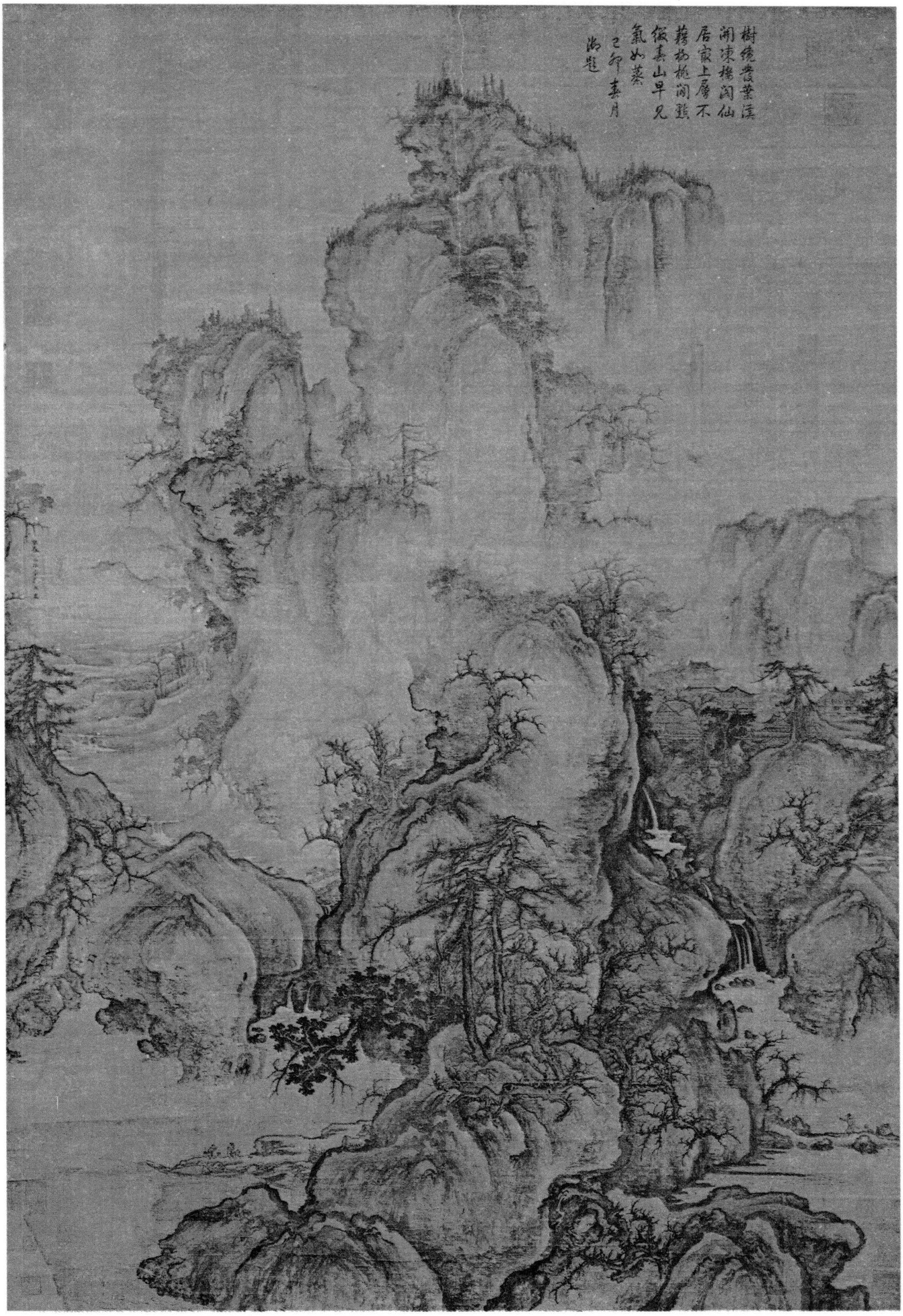

36. Kuo Hsi (ca. 1020–80): "Early Spring." Detail of a hanging scroll dated 1072; ink and slight colour on silk. Ht. of whole picture 158.3 cm. Sung Dynasty. National Palace Museum, Taipei.

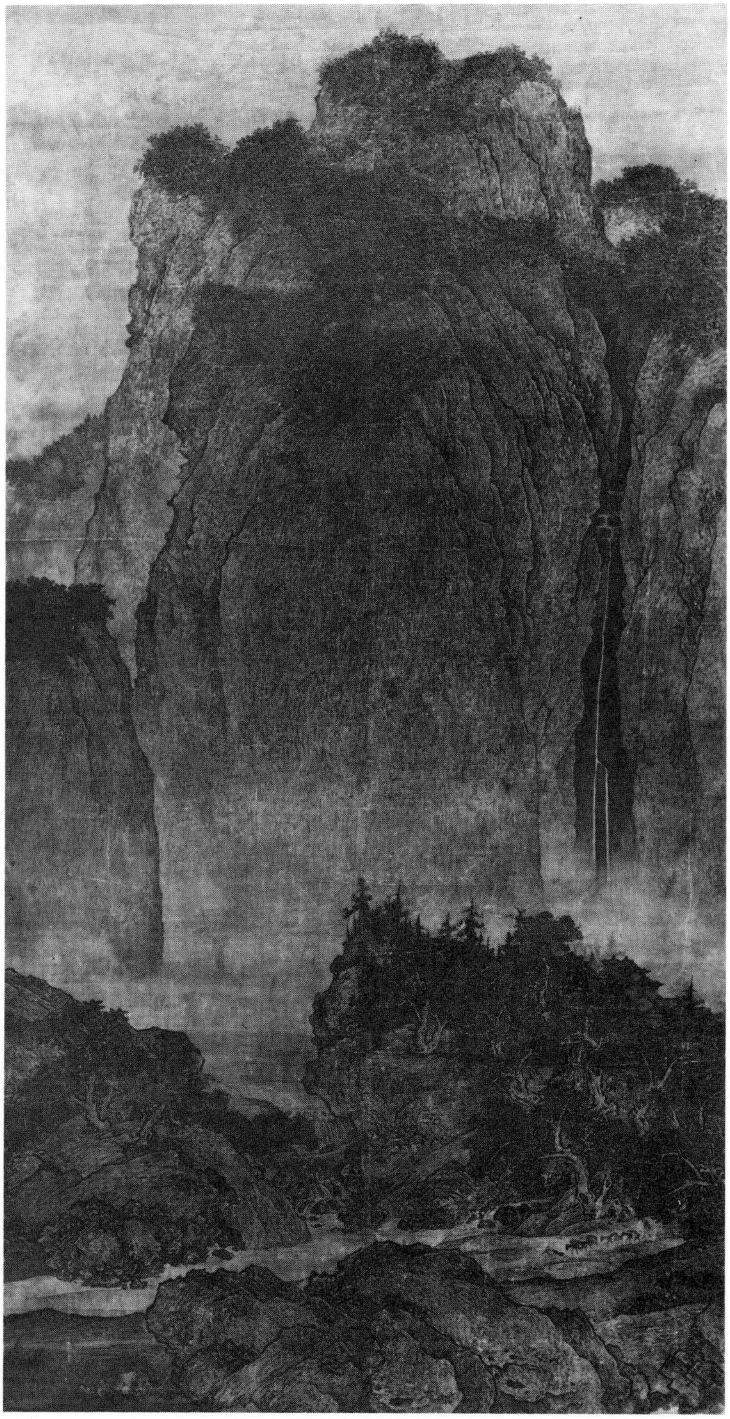

37. Fan K'uan (early eleventh century): "Travelling amid Mountains and Streams." Hanging scroll; ink and slight colour on silk. Ht. 206.3 cm. Sung Dynasty. National Palace Museum, Taipei.

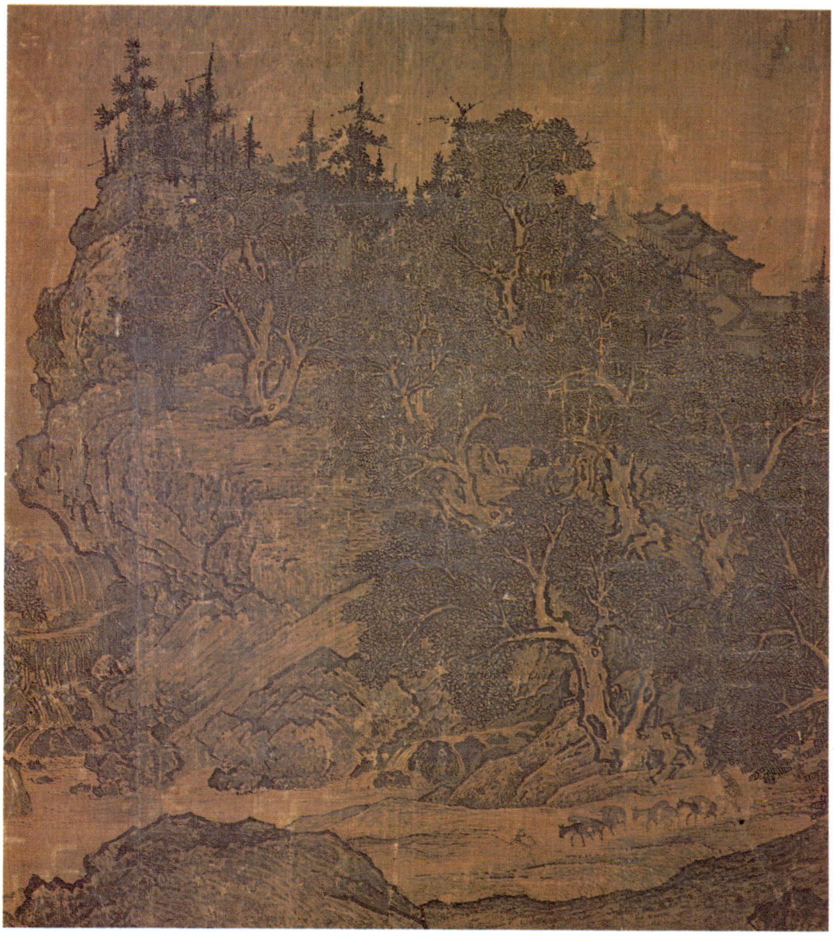

38. Detail of Fan K'uan, "Travelling amid Mountains and Streams."

closely, as if one could walk right into them. We have to stand back from Kuo Hsi, not because his technique is impressionistic, but because he is above all a great decorator. Perhaps it was this that led the fastidious, not to say pernickety, Emperor Hui-tsung (1100–1125) to consign his paintings to a palace storehouse, whence many were rescued by more discriminating collectors.

The search for absolute truth to nature that reached its climax in the eleventh century is best seen in what is possibly the only surviving work of Fan K'uan, a recluse of the early years of the Sung, whose signature on *Travelling amid Mountains and Streams* (Plates 37 and 38) was only recently discovered, hidden among the leaves of one of the trees in the lower right corner. No small reproduction, no words can do justice to this formidable work. A cliff rises sheer in front of us, its base lost in the mists that hover

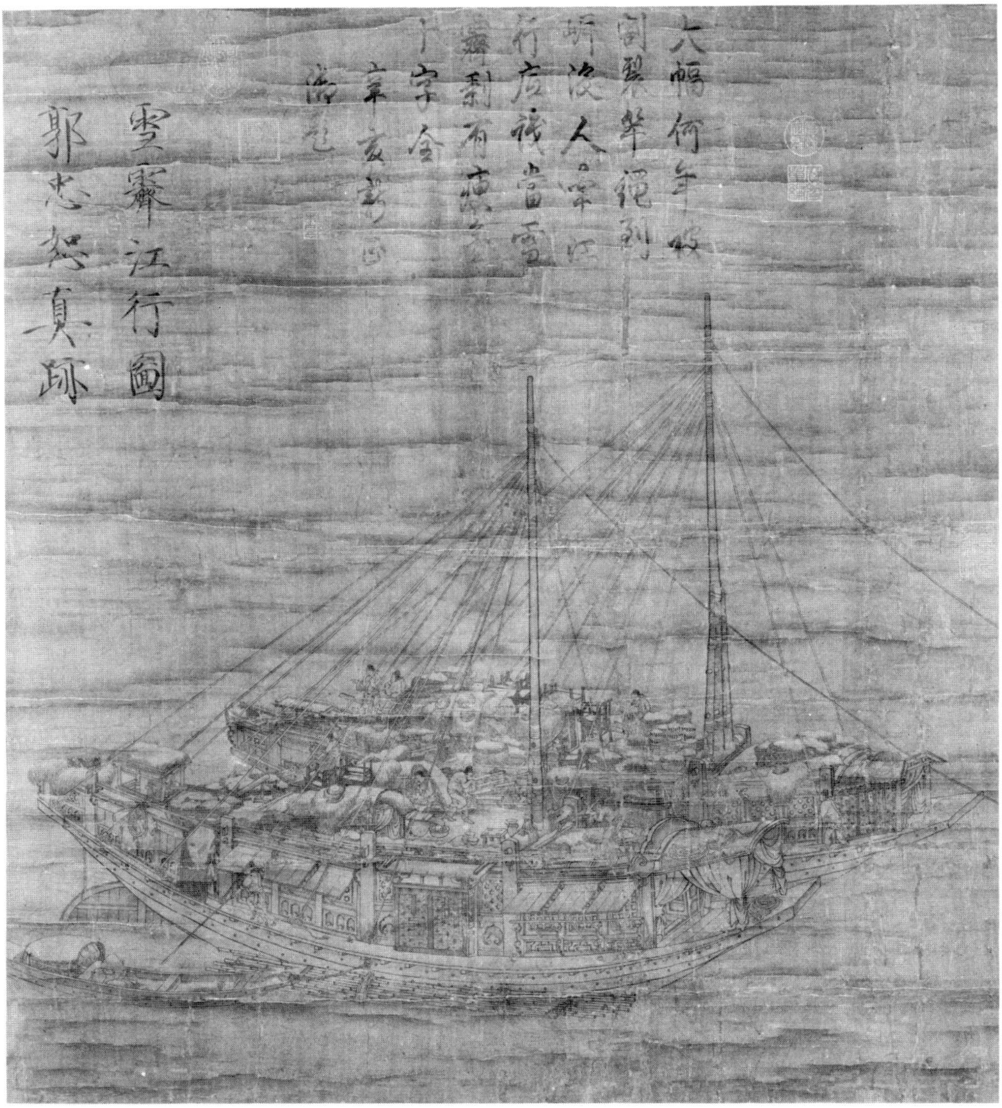

39. Attributed to Kuo Chung-shu (died 977), but more likely a work of the eleventh century: "Travelling Up-river in Midwinter." Hanging scroll; ink and slight colour on silk. Ht. 74.1 cm. Sung Dynasty. National Palace Museum, Taipei.

over the waterfall at its feet. From the dense wood that clothes a rocky spur comes a train of donkeys bearing firewood, while beyond, the roof of a temple rises above the trees. Never for a moment does Fan K'uan's brushwork slacken. He takes no shortcuts; every leaf is set down, every twist of root and branch seems to be carved out with angular strokes of great power, as if he were wielding not a brush but a knife. This is not a picture to stand back from, grand as it is, but to lose oneself in. Fan K'uan's aim is to make us feel that we are not looking at a picture at all but actually standing on those rocks beneath that great cliff, until, as we gaze on it, the sounds of the world about us fade away, and we hear the wind in the trees, the thunder of the waterfall, the clatter of hooves on the stony path.

Nothing escaped the eye of these northern realists. Although many of them were poets and scholars, no detail was beneath their notice. The painter of the marvellous scroll in Plate 39 shows an intimate knowledge of how river boats are built and equipped, and gives so vivid a sense of a river journey in North China in the depths of winter that it makes us shiver to look at it. We must try to imagine this picture as it must have looked before it was cut down, when it was probably mounted on a standing screen, with the heavy woven bamboo hawsers, as thick as a man's arm, sweeping down to a foreshore on which a team of harnessed haulers would be clawing their way over the rocks.

This extraordinary painting is attributed in the inscription above to an extraordinary man—Kuo Chung-shu (d.977), a scholarly prodigy who after a fight with a censor was banished and became a wanderer and a drunkard. Brought back into the emperor's service, he stole and sold official papers, was flogged and banished again, and on his way to Shantung suddenly stopped at the roadside, dug a small hole, stuck his head in it, and died. One would expect such a man to paint wild pictures in the manner of the T'ang ink-flingers—which he did when he was drunk. But in his sober intervals he was a master of *chieh hua* ("ruler painting"), that difficult art in which the intricate detail of Chinese architecture is rendered with painstaking accuracy. In spite of the imperial inscription, it is not known for certain who painted this picture; but the attribution to Kuo Chung-shu is not impossible, for there is reason to think that the intense realism that reached a climax in the eleventh century had already been attained in his day.

Perhaps the last great monument of Northern Sung realism is a handscroll, painted between 1100 and 1125, which depicts life along the river outside the capital at the time of the Ch'ing-ming festival in early summer (Plate 40). The painter takes us on a leisurely walk by the riverside, over the bridge, through the city gate, and into the busy streets, as though he were tracking with a movie camera. The painter, Chang Tse-tuan, shows complete mastery of shifting perspective, foreshortening, shading, and other realistic techniques that were about to be abandoned, not to appear again in Chinese painting until the arrival of the Jesuits in the seventeenth century.

Some Chinese scholars think this picture was painted in Kaifeng shortly before it fell to the Jurchen in 1127; but there is also a tradition that soon after the court was reestablished at Hangchow the emperor held a painting competition in which the contestants were required to recreate life in the capital from which they had been driven, and that Chang Tse-tuan (who, incidentally, was no humble craftsman but a scholar and a gentleman) was the winner. The truth will probably never be known, but if this is indeed based only on the painter's memories, its realism is all the more remarkable.

Whence came this passion for truth? It was not merely a reaction against the extravagant, undisciplined gestures of the late T'ang expressionists. It was rather a reflection of the restoration of Confucian seriousness to affairs. Probably at no time in Chinese history was the belief so strong that through reason and study one could come to an understanding of the world; and at no time was debate among scholars and civil servants more lively and intense. This was the great scientific age in medieval China. "Whenever one follows up any specific piece of scientific or technological history in Chinese literature," wrote Joseph Needham, "it is always at the Sung dynasty that one finds the major focal point." The philosophy formed of a fusion of Buddhist metaphysics and Confucian ethics that the West calls Neo-Confucianism stressed the importance of a rigorous study of this world as a path to the understanding of the Whole. As the great twelfth-century Neo-Confucian scholar Chu Hsi wrote, "The student must, for all the separate things in the world, proceed, by means of the Principles already known to him, to gain a further exhaustive knowledge of those others (with which he is as yet unfamiliar), in this way seeking to extend his knowledge to the furthest point. When one has exerted oneself for a long time, finally a morning will come when complete understanding will open before one."* To this end, "the concentrated and intensive" investigation of things, with complete sincerity, was the first step, and nothing was entirely irrelevant. This study was not

**Ta-hsüeh chang-chü* (*Commentary on the Great Learning*), quoted in Fung Yu-lan, *A History of Chinese Philosophy*, vol. 2 (Princeton, N.J., 1953), p. 561. Translated by D. Bodde.

scientific in the Western sense, but it did involve a serious concern with one's experience of the world at all levels, which is undoubtedly reflected in Northern Sung painting.

Why, then, were those realistic techniques abandoned, as abandoned they were? This is one of the most fascinating questions in the study of Chinese art. It seems to be bound up with the question, so often asked nowadays, of why China never developed a systematic science. I have suggested that the retreat from realism was connected with the growth of a vocabulary of pictorial conventions; but of course that is only a partial explanation, for the need for these conventions has itself to be explained. The reason is to be sought, I think, at a much deeper level—in the Chinese view of what constitutes true knowledge and understanding of the world. Central to Neo-Confucian teaching was the concept of *li*, "principle." Everything has its *li*: there is a *li* of good government, a *li* of relations between father and son, a *li* of the wind and the storm, a *li* of rocks and of bamboo. If only one could, by intensive study, grasp the *li* of individual objects and phenomena, one could eventually come to an understanding of the universe.

40. Chang Tse-tuan (late eleventh to twelfth century): "Going Up-river at Ch'ing-ming Festival Time." Detail of a handscroll; ink and slight colour on silk. Ht. 25.5 cm. Sung Dynasty. Palace Museum, Peking.

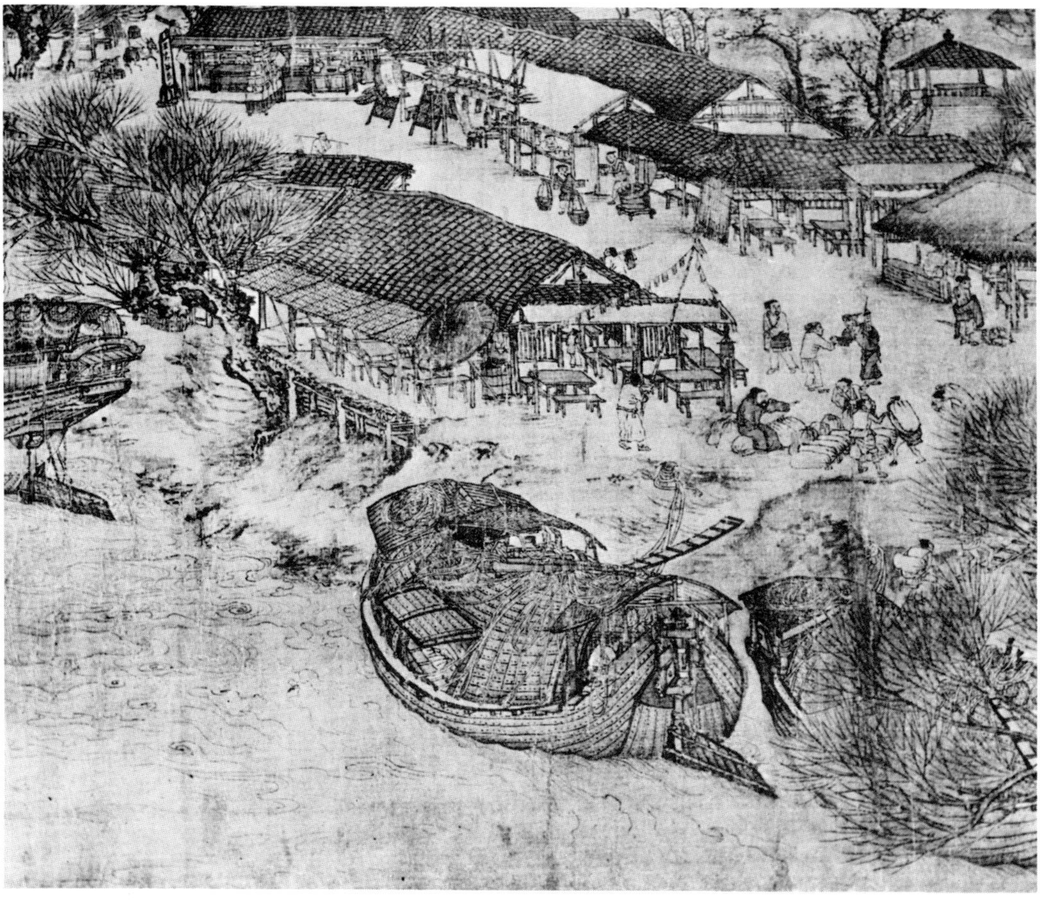

Was it the discovery that the *li* of things could be grasped not by study but, in the last analysis, only by intuition that led to the failure to develop systematic science beyond the accumulation of observations? Was it that Chinese astronomers found it increasingly difficult to reconcile their observations with traditional cosmology? Was it that the more rigorously one investigated specific things and events, the harder it became to fit them into a general scheme, such as the traditional 64 hexagrams of the *I-ching* (which, it was believed, could explain all phenomena)? Was it that, as Neo-Confucianism developed into a state cult, instead of stimulating the mind toward investigation, it actually forced it toward orthodoxy and submission to authority? Joseph Needham has suggested that the failure occurred because Chinese thinkers—and Needham is speaking of the Taoists, the only group that toyed with scientific experiment— "were groping after an Einsteinian world picture without having laid the foundations for a Newtonian one."* I would put it the other way about, and suggest that precisely because they had arrived centuries earlier at a unified, Einsteinian view, they found it impossible to develop a Newtonian one. If observation could not be reconciled with the world view, then one must cease to observe; for the synthetic world view was the better view, making for unity and social harmony, whereas analysis was divisive. If the artist's observation—of the variation in, shall we say, the texture of individual rocks or the bark of individual trees—did not match the schemata he was developing to represent rocks or bark, then it was the schemata that must be preserved because, as Ching Hao realised when he spoke of the function of "thought" in art, they contained all that was essential and typical. Once this decision was taken, the abandonment of realism and the development of a formalised pictorial language was inevitable.

A lack of confidence in the scientific approach is expressed even by Shen Kua himself, whom we have already encountered as an art critic, and whom Needham has called "one of the greatest scientific minds in Chinese history." For it was Shen Kua who criticised the great Li Ch'eng for paying too much attention to scientific perspective in drawing buildings—as he put it, for "painting his eaves from below." Shen Kua says that what (to the Western eye) is "correct" perspective is all very well, but surely the true painter should not concern himself with "the angles and corners of buildings." (He is objecting to the kind of perspective that the unknown painter of the gateway in Plate 41 is attempting.) Landscapes, he says, have to be viewed "from the angle of totality to

*In *The Grand Titration: Science and Society in East and West* (London, 1969), p. 311.

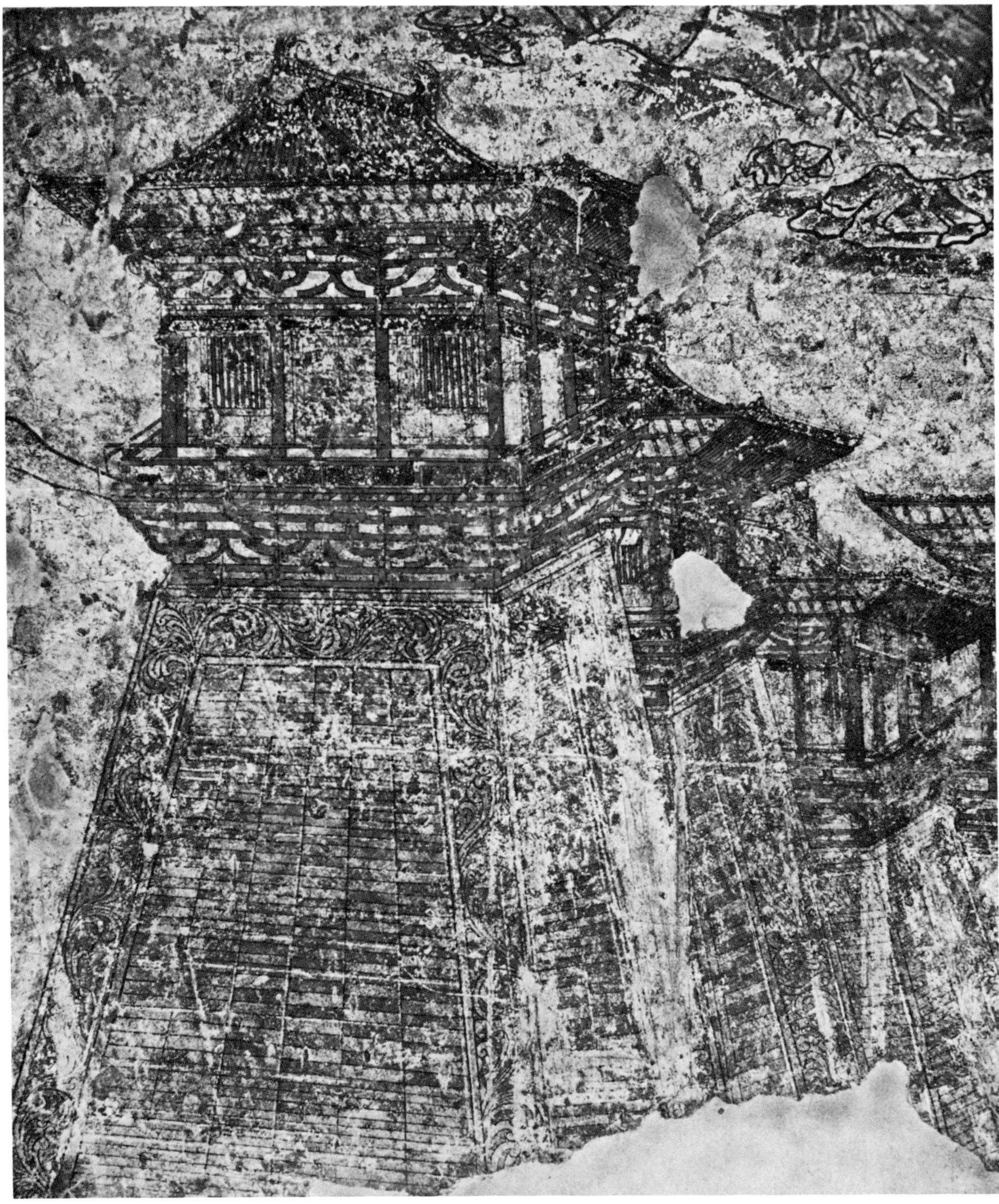

41. *Ceremonial gate tower. Wall-painting in the tomb of Prince I-te (706), near Sian. T'ang Dynasty.*

grasp the whole"—in other words, with a shifting perspective that does not limit the viewer to a fixed point but moves, like the gardens of suburban houses we see from the window of a moving train, creating a continuous series of vanishing points. The painter, Shen Kua says in effect, should paint what he knows is there, not just what he sees from one place.

If the great scientist had so little faith in the scientific application of the laws of perspective, how much less must they have been valued or understood by the literati as a whole! By the twelfth century, moreover, Neo-Confucians were becoming less confident than they had been that the study of the phenomenal world would lead to the truth. For Chu Hsi, study was important because it led to knowledge, not of the external world but of the self. From his day to the twentieth century, Chinese thought has been dominated by this concept of the purpose of knowledge, which at its best is noble and austere, but at its worst an excuse for intellectual laziness and timidity.

There was yet another reason for the retreat from realism, and that was a social one. In the Sung Dynasty, partly perhaps because of the high prestige accorded the scholar, the gap between the educated man and the rest of society began to widen, and scholars began to feel that it was beneath their dignity as gentlemen to know how a waterwheel was constructed (much less to construct one themselves), to depict the daily life of the common people (except in a humorous way), or to soil their fingers with any implement more utilitarian than a writing-brush. When the Mongol conquest of 1279 drove them into exile or seclusion, they were to derive much comfort from this conviction of their own superiority.

The effects of the unwillingness to accept the implications of a scientific approach to nature only gradually became apparent in landscape painting, however. There was no sudden break with the monumental realism that Fan K'uan and Kuo Chung-shu had forged; their styles were instead gradually frozen, as it were, into an official court style. The man most directly responsible for this freezing process was the enormously influential Li T'ang, doyen of the imperial academy under the Emperor Hui-tsung, who was himself a skillful academic painter and perhaps the first imperial patron to exert a dictatorial control at court over artistic styles and techniques. Between them, Li T'ang and the emperor did more than anyone else to create a gulf between officially approved court art and the kind of painting that scholar-gentlemen did for their own pleasure. A painting many experts believe to be the work of Li T'ang—it bears his signature and a date equivalent to 1124—*Whispering Pines in the Mountains,* is a coldly monumental work (Plate 42). Here it seems that the intense

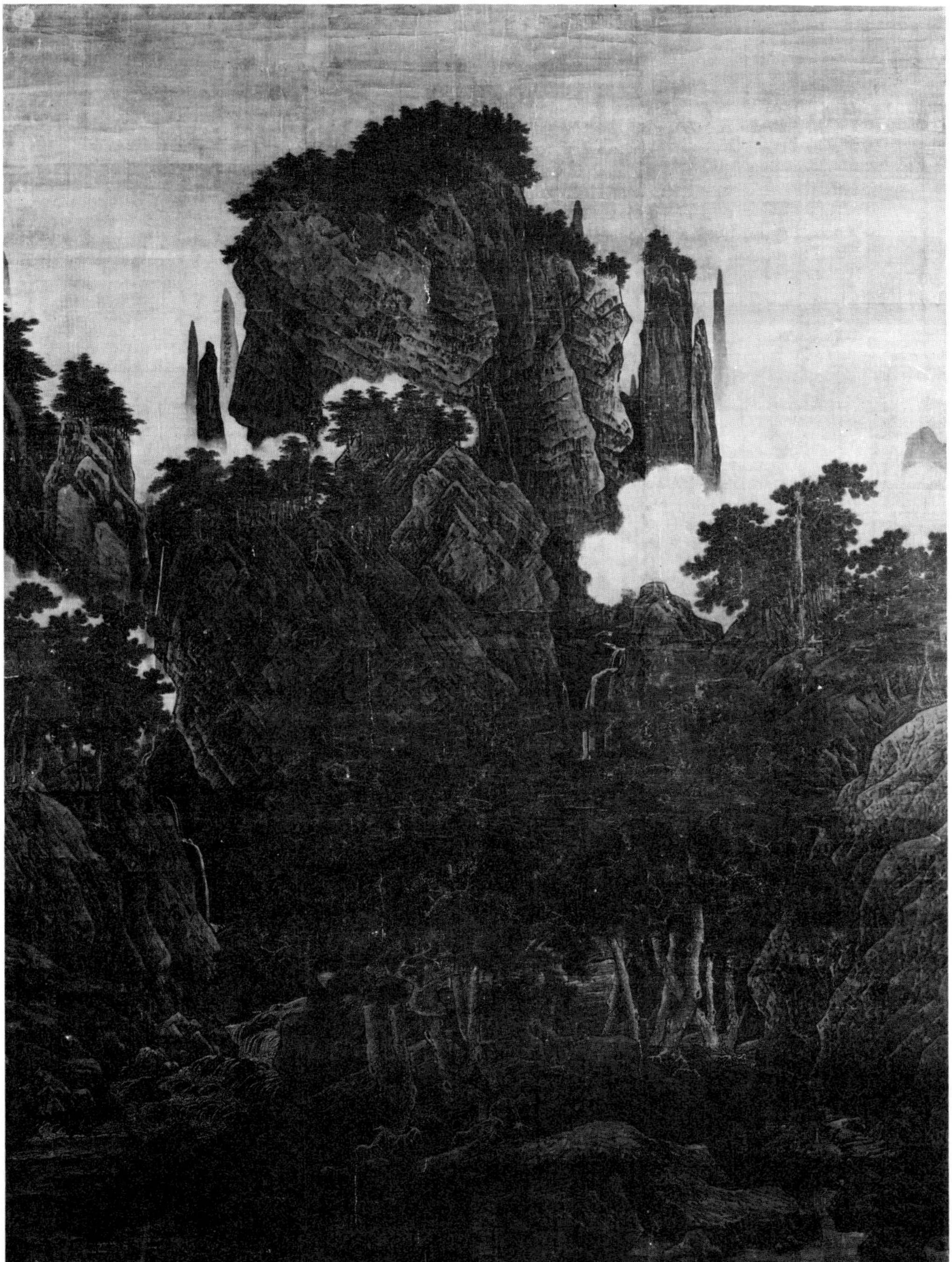

42. Li T'ang (ca. 1050–ca. 1130): "Whispering Pines in the Mountains." Hanging scroll dated 1124; ink and colour on silk. Ht. 188.7 cm. Sung Dynasty. National Palace Museum, Taipei.

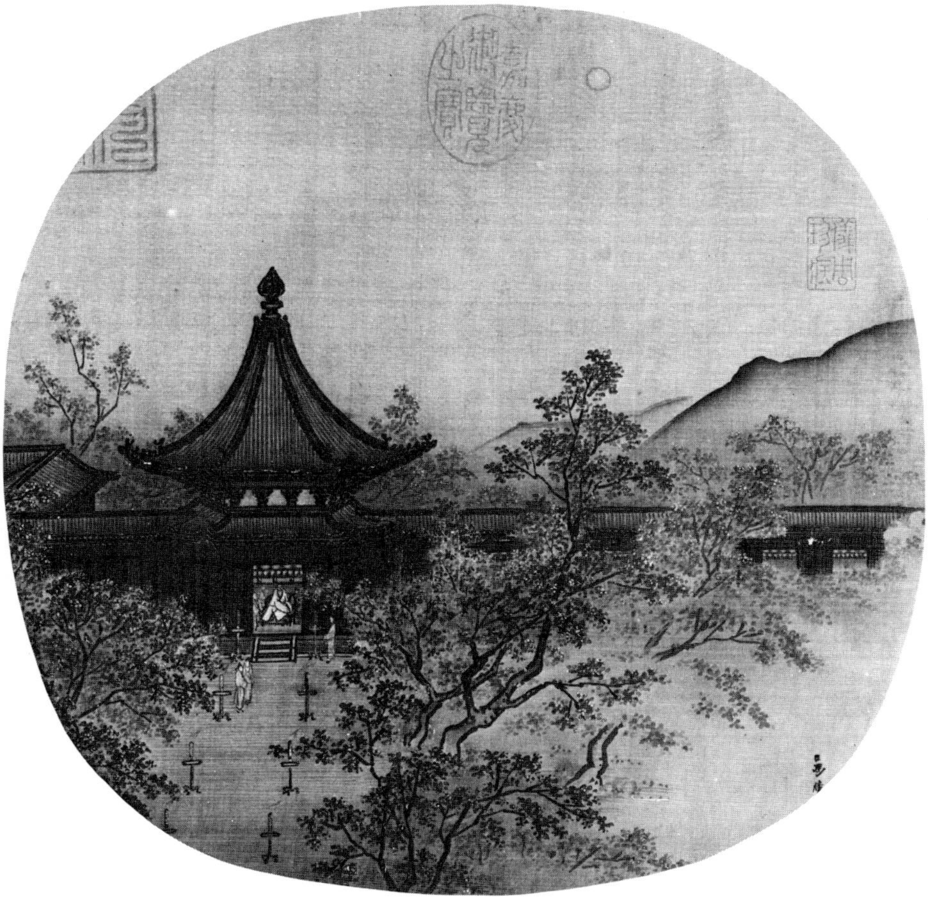

43. Ma Lin (early thirteenth century): "Waiting for Guests by Lamplight." Fan painting: ink and slight colour on silk. Ht. 24.8 cm. Southern Sung Dynasty. National Palace Museum, Taipei.

yet sensitive brushwork of Fan K'uan has hardened into a formula. The emphasis is on disciplined brushstrokes, specifically on a short, chopping texture-stroke (*ts'un*) done with the side of the brush, appropriately called the "small ax-cut *ts'un*," with which Li T'ang hacks out the facets of his cliffs as if he were trimming a beam with a hatchet. It is not hard to see how this could become an official style, and one that could with practice be easily imitated. It is completely impersonal.

Li T'ang was an old man when, in 1127, the Sung capital was sacked by the Jurchen, and the former emperor Hui-tsung and 3,000 members of his court were carried off as prisoners into the desert. Li T'ang for some reason was not among them, but fled south, joining the remnant of the Sung court that eventually took refuge in what they were sure would be only their temporary capital at Hangchow. In these lovely surroundings they pulled together what they had been able to salvage of the old court culture and art, and dedicated themselves to preserving it against the day of their inevitable return to the north. But the years went by, and that day never came. The generation of the refugees died off, and although Hangchow grew into the rich and prosperous city Marco Polo was later to describe, thinking people may have felt an increasing sense of unreality as the forgotten armies on the northern frontier strove in vain to recover the lost provinces.

Thus it is not at all surprising that the painting of the Southern Sung period, which lasted from 1127 until the Mongol conquest of 1279, presents a great contrast to what we have been looking at so far. Gone is the monumental strength, the passion for truth, the confident acceptance of things as they are. The painters of the Southern Sung academy sometimes seem almost to be afraid of the light of day. Their themes are lamplight in the women's apartments, a court festival at night, a banquet where the host waits, it almost seems in vain, for the guests to arrive while burning candles in the garden lest the flowers should know that night has come and close their petals in sleep (Plate 43). The landscape has a beauty so fragile that it seems it would shatter at a touch, or if we tried to come too close would dissolve before our eyes—which is, in fact, what it finally did. The spectacular bore on the river at Hangchow is viewed at night; and a

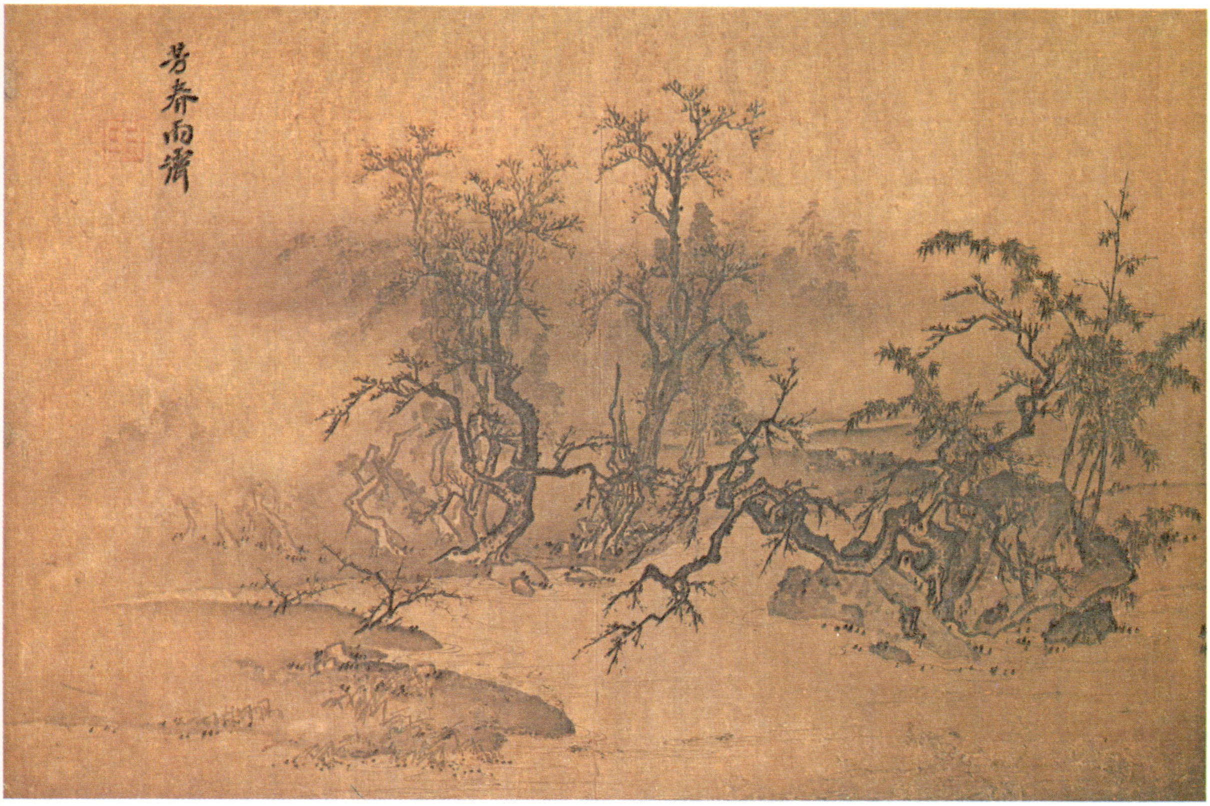

44. Ma Lin (early thirteenth century): "Fragrant Spring: Rain Clearing." Album-leaf; ink and slight colour on silk. Ht. 27.5 cm. Southern Sung Dynasty. National Palace Museum, Taipei.

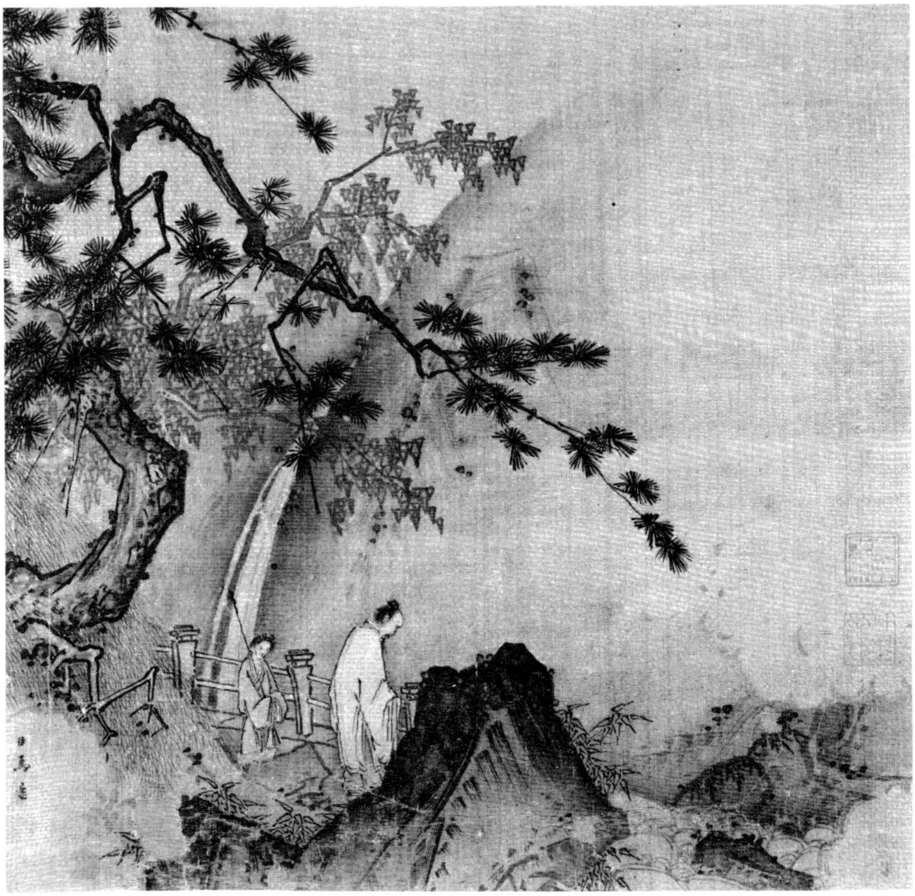

45. Ma Yüan (active 1190–1225): "Scholar by a Waterfall." Album-leaf; ink and slight colour on silk. Ht. 25 cm. Southern Sung Dynasty. Metropolitan Museum of Art, New York.

painting of a gentleman sitting in silence gazing out over a misty lake under a full moon evokes feelings not of exhilaration and release, but of regret and loneliness. Even the spring blossoms on the ancient plum trees by the waterside (Plate 44) seem to express a poignant yearning, a struggle for survival rather than a joyful sense of renewal.

I do not know if I am reading too much into these haunting pictures, and I have perhaps deliberately chosen ones that convey this mood. There are more cheerful ones; but it is those dream landscapes suffused with a poetic melancholy that seem most characteristic of the Southern Sung. The painters who in the decades on either side of the year 1200 created this exquisite style—notably Ma Yüan (Plate 45), his son Ma Lin, and Hsia Kuei—were all very close to the throne and members of the academy. They derived their style ultimately from Li T'ang, converting his tight

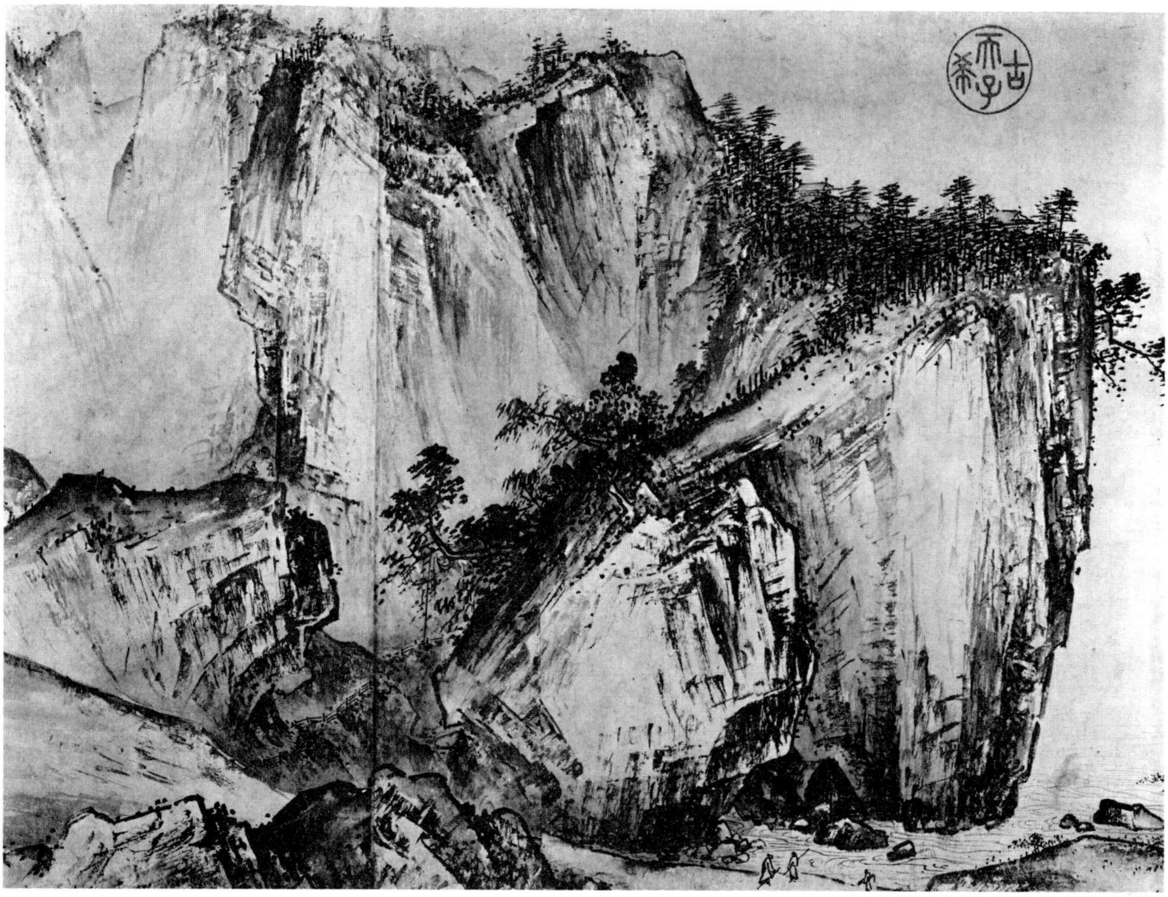

46. *Hsia Kuei (active ca. 1200–1230): "Pure and Remote View of Hills and Streams." Detail of handscroll; ink on paper. Ht. 46.5 cm. Southern Sung Dynasty. National Palace Museum, Taipei.*

"small ax-cut *ts'un*" into the broader and more pictorial "big ax-cut *ts'un*," making effective use of silhouettes and dark ink accents, pushing the foreground over to one corner to open up an unlimited vista into the haze, where the distant mountains seem to float like clouds in the evening light.

The style of Ma Yüan and Hsia Kuei (Plate 46) soon became popular in and around the court, partly because these artists were patronised by the emperor and empress, who sometimes deigned to write couplets on their fans and album leaves, but partly too because it had such an immediate and obvious appeal. It travelled to Japan, where it gave birth to an important tradition in landscape painting, the Kanō school; in the West it came to represent, to Laurence Binyon, Ernest Fenollosa, and other early enthusiasts, the very quintessence of the Chinese pictorial genius.

The Chinese themselves, however, look on things rather differently; and in the twelfth and thirteenth centuries not everyone shared these exquisite feelings, or expressed them in such conventional terms. There were southern scholars and country gentlemen to whom the loss of the northern provinces must have meant very little. They lived far from the court in their mansions and cottages in this most beautiful and hospitable region, accepting the procession of the seasons and each other's companionship with untroubled joy. Something of their contentment comes across in a sequence of Vergilian nature poems by the twelfth-century poet Fan Ch'eng-ta, of which I will quote but one stanza in Gerald Bullett's rendering—one of the rare examples of the successful use of rhyme and regular metre in translations from the Chinese:*

Few come this way, and if a stranger should,
See how the birds dart off, into the wood!
Shadows of dove-grey dusk the hills obscure,
And gathering reach my faggot-builded door.
In a boat light as a leaf, still visible,
My lad-of-all-work plies his single scull.
Alone I weave my fence, of little bamboo,
And ducks go primly homeward, two by two.

We find this serene, unadorned utterance in painting, too: not in the brilliant brushwork of Ma Yüan or Hsia Kuei, but in the art of the scholarly amateurs whose work has almost, but not quite, disappeared. These gentlemen expressed a view about what painting was, and what it was for, that later tradition credited to the T'ang painter-poet Wang Wei. But Wang Wei, so far as we know, never put it into writing; rather, it was the small coterie of amateur painters and calligraphers gathered around the great scholar, poet, painter, and administrator Su Shih (better known as Su Tung-p'o; 1037–1101) who first expressed it as a coherent philosophy of art.

Su Tung-p'o and his friends put forward what was then the revolutionary idea that the purpose of painting, or at least the kind of painting that was suitable for a gentleman, was not to depict things—that could be left to the professionals—but to express the painter's own feelings. "I write," he quotes a painter friend as saying, "to express my mind and paint to set forth my ideas, and that is all." Another painter of this time said, "I make paintings as a poet composes poems, simply to 'recite my feelings and nature.' " Painting and poetry were two ways of saying the same thing, as Su Tung-p'o made clear in his famous couplet on Wang Wei (Wang Mo-chieh):

*Gerald Bullett, *The Golden Years of Fan Ch'eng-ta* (Cambridge, 1946), p. 20.

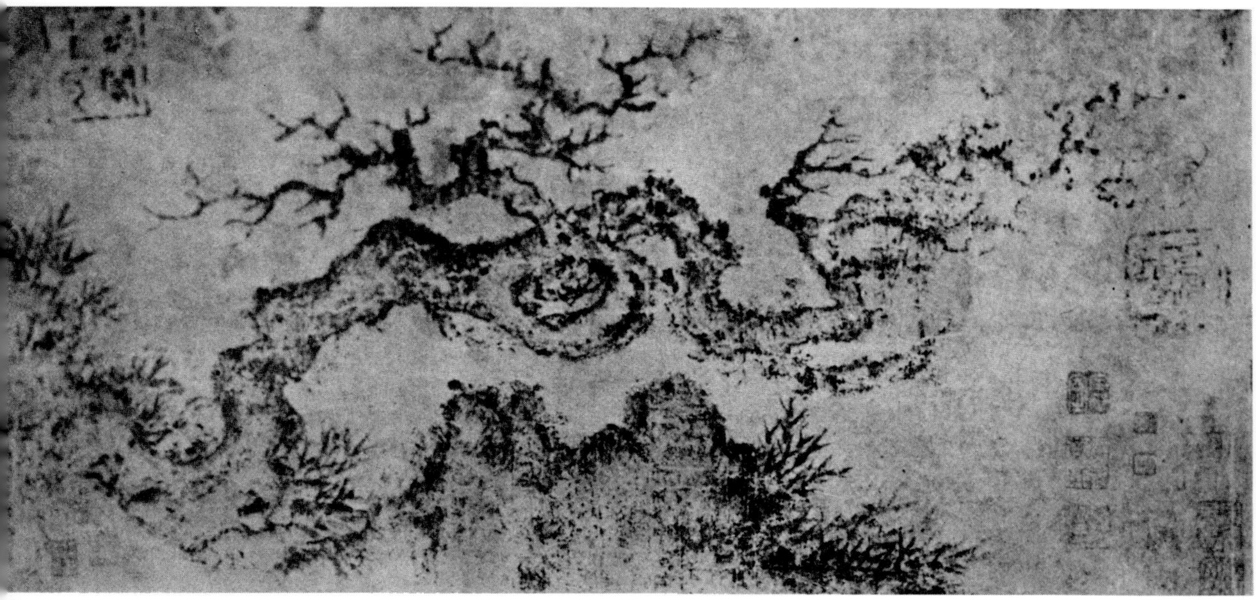

47. Attributed to Su Tung-p'o (1037–1101): "Bare Tree, Bamboo, and Rocks." Handscroll; ink on paper. Ht. 23.4 cm. Sung Dynasty, Palace Museum, Peking.

When I savour Mo-chieh's poems, I find paintings in them;
When I look at Mo-chieh's paintings, there are poems in them.

These scholar-gentlemen maintained that good painting could not be imitated because it was the expression of the thoughts and feelings of an individual. With this intensely personal attitude there went a new detachment from "things." Su Tung-p'o spoke not of "concentrated and intensive study," but of merely "borrowing" the forms of rocks, mountains, and trees to "give lodging" for the moment to his feelings. As can be imagined, the merits of their paintings are much harder to appreciate than those of the Ma Yüan–Hsia Kuei school. They do not go halfway to meet us with their brilliance of brushwork or obvious romantic mood. Their virtues are those of the Confucian gentleman—unaffected, detached, reticent, sometimes whimsical, sometimes austere—and are expressed with the touch of a calligrapher, the taste of an amateur and a poet. Indeed, in their eagerness to show that they were not professionals, these painters sometimes pretended, following the august precedent of Wang Wei, that they were not really painters at all but were merely having a clumsy shot at it or, as they put it, "playing with ink"; moreover, as they were communicating only with each other, nothing had to be spelled out. A mere hint was enough.

Their kind of painting could find no place in a court dominated by the fashionable art of the Ma Yüan–Hsia Kuei school. In any case, these

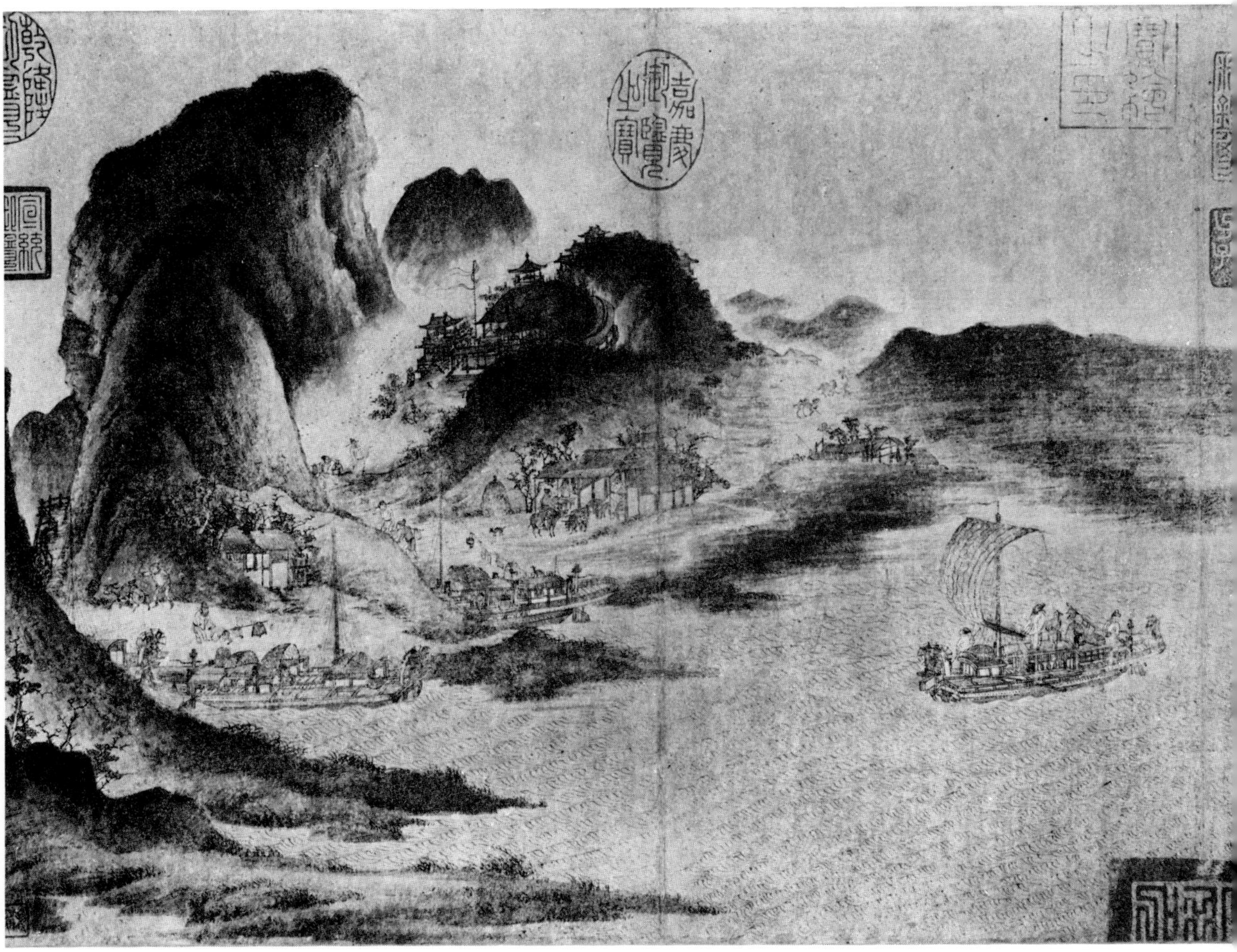

48. Anon (eleventh-twelfth century): "Market Village by a River." Album-leaf mounted as a handscroll; ink and slight colour on paper. Ht. 28.6 cm. Sung Dynasty. National Palace Museum, Taipei.

artists preferred to paint, as they wrote, in ink on paper, and to circulate their essentially modest pictures only among themselves. As a result their works were inevitably lost by their descendants. Only a tiny handful of paintings by, or attributed to, the Sung literati have survived to bear witness to the existence of this new kind of painting. Very characteristic in its hoary roughness, sparing use of dry ink, and uncompromising lack of any seductive quality is the simple sketch of a bare tree with rocks and young bamboo attributed to Su Tung-p'o himself (Plate 47), which came to light in the 1950's. Yet although bamboo, as a symbol of the pliant but unbreakable spirit of the scholar-official, was to become a favourite theme among the literati, their greatest love was always landscape.

One of the most exquisite treasures in the National Palace Museum in Taipei is an album-leaf on paper (Plate 48) called *Market Village by a River,* believed to be a work of the eleventh or twelfth century. It depicts a small, crowded boat in which a gentleman stands conspicuously erect, his head high, his air expectant; the boat is approaching a village by the waterside at which more boats are moored; there are wineshops along the shore and a temple on the distant hillside. Every minute detail of the boats and houses is rendered with captivating accuracy, from the chicken coops to the laundry hanging on the line. The towering crags are derived from the manner of Fan K'uan and Li Ch'eng, but the softly rendered foreground and impressionistic, carelessly smudged-in distance seem to hint that the artist was not ignorant of the tradition of Tung Yüan and Chü-jan. Camels coming down the distant road show that this is a North China scene, while the theme of the scholar standing in the boat (Is it the poet T'ao Yüan-ming coming home, and is that one of his friends in the valley waiting to welcome him?) suggests that this is the work of a scholar and a gentleman, perhaps Chang Tse-tuan himself. For with

49. Attributed to Chiang Tsan (twelfth century): "Verdant Mountains." Detail of a handscroll; ink on paper. Ht. 32 cm. Southern Sung or Yüan Dynasty. Nelson-Atkins Gallery of Art, Kansas City, Mo.

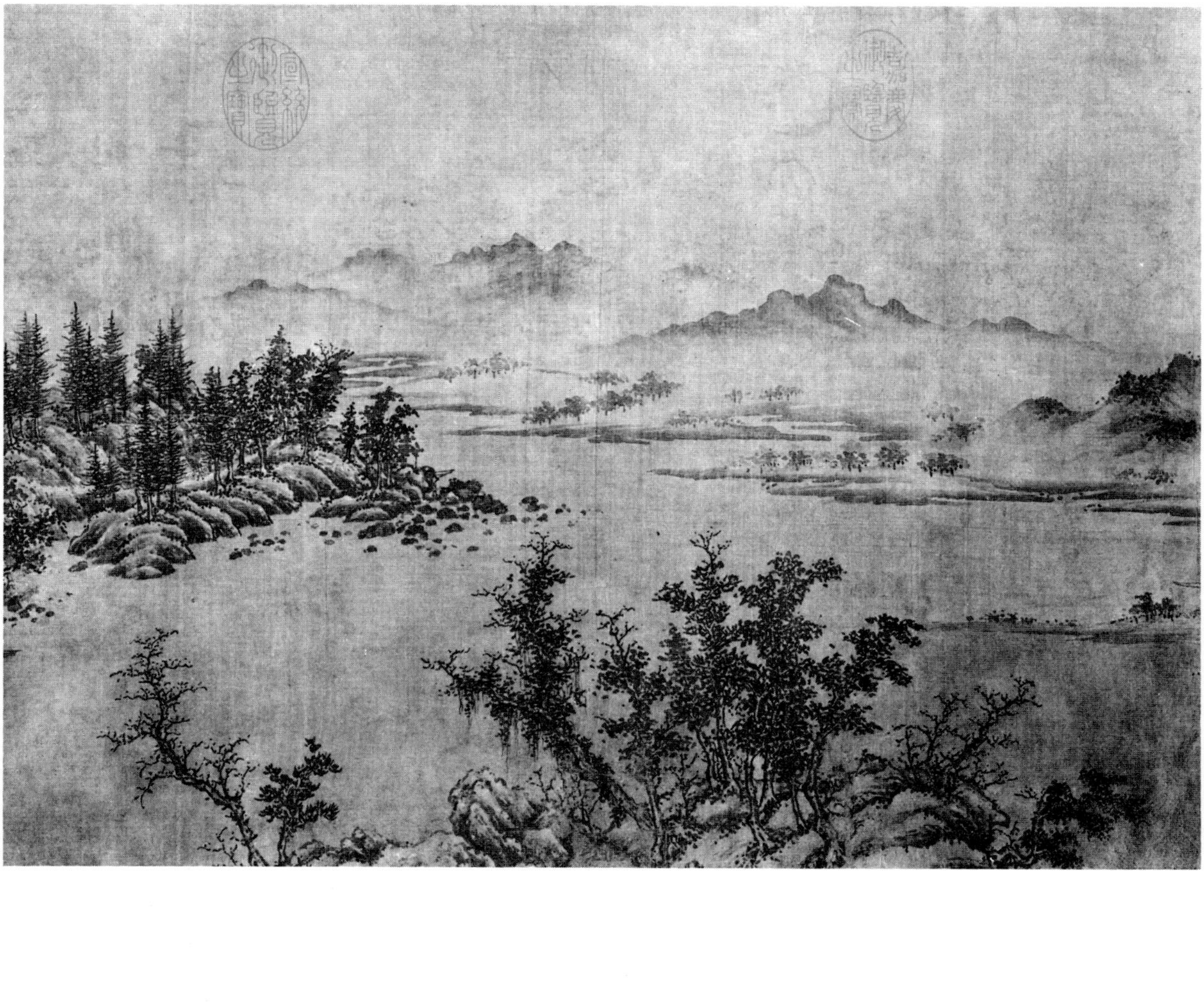

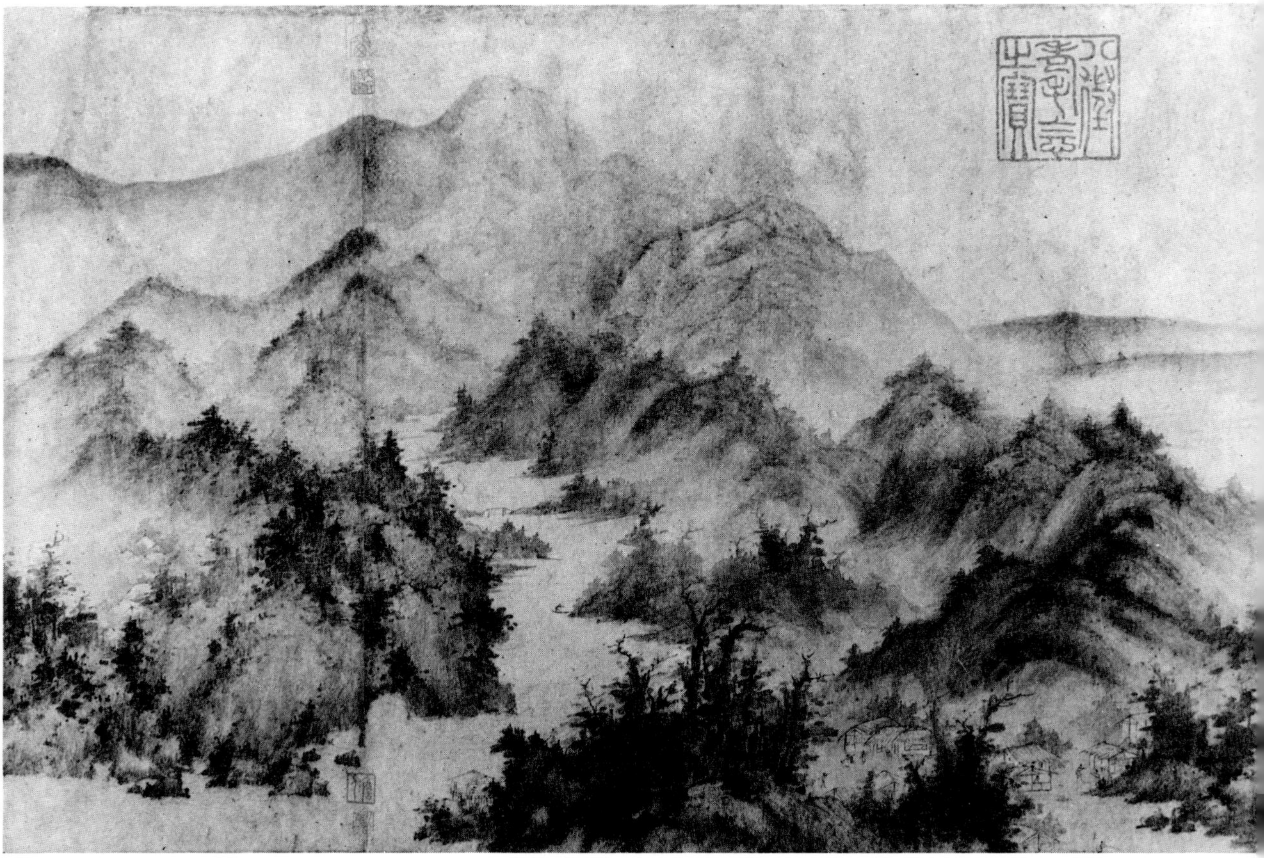

50. Li (full name unknown): "A Dream Journey on the Hsiao and Hsiang Rivers." Detail of a handscroll; ink on paper. Ht. 30.3 cm. Southern Sung Dynasty. National Museum (Tōyōkan), Tokyo.

the example of the Ch'ing-ming scroll (Plate 40) before us, we need not assume that all gentlemen's painting abandoned pictorial realism as soon as Su Tung-p'o spoke.

But Su Tung-p'o's ideas were spreading, and there must have been hundreds of gentlemen living in and around Hangchow in the twelfth and thirteenth centuries who looked on painting merely as a pastime, and were inspired by the same ideals. One of the very few that we know anything about was an extremely shy scholar named Chiang Tsan, who was summoned reluctantly to court and died—perhaps of sheer fright—on the night before his first audience with the emperor. Had he lived, would the "literary style" have become fashionable at court? It hardly seems likely; the influence of the academy was too strong. It is very doubtful that any of Chiang Tsan's paintings have survived; the lovely picture attributed to him now in Kansas City (of which a detail is shown in Plate 49) is probably a free copy of the Yüan Dynasty. Even so, it shows clearly in its broad, free handling, in its use of wet ink to suggest atmosphere, and in its reticence how much these southern gentlemen-painters must have owed to Tung Yüan and Chü-jan.

Even more elusive is the painter of the wonderful landscape illustrated in Plate 50. It is called *A Dream* [literally "Couch"] *Journey on the Hsiao and Hsiang Rivers.* Whether the painter ever visited that part of Hunan it is impossible to tell, since nothing is known about him except that his family name was Li. But these rivers had become an inspiration to painters from the time that the eleventh-century master Sung Ti, a friend of Su Tung-p'o, had painted his famous *Eight Views of Hsiao and Hsiang.* The source of Li's style, like that of Chiang Tsan's, is "Tung and Chü," as they were called; but here Li has created, almost entirely in ink wash (there are scarcely any lines in the picture at all), a panorama in which the mist out of which the hills and trees emerge seems to be more real, more tangible than the hills and trees themselves. He manages to suggest that this is a visionary projection of the painter's mind, rather than a remembered landscape. Many educated men at this time were influenced by the idealistic schools of Mahāyāna Buddhism, which held that all appearance is illusion, Māyā, a mere outward and ever-changing manifestation of transcendent reality. The idea that the world of the senses is illusory must have had great appeal to men of a sensitive, inward turn of mind, who increasingly sought refuge from the decay around them with the Zen monks in their quiet monasteries across the lake.

The line between the intuition and spontaneity of the scholar-painter and that of the Zen artist is a fine one, but it is there. For what the Zen master sought was to express, not himself, but a reality that denied the self, by his arbitrary choice of subject matter and his technique of broken washes to reveal the underlying unity of all things, and by the flash and daring of his brushwork, to suggest, by analogy, what the sudden, irrational experience of Zen illumination was like. At the same time, the Zen painter, like the Zen teacher, deliberately gives us a series of visual shocks to shake free our locked-in consciousness. It is no accident that he chose as his technical language not the relaxed and highly personal styles of the literati but those of the Southern Sung academy. For the academic style, like the Zen method of teaching, is both disciplined and impersonal. As in the act of meditation, its sharpness of detail fixes the viewer's attention on a significant point while the world around dissolves in mist and silence.

In Mu-ch'i's *Sunset Glow on a Fishing Village,* one of the *Eight Views of the Hsiao and Hsiang Rivers* (Plate 51), the mountains hang before us as though they would melt away at any moment into the all-enveloping mist. But the painter wills that they shall not. The dark accents provided by the tree trunks and distant roofs are too sharp to be true to nature.

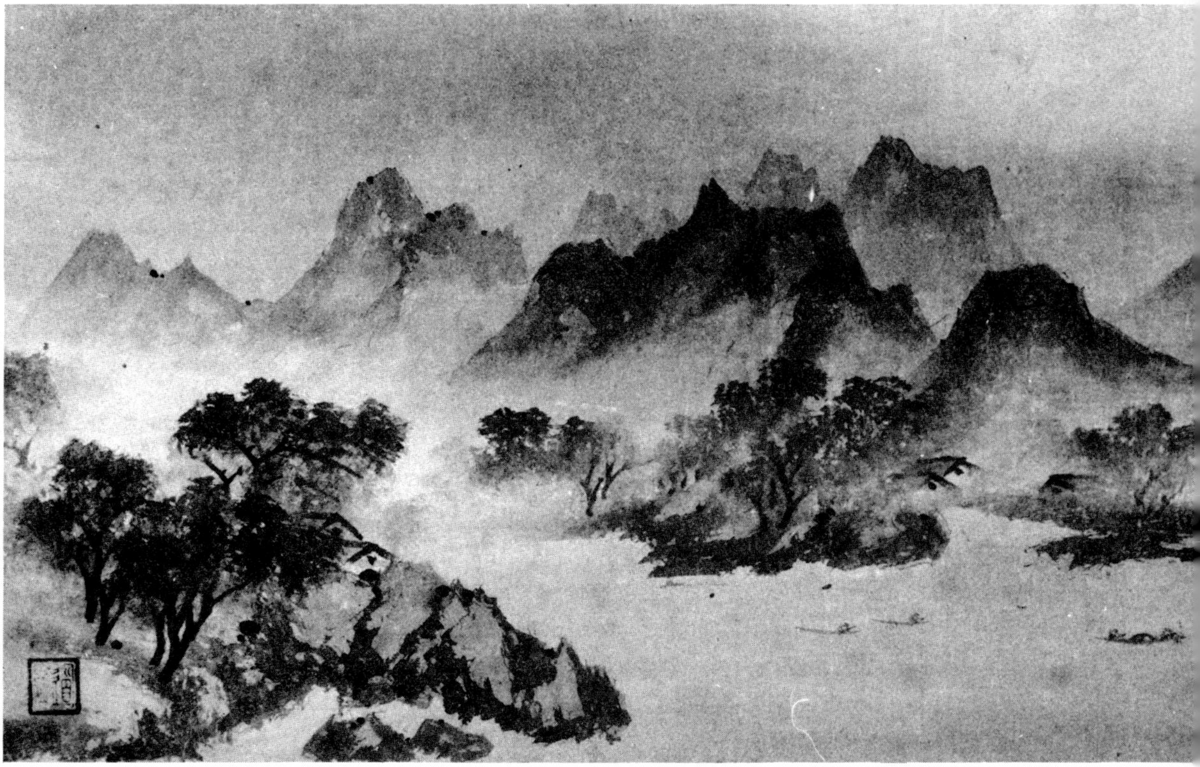

51. Mu-ch'i (mid-thirteenth century): "Sunset Glow on a Fishing Village"; one of his "Eight Views of Hsiao and Hsiang." Detail of a handscroll; ink on paper. Ht. 33.2 cm. Southern Sung Dynasty, Nezu Art Museum, Tokyo.

Their purpose—and the purpose of the ink dots the artist set down at the last moment with lightning and instinctive swiftness on the edges of rocks and distant mountains—is not only to accent the visual rhythm in a very lively way, but also, like the raps of the Zen master's stick on the head of the inattentive pupil, to fix our eyes so that they do not simply wander idly over the misty landscape. These dots and accents seem to say to us that meditation, even upon nature at its loveliest, is a strenuous business, demanding constant attention. Yet as in meditation, the end of the painter's effort, and of ours, is to come to a state of unutterable peace.

We might think that the dissolution of the landscape into an all-enveloping haze could be carried no further than this, but an obscure thirteenth-century monk named Yü-chien, or Ying Yü-chien, achieved it by smearing and splashing ink onto the paper in a state of high excitement and then, like the late T'ang eccentrics, adding a few deft touches with the brush that not only transformed his gestures into a picture of countrymen coming home to their village at dusk but also created a marvellous pictorial analogy to the Zen experience in which form is manifest out of the formless, unifying Void (Plate 52). But a point on the road to illumination is eventually reached when even this kind of painting

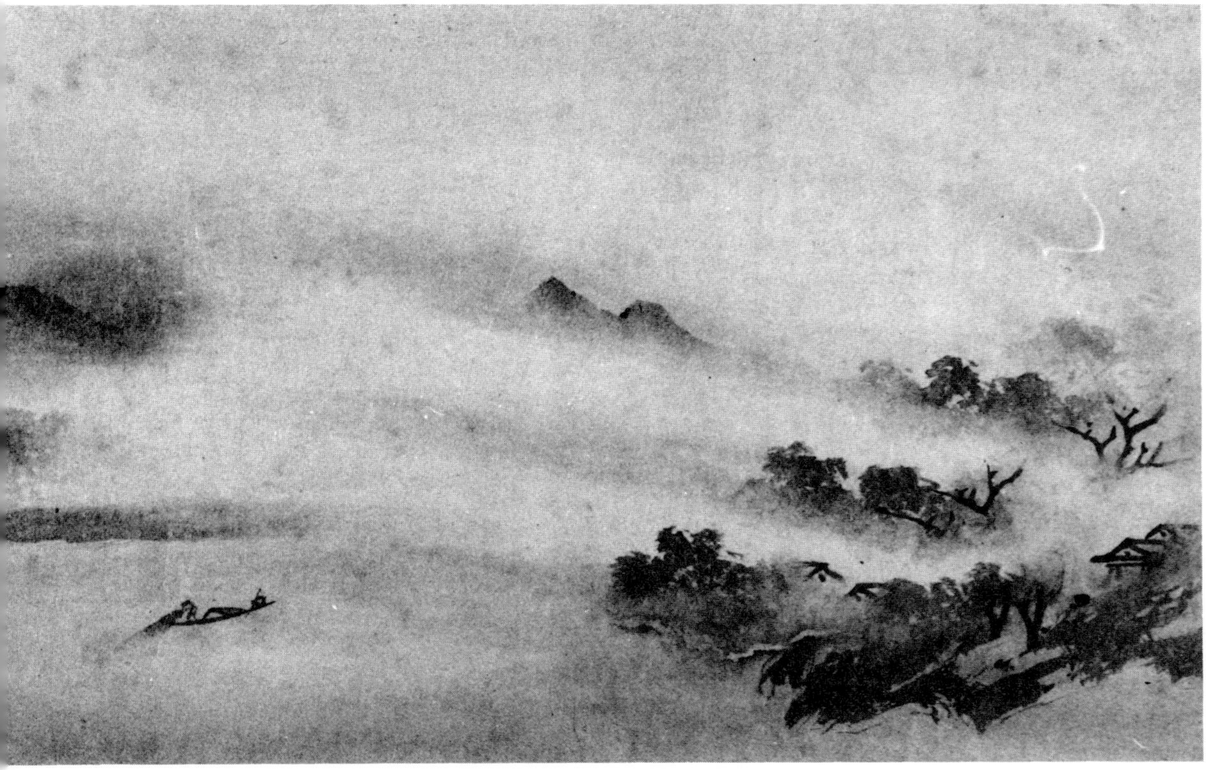

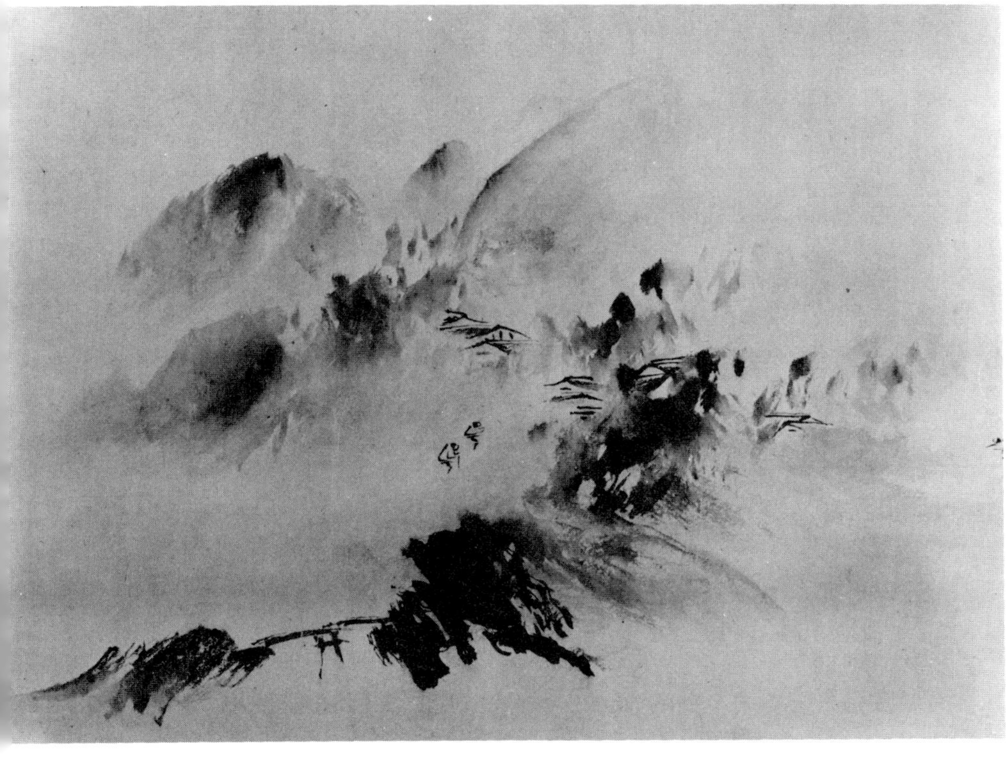

52. *Attributed to (Ying?) Yü-chien (thirteenth century): "Returning Fishermen," one of his "Eight Views of Hsiao and Hsiang." Handscroll; ink on paper. Ht. 30.6 cm. Southern Sung Dynasty. Commission for the Protection of Cultural Properties, Tokyo.*

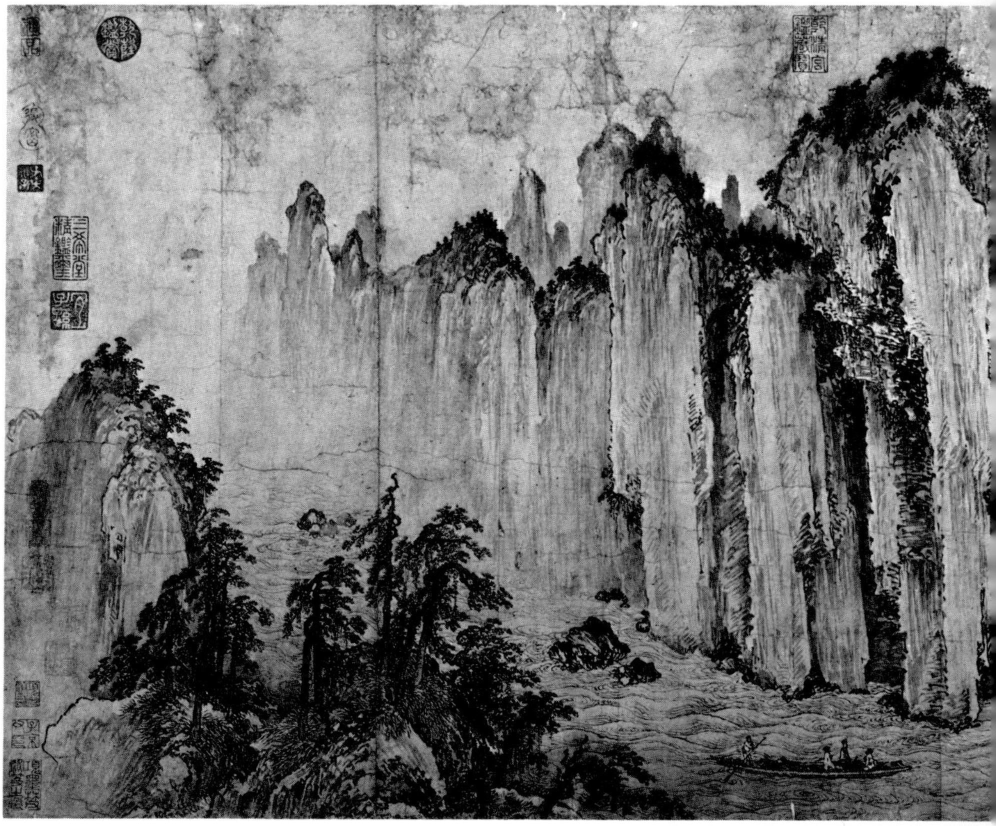

53. Wu Yüan-chih (active ca. 1190–1200): Illustration to the "Red Cliff Ode" of Su Tung-p'o. Handscroll; ink on paper. Ht. 50.8 cm. Chin Dynasty, about 1195. National Palace Museum, Taipei.

ceases to be any help. At that point art, and indeed all forms of communication, are left behind, and the spirit journeys on alone.

The retreat from the "real" world expressed in very different ways in Zen and in the teachings of the later Neo-Confucianists was hastened by a general failure of nerve, a sense of despair, that deepened as the Sung dragged out its last years and the Jurchen armies, already in occupation of all North China, pressed farther and farther into Sung territory. The Jurchen by this time were no barbarians, however. Like other invaders before them they had become completely sinicised, calling their dynasty Chin. At their northern court the arts flourished, and as we would expect the inspiration of the landscape painters was not Ma Yüan but the monumental style of the Northern Sung masters, which had lingered on in the north. But when we look carefully at Wu Yüan-chih's splendid panorama depicting Su Tung-p'o and his friends drifting in their boat under the Red Cliff (Plate 53), we cannot help noticing a subtle difference. For the artist models his cliffs with long straight strokes and repeated slanting cross-hatchings that are never found in "proper" Chinese painting and

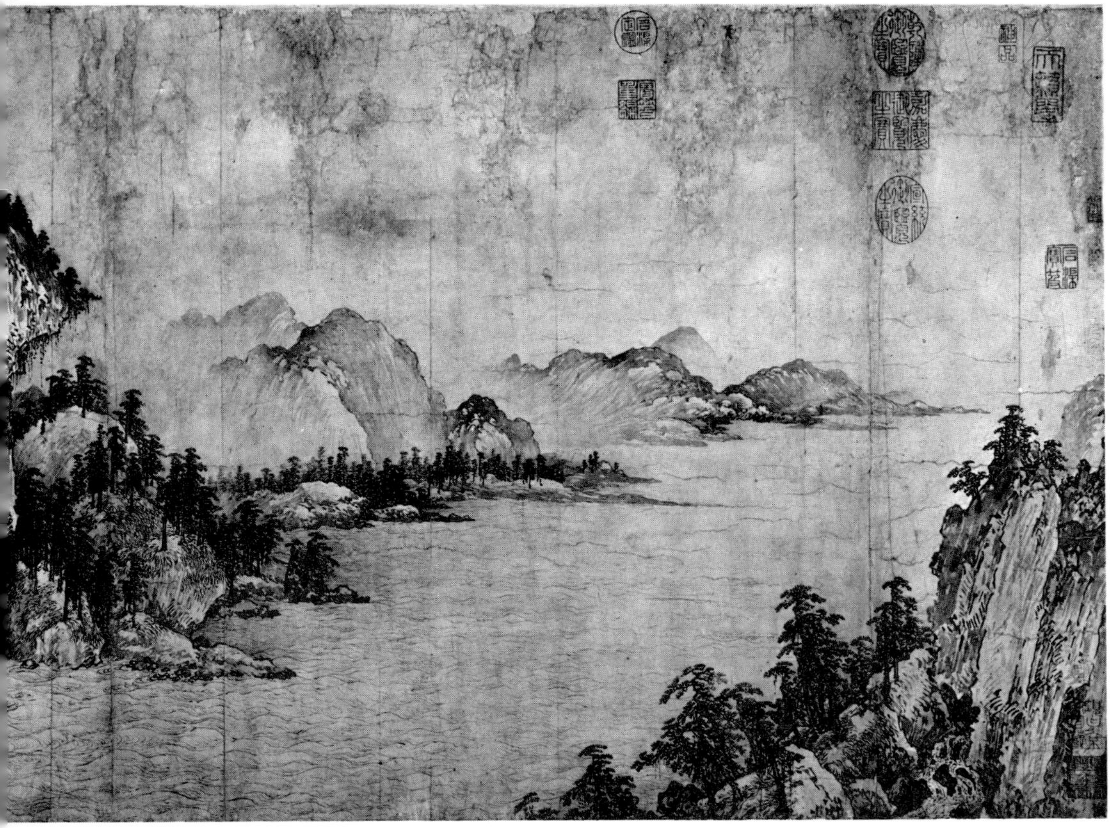

that give these cliffs a curiously Western look, as if they had been drawn with a pen. This small but telltale symptom of decline seems to suggest that, cut off from the mainstream of Chinese painting in the south, the inspiration of these northern masters was drying up, and they were beginning to resort to technical shortcuts. If we could explore thirteenth-century painting beyond Chin territory into neighbouring Korea, we would find these same tendencies toward a mechanical repetition of inexpressive brushstrokes carried still further. Chinese calligraphy was a demanding discipline: once removed from its influence, Far Eastern painting takes very different directions, or develops bad habits.

For several decades in the thirteenth century the Chin stood between the dying Sung and the Mongol horde to the north, who now prepared for their final onslaught not only on the Chin but on the remnant of the Sung empire itself. Civilisation as the Chinese gentlemen had known it was about to be blotted out. The effects of this disaster were to leave their mark on Chinese landscape painting for over 500 years.

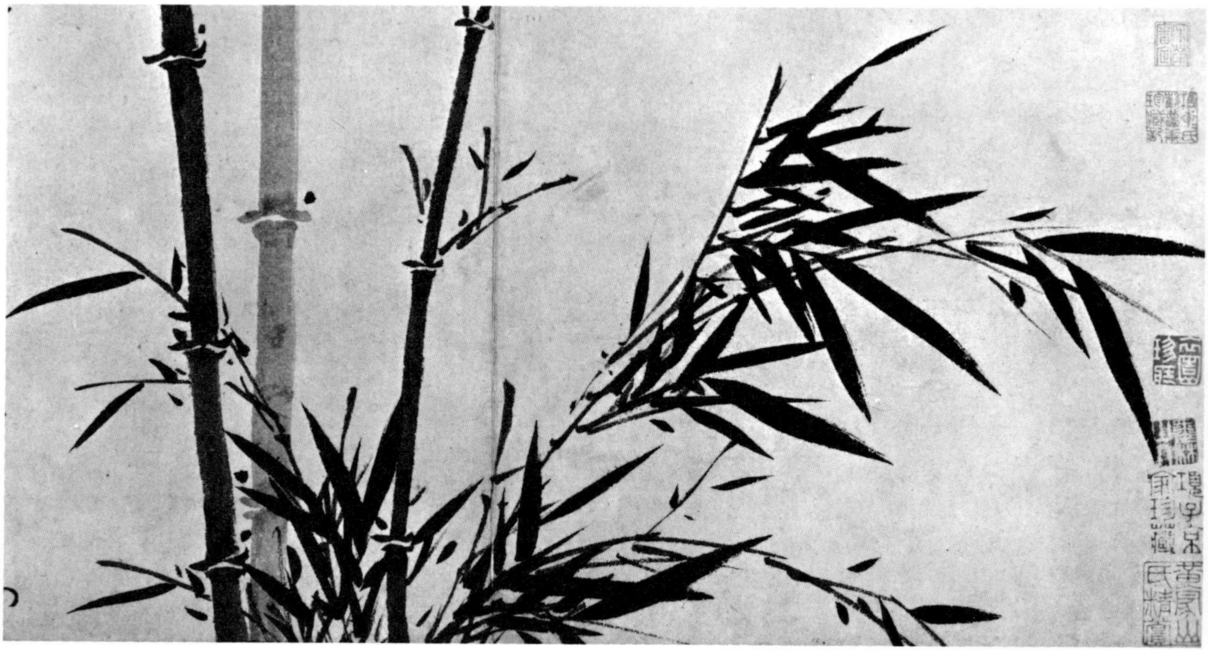

IV Withdrawal and Renewal

The Yüan Dynasty, 1279-1368

Detail of Plate 54 (p. 93): Wu Chen, Bamboo.

On a dark day in the middle years of the fourteenth century, a scholar named Sung Lien found on the wall of an old building a painting of two pine trees by the great Sung Dynasty master Kuo Hsi. Taking a brush, he wrote on the wall beside it, "Holding a candle to look at this painting of two pines . . . it is exquisite in its delicate beauty. The brushwork is simple, the conception tranquil. The flavour is subtle and elegant. One has a sense of pride triumphant over wintry chill, and of moral integrity" —strange words to write about a painting of pine trees, until one remembers that the pine tree, particularly in winter, had become a symbol of endurance in adversity; that when Sung Lien saw this faded masterpiece the Mongols and their attendant rabble of stinking Tibetans, Uighurs, and Tanguts were in occupation of his country; and that painters and scholars were then experiencing such suffering as they had never known before.

This was the China that Marco Polo saw from the top, during his twelve years' service with Kubilai Khan. The glittering palaces he described were built and decorated by Chinese craftsmen and painters who were treated, at least to begin with, as little more than slaves. The Mongols viewed the literati with profound suspicion as the one class that might challenge them. The examination system was suspended; for some years it was impossible for a Chinese scholar, particularly a southerner, to get more than the most menial job; and the southern landed gentry were taxed beyond endurance.

The scholars had in fact been forced into an impossible position. The "correct" Neo-Confucian doctrine propounded by Chu Hsi demanded that they be absolutely loyal to the emperor, however barbarous or corrupt he might be. A scholar might at the risk of his life reprove him, but must never desert him. The far older Confucian morality, going back to Mencius, taught that the scholar's highest loyalty was to virtue, and that under intolerable conditions he was justified in withdrawing his services. What, then, should he do? There was no "right" answer, and the Mongol occupation of 1279 paralysed the scholars into inaction. At first they had little choice, since there was no place for them in the administration anyway. Their dilemma came when the enlightened Kubilai Khan attempted to woo them back into public service. Most refused, and sank into obscurity. Why, we might ask, was there so little active resistance? Undoubtedly what Frederick Mote has called the scholars' "low potential for political action" was the result partly of Neo-Confucian brainwashing, partly of their contempt for the profession of arms. Their weapon was the writing brush—even, in an oblique sort of way, the painting brush.

Now no longer did the scholars set the tone at court as they had in the T'ang and Sung, establish standards of taste, engage with the emperor in poetry competitions, or help him form an art collection. They were left out in the cold, and court art was produced by professionals far down on the social ladder. If the founder of the succeeding Ming Dynasty, who drove out the remnant of the Mongol regime in 1368, had been a man of even ordinary humanity, he might have restored the literati to their old place at court. But the first Ming ruler, the Hung-wu Emperor, was more brutal than the worst of the Mongol rulers. Scholars who could escape fled from his presence, and so the gulf between them and the court, and between scholarly taste and courtly taste, widened still further, to become a permanent feature of Chinese traditional culture. At the beginning of the Yüan (1279), artists still gathered in Hangchow, the "Quinsai" that Marco Polo called the greatest city in the world. But

Hangchow declined, and never fully recovered from two great fires in 1341 and 1342. Now more and more artists, poets, and scholars were settling in the towns further north around Lake T'ai, particularly in Wu-hsi and Soochow, the prosperous centre of a little world of lakes and rivers, towns and rich farmland—so rich, in fact that 90 percent of all the taxes collected by the Mongols came from this area (see map on p. xiii). Until the nineteenth century, this part of Kiangsu remained the cultural hub of China, where the painters and poets could pursue their interests for the most part untroubled by the barbarous emperors and vindictive eunuchs of Peking.

Yet the arm of imperial authority was very long indeed, and at the beginning of the Yüan Dynasty any form of protest was an act of courage. Among the heroic literati of the late fourteenth century was Cheng Ssu-hsiao (1241–1318). A devoted Sung loyalist, he would have committed suicide, but his duty to his widowed mother forbade it. A poem he wrote ends:*

> I want to die, but cannot die and be a filial son;
> I must live, but cannot live and be a loyal servitor.

He lived; but his hatred of the Mongols never abated. In company he would never sit facing north, toward the capital; and he found in painting a way of expressing his feelings about the Occupation. He painted orchids floating as if in midair, rootless like himself, the very ground beneath them torn away by the invaders. Seldom can a passionate patriotism have been expressed with such exquisite obliqueness!

In the art of bamboo painting, which came into its own in the Yüan Dynasty, the scholars might be said to have been protesting, too—or at least making a gesture. For the bamboo had come to be regarded as a symbol of the scholar himself—bent, perhaps, but never broken by adversity. Bamboo painting makes the same demands on its practitioner as does calligraphy, and so was the natural subject for the scholar's brush. In the hands of the great masters it becomes an art almost of pure form, one in which, as in calligraphy, movement, balance, rhythm, and mastery of ink are supreme; yet it still must convey the endless variety and springing life of the living plant. Bamboo is not properly a branch of Chinese landscape painting, but it plays so great a part in the painter's awareness of the natural world that we must include at least one example (Plate 54), by the poet-painter Wu Chen (1280–1354), whose landscape we will look at in a moment.

*Frederick Mote, "Confucian Eremiticism in the Yüan period," in Arthur F. Wright, ed., *The Confucian Persuasion* (Stanford, Calif., 1960), p. 235.

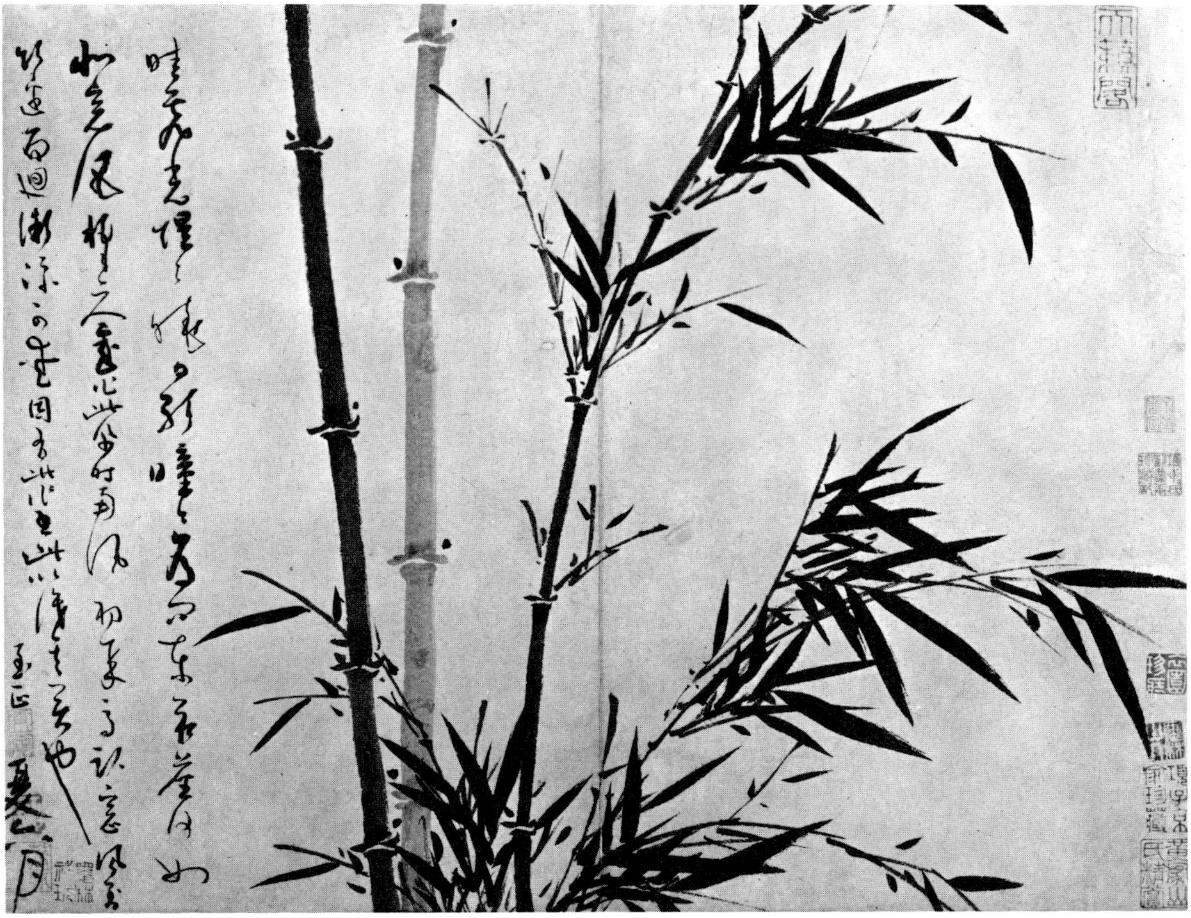

54. Wu Chen (1280–1354): Bamboo. Leaf from an album dated 1350; ink on paper. Ht. 42.9 cm. Yüan Dynasty. National Palace Museum, Taipei.

An air of such serenity and detachment as this picture wears was not easily achieved. For the scholars, the present was bleak, the future held no hope. Only the past could be contemplated with any pleasure: not the immediate past, of course, for the Southern Sung had been weak and decadent. They looked much further back, to the days when China had been free and strong, and felt that it was their task to rediscover and uphold the ancient virtues. They spoke of *fu ku*, "restoring the past," as the only hope for the future. For certain painters at the end of the fourteenth century this meant deliberately choosing to paint in the styles of those far-off happier times, even if the painters had a rather hazy idea of what those styles had been. T'ang and Sung critics had been convinced that the painting of their own epoch was better, more advanced, than that of former ages. Now, for the first time, that confidence in the progress of art is gone, and there creeps into the thinking of the literati the insidious idea that only by reaching back into history for inspiration can poetry and art flourish. Free spirits will from time to time transcend this fixation on the past, or rebel against it, but from now on it is to lend a very particular kind of colour to the arts in China. In the Yüan, however, this antiquarianism must be considered as a positive attitude, and not a negative one, for by their repudiation of the present and of the immediate past the literati were making a commitment to a certain standard of personal and artistic conduct.

Ch'ien Hsüan (ca. 1235–after 1301) was a young official when the Southern Sung Dynasty collapsed around him, and he retired into private life. He painted birds, flowers, and squirrels in a style not very different from that of the Southern Sung academy. In his landscapes, however, he leaps back not decades but centuries. Ch'ien Hsüan's painting of the great fourth-century calligrapher Wang Hsi-chih contemplating his geese—whose gracefully curving necks were supposed to have inspired his own supple handwriting—is the sort of picture that only a few of his most intimate friends such as Chao Meng-fu would have appreciated (Plate 55). Ch'ien Hsüan has deliberately chosen the archaic style, the "green and blue" manner of the T'ang court painters Li Ssu-hsün and Li Chao-tao, which he handles with wit and charm. If we did not know that he was an extremely skilful painter, might we not take the stiffness of the drawing, the awkward handling of the roofs, the monotonous array of the leaves for sheer incompetence? Ch'ien Hsüan was prepared to take that risk, because he had something important to say about the state of painting in his own day: that only by rejecting the meretricious skills and conventional sentiments of the Southern Sung could painting recover its lost innocence and find its true path again. Naiveté—we can hardly call it awkwardness—was a mark of the artist's sincerity and integrity.

Chao Meng-fu (1254–1322) was a brilliant, ambitious young man who, after resisting the allurements of Kubilai Khan for ten years, capitulated, went up to Peking, and rapidly rose in the civil service. His decision to collaborate always haunted him, and at first cost him many friends. His old teacher Ch'ien Hsüan was never reconciled to it, and later generations of scholar-painters, though they acknowledged his formidable talents as an administrator, scholar, calligrapher, and painter and admitted how much he had done to mitigate the lot of the Chinese scholar class under the Occupation, could never forgive his defection, so that he was never numbered among the Four Great Masters of the Yüan Dynasty.

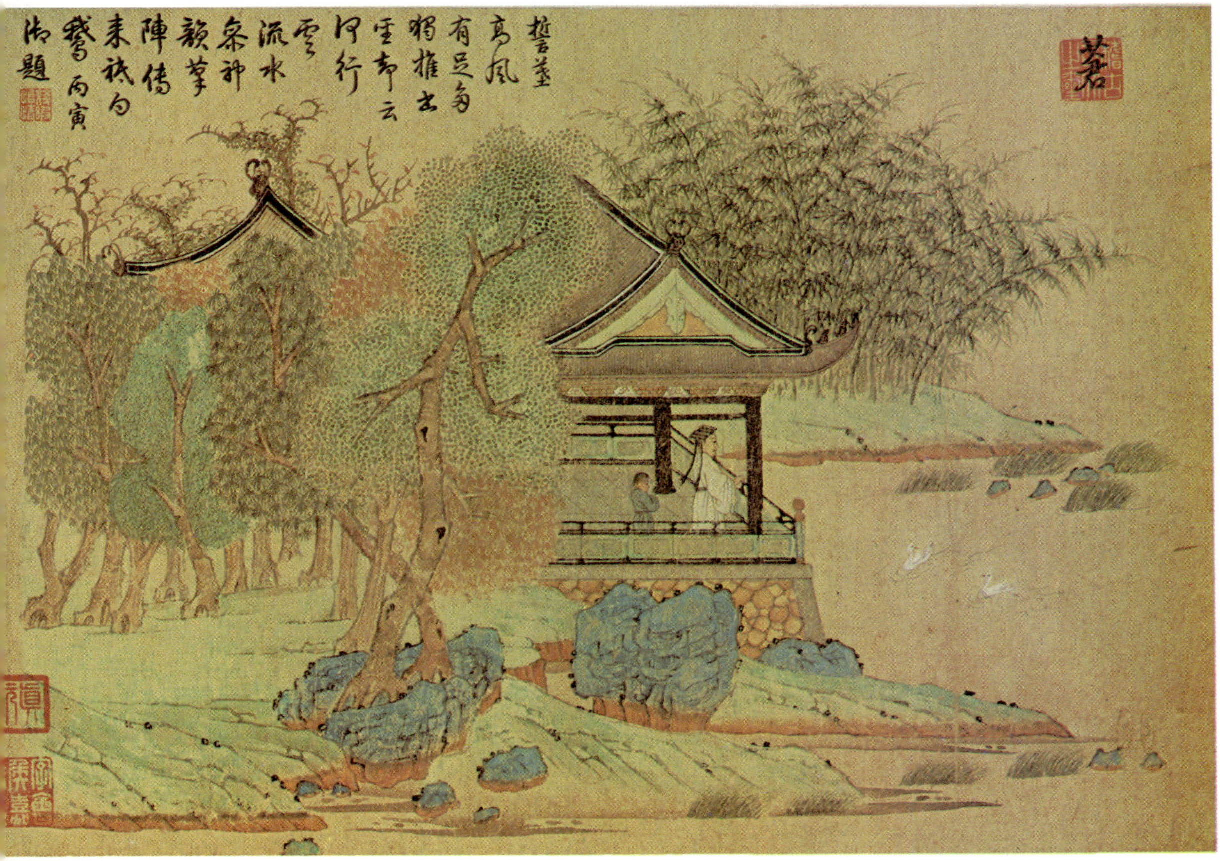

55. Ch'ien Hsüan (ca. 1235–after 1301): "Wang Hsi-chih Watching Geese." Detail of a handscroll; ink and colour on paper. Ht. 23.2 cm. Yüan Dynasty. Metropolitan Museum of Art, New York.

Like Ch'ien Hsüan, Chao Meng-fu believed that only by restoring the spirit of the past (rather than merely the styles of the past) could art, like Chinese culture itself, recover its standing. He is said to have written these words on a picture in the year 1301: "The most precious quality in a painting is 'the spirit of antiquity,' *ku i*. If it is not present, the work is not worth much, even though it is skilfully done. Nowadays, people who paint with a fine brush in a delicate manner and lay on strong and brilliant colours consider themselves skillful painters. They are absolutely ignorant of the fact that the works in which the spirit of antiquity is wanting are full of faults and not worth looking at. My paintings may seem to be quite simply and carelessly done, but true connoisseurs will realise that they are very close to the old models and may therefore be considered good. This is told for real connoisseurs and not for ignoramuses."*

But how could Chao Meng-fu be so sure that his paintings were close to the old models? In fact, he was in a unique position to know. For as Secretary to the Board of War, President of the Imperial Academy of Letters (Hanlin), and a senior provincial administrator he spent the years between 1286 and 1295 in North China, where he acquired a large collection of old masters, many no doubt gifts from people anxious to get on the right side of him. His collection came to include landscapes by Wang Wei, Li Ch'eng, Li Ssu-hsün, Wu Tao-tzu, and Tung Yüan, and he brought it back to Hangchow with him when he retired in 1295. To painters searching for models, and filled with the ideals of *fu ku* and *ku i*, these ancient masterpieces must have come as a revelation.

One of the first things Chao Meng-fu did after he got home was to paint a panorama of a friend's native place in Shantung. His friend had never seen it, but Chao had been posted there as Lieutenant-Governor. He explains in his inscription why he painted this picture of Mount Hua, which he notes rises quite isolated in a most unusual way (Plate 56). A friend wrote a colophon on the picture in which he says that Chao's painting and calligraphy are exquisite in every sort of way, "with a purity of conception that is very appealing. There is no breath of artisanry. Could anyone say that it is not a masterpiece," he asks, "like the Lan-t'ing script of Wang Hsi-chih, and the Wang-ch'uan panorama of Wang Wei? Chin-hsi (the owner) has a treasure indeed."

This fascinating picture (known as *Autumn Colours on the Ch'iao and Hua Mountains*) contains stylistic allusions to Wang Wei himself, to the southern ink landscapes of Tung Yüan, and, in Chao's choice of bright colours to the ancient northern style of Li Ssu-hsün and Li Chao-tao (a tribute, perhaps, to his master Ch'ien Hsüan?). It thus playfully brings together the scholarly and the courtly styles in the same picture. Chao's handling is deliberately naive. A Ming writer tells us that the Yüan painters "were all men of great virtue and succeeded in concealing their technical skill. They were afraid of becoming famous through their painting and of not being able to avoid the entanglements of the world. Only Chao Meng-fu stood out brilliantly [i.e. he did not become a recluse] and competed with the famous masters of the T'ang and Sung periods. He was very bold, but when he became a high official, he must nevertheless

*Osvald Sirén, trans., *Chinese Painting: Leading Masters and Principles* (London, 1958), vol. 4, p. 19.

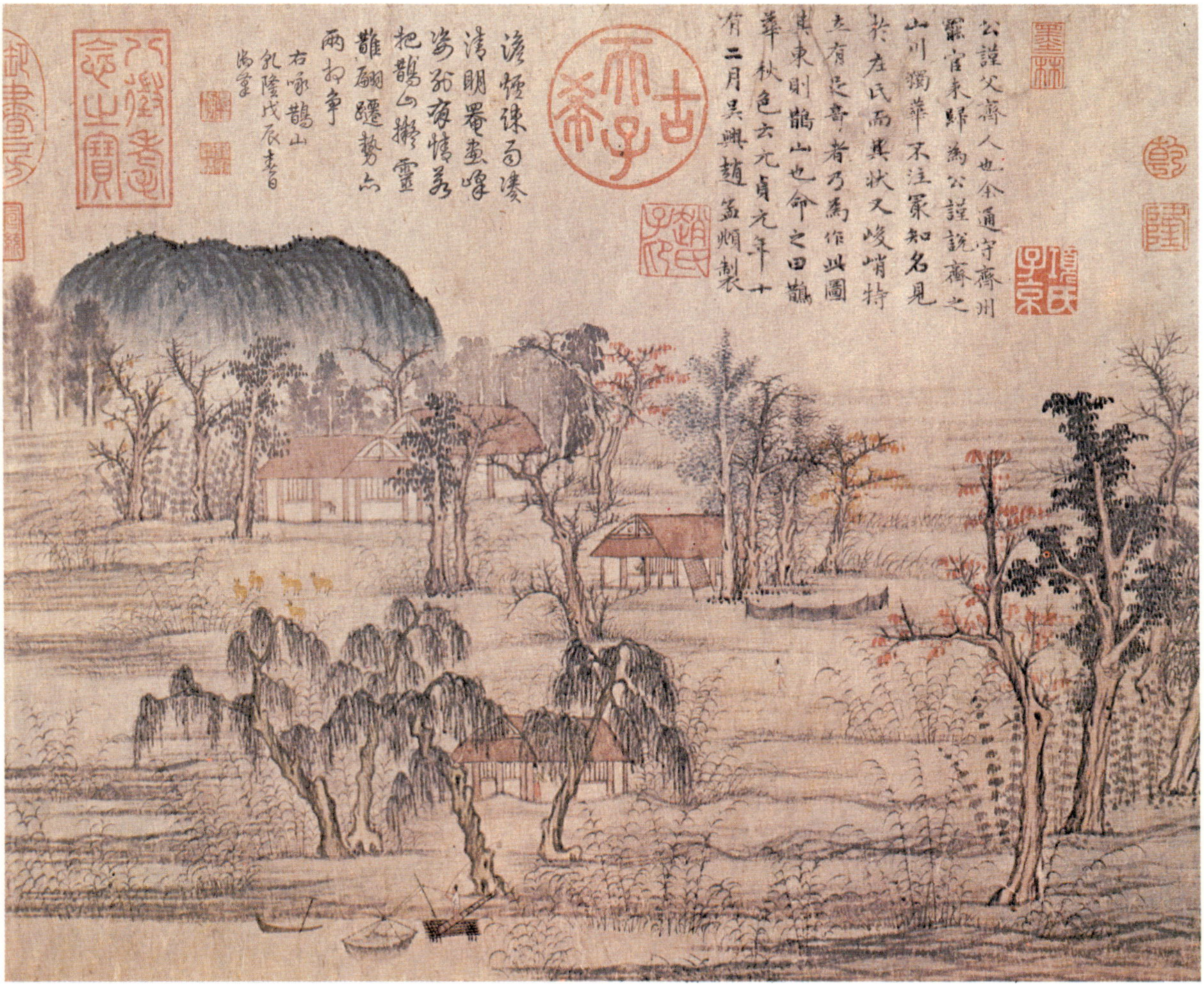

56. Chao Meng-fu (1254–1322): "Autumn Colours on the Ch'iao and Hua Mountains." Detail of a handscroll dated 1295; ink and colour on paper. Ht. 28.4 cm. Yüan Dynasty. National Palace Museum, Taipei.

have found his great skill in art an embarrassment."* This interesting comment suggests that the assumed clumsiness of the scholar-painters may not have been the pose of amateurs, but may also have been a device to ensure against their being conscripted by their Mongol masters into the ranks of the court painters. Chao Meng-fu, who has been aptly called "a man of facile genius," would have been particularly vulnerable in this respect.

Seven years after painting *Autumn Colours*, Chao Meng-fu did a

*Ku Ning-yüan, *Hua yin*, translated by O. Sirén, *The Chinese on the Art of Painting* (New York, 1963), p. 162.

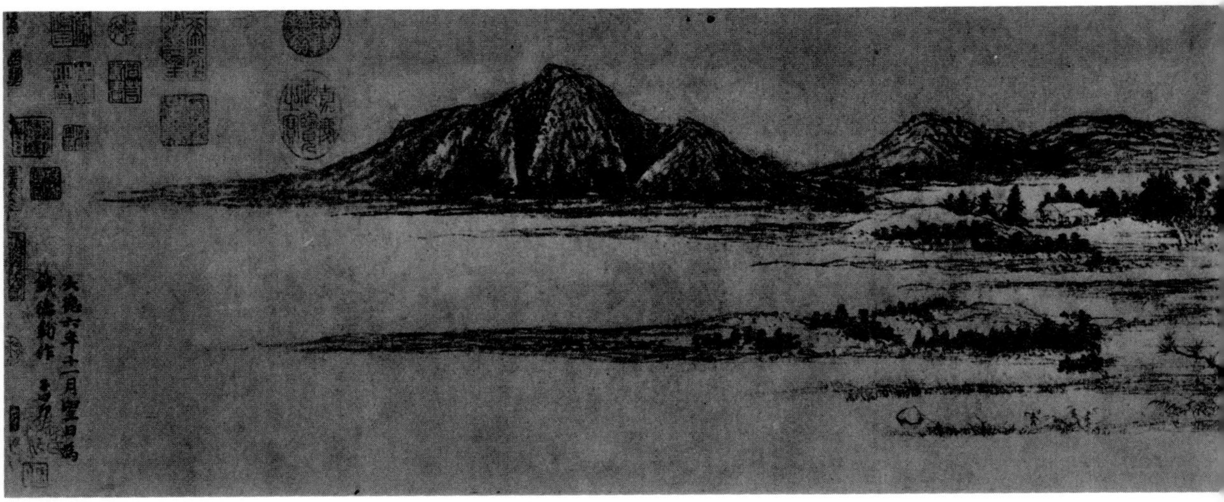

57. Chao Meng-fu (1254–1322): "The Village by the Water." Detail of a handscroll dated 1302; ink on paper. Yüan Dynasty. Palace Museum, Peking.

landscape scroll known as *The Village by the Water* (1302), a picture that turned up in China only a few years ago (Plate 57). The change is remarkable. The painting is southern in style and subject; the inspiration in Tung Yüan is obvious, in Wang Wei somewhat less so. But here are none of the whimsical archaisms of *Autumn Colours*. The brushwork is free and spontaneous, the style relaxed and unaffected, breathing the life of the southern hills and lakes. With this picture, whose authenticity is attested by no fewer than 50 colophons of the fourteenth century, Chao Meng-fu opened up a new path for the scholar-painters, showing how it was possible to find inspiration both in nature and in the past. Here, at last, was a way forward; and the influence of his achievement, not only on the scholar-painters of the fourteenth century but on landscape painting in China right up to the present day, has been incalculable. Chao Meng-fu could have said of himself, as Cézanne said, "I am the primitive of the way I have discovered."

The Yüan masters not only created a new kind of painting but bore witness through their art to the triumph of the Chinese spirit over the tragedy of the times. These men are often called hermits or recluses. But eremitism did not necessarily mean totally shutting oneself off from the world—it could simply mean refusing to become an official, becoming what was called an "urban recluse," and living as a private person as best one could. Huang Kung-wang (1269–1354), the greatest of the Four Great Masters of the Yüan Dynasty, took a junior official post in the Yüan administration; was arrested, imprisoned, and dismissed; retreated to Chekiang; supported himself as a druggist—a typical occupation for a

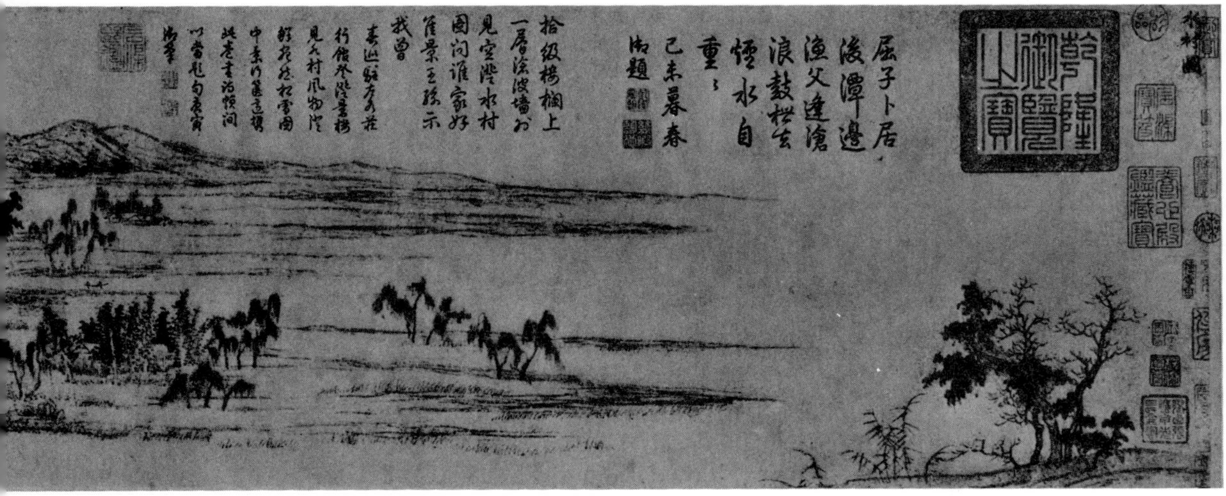

man with Taoist leanings; and then opened a small school of the Three Doctrines (Confucianism, Taoism, and Buddhism) in Soochow. His later years he spent peacefully living along the Fu-ch'un River southeast of Hangchow. He was a poor man, a Ming critic said, "who lived in a cottage that did not shut out the rain and the cold, but there he sat cross-legged, humming poetry."

One day in 1347, Huang Kung-wang took his brush and a long sheet of paper, and in a surge of high exhilaration sketched out a panorama of the scenery along the Fu-ch'un River (Plate 58). He writes in his inscription that he left it behind in his mountain retreat on his trips into the outer world, only returning to add touches and details, or to make corrections, when he felt really inspired. Three years later, feeling that he could do no more, he inscribed it to the friend to whom he had promised it, a Taoist called Mr. Useless. It is only by a miracle that the scroll has survived, for a seventeenth-century owner on his deathbed ordered it thrown on the fire; a nephew rescued it in the nick of time, but the opening section was damaged and cut off. The damaged beginning is now in Peking, while the main part of this wonderful work is in the Palace Museum collection that was taken to Taiwan in 1948.

The Fu-ch'un River panorama is monumental in its conception, yet utterly free and spontaneous in its execution. Like Cézanne, Huang Kung-wang never put brush to paper except in response to intense feeling; he thought nothing of finish or effect, not hesitating to go back to add a tree or a rock as instinct told him, so that in places the picture has that almost fumbling quality the scholar-painters came to regard as the

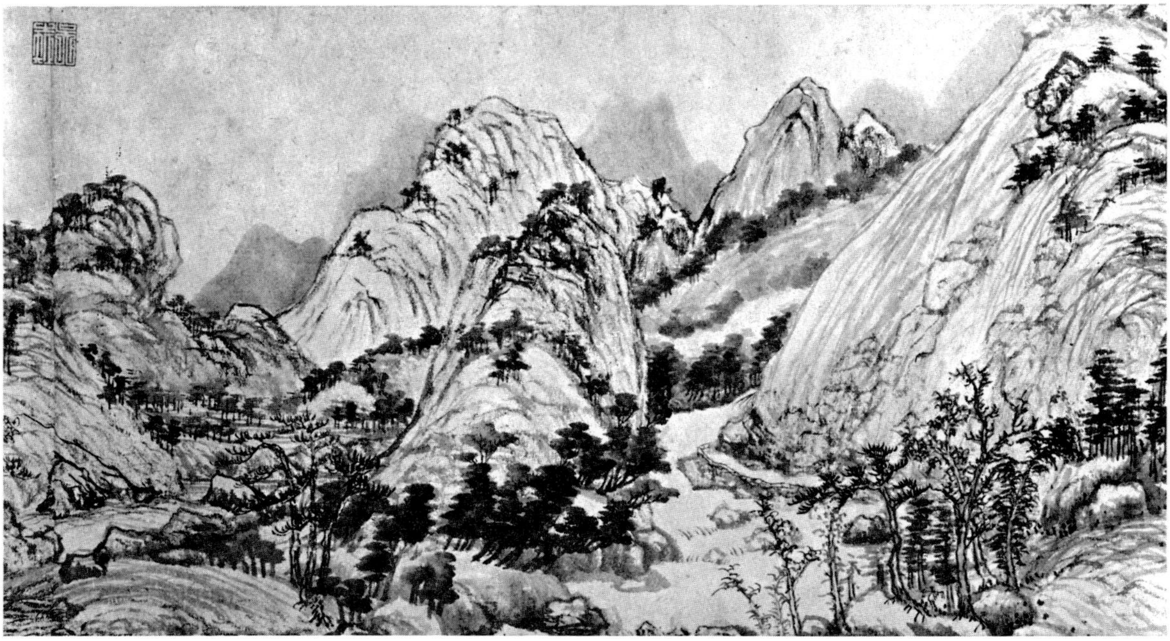

58. Huang Kung-wang (1269–1354): "Dwelling in the Fu-ch'un Mountains." Detail of a handscroll completed in 1350; ink on paper. Ht. 33 cm. Yüan Dynasty. National Palace Museum, Taipei.

mark of complete artistic integrity. The huge, wavelike heaving of the mountains, the light touches of the brush, the subtle play of delicate shades of ink, the luminous atmosphere—all seem to bear witness not only to the character of this relaxed and generous-hearted man, whose complexion remained clear, a friend said, and whose eyes remained bright into extreme old age, but to the triumph of the human spirit in times of national and personal catastrophe.

A very different kind of man was Huang Kung-wang's young friend Ni Tsan (1301–74). Ni Tsan, who inherited the family fortune when he was 27, came from one of those merchant families in Wu-hsi whose wealth had bought them gentry status. He was a man of leisure, a bibliophile and collector, fussy about cleanliness to the point of eccentricity, a little arrogant—just the sort of southern gentleman of the moneyed class to be mercilessly squeezed by the Mongols. When his estate was crippled by taxation he either sold it or distributed it among his relatives and took to a houseboat, spending years drifting among the lakes and rivers around Wu-hsi, staying in monasteries or with friends, painting when the mood took him, and even from time to time selling his paintings—something that only dire necessity would have let him stoop to. His range as a landscape painter is very narrow, for he painted essentially the same composition over and over again: a foreground with trees, an expanse of water, and

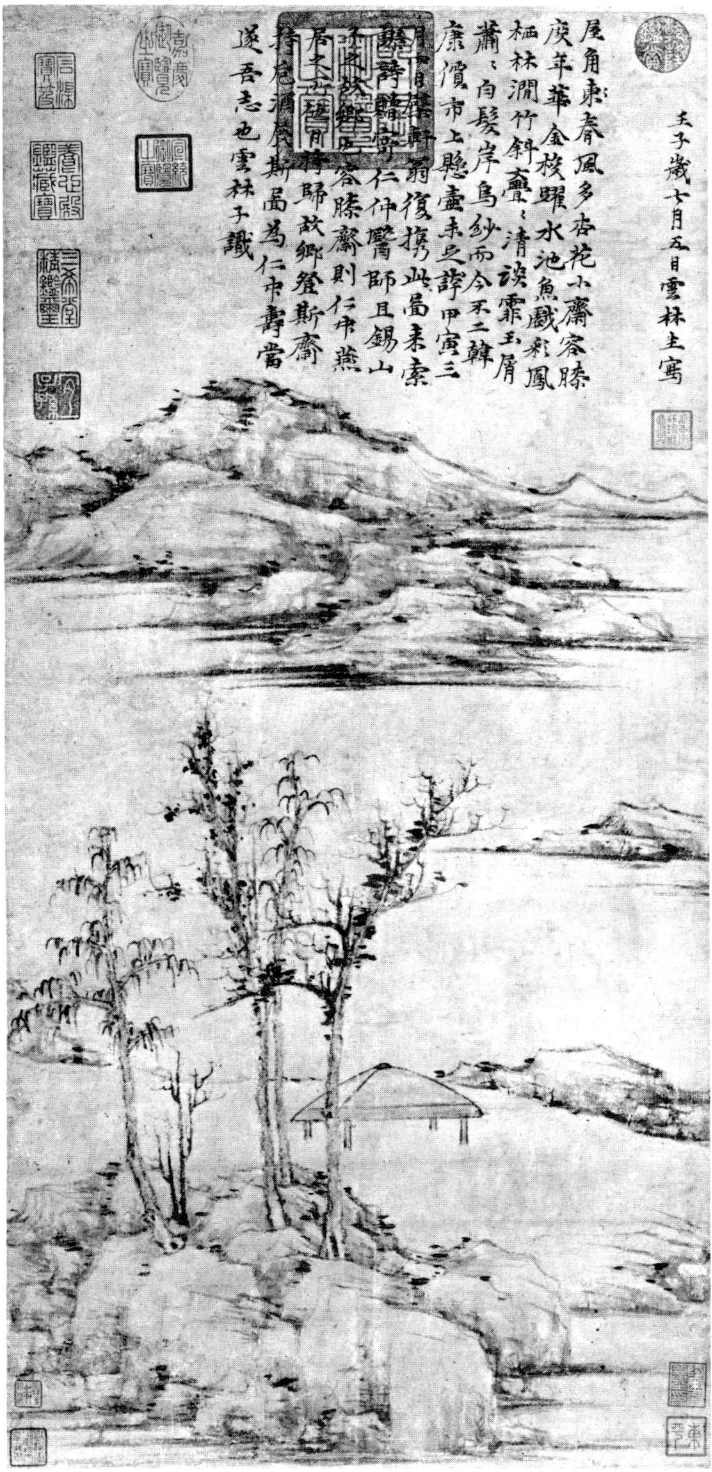

59. Ni Tsan (1301–74): "The Jung-hsi Studio." Hanging scroll painted in 1372, inscribed by the artist in 1374; ink on paper. Ht. 73.3 cm. Yüan Dynasty. National Palace Museum, Taipei.

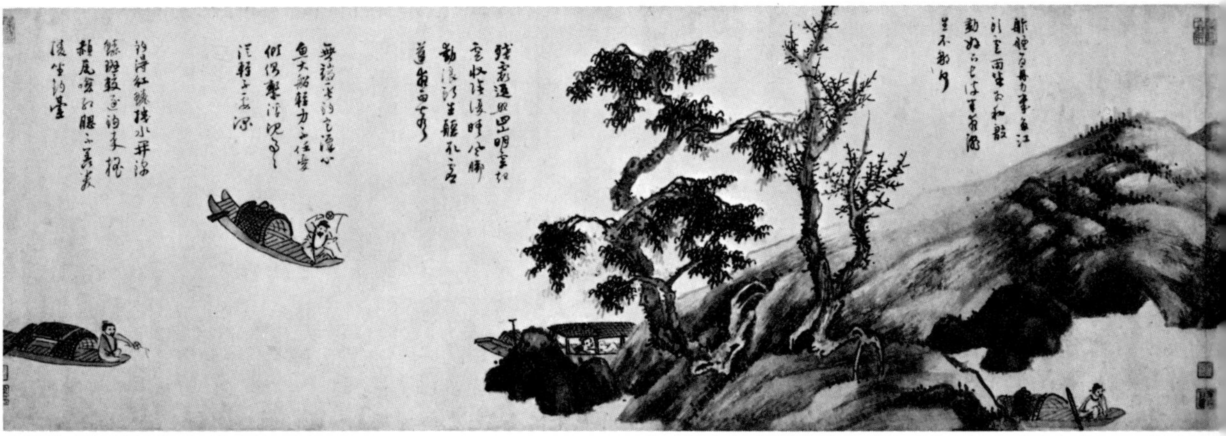

60. Wu Chen (1280–1354): "The Fishermen." Handscroll; ink on paper. Ht. 24.8 cm. Yüan Dynasty. John M. Crawford Collection, New York.

distant mountains. Among his surviving paintings only the earliest, of 1339, has a figure sitting in the pavilion in the foreground. In later paintings the foreground is always empty—for, as he explained to a friend, "I don't know that there is anyone around in the world." Besides, the foreground figure must have seemed an obvious and conventional device to this extremely fastidious painter.

There is a cool, almost unearthly detachment about Ni Tsan's landscapes, an austere serenity that goes less than halfway to meet the viewer yet draws him into the picture in a mysterious way, to take his seat in that untenanted shelter by the waterside. The careless abundance of Huang Kung-wang and the skill of the professionals are alike foreign to Ni Tsan. He used ink, it was said, as sparingly as if it were gold. A great seventeenth-century painter said of him, "The paintings by Master Ni are like waves on a sandy beach, or streams between stones which roll and flow and issue by their own force. The air of supreme refinement and purity is so cold that it overawes men. Painters of later times have imitated only the dry and desolate, or the thinnest parts, and consequently their copies have no far-reaching spirit."* One of his noblest and simplest compositions is *The Jung-hsi Studio* of 1372 (Plate 59). The long inscription was added two years later, when the owner asked him to dedicate it to a friend who had a studio of that name. This shows that when Ni Tsan painted it he had no particular place in mind at all: it was just an ideal, almost abstract, landscape, an expression of his own detachment from worldly things. It only became a picture of the Jung-hsi studio when Ni Tsan wrote on it.

*Osvald Sirén, *Chinese Painting*, vol. 5, p. 164. This is taken from a colophon on a painting by Shih-t'ao, in the Abe Collection, Osaka Museum of Art.

Up to this moment the artist's inscription consisted of little more than a signature and perhaps a date. But now it grows until it sometimes becomes almost as important as the painting itself. This is not just because the artist is a scholar and a poet. That is nothing new. What is new is the abstract and completely generalised character of his paintings. He is no longer depicting the real world, still less a particular place. If he wants to show that he has a particular spot in mind he can only do it by his inscription; there is no other way. Writing on the painting, therefore, far from spoiling it actually enhances it, for the poem gives it added meaning, carries the idea "beyond the image," as the critics put it. Moreover, a work that combined the three arts of poetry, calligraphy, and painting was considered triply excellent.

Something of the calm and serenity of Ni Tsan, but expressed with greater warmth, we find in the third of the Four Great Yüan Masters, Wu Chen (1280–1354). He made a living of sorts as a diviner and fortune-teller, and tried to be a philosopher; but, as with Oliver Edwards, he found that cheerfulness was always breaking in, as witness the poem he wrote on a delightful sketch in the Crawford Collection:*

> To the west, the village of red leaves,
> The last light of the day is lingering.
> By the sandbanks of the golden reeds,
> The faint vestige of the moon just appears.
> So lightheartedly pull the oar, and let's return;
> Hang up the rod, and fish no more.

In fact, I doubt if Wu Chen had been fishing at all; the rod was just a pretext for doing nothing, as it was to the Chinese poet who never baited his hook. A critic called Wu Chen's landscapes "profound and remote, with a leisurely and relaxed feeling"—which perfectly describes them. Wu Chen's acceptance of the world has a geniality about it entirely lacking in the austere Ni Tsan, not because he puts people in his landscapes—for he seldom does—but because his easy contours and liberal yet subtle use of ink washes are warm and appealing (Plate 60). Yet he, too, cared nothing for fame and success. He knew that few people understood his "splashing around in his inkstone pond," as he called it; but when his long-suffering wife told him that all the collectors were calling at the house of Sheng Mou, a popular painter who lived next door, he calmly replied, "it won't be so in twenty years' time." It took longer than that, and it is easy to see why the picture-buying public would have preferred

*Sherman E. Lee and Wai-kam Ho, trans., *Chinese Art under the Mongols: The Yüan Dynasty (1279–1368)* (Cleveland, Ohio, 1968), No. 251.

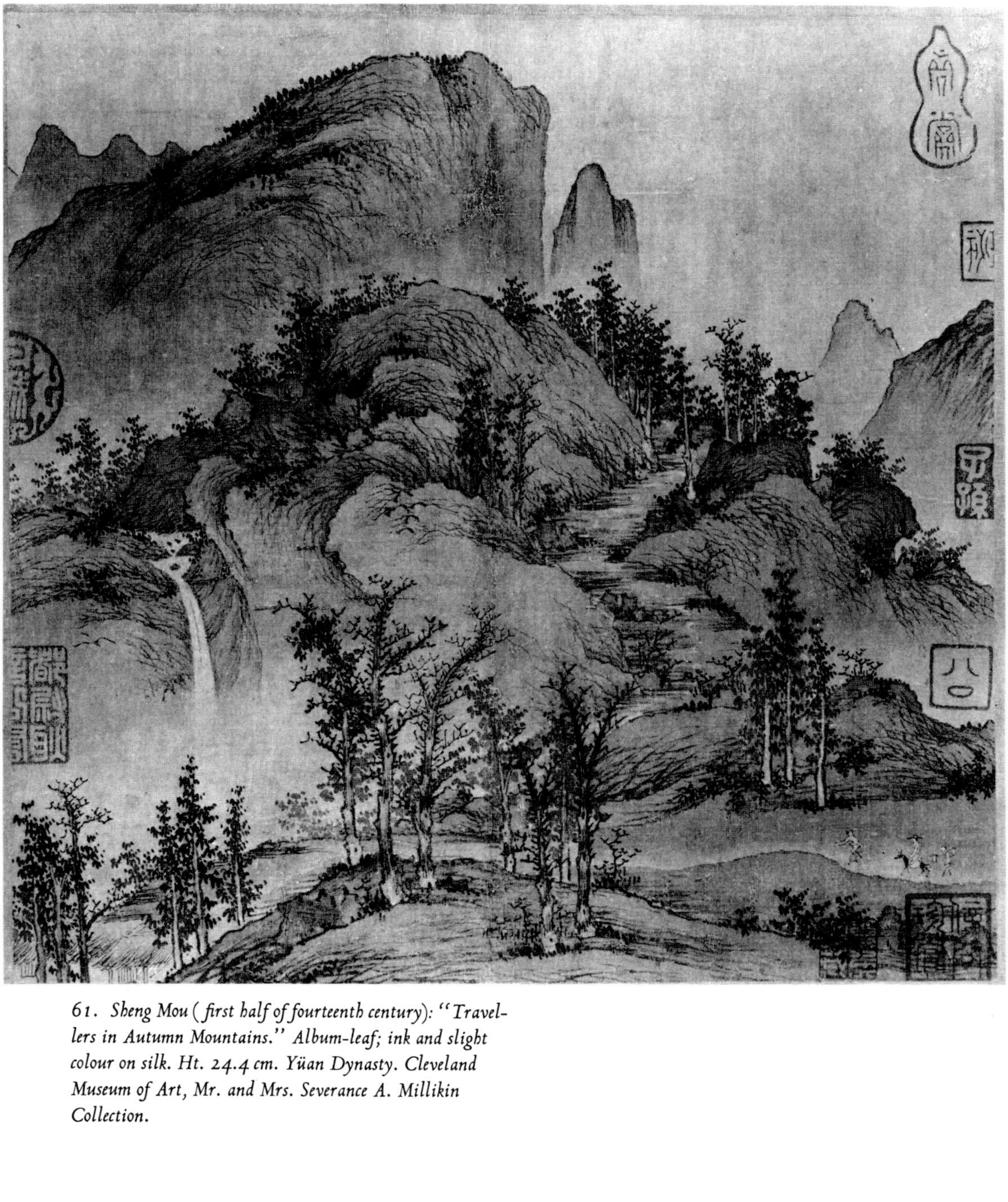

61. Sheng Mou (first half of fourteenth century): "Travellers in Autumn Mountains." Album-leaf; ink and slight colour on silk. Ht. 24.4 cm. Yüan Dynasty. Cleveland Museum of Art, Mr. and Mrs. Severance A. Millikin Collection.

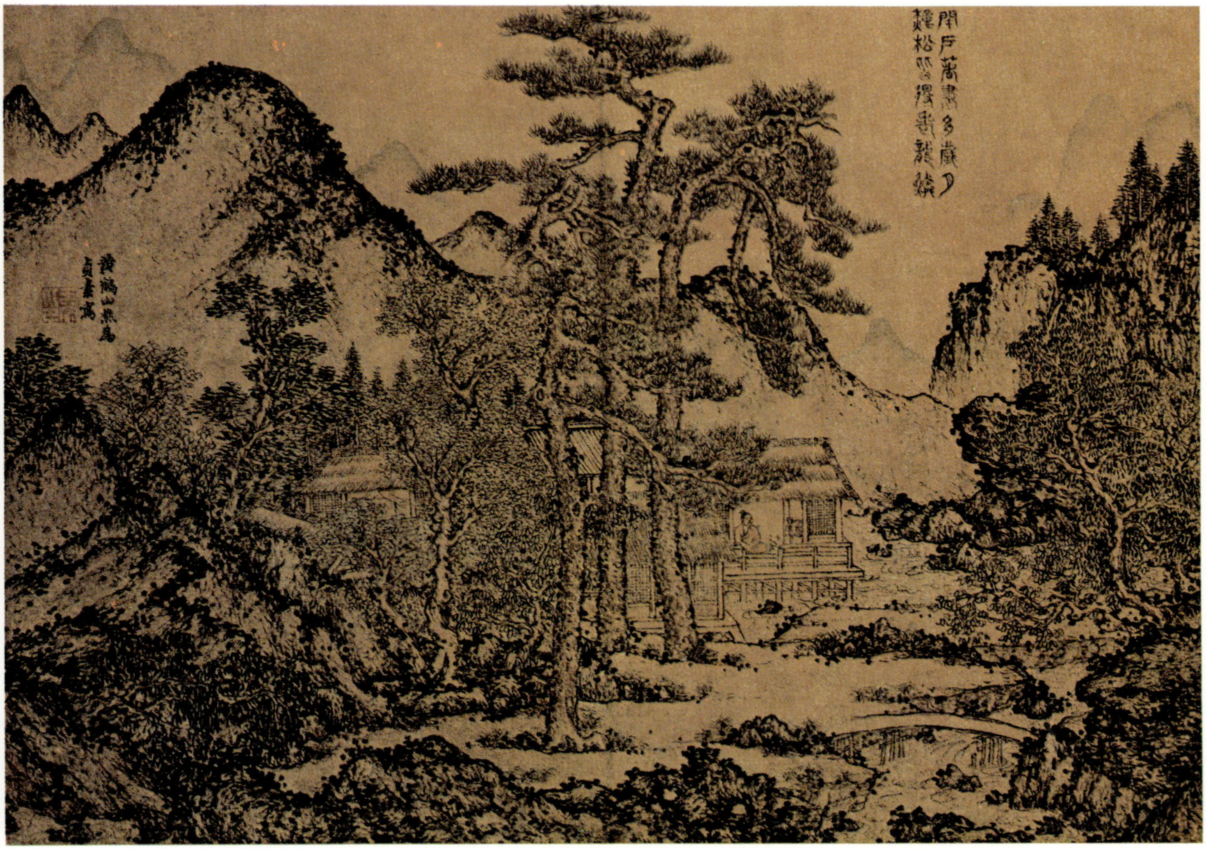

62. Wang Meng (ca. 1308–85): "Writing Under the Pine Trees." Double album-leaf mounted as a hanging scroll; ink and slight colour on paper. Ht. 38.7 cm. Yüan Dynasty. Mrs. A. Dean Perry Collection, Cleveland, Ohio.

Sheng Mou, son of a Sung academician, who skilfully combined the styles of several classic masters (Plate 61) and filled his pictures with interesting details and rather fussy brushwork.

When first we look at the works of the fourth of the Yüan Masters, Chao Meng-fu's grandson Wang Meng (ca. 1308–85), we wonder just where he fits in, for both his style of painting and his career seem to set him apart. He held a minor post in the decaying Yüan administration and re-entered government service as soon as the Mongols were driven out and the new Ming Dynasty was established. He was interested in politics and military affairs—dangerous pursuits in those uncertain times—found himself on the wrong side in a great power struggle, was arrested for alleged treachery, and died of starvation in prison.

Wang Meng's style is without precedent (Plate 62). His brushwork is tight and restless, where Huang Kung-wang's and Wu Chen's are relaxed; his textures are congested and careful, where Ni Tsan's are spare

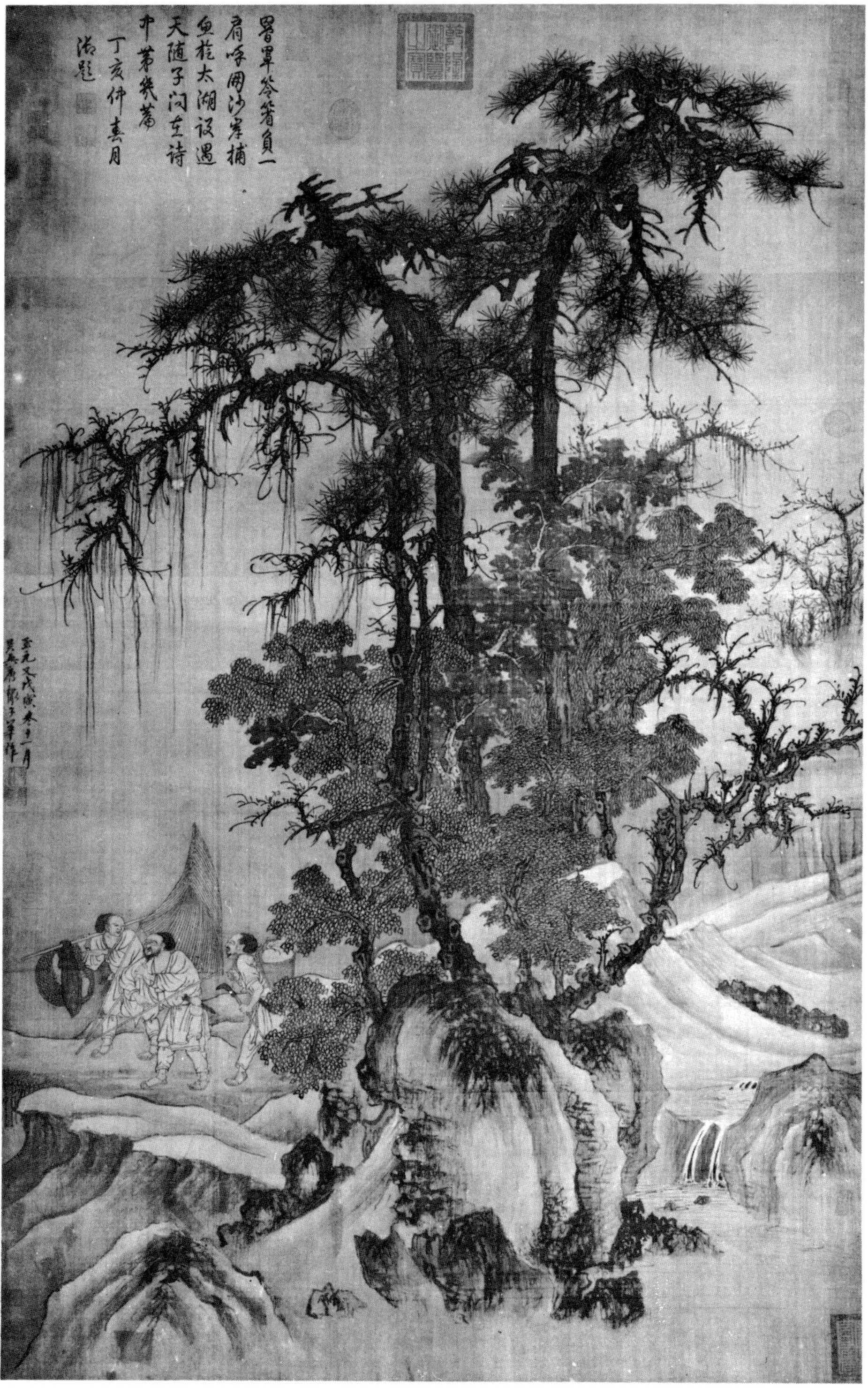

63. T'ang Ti (1296–1340): "Fishermen Returning on a Frosty Bank." Hanging scroll dated 1338; ink and slight colour on silk. Ht. 144 cm. Yüan Dynasty. National Palace Museum, Taipei.

and dry; his landscapes are worked over with an intensity that is the very antithesis of the serene understatement of his great contemporaries. Yet a Ming Dynasty critic wrote on one of Wang Meng's pictures: "His brush is refined and his ink wonderful like those of Wang Hsi-chih [the great fourth-century calligrapher]. His heart is pure like that of Tsung Ping. His strength is sufficient to carry a bronze ritual tripod. There has been no one like him for a hundred years."* And a later critic praised him for his concentration, purity, and refinement. Certainly the completeness of realisation in Wang Meng's landscapes—such as the beautiful album-leaf painted for his friend, the painter's Ts'ao Chih-po—is a great help to Westerners who find Ni Tsan and Wu Chen empty or excessively bland. Moreover, his use of colour comes as a refreshing change from their austere monochrome. Perhaps what the scholar-painters found so admirable in Wang Meng was his total absorption in the language of painting to the exclusion of all else. Here again, but in a very different way, we are reminded of Cézanne.

I have of course given a very simplified view of landscape painting in China during the Yüan Dynasty. I have said nothing about the many survivals of Sung academy painting; about the exaggerations and distortions of what we might call "post-Zen" Buddhist painting; about men like Kao K'o-kung, who recreated the misty landscapes of Mi Fu, or T'ang Ti (Plate 63), whose towering landscapes have often been taken for authentic works by Li Ch'eng and Kuo Hsi, or Ts'ao Chih-po, wealthy friend of Huang Kung-wang and Ni Tsan, who perhaps came closest to capturing the spirit of the antique in the way that the Four Great Masters did. Still less have we been able to concern ourselves with the professionals, who by this time were able to exploit almost the whole tradition to their own decorative ends. For it was not they who salvaged Chinese landscape painting from the wreckage of the Occupation; rather it was a handful of heroic individuals who rose above the misery of their condition and, by a passionate reinterpretation of what they found best in their past, created a new kind of painting for the future. Their example was to sustain and inspire landscape painters until modern times.

*Chang Ch'ou, *Ch'ing-ho shu-hua-fang*, translated by O. Sirén in *Chinese Painting*, vol. 4, p. 86.

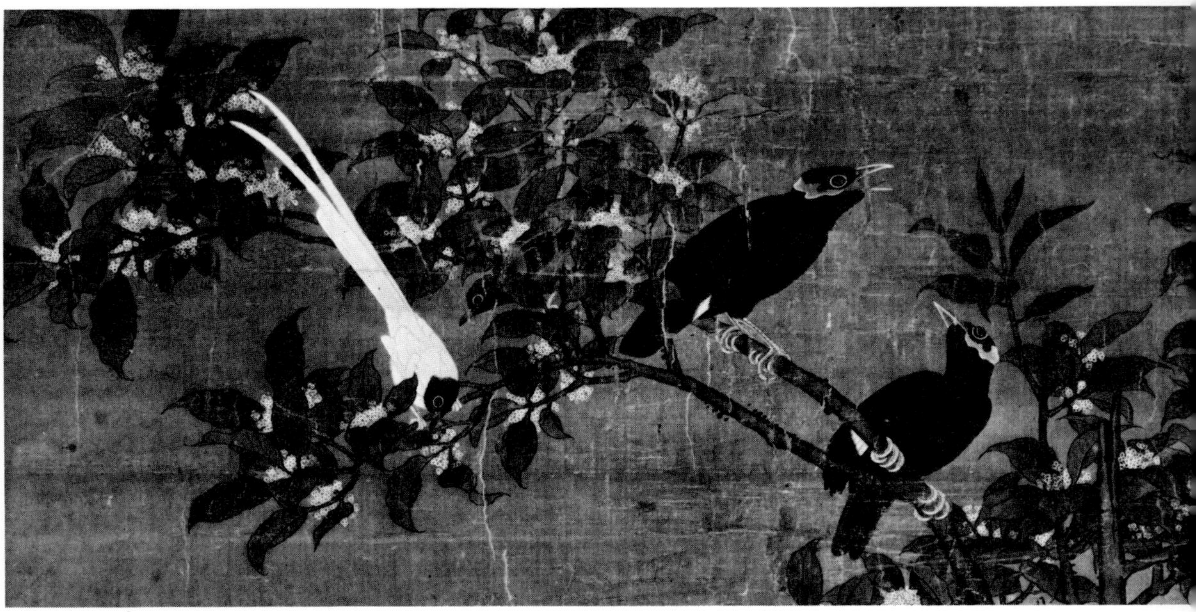

V Achievement and Crisis in Scholarl

The Ming Dynasty, 1368-1644

Detail of Plate 65 (p. 112): Lü Chi, "Winter."

It is impossible to imagine a European painter stopping to consider whether to paint his next landscape in the manner of Salvator Rosa, Claude, or Ruysdael. But by the fifteenth century such a choice for the Chinese painter had become not only possible but unavoidable. For the sources of his inspiration had changed, and it was now more and more often the case that he had far more experience of looking at pictures than he had of looking at nature. We can only really understand the painting of the Ming and Ch'ing dynasties if we know what it was that made the painter so excessively aware of the history of style, and led him again and again to paint nature not as he saw it but through the eyes of Tung Yüan, Huang Kung-wang, or Ni Tsan. If, despite this accumulation of art-historical scholarship, his paintings are still so full of natural beauty, that is because he was not only a painter and a scholar but a Taoist and a poet as well.

The freedom to choose was not, as one might have thought, a gift

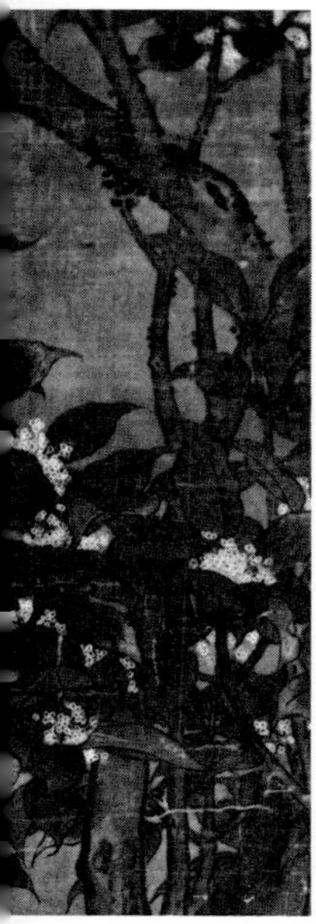

ainting

brought by liberation from the Mongol yoke and the establishment of a native dynasty, the Ming, in 1368. Far from it. Indeed, as I suggested in the last chapter, the first decades of the Ming, under the ferocious Hung-wu emperor, were a time when court painters and scholars everywhere lived in terror of their lives—a terror that increased as the emperor, once a shrewd judge of men, degenerated into a pathologically suspicious tyrant who would have a court artist cruelly done to death (being cut in half was one method) for the most trivial breaches of the regulations. For a short time under the Hsüan-te emperor (1425–35), himself a benign and moderately talented painter, imperial patronage was something to be courted rather than feared; but increasingly the court became dominated by the eunuchs, the curse of the Ming, and the scholar-painters kept well away from Peking. Indeed, by the mid-fifteenth century there were few inducements for them to quit the stable, prosperous world around Soochow, with its famous gardens such as the Cho-cheng-yüan, The Garden of the Clumsy Politician (Plate 64), in which an educated man could cultivate his tastes in peace and freedom. To secure the status of a gentleman he did not even have to pass the state examinations, although many, in the hope of an official career, wasted the best years of their lives trying to master the sterile complexities of the "eight-legged essay," an ordeal that only one in a hundred survived. But one could also acquire gentry status, even a degree of sorts, simply on the basis of one's scholarly and social standing; then, provided one had a private income, one could live like the painter Shen Chou, comfortably at home. The officials, on the other hand, were shunted about from pillar to post, amassing wealth in the process but constantly being torn away from their friends, with whom they kept in touch over the years by the exchange of letters, poems, and, if they had any talent at all in that direction, paintings.

This is the era of the great private collections, when wealthy men such as the miserly Hsiang Yüan-pien (1525–90) could amass a collection far bigger and better than that of the emperor himself; and it is a sign of the social mobility of the age that Hsiang, whose fortune was based chiefly on a string of pawnshops, could hobnob with the gentry, acquiring prestige as a connoisseur. For the Chiang-nan region, and Soochow particularly, had now become the artistic centre of China. There cata-

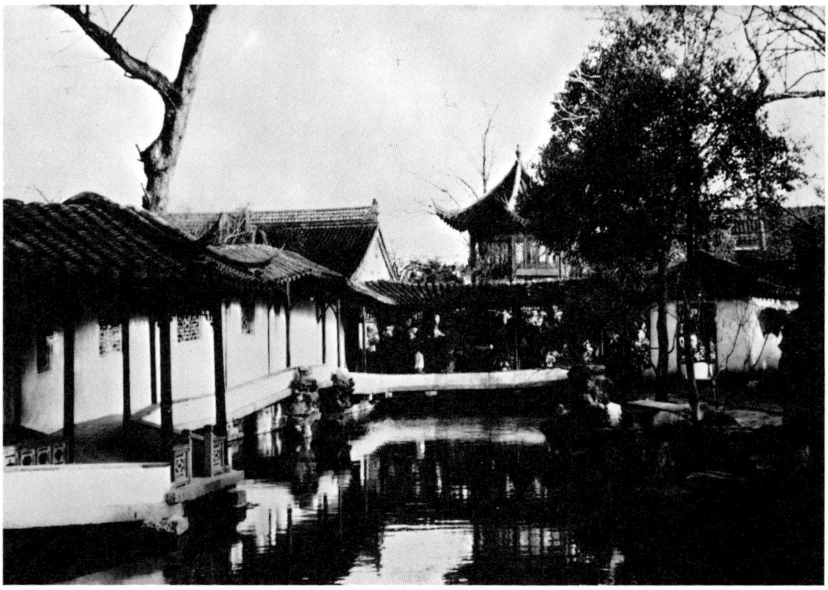

64. The Garden of the Clumsy Politician, Cho-cheng-yüan, Soochow. Photograph by Ramond Dawson.

logues were compiled, stylistic lineages traced, masterpieces copied (and forged in huge numbers), colophons written, and seals carved, applied, and deciphered. Around and even on the painting accumulated a literature of critical appreciation—as it passed through the hands of scholars, poets, and experts—that made the scroll not just a work of art and of scholarship but a witness to the ties that bound members of the intelligentsia together.

Not only did there grow up a scholarship of painting, but painting itself became a scholarly activity. How much the artist actually knew about the history of painting depended upon whom he knew and what private collections were open to him, for there were no museums in China until well into the twentieth century. We read many heartrending stories of the delights and disappointments, the surprises and frustrations when a long-heard-of masterpiece was at last before the painter's eyes, only to turn out to be a wretched fake, or worse still, to be snatched away by its anxious owner before the painter could finish copying it—for copying these rarely seen works was the best way to study them, and an important way of keeping the tradition alive.

I would not like to suggest that the Ming scholar-painters were mere pedants or *pasticheurs*, shopping around for styles. But if they were industrious and persistent, they did acquire an encyclopedic knowledge of the history of painting. When it came to choosing a style, much depended upon your position in society, how well educated you were, whom you knew, where you lived. If you lived in Nanking, for instance, you enjoyed the patronage of rich merchants and officials of a subsidiary court a good deal more relaxed than that of Peking; if you lived in Soochow, you became steeped in the scholarly ideals of the Yüan Masters, and your models would be Huang Kung-wang, Ni Tsan, and Wu Chen; if you lived in the old Southern Sung capital of Hangchow, you naturally felt more comfortable in the tradition of Ma Yüan and Hsia Kuei. Around the year 1500 the range of styles the artist could draw upon was as wide as that of the tradition itself; none yet bore a special cachet in the eyes of the critics, nor was any yet condemned.

But it was not just a matter of choosing freely among a number of different styles. In a very special sense, the style was the man. For it was in the way he painted, as much as in what or where he painted, that the artist proclaimed where he stood. Sometimes it was not even that. It might be just a matter of how he felt at the moment he took up the brush. Just as the amateur pianist sitting down at the piano pauses to select a volume of Bach or Debussy according to his mood, so might the Chinese painter say to himself "I feel like doing a Huang Kung-wang, or a Ni Tsan, today." Having chosen a style, imperceptibly, unconsciously, he loses himself in that master and becomes one with him. So if the painter's sense of history still bound him to tradition, his choice within the tradition was wide. This was a freedom very different from that of Ruysdael or Constable, but a kind of freedom nonetheless.

We could illustrate this by scanning, as it were, the spectrum of painting between 1450 and 1550, from the court artists and professionals on the right to the individualists and eccentrics on the left—although the latter are as yet rare and isolated. We could consider the out-and-out professionals like Lü Chi (Plate 65), whose job it was to fill the palace halls with landscapes and birds and flowers in a decorative coloured style derived from the Southern Sung academy. Moving a little to the left, we could consider the work of Tai Chin, who escaped from the jealousy of rival painters at court to struggle for a living in Hangchow. For a time he even had to flee to distant Yunnan. One would have thought that he had had enough of court life, but he later returned to Peking under a happier regime for a brief autumnal glory. If we compare his *Life of the Fishermen* (Plate 66) with a painting of a similar subject by the real recluse Wu Chen (Plate 60), we cannot help noticing a subtle difference: how relaxed and assured is Wu Chen's touch, how solid his forms, how naturally his poems become part of the whole work of art; while Tai Chin the professional cannot help trying to be realistic in the Sung manner, his spiky

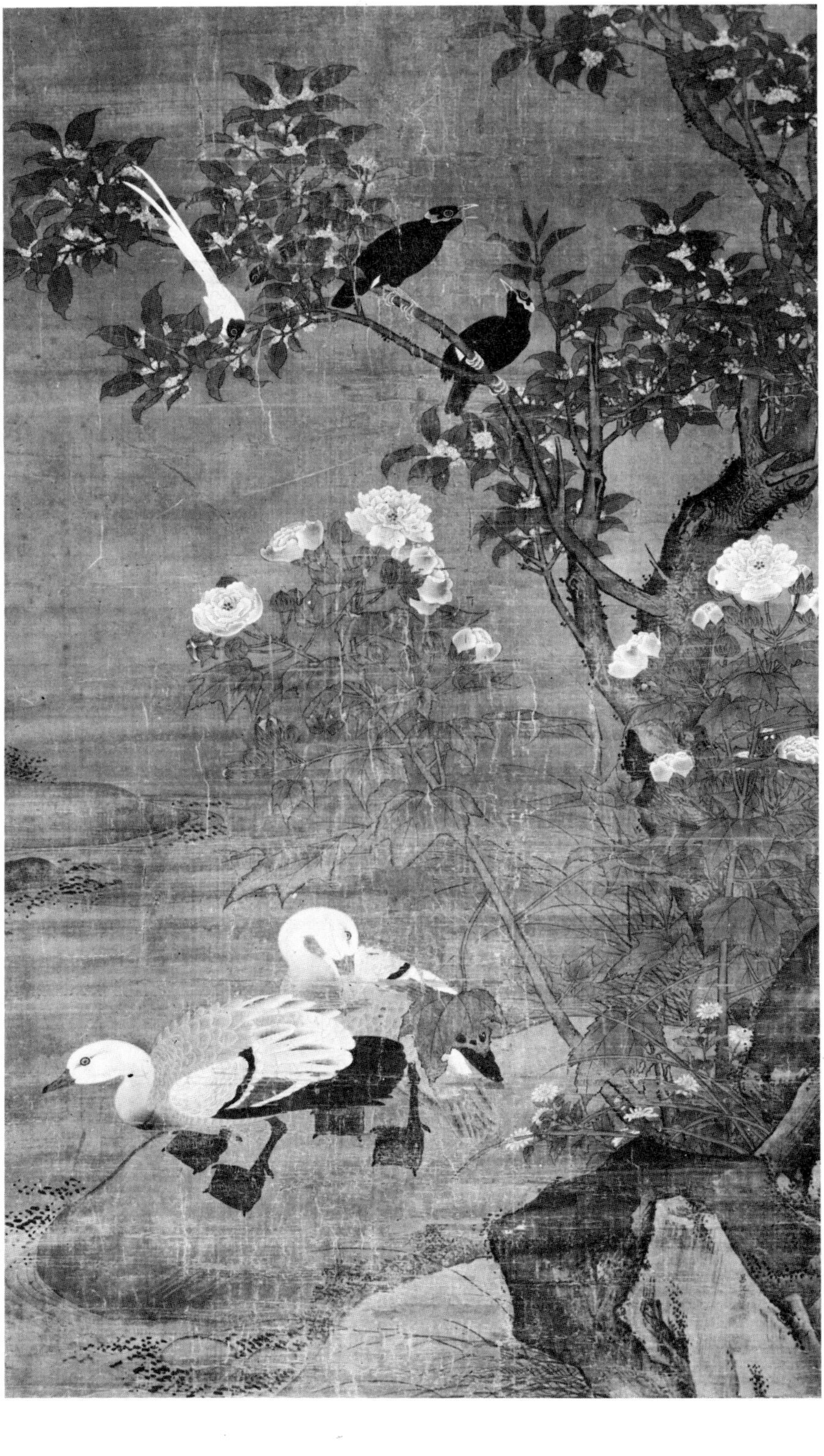

65. Lü Chi (active ca. 1480–1510): "Winter," from a set of landscapes of the "Four Seasons." Hanging scroll; ink and colour on silk. Ht. 175.2 cm. Ming Dynasty. National Museum (Tōyōkan), Tokyo.

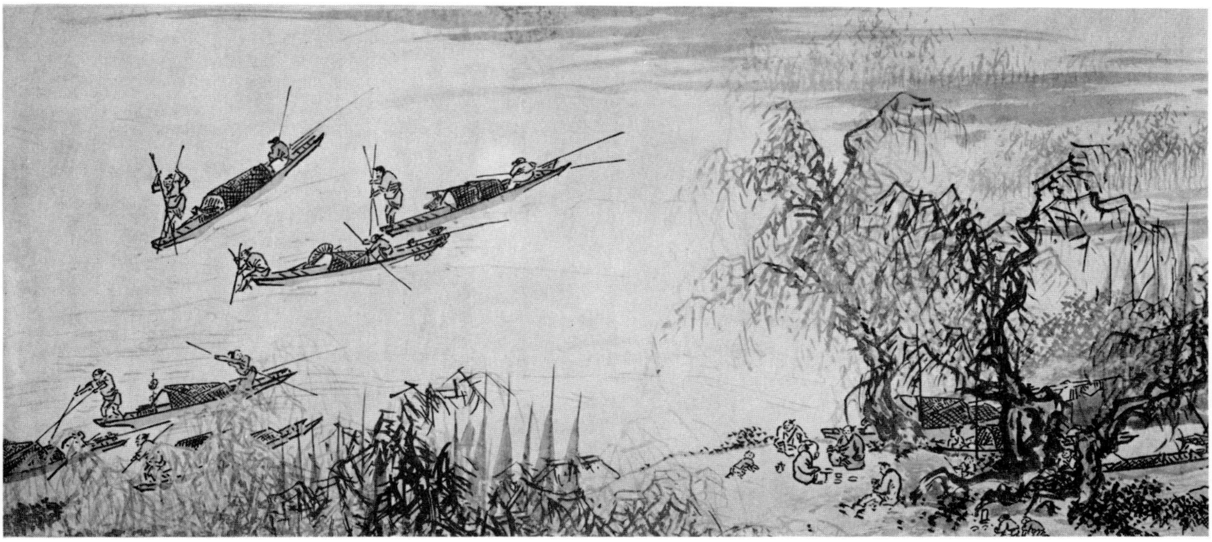

66. *Tai Chin (ca. 1388–1462): "The Life of the Fishermen." Detail of a handscroll; ink and colour on paper. Ht. 47 cm. Ming Dynasty. Freer Gallery of Art, Washington, D.C.*

brushwork suggesting the last gasp of the great academy tradition of Ma Yüan and Hsia Kuei. Tai Chin was only one, although by far the best, among hundreds of professional painters who drew upon the Sung academy style. Later critics condemned the vast majority of their works, with a good deal of justice, as flashy and vulgar: the sort of thing suitable for a rich merchant's reception hall, perhaps, but not for the library of a gentleman.

The flavour of professional brilliance, more firmly controlled perhaps, hangs too about the work of Ch'iu Ying, a successful artist in Soochow who painted, in a style of exquisite refinement, landscapes with figures on which his scholarly friends would sometimes write poems. A picture such as his *Conversation Under the Wu-t'ung Trees,* a delightful expression of the theme of scholarly friendship (Plate 67), seems to bridge the gulf between the professional and the amateur, making nonsense of the intellectual class distinction that beset Chinese culture for so much of its later history.

Professional in technique, scholarly in content: later critics taught that such a mixture was unacceptable. Yet who but a bigoted theorist could deny the intensity of feeling in such works as the marvellous *Eastern Sea,* a scroll that bears the signature of Chou Ch'en (Plate 68). An obscure Soochow professional who died soon after 1535, Chou Ch'en clearly got his way of drawing trees, rocks, and waves from the Sung academicians, above all from Li T'ang and Hsia Kuei. The picture is full of drama and restless movement. We can hear the thunder of the waves, the howl of the wind in the storm-tossed branches. Yet, still amid the tempest, gazing calmly out from his study window sits a scholar waiting for the friend who makes his hazardous crossing of the torrent not far away. The villagers must be taking refuge from the storm, but the two gentlemen accept it, even revel in it. Though nature is often awe-inspiring in Chinese landscape painting, nowhere but in the work of Kung Hsien is it frightening, haunting, or alien, as it is in Grünewald or Böcklin. The Chinese understands that the chaos around him is in the natural order of things, and his mind is at peace.

Sometimes a personal disaster, such as the one that struck down T'ang Yin (1470–1523), cast a scholarly amateur into the ranks of the professionals. A brilliant student who came first in the local examinations, T'ang Yin went up to Peking for the metropolitan examinations and there was implicated in a cheating scandal. He returned in disgrace to Soochow, where he was compelled to support himself with his brush for the rest of his life. He could paint in the free style of the literati, for he was a scholar and a poet himself; but he could and did paint in a far more professional manner, for after all those were the pictures that sold. He lived the life of a bohemian between the monasteries, wineshops, and brothels of Soochow, gradually becoming estranged from his rather prudish friend Wen Cheng-ming, of whom more below. He painted erotic pictures and wrote mildly erotic verse:*

> Last night the cherry apple
>   deflowered by the first rain-drops
> Its fallen petals slight and frail
>   their beauty almost articulate
> My mistress rising early
>   leaves her bedroom
> In her hand a mirror
>   to admire her painted cheeks
> She asks me, "which is prettier
>   the petals or my complexion?"
> To her question I reply
>   "They win by innocence."
> At hearing this my mistress
>   displays a charming anger
> Refusing to believe dead petals
>   surpass a real live person.
> She crumbles a handful of blossoms
>   to throw in my face—
> "Tonight, my dear," she says
>   "sleep with the flowers."

*John Scott, trans., *Love and Protest: Chinese Poems from the Sixth Century B.C. to the Seventeenth Century A.D.* (New York, 1972), p. 137.

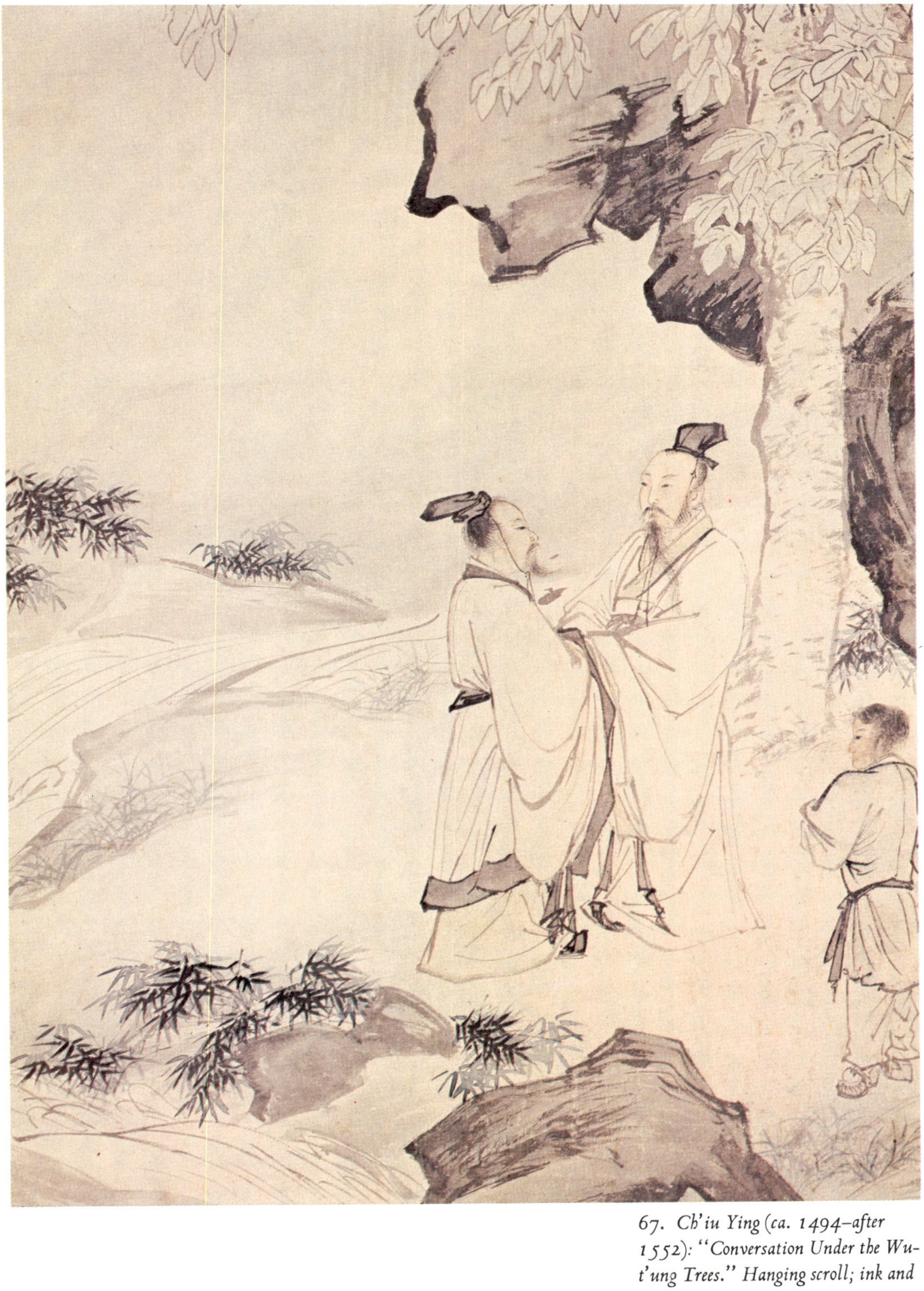

67. *Ch'iu Ying (ca. 1494–after 1552): "Conversation Under the Wu-t'ung Trees." Hanging scroll; ink and colour on paper. Ht. 279.5 cm. Ming Dynasty. National Palace Museum, Taipei.*

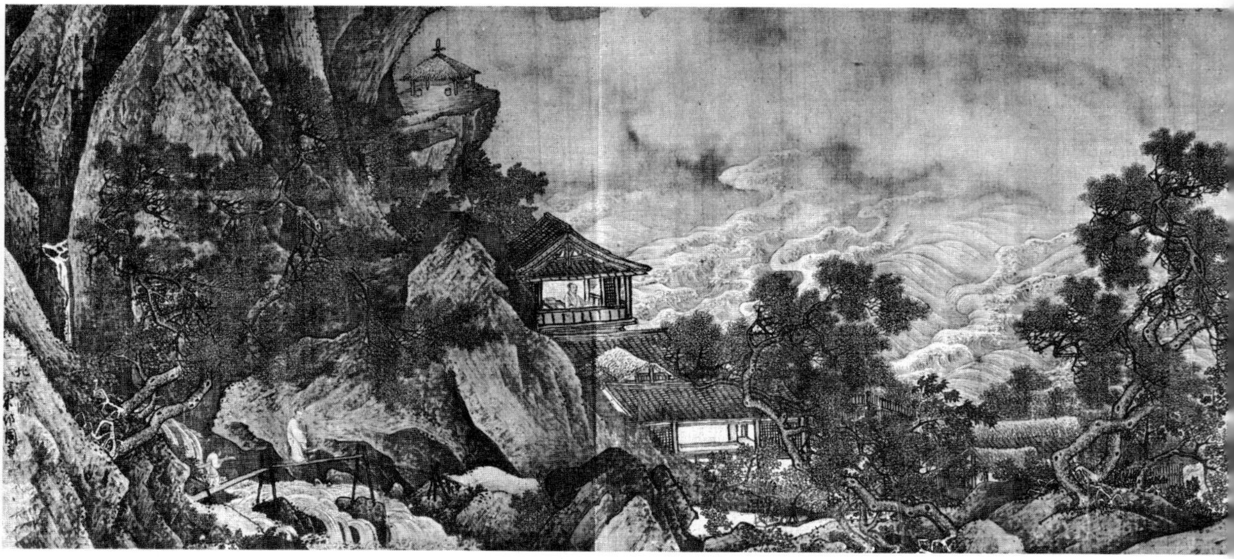

68. Chou Ch'en (died after 1535): "The Eastern Sea." Part of a handscroll; ink and slight colour on silk. Ht. 29 cm. Ming Dynasty. Nelson-Atkins Gallery of Art, Kansas City, Mo.

T'ang Yin's *Murmuring Pines on a Mountain Path* (Plates 69 and 70) would seem at first sight to be a more serious performance altogether. It is a huge composition in the grand Northern Sung manner, full of fine detail, displaying a masterly control of line and wash. The whole effect, though spectacular, is nonetheless a little artificial. The scholar pausing on the bridge, head thrown back, to gaze at the waterfall above him suggests the eighteenth-century English gentleman in a Picturesque landscape, pausing at a turn of the path to admire a composition that reminds him of Claude or Salvator Rosa. We can almost hear our scholar exclaiming "Ah! A perfect Li T'ang!" and strolling on. It is a virtuoso performance with the brush, done to evoke admiration rather than to inspire any deep thoughts about the cosmic *ch'i*, the vital force that animates both nature and the artist.

Moving further to the left, or rather, perhaps, to dead centre, we come to the towering figure of Shen Chou (1427–1509), the great humanist, country gentleman, poet, and painter, who so dominated the art world of Soochow that he is considered the leader, if not the founder, of the Wu school of landscape painting—Wu being the old name of the area in which Soochow lies. In fact, he was only one of the great luminaries in a tradition that can be traced back many centuries. We could indeed, in scanning Shen Chou's work, cover almost the whole range of landscape painting in these settled years of the middle Ming, beginning with his academic paintings in the archaic "green and blue" style and

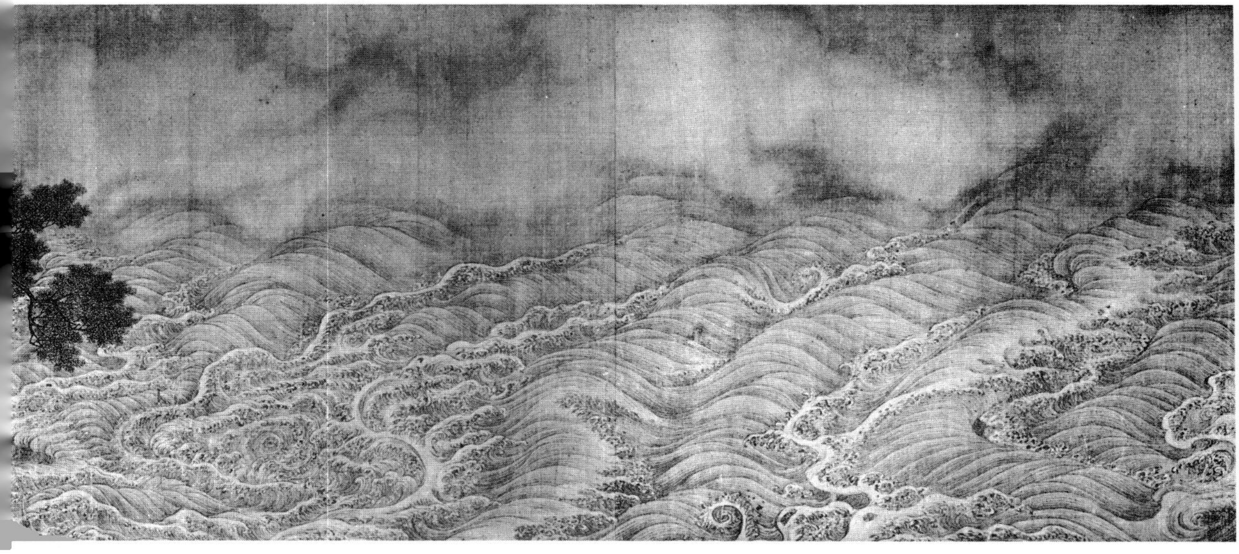

passing through works in the manner of the Northern Sung masters to a brilliant concoction based on the fusion of two scrolls by Ma Yüan and Hsia Kuei. We find reflections of his great love, Huang Kung-wang (whose scroll *Dwelling in the Fu-ch'un Mountains* [Plate 58] Shen had owned and copied), and of the other great Yüan Masters—Ni Tsan, Wu Chen, and Wang Meng. It was Wang Meng's style that he borrowed for that grand tribute to his teacher, *Towering Mount Lu* (Plate 7)—his diploma picture, as it were—that I referred to in the Introduction. On the styles of these masters he played endless variations, transforming them by the sheer force of his personality into works that are uniquely Shen Chou. One has only to compare his landscape of 1484 (Plate 71) with Ni Tsan's *Jung-hsi Studio* (Plate 59) to see how he has humanised that austere composition, inserting the delightful nonfishing fisherman chatting with his friend in the shelter by the waterside; and how what a critic called his "forceful hand" has prevented him from quite achieving the Yüan Master's severe understatement. When he was "doing a Ni Tsan," his teacher, it is said, would cry out, "Enough! enough!" Yet that same critic said that Shen Chou was the only Ming painter who came anywhere near understanding Ni Tsan.

The almost casual ease with which Shen Chou gathered the tradition to himself and, without doing it violence, made it express his own vision of the world is not matched by any other Ming artist. We see it best of all perhaps in his album-leaves, such as the delightful *Poet on a*

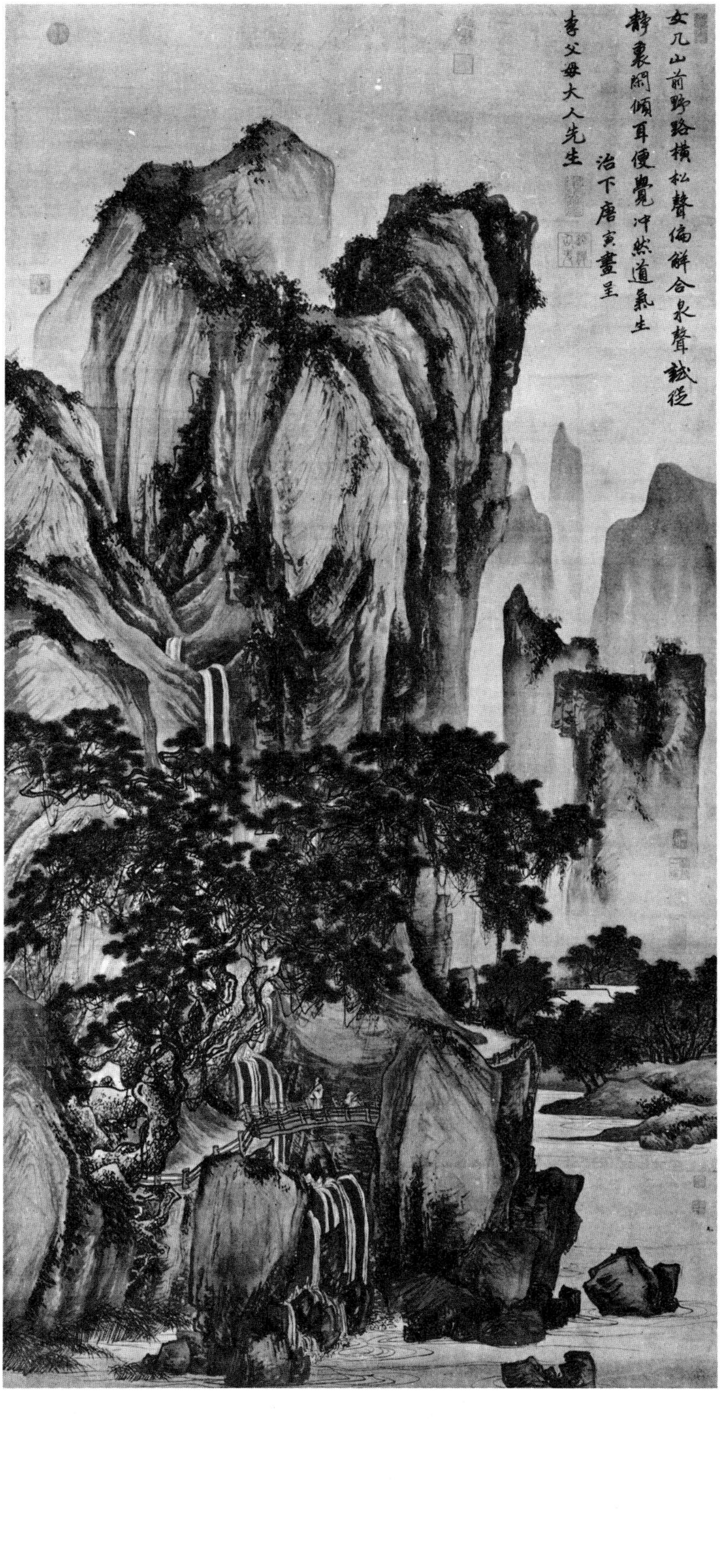

69. *T'ang Yin (1470–1523): "Murmuring Pines on a Mountain Path." Hanging scroll; ink and slight colour on silk. Ht. 194.5 cm. Ming Dynasty. National Palace Museum, Taipei.*

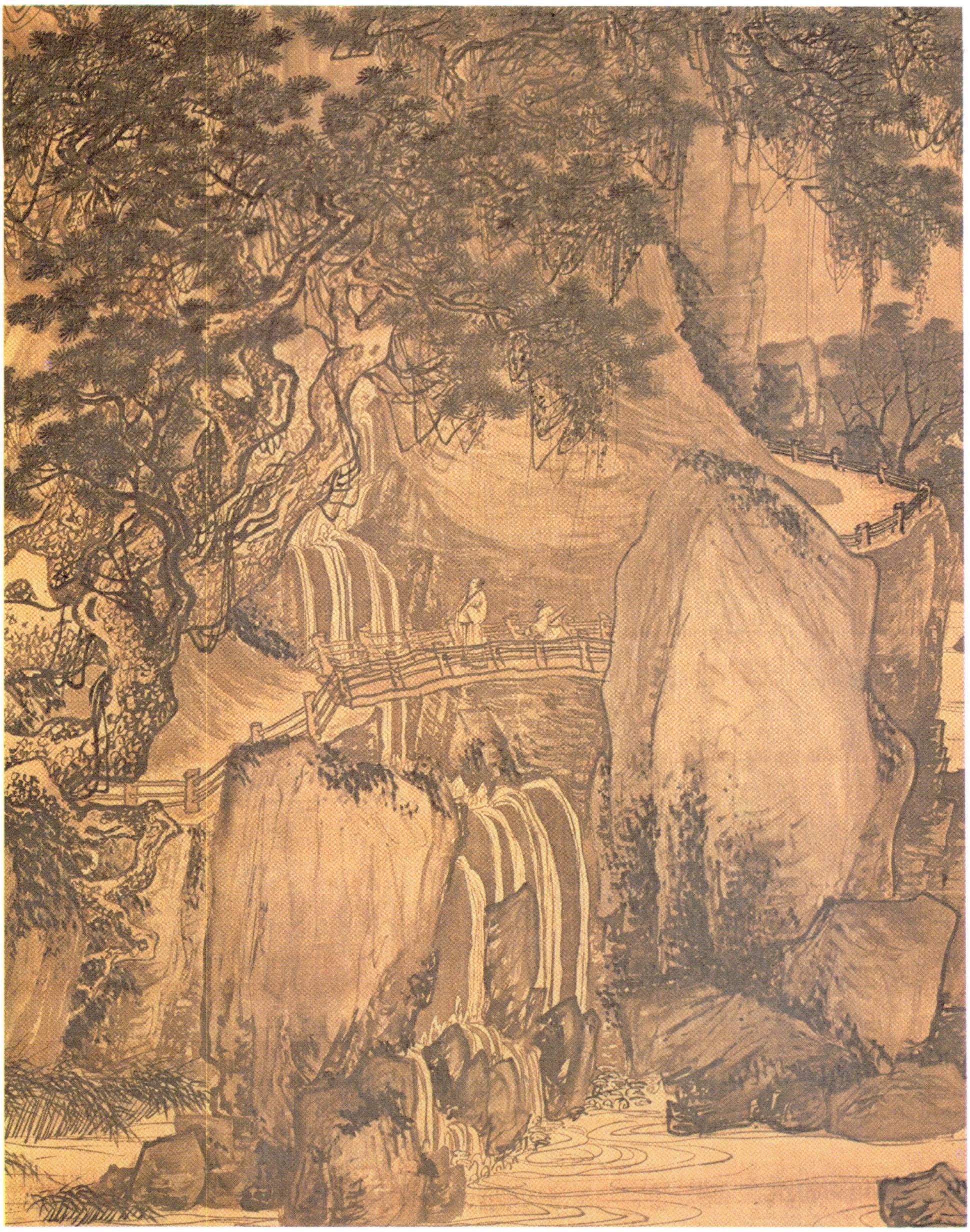

70. Detail of T'ang Yin, "Murmuring Pines."

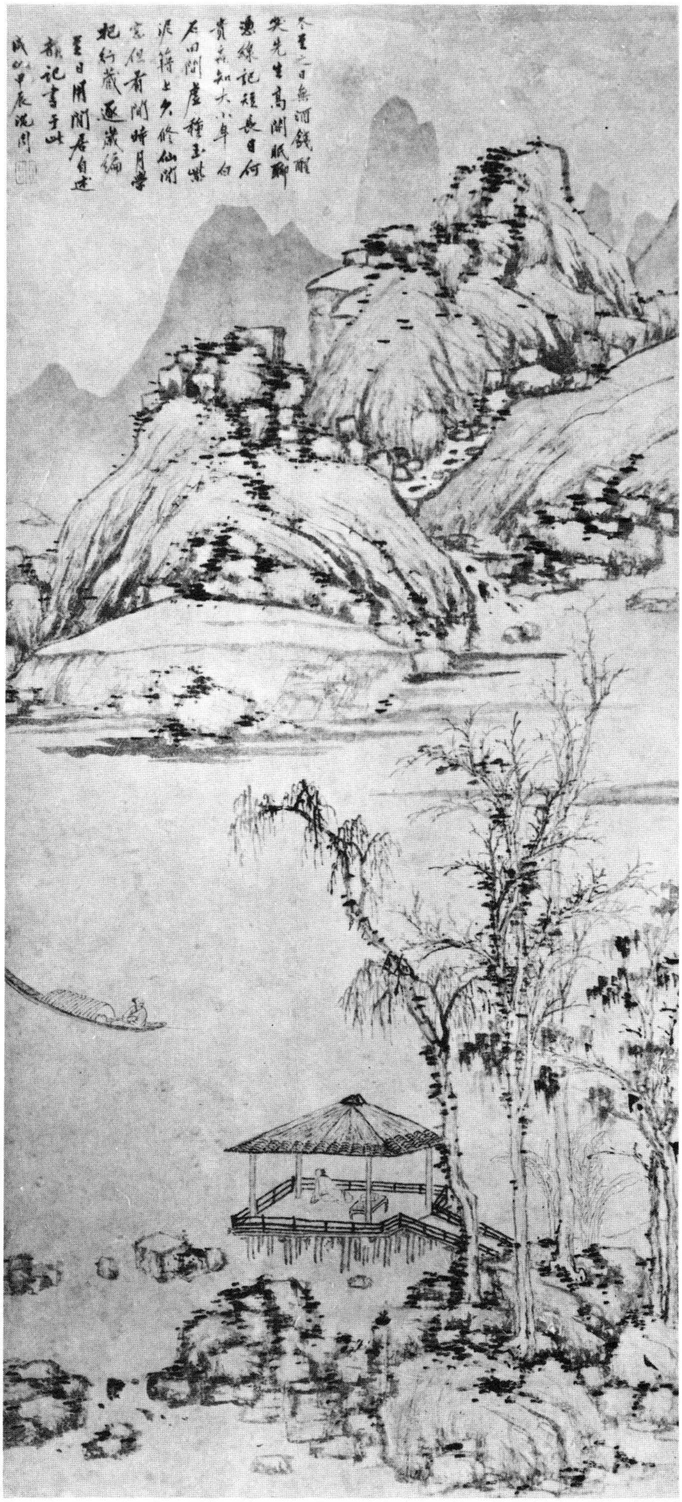

71. Shen Chou (1427–1509): Landscape in the manner of Ni Tsan. Hanging scroll dated 1484; ink on paper. Ht. 140 cm. Ming Dynasty. Nelson-Atkins Gallery of Art, Kansas City, Mo.

Mountaintop (Plate 72), to which he penned a verse that has the effect of focusing the viewer's attention, inviting him to identify himself with the solitary figure gazing out over the clouds:*

White clouds like a belt
  encircle the mountain's waist
A stone ledge flying into space
  and the far thin road
I lean on my bramble staff
  and gazing into space
Make the note of my flute
  an answer to the sounding torrent.

It all looks simple enough, but what would-be imitators found to their cost is that Shen Chou, unlike so many Ming masters, is in fact inimitable—in the extraordinary clarity and firmness of his forms; in the simplicity of his figures, which are so full of character; in the strength of his line; and in the lively and unhesitating touch of his dots (*tien*), which provide accents, rhythm, and unifying texture. Although he had few pupils, many later artists felt his influence, which was wholly beneficial.

Shen Chou's sixteenth-century followers were either much narrower in range or, like Wen Cheng-ming (1470–1559), positively encyclopedic. Wen Cheng-ming was an accomplished scholar, poet, and calligrapher, who longed for the high career that success in the civil service examinations would bring him but hated the examinations. Ten times did he sit for the second degree, and ten times did he fail. At the age of 52 he was finally given a job as a hack historian in Peking simply on the basis of his scholarly reputation. Resented by his colleagues as an interloper, he stuck it out for three years and then returned, sadly disillusioned, to Soochow. There he spent the rest of his life as what we might call a "professional amateur," supporting himself by teaching, painting, writing poetry, and executing commissions for calligraphy, eulogies, and epitaphs. It was he who developed his teacher Shen Chou's grand synthesis into an encyclopedia of styles and techniques suitable for a gentleman. He admired Li Ch'eng as much as Tung Yüan, and the great eclectic Chao Meng-fu even more than Huang Kung-wang or Ni Tsan. Through his son, his nephew, and his many pupils he passed on a standard of punctilious artistic and personal behaviour that was scarcely to be equalled in later years.

What is surprising is that Wen's eclecticism should have produced

*Richards Edwards, *The Field of Stones* (Washington, D.C., 1962), p. 40.

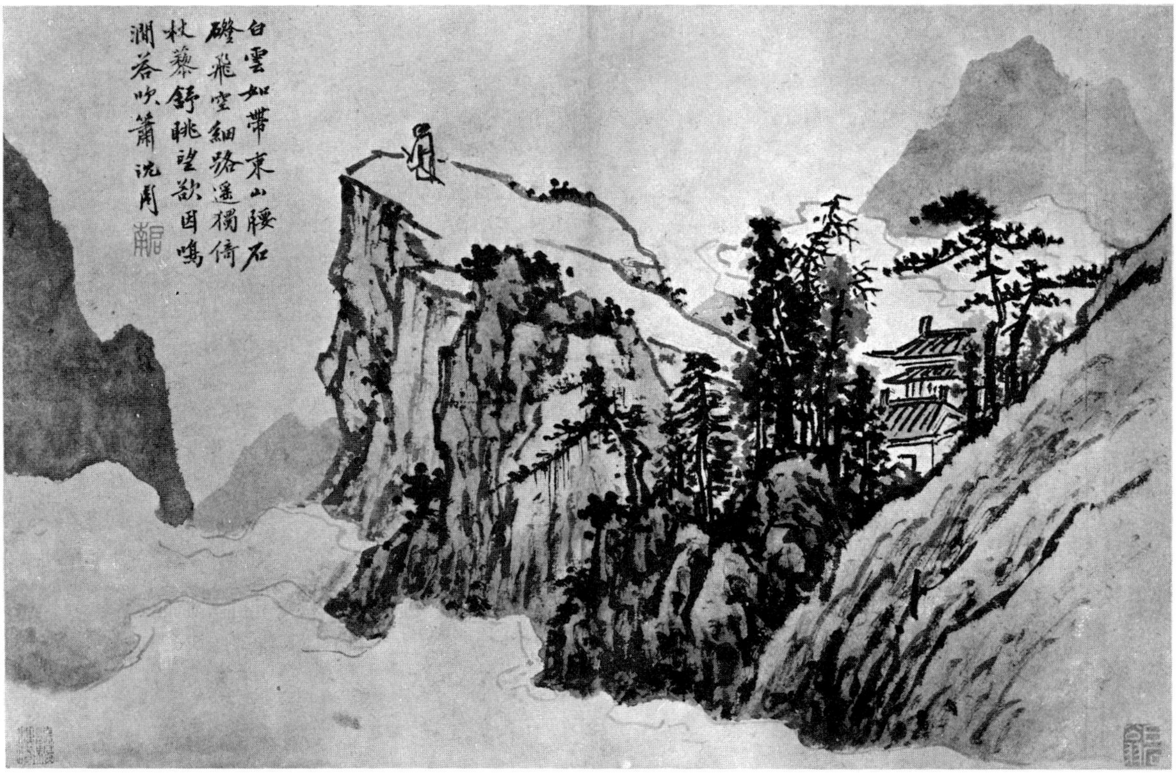

72. Shen Chou (1427–1509): "Poet on a Mountaintop." Album-leaf; ink on paper. Ht. 39 cm. Ming Dynasty. Nelson-Atkins Gallery of Art, Kansas City, Mo.

works of such lyrical beauty as *Saying Farewell to a Friend* (Plate 73), painted in 1531. Perhaps the subject had something to do with it. For this is no mere exercise in the manner of Chao Meng-fu or Wang Meng, although the stylistic references are there; it was painted as a farewell present for his old friend Wang Ch'ung, when the latter came to say goodbye before he left Soochow. The artist shows the two friends sitting in his garden. They have drawn a little aside—suggested how delicately by placing them at the edge of the picture!—while their servants chat under the trees, for this is their farewell, too. We can imagine that few words were exchanged, and that for the most part they sat in silence, thinking of the past and of the future. An evocation in art of the sadness of parting could hardly be more restrained, or more poignant. This exquisitely simple picture is a perfect example of the use to which the literati so frequently put the arts: not just to express one's feelings, but to express them for a particular person. Rarely in Western art—van Gogh is a wonderful exception—do we find that sense of intimate communication through painting with someone dear to the artist. To say that this

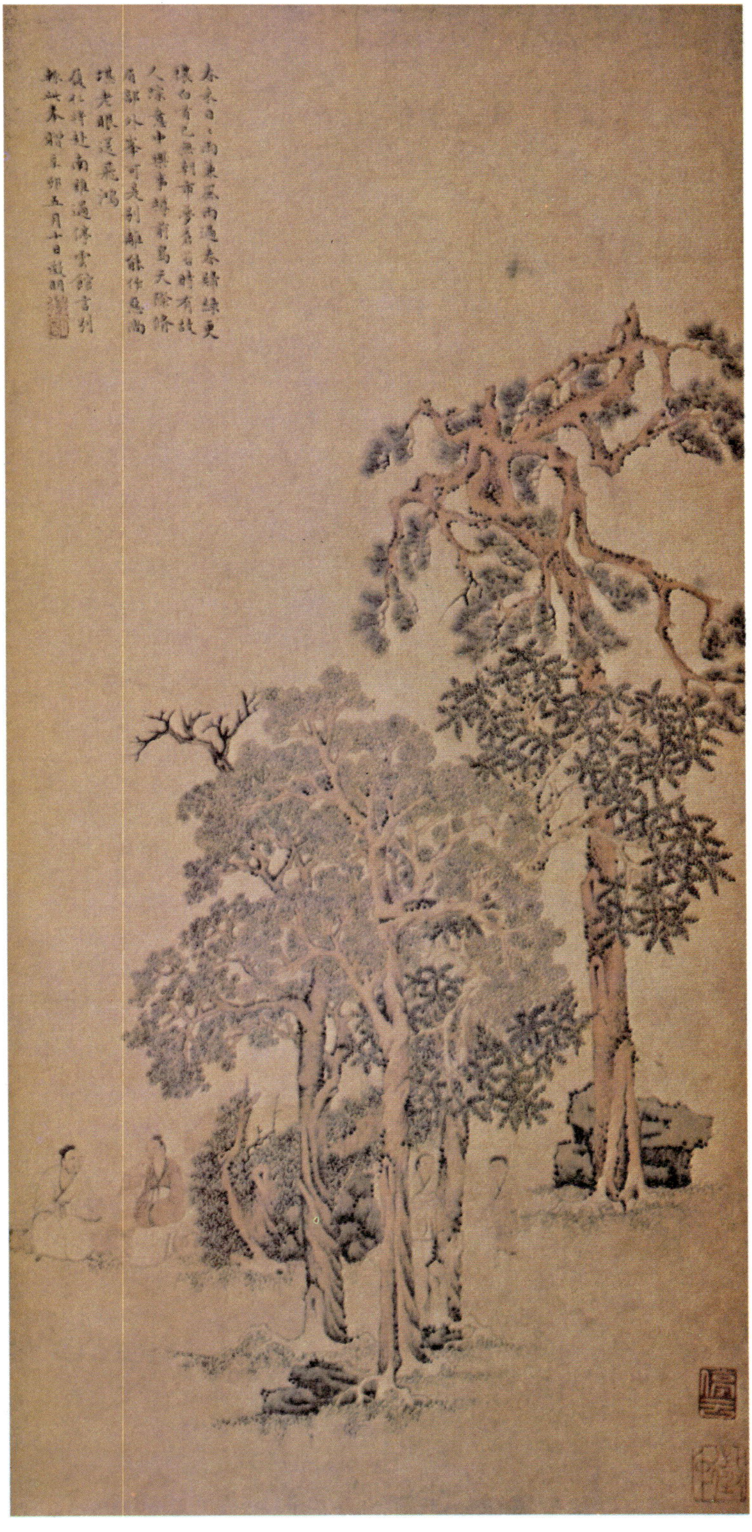

73. *Wen Cheng-ming (1470–1559): "Saying Farewell to a Friend." Hanging scroll dated 1531; ink on paper. Ht. 50.2 cm. Ming Dynasty. Dr. Franco Vannotti Collection, Lugano, Switzerland.*

purely human feeling is not an element in the beauty of the whole presented work would be to show a real impoverishment of spirit.

But there was another side to Wen Cheng-ming, which comes out from time to time in his remarkable studies of cypresses, pine trees and junipers, some of which he painted in his eighties. The ancient trunks, twisting and writhing with a life of their own, are not just a symbol of the indomitable spirit of old age, although they are certainly that; they reveal a passion for pure form that is new to Chinese painting. Wen Cheng-ming does not, like some painters of the last years of the dynasty, exploit form for a display of the self, as does Wu Pin, for example, in the contorted landscape (Plate 78) that we will turn to in a moment. Wen Cheng-ming's passion is governed by his feeling for the tree itself, and thus the painting holds a balance between the claims of nature and the artist's own urge for self-expression. Perhaps it is just this balance that makes the art of the middle Ming period so profoundly satisfying. However much Wen Cheng-ming had thought about style and technique before he started to paint—and it would be surprising if Ching Hao and Li Ch'eng were not there, lurking somewhere just below the level of his conscious mind—in the very act of painting, as in the act of playing the piano, there was no conscious thought, only intuition and feeling translated immediately into form. In that act, the life of nature and the life that is in the artist are fused, and the result is a work not of art-historical scholarship, but of art.

When these painters were not painting, they were looking; but even more were they reading, thinking, discussing the philosophical ideas that were running like an electric current through the southern intelligentsia during the sixteenth century. Wen Cheng-ming would certainly have been familiar with the ideas of his great contemporary, the philosopher Wang Yang-ming (1472–1529), whose theories about what kind of knowledge was valuable represented the climax of a movement away from the study of the external world and a revolt against the arid pedantry of the examination system that had defeated Wen Cheng-ming and many other ambitious scholars. The founders of Neo-Confucianism, it will be remembered, had stressed the value of intense study of the world as a path to understanding, and I suggested that this confidence in the evidence of the senses was reflected in the realism of Northern Sung landscape painting. But in the Southern Sung the emphasis was already shifting from the object of the mind's investigations to the mind itself. Wang Yang-ming and his school now carried philosophical idealism to its logical limits, to the point of neglecting the world of sensory experience.

Wang himself said that to grasp the *li* of things was impossible. He wrote how, in exile in the south, he had spent seven days and nights trying by sheer concentration to grasp the *li* of the bamboo outside his house. It left him exhausted and ill. At the time he thought he had failed to grasp it because he lacked the will. But later, he said, he came to understand that no one can investigate everything in the world. Investigating things meant "investigating one's own body and mind."

This doctrine, which had a great appeal to sixteenth-century scholars, turned men's thoughts away from nature and inward upon themselves. It did not make them ineffective as officials and administrators, for they kept their careers as practical men of affairs separate from their philosophical speculations, which, like their poetry and painting, they indulged in after office hours, so to speak. But it profoundly affected their attitude to knowledge. The clue to the meaning of things was to be found, they felt, not "out there" but within. Nature and the painted forms of nature, to men of this persuasion, were significant only insofar as they had a place in the knowing mind; and the landscape painting of these men was a reflection of that mind. Wen Cheng-ming reveals in his *Cypress and Rock* (Plate 74) the true painter's eye, a very different form of apprehension from that of the idealist philosopher; but the picture can hardly be called realistic in the sense that Northern Sung painting was. There is no doubt that from this time forward external points of reference are increasingly abandoned by the landscape painters, and a new kind of abstraction appears that we shall see revealed at its purest and most intense in the strange landscapes of Tung Ch'i-ch'ang (Plate 80). Wen Cheng-ming's nephew Wen Chia even went so far as to maintain that that great monument of Sung realism, the Ch'ing-ming scroll (Plate 41), was "not a fitting object for a gentleman's collection." It was too realistic.

We may see this passionate concern with what kind of knowledge was important not—or at least not yet—as a failure of nerve but as a reflection of a particularly settled and secure period in Chinese history, when the expression of men's thoughts in art could be abstract, generalised, intuitive, inward, without any loss of power. It was a precious, and precarious, moment that produced Shen Chou and Wen Cheng-ming, Wang Yang-ming and his disciples and opponents, a moment of great freedom and intellectual excitement, when philosophy and ethics were debated literally in the marketplace and from his travelling cart the peripatetic philosopher Wang Ken proclaimed his doctrines of absolute liberty and of the common man as sage. Some of the most brilliant men of

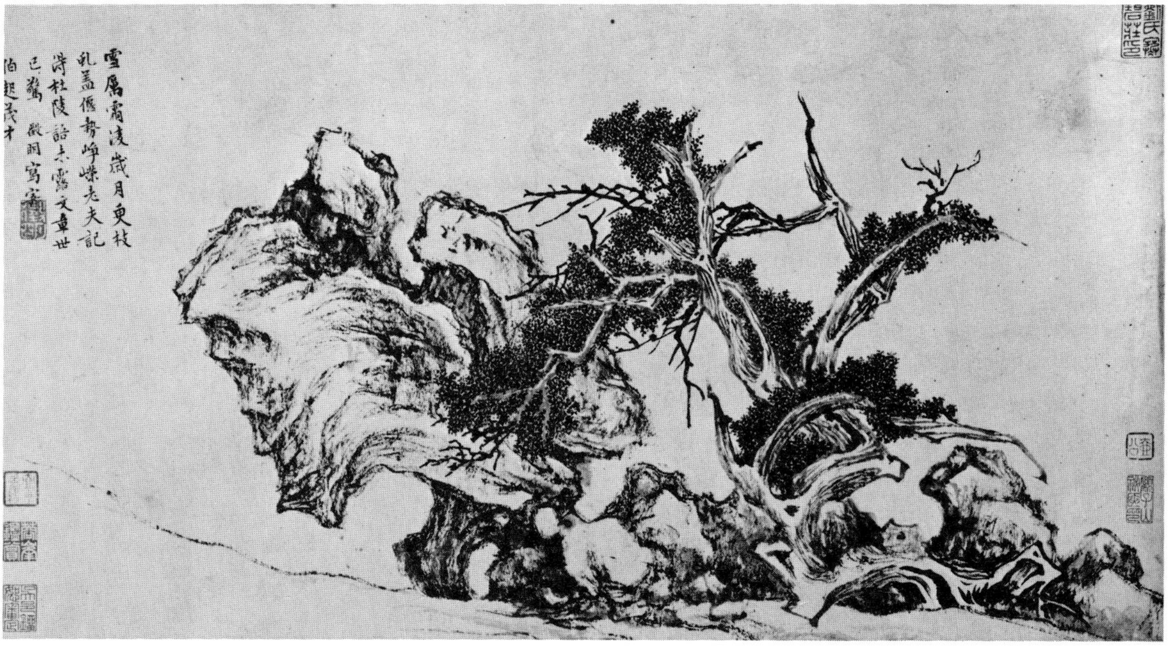

74. Wen Cheng-ming (1470–1559): "Cypress and Rock." Handscroll dated 1550; ink on paper. Ht. 26 cm. Ming Dynasty. Nelson-Atkins Gallery of Art, Kansas City, Mo.

the day came of humble stock: Wang Ken's father was a salt farmer, T'ang Yin's a grocer or a restaurateur.

The achievements of these climactic years, roughly between 1480 and the death of Wen Cheng-ming in 1559, carried art forward on its own momentum into the second half of the century, when many of the most talented painters were Wen Cheng-ming's relatives, pupils, and followers. But by now Soochow was no longer the hub of this artistic world, for the ideas that had crystallised there were current, if in diluted or corrupted form, wherever a painter took up the brush. But a change was coming, not unconnected with the rot that had already set in at court before the end of the fifteenth century and was gradually spreading outward and downward through the official class, even to stain the ivory towers of Soochow. As authority in the person of the emperor and his court became increasingly corrupt, defiance of authority became a positive moral stance. It could also in less responsible hands become mere lawlessness.

Thus in the last decades of the dynasty was the intellectual and artistic integrity of the Ming undermined, the scholar class fragmented. We cannot pretend that, in China at least, art and politics were not often intimately connected. Painters were scholars; scholars were officials or related to officials; and officials, whether they liked it or not, were inextricably bound up with the health and fate of the dynasty, on which their own careers, even their very lives, depended. So we are justified in looking on the art of the last 50 years of the Ming as a reflection of the state of the country as a whole.

Not all of it was turbulent, or wayward, by any means. Look, for instance, at the detail from a handscroll by Shao Mi (1626–60), one of the last great figures of the Soochow twilight (Plate 75). Do we feel a certain looseness of form, a lack of that firmness and discipline that are never lacking in Shen Chou and Wen Cheng-ming? Perhaps; but this picture still breathes an air of lyrical freedom quite untarnished. Shao Mi's response to the Yüan Masters—for instance to Ni Tsan in the distant mountains—is more casual and friendly than Wen Cheng-ming's, and the picture is not only intensely alive but beautiful in the spontaneous disposition of its forms.

The catching of an idea in its flight is hard to sustain in a long handscroll; yet Shao Mi achieved it, as once Huang Kung-wang had on a far grander scale. More often it was set down on a fan or an album-leaf, and bound sets of these leaves would be exchanged among friends. The album-leaf is the perfect format for the sudden inspiration, the theme and variations on the styles of several masters, the scholarly note, the present to a friend or an official. I can only illustrate two of the innumerable album-leaves that were produced by professionals and amateurs from the Ming Dynasty on, reflecting two very different attitudes to art. The first is a simple landscape from an album of 1642 by the Hangchow painter Lan Ying (Plate 76). His brief inscription says that he did it in the manner of the Yüan artist Ts'ao Chih-po. Behind Ts'ao Chih-po, the connoisseur would catch the allusion to the pine trees of Li Ch'eng and Kuo Hsi; but the freshness of this lovely work, its luminous atmosphere, its simplicity and charm, show that Lan Ying carries his burden of art-historical scholarship very lightly.

But as the freedom of the early 1500's gave way to the chaos of the 1600's, the tone of late Ming painting became less cheerful and lyrical than in these works by Shao Mi and Lan Ying. Something of this changed atmosphere is reflected, perhaps, in the album-leaf (Plate 77) by Yang Wen-ts'ung (1597–1646). The carelessness of this sketch is certainly no mark of Yang's own moral disintegration, for he was to be one of the heroes of the Ming resistance to the Manchus, to die under the executioner's ax, defiant to the last. But it does perhaps reflect the *stylistic* breakup of Ming painting, a cavalier attitude to tradition and to

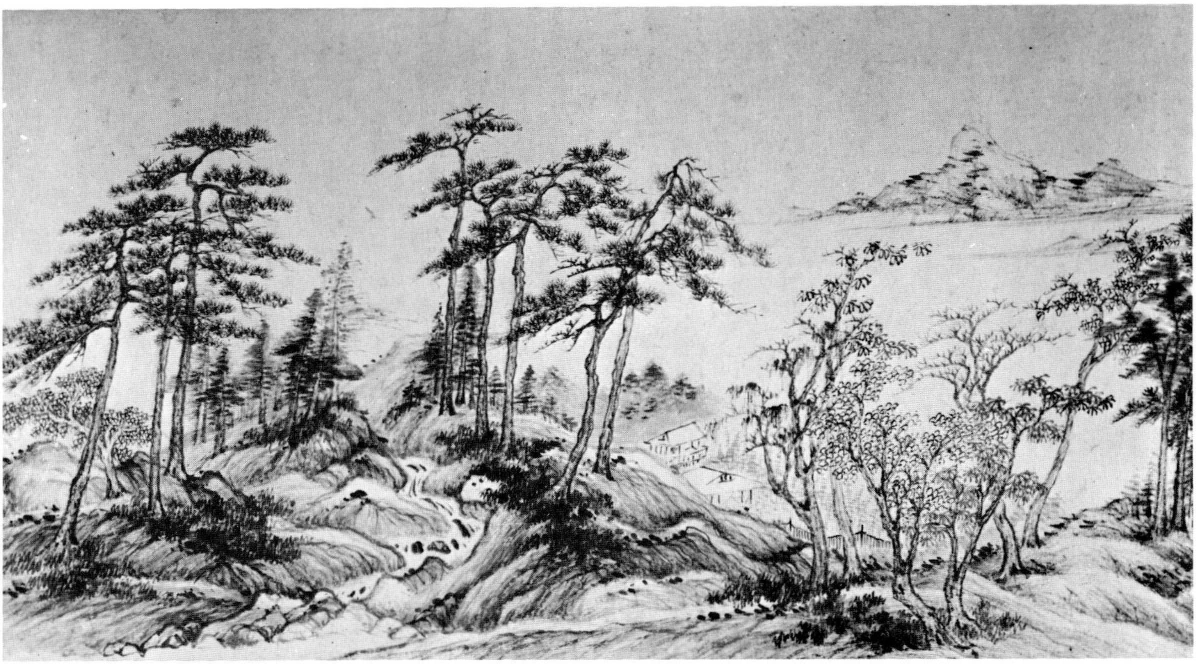

75. Shao Mi (active 1626–60): Landscape. Detail of a handscroll dated 1620; ink and slight colour on paper. Ht. 26.1 cm. Abe Collection, Osaka Municipal Museum, Japan.

the acceptable canons of good brushwork that would not have been permitted in the studio of Wen Cheng-ming.

There are obvious dangers in picking out paintings that seem best to illustrate the theme of restiveness, anxiety, and disintegration; Yang Wen-ts'ung's sketch, probably done simply for a friend, could just as well be an illustration of his own energy and independence. Yet there is no doubt that things were happening to landscape painting that could not have happened 50 years earlier, and the state of mind of the painter and his circle cannot be ignored. Once again, as in the Yüan, the watchword was *fu ku*, "restore the past." Speaking of literature, the critic Li Meng-yang (1473–1529) had insisted that "Prose must be Ch'in or Han, and poetry must be High T'ang—anything outside that is not worth talking about." Such dogmatism was now to appear in art criticism also; but meantime just what *fu ku* meant was for each painter to decide for himself. Yet could one restore the past without either distorting it or merely copying it?

Just how difficult it was to avoid these pitfalls we can see from the work of Wu Pin (active between 1583 and 1626), a professional painter from Fukien who settled in Nanking. He belongs among the many who sought inspiration in the great Northern Sung masters. But look what he

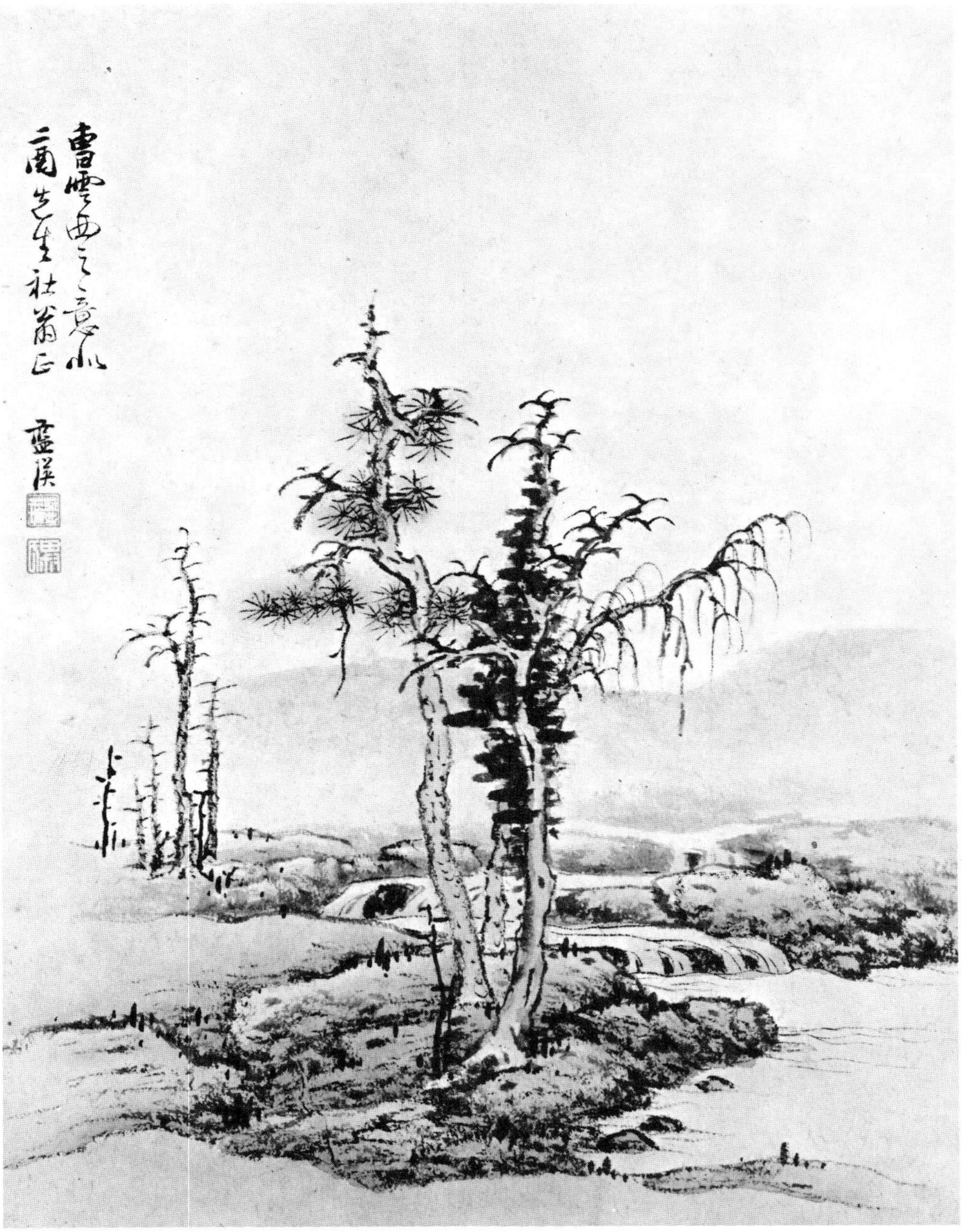

76. Lan Ying (1585–after 1660): Landscape in the manner of the Yüan master Ts'ao Chih-po. Leaf from an album dated 1642; ink and slight colour on paper. Ht. 31.6 cm. Ming Dynasty. Metropolitan Museum of Art, New York, Sackler Fund.

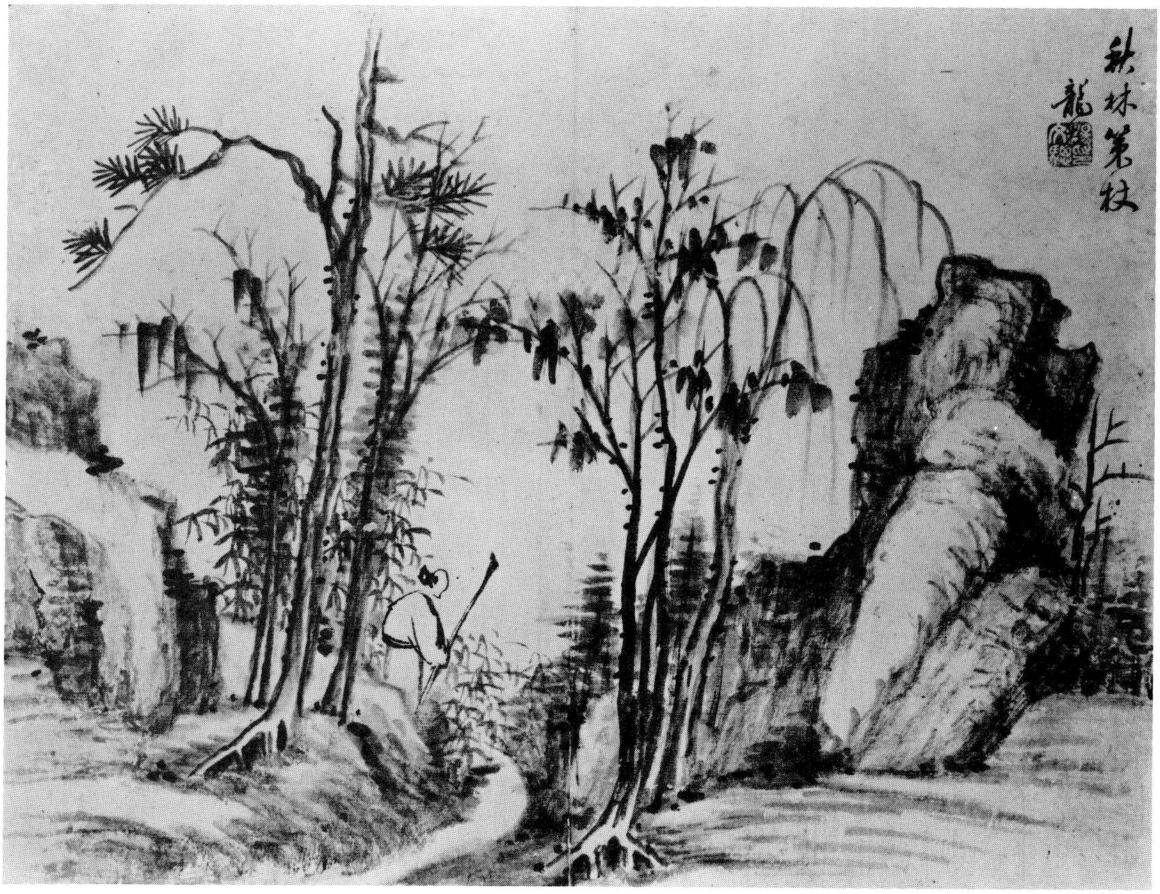

77. Yang Wen-ts'ung (1597–1646): "Woods in Autumn." Album-leaf dated 1638; ink on paper. Ht. 23.9 cm. Ming Dynasty. Abe Collection, Osaka Municipal Museum, Japan.

does with the monumental realism of Fan K'uan! His coldly calculated distortions (Plate 78), his fantastic pinnacles and flying rock bridges belong to no landscape in nature, nor are they a distillation of the artist's experience of looking at Fan K'uan. They seem rather to mock their model, to proclaim that even the great masters can be abused for the sake of creating something original or startling. For Wu Pin, at least in this phase of his career, nothing seemed to be sacred. Not here, surely, lay the path to salvation, the restoration of probity to art.

But between the careless sketch and the calculated distortion there was a third way, which lay through deep study to a reverend understanding of the old masters, fortified by an awareness of one's obligation to preserve the tradition not by copying it but by creatively reinterpreting it in the light of one's own experience—and here one's knowledge of the art of Shen Chou and Wen Cheng-ming could not help but play a part. In his finest surviving work (Plate 79), the huge *Paradise Landscape of Yang-so* (a beautiful district in Eastern Kiangsi), painted in 1625, Mi Wan-chung shows how both the monumental composition and the spirit of the Northern Sung masters could be recaptured in a language of the brush that is made more human and appealing by the example of Shen Chou. If we were to look for a parallel in the realm of ideas, it would be in the thought of the philosopher and poet Wang Shih-chen (1526–90), who was a leader of the northern revival of classical learning as a corrective to the intellectual anarchy into which the followers of Wang Yang-ming, with their doctrine of total freedom, were leading the southern intelligentsia.

Mi Wan-chung was not alone in going back to Fan K'uan. Many painters at this time turned to him and to Li Ch'eng, and even to the stars of the Southern Sung academy, Ma Yüan and Hsia Kuei, to light them on their way through the gathering darkness. Indeed, by 1600 there was no major master whose work might not provide a model, and the extraordinary range of late Ming painting shows how artists were casting about for a way forward. Debate on whom one should follow was lively and intense, for what the painters were debating was not just questions of artistic style, but of their own position, their own identity in relation to Chinese culture as a whole. In this controversy there was certainly an element of the old north-south dialectic, the stern northern revivalists looking upon the southern tradition as interpreted in Soochow as too soft, luxuriant, and corrupting.

It was at this moment that there appeared on the scene, at Sung-chiang near Soochow, a critic and painter of enormous intellectual force and influence who cried "halt" to what he considered a quite undiscriminating use, or abuse, of the past by the painters of his day. To Tung Ch'i-ch'ang (1555–1636) there was, for the scholar and gentle-

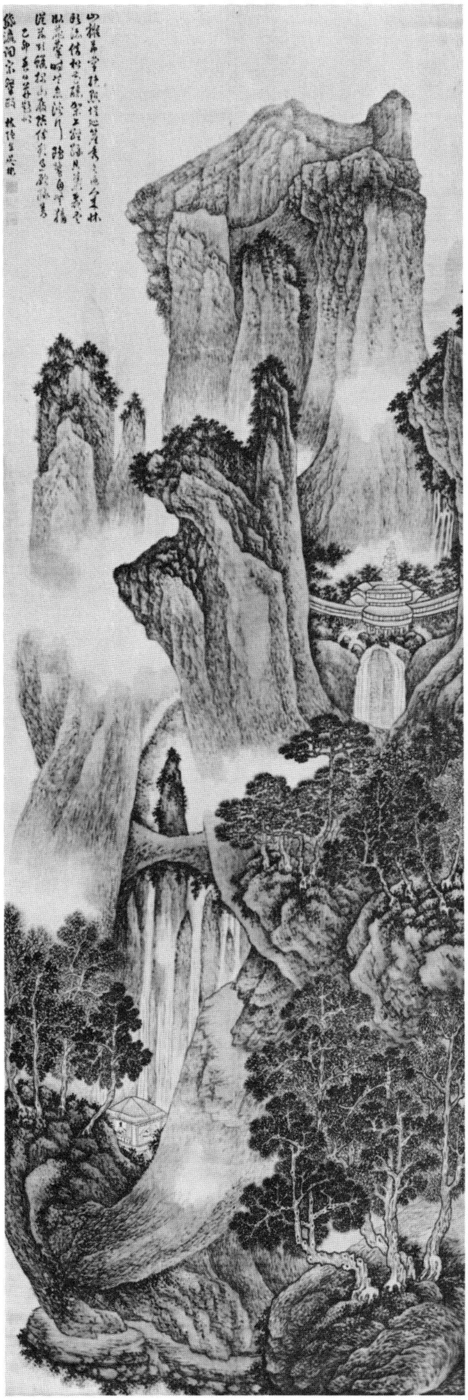

78. Wu Pin (ca. 1568–1626): "Streams and Hills far from the World's Din." Hanging scroll dated 1615; ink and slight colour on silk. Ht. 255 cm. Ming Dynasty. Hashimoto Sueyoshi Collection, Osaka, Japan.

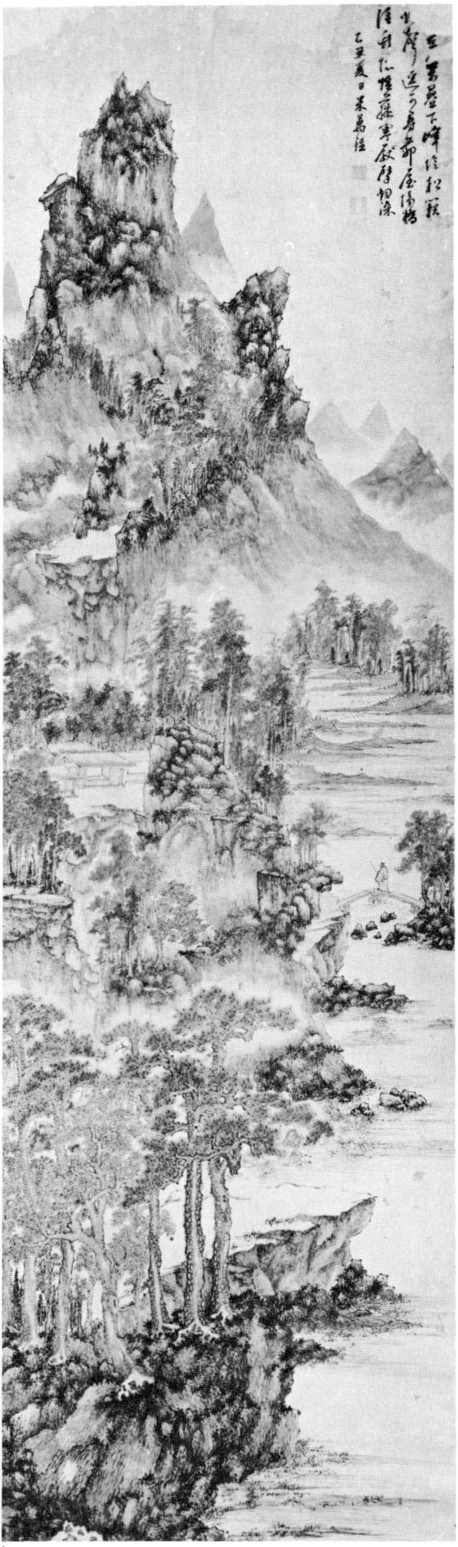

79. Mi Wan-chung (before 1575–1628): "The Paradise Landscape of Yang-so." Hanging scroll dated 1625; ink and slight colour on paper. Ht. 325 cm. Ming Dynasty. Stanford University Museum of Art, Stanford, California. Gift of the Committee for Art.

man, only one true artistic lineage, and it did not include professionals like Ma Yüan and Hsia Kuei. As an official Tung Ch'i-ch'ang was incorruptible, but scarcely popular, his severe conduct of the examinations when he was Commissioner of Education being the subject of a student demonstration that has a very modern ring. A wealthy landowner, he was hated by his tenants, who burned down his house because he appropriated the wife of one of them. Today, in a room in the Nanking Museum devoted to peasant revolts at the end of the Ming Dynasty, he is held up, with statistics, as one of the three most rapacious landlords of the Nanking area.

Yet, to a generation slipping into aesthetic anarchy he could still speak with a voice of formidable authority. In his short pamphlet *Hua shuo,* "Discussion of Painting," Tung Ch'i-ch'ang, whose knowledge of the art was prodigious—he had as a youth been a tutor in the house of that greatest of collectors, Hsiang Yüan-pien—stated as a historical truth that there were two traditions of landscape painting. One was the school of the professionals and court painters, founded by the T'ang masters Li Ssu-hsün and Li Chao-tao, and including Li T'ang, Ma Yüan, Hsia Kuei, and Tai Chin. For reasons we need not go into here, and which have nothing to do with geography, he called this the Northern School. The Southern School, he said, had been founded by Wang Wei, and included Tung Yüan, Chü-jan, Li Ch'eng, the Four Great Masters of the Yüan, Shen Chou, Wen Cheng-ming, and, by implication, himself. For the gentleman, this was the only way to paint landscapes. To understand why he was so dogmatic, we must see him as a champion of an embattled class of literati who were being increasingly persecuted by the court and the eunuchs. He was appealing to the scholar painters to close ranks, to present a united front and to return to the pure

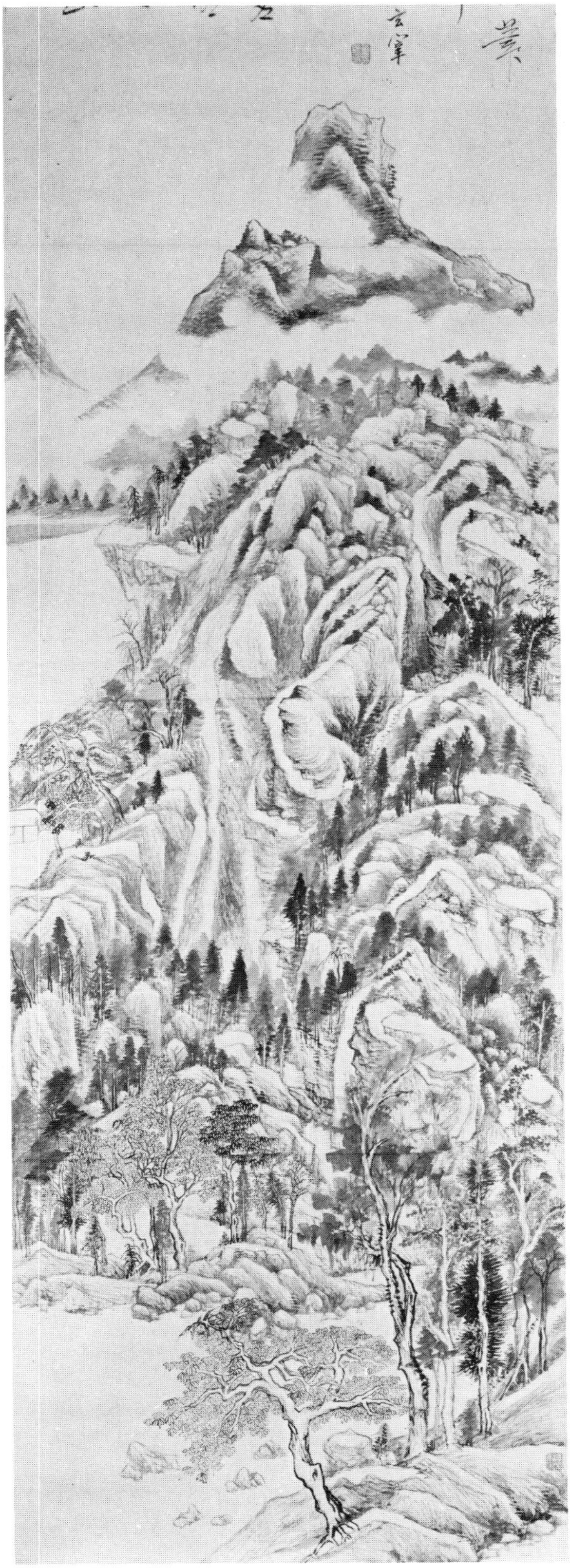

80. *Tung Ch'i-ch'ang (1555–1636): "The Ch'ing-pien Mountains." Hanging scroll dated 1617; ink on paper. Ht. 217 cm. Ming Dynasty. H.C. Weng Collection, New York.*

fountainhead of scholarly painting in Wang Wei. Wang Wei was a shadowy figure indeed, more of an ideal than a reality; but when Tung Ch'i-ch'ang said, in effect, "Just take Wang Wei, Tung Yüan, Huang Kung-wang, and Ni Tsan as your guiding lights, and you'll be all right," he was giving his contemporaries a programme that was easy to follow, the more so because it seemed to justify their ingrained belief that they were the elite.

Painters who slavishly obeyed this manifesto, however—and in the late Ming and throughout the Ch'ing they were legion—had forgotten something else that Tung Ch'i-ch'ang had said: that it was easy to copy an old master, difficult to transmit his spirit. Above all, Tung Ch'i-ch'ang insisted, be yourself, and whether you start from nature or from the old masters, you will be truly creative. "When Chü-jan studied Tung Yüan, Mi Fu studied Tung Yüan, Huang Kung-wang studied Tung Yüan," he wrote, "they all followed the same model. Yet they were not like one another. But when ordinary people make faithful copies, they do not transmit anything to posterity"—for they put nothing of themselves into their work. And Tung Ch'i-ch'ang practices what he preaches. For though in his inscriptions he tells which masters inspired him, he so transforms their style through the sheer force of his personality that his reinterpretation becomes a profoundly original work, beside which Shen Chou and Wen Cheng-ming seem positively conventional. His vision of *The Ch'ing-pien Mountains* (Plate 80) is no landscape to wander in, even to contemplate with easy pleasure. Tung Ch'i-ch'ang makes no concessions to the viewer; there is none of the fantasy and surrealist distortion of Wu Pin, which Tung Ch'i-ch'ang would no doubt have thought meretricious; nor is there any poetic feeling, any intimation of eternity—matters about which this coldly intellectual artist seems to have been entirely neutral. The impact his painting makes is a purely formal one, through the way in which he violates the laws of nature and of space, thrusting up form against form, plane against plane, to confront us. He seems to be saying, amid the growing cultural anarchy around him: "Here, in the language of pure form, is one realm where the rule of law is absolute." And the more formal and abstract his painting becomes, the more powerful a protest it makes against the state of art in his day.

It is not to be expected that many of Tung Ch'i-ch'ang's followers understood him. In some respects his legacy to the painters of the Ch'ing Dynasty, which came to power in 1644, was disastrous, instilling in all but the most independent a slavish devotion to the "party line" that he had laid down for them, reinforcing their conviction of their own superiority, and, worse still, making it even harder for them to look at nature except through the eyes of the masters he prescribed, or indeed, of himself. But at least he prescribed noble examples for them to follow, while he inspired those who did understand him to flights of great imaginative power. The result, in the hundred years following his death in 1636, was some of the most exciting painting in the whole history of Chinese art.

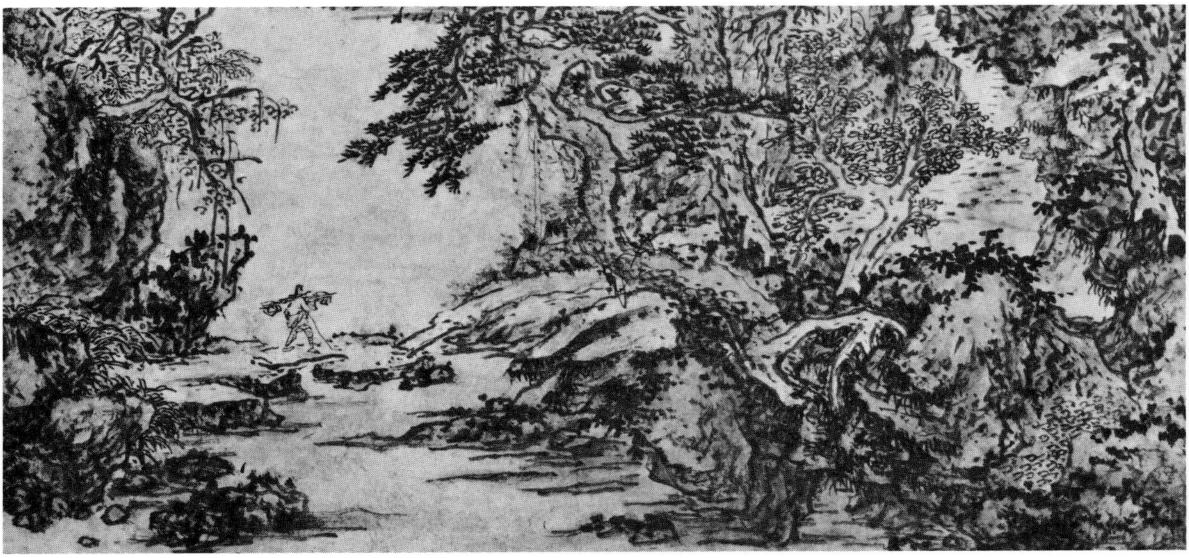

VI Authority Challenged and Triumphant
The Ch'ing Dynasty, 1644-1912

Detail of Plate 89 (p. 149): Shih-ch'i, "Climbing Wooded Mountains at Dusk."

The story of Ming landscape painting ended with the dominating figure of Tung Ch'i-ch'ang, whose influence, both as a revolutionary and as a passionate restorer of traditional values in art, was as great upon the conservatives as upon the avant-garde. His impact was certainly heightened by the chaos that attended the Manchu conquest of 1644. The Manchus were anxious from the start to draw the best Chinese talent into the administration; but the new dynasty began with twenty years of civil war as the Manchus hunted down the Ming loyalists, who viewed their coming with the same horror as that with which their forebears had watched the coming of the Mongols. It was not until the accession of the K'ang-hsi emperor in 1662 that the young scholars began once again to flock to the examination halls.

The Ming loyalists, called *i-min*, literally "men left over" (from the previous dynasty), faced the same agonising choice between withdrawal and collaboration that had faced their predecessors in the thirteenth century. There were some heroic campaigners, a handful of suicides, a far larger number who retired to the safe obscurity of a Buddhist monastery or a cottage in the hills. Once again, as under the Mongols, here and there the true Chinese spirit proclaimed itself, triumphing over the times—although when one considers the vastness of China and the size of the scholar class, the number of these courageous and independent men was astonishingly small. Yet even if they survived, their world was shattered.

Supreme among the painters who soared above the storm was Hung-jen, who after the Manchu conquest fled to Fukien, shaved his head, and became a monk. Not surprisingly, he took as his model the greatest recluse of all, Ni Tsan. He said of himself, however, that he fell far short of Ni Tsan: "I am incapable" he wrote on an album-leaf, "of mastering his style, so I have only followed his simplicity. Those who emulate the Perverse Old Man should not take me as their standard." Yet we would say of his austere landscapes, as was said of Ni Tsan, that "their air of supreme refinement is so cold that it overawes men." Such is the quality of Hung-jen's line that his mountains (Plate 81) seem to take form before our very eyes, to hover in the air, monumental for all their frailty. Hung-jen being a devout Buddhist, it is perhaps not stretching a point to see these ethereal landscapes as an expression of the Buddhist idea that all phenomena, the very evidence of the senses itself, are illusion, *māyā*, akin to a dream. As such, no wise man should feel either attachment or antipathy to the world of his experience. To express this notion of illusion and nonattachment in the visible forms of mountains, rocks, and trees in such a way as to move us by their beauty would seem to be impossible. Does Hung-jen achieve it because, being Chinese, he is not only a Buddhist but also a Taoist, to whom nature is no mere illusion but a manifestation of the Real, to be identified with and felt in his innermost being? If we could, by sympathy and intuition, probe to the heart of this mysterious duality, we might come some way toward understanding the mind of the Chinese landscape painter.

Nothing could be further from the rarified atmosphere of Hung-jen's towering mountains than the landscapes of Kung Hsien, another Ming patriot of the seventeenth century, who may for a time have been a member of the anti-Manchu intellectual underground, and who was for a number of years a hunted, haunted man. Rare is it in Chinese painting for an artist to lay bare his tortured spirit as Kung Hsien does in his extraordinary *Thousand Peaks and Myriad Ravines* (Plate 82), painted around 1670. Kung Hsien speaks, in an inscription he wrote on a lost painting

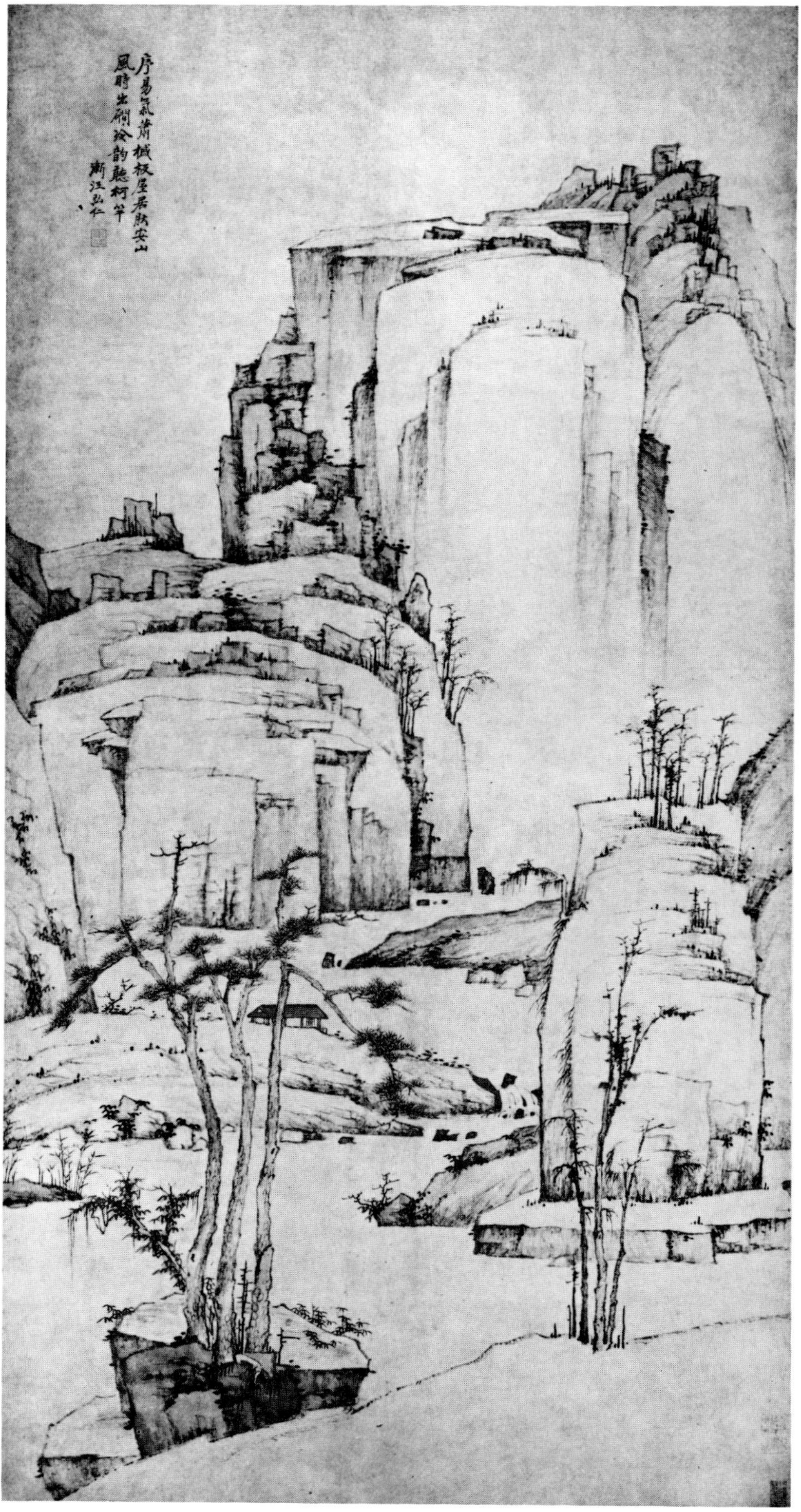

81. Hung-jen (1610–64): "The Coming of Autumn." Hanging scroll; ink on paper. Ht. 122 cm. Ch'ing Dynasty. Honolulu Academy of Arts, Honolulu, Hawaii.

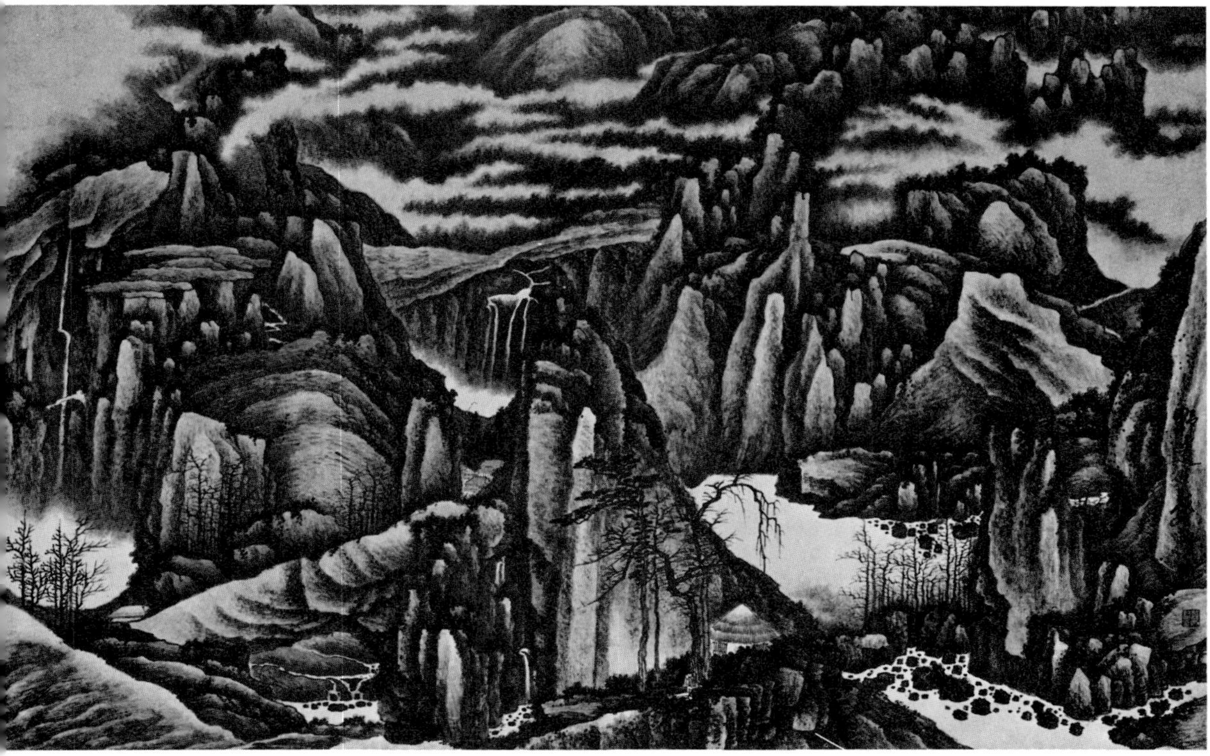

82. Kung Hsien (1620–89): "A Thousand Peaks and Myriad Ravines." Hanging scroll; ink on paper. Ht. 62.3 cm. Ch'ing Dynasty. Charles A. Drenowatz Collection, Museum Rietberg, Zürich, Switzerland.

of blasted trees on a desolate heath, of "a world gone corrupt," and there can be little doubt that the dehumanised, shut-in landscape we see here symbolises not only the desolation of China raped by the Manchus but the state of mind of a man who, for political or private reasons or both, had literally nowhere to turn. When we pass from this grimly impressive painting to a monumental landscape Kung Hsien painted fifteen years later (Plate 83), we find that the tension has relaxed. Something of the awful solemnity of the earlier work remains, but now it is distilled into a tranquil, almost dreamy grandeur that wonderfully expresses the peace of mind that Kung Hsien seems to have found, all passion spent, in his last years.

For in the last decades of the seventeenth century even the most dedicated Ming loyalist must have felt that, apart from the fact that the regime was Manchu and not Chinese, there was very little to protest about. Under the K'ang-hsi emperor (1662–1722), one of the most intelligent and just rulers who ever sat on the Dragon Throne, China entered a long era of peace. The scholars and painters settled down to enjoy life, wanting nothing more than that it should continue thus forever. There

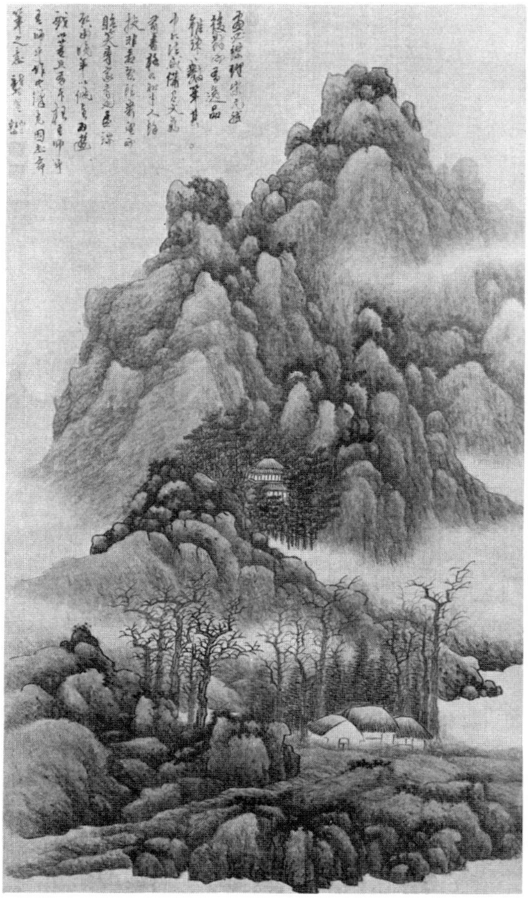

83. Kung Hsien (1620–89): Landscape in the manner of the Southern Masters. Hanging scroll dated 1684; ink and slight colour on silk. Ht. 99.5 cm. Ch'ing Dynasty. Honolulu Academy of Arts, Honolulu, Hawaii.

was no impulse to rebel, and in any case the Manchus kept a strict eye on them; drunkenness and eccentricity were one thing, political protest something else, and the censors were ever watchful. Gradually, however, as with every other dynasty, the momentum drained out of the Ch'ing and a deadening uniformity began to settle over Chinese cultural life, from which, increasingly, the deviants were not the rebels and patriots—the time for that was still far away—but the dropouts and professional eccentrics.

The orthodoxy of the eighteenth century was personified in the Ch'ien-lung emperor (1736–96), a man of tireless energy, a voracious art collector, a niggardly and opinionated connoisseur, an unstoppable writer of inscriptions and stamper of seals who was determined, as a function of his imperial role, to leave his indelible mark upon China's artistic legacy. His seals almost obliterate some of the finest paintings in the imperial collection, which now grew to such enormous size that there

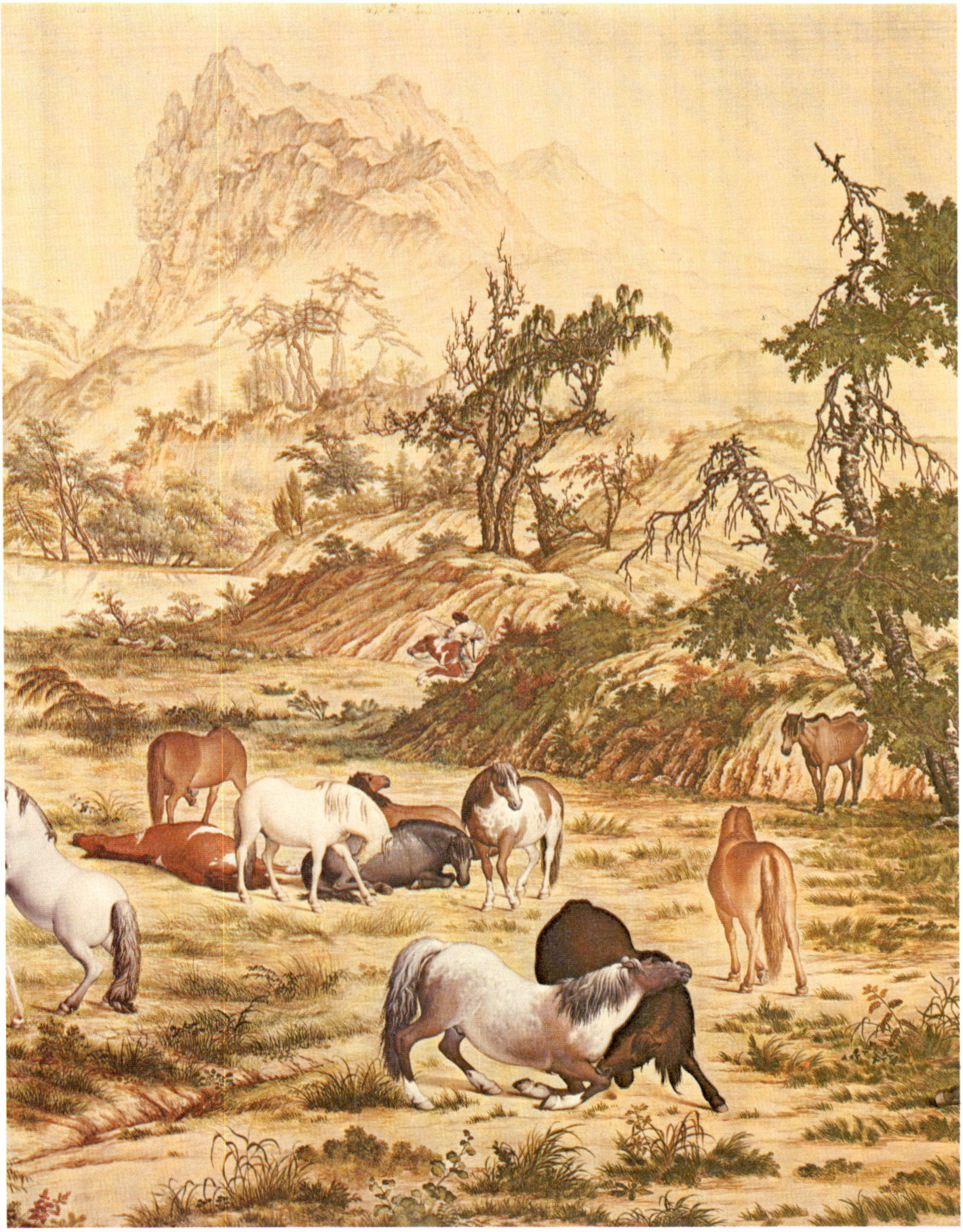

84. Lang Shih-ning (Giuseppe Castiglione, 1688–1766): "A Hundred Horses in a Landscape." Detail of a handscroll dated 1728; ink and colour on silk. Ht. 95 cm. Ch'ing Dynasty. National Palace Museum, Taipei.

were few ancient masterpieces that were not gathered behind the high walls of the Forbidden City, shut away forever from the painters who might still have studied them had they remained in private hands. The Ch'ien-lung emperor kept an array of artists and copyists busy in the palace studios and was a feeble painter himself, who did not really appreciate the painting of the scholars. What he liked best was realism, professionalism, fine craftsmanship. For many years one of his favourite painters was not Chinese at all, or even Manchu, but an Italian Jesuit brother, Giuseppe Castiglione, who had arrived in 1715 from Genoa, served under K'ang-hsi and Ch'ien-lung's father, the Yung-cheng emperor (1723–35), and remained a favourite at court until his death in 1766.

Although the darling of Ch'ien-lung, Castiglione (or Lang Shih-ning, as he was known in China) was a very minor member of the court, forced like the other Jesuits to devote his life not to decorating Christian churches, as he had hoped, but to designing rococo pavilions and painting decorative panels for the emperor's country palace, the Yüan-ming-yüan. As one of his French colleagues bitterly wrote home, "It is hard to convince myself that all this is for the glory of God." But until the news of the dissolution of the Jesuit order reached China in 1774, they stuck it out, creating a school of Sino-European painting that represents the Ch'ien-lung emperor's one original contribution as a patron of art. The detail of Castiglione's *tour de force*, the *Hundred Horses* scroll in the Palace Museum collection in Taipei (Plate 84), shows how brilliantly he mastered the Chinese technique, combining it with a degree of realism that was viewed with reluctant astonishment by his Chinese colleagues at court, and that was vastly admired by the emperor himself.

Castiglione's Sino-European style had no impact on the literati, however. They may have been impressed by Gherardini's illusionist frescoes in the Catholic cathedral in Peking because they were so utterly different from their own art and could not possibly be measured against it; but Castiglione's synthesis was more insidious in its appeal and therefore the more firmly to be rejected. It was not the kind of thing a gentleman should stoop to, for, as one of the literati said, "These painters have no brush-manner whatsoever; although they possess skill they are simply artisans and cannot be classed as painters." Intellectual snobbery was a traditional Chinese vice, but these literati were right to recognise a potential challenge to their whole way of seeing the world and of expressing their thoughts and feelings in the language of the brush.

In any case, the scholar-painters were by now so deeply imbued with the doctrines of Tung Ch'i-ch'ang that they had no need to look to the West for inspiration. Scarcely, it seems, did they look at nature. For

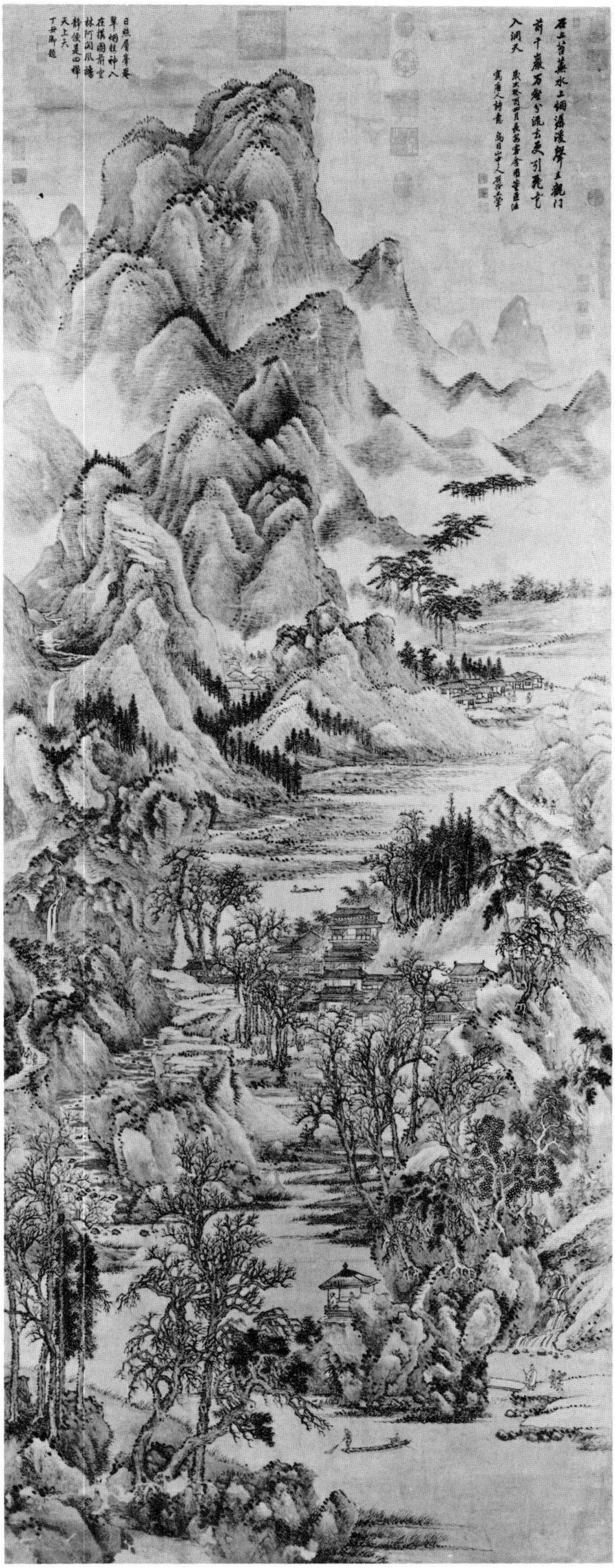

85. Wang Hui (1632–1717): "Countless Peaks and Vales," in the manner of Tung Yüan and Chü-jan. Hanging scroll, dated 1693; ink and slight colour on paper. Ht. 254.1 cm. Ch'ing Dynasty. National Palace Museum, Taipei.

Tung Ch'i-ch'ang had shown them how art could be constantly revitalised by drawing at the fount, not of nature, but of the tradition itself. Literally interpreted, this doctrine produced a host of slavish imitators of the past, who clung to the dictum of the master: "Someone has said that each must found his own school. But that is not correct. Thus, for example, the willow trees should be made after Chao Po-chü, the pine trees after Ma Ho-chih, the dead branches after Li Ch'eng. . . . Even though a painter should make variations of these types, he cannot depart from them. How can anyone put the ancient methods aside and start on his own?" No Ch'ing painter carried out this manifesto more scrupulously than Wang Hui (1632–1717). A virtuoso landscapist of enormous output, he maintained the style of a gentleman while actually supporting himself as a copyist and painter in the manner of the old masters. His pastiches of such great classical exemplars as Li Ch'eng breathe an air of such hoary antiquity that until very recently Chinese museum authorities accepted them as truly ancient works. Sometimes he rose above his prodigious facility, as in the splendid landscape *Countless Peaks and Vales* of 1693 (Plates 85 and 86), but he was too prolific to reach this level very often.

When the tradition begins thus to feed upon itself, we may expect the results to be disastrous. That so high a level was maintained was owing to the years of training with the brush that every painter went through. Inspired these works are not; but they are seldom less than pleasing and always very well painted, and that is something, after all. For the more gifted spirits, the past was a very real source of inspiration. The weight of tradition was tremendous, and—their education being what it was—they could not escape from it. They confronted the past, struggled with it, and came each to have his own working relationship with it; and it is the variety of their responses to that challenge, about which they are often obsessively articulate, that gives early Ch'ing art, and indeed early Ch'ing culture in general, its particular tension and fascination.

Ever since the *yang-yin* dualism was first set down in the third century B.C., the Chinese have been fascinated by the dialectical process. The conflict between the claims of the present and those of the past is but one of many dialectics at work in the mind of the educated man: between the Confucian in him and the Taoist; between orthodoxy and individualism; between the past as inspiration and the past as burden; between the demands of society and the demands of the self; between stability and change; between objective study and inner illumination. For the artist especially, there were the tensions between art as representation and art

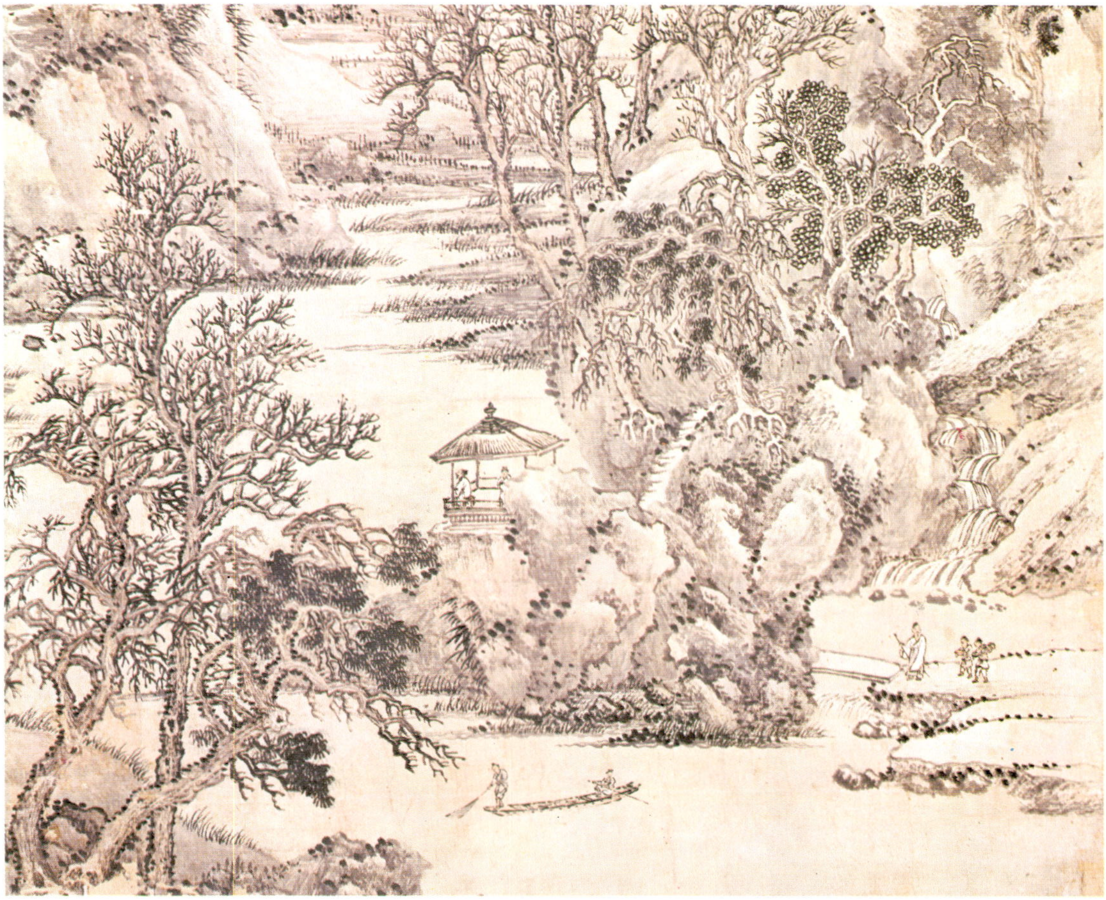

86. *Detail of Wang Hui, "Countless Peaks and Vales."*

as expression; between craftsmanship and spontaneity; between the universal and the particular statement; between nature as seen by the old masters and nature as seen by the artist himself. In the psyche of each individual painter these opposing ideals, impulses, loyalties were constantly struggling against each other, keeping his mind and his imagination alive. It was not a matter of absolute choice, for surrender in one direction would lead to a deadening of the artist's spirit, in the other to anarchy. It was only in the late eighteenth and nineteenth centuries, when loss of faith in the very dialectical process itself produced a failure of confidence in the educated class, that the dynamic reciprocal action slowed down and the vast, antiquated engine of Chinese civilisation ground to a halt.

By then, the past had smothered the creative fires. But for the first century of the Ch'ing it was the fuel that fed them, and the great engine pulsated with energy. For the chief among the early Ch'ing masters were no slaves to tradition. As the eighteenth-century scholar Fang Hsün put it, "When copying ancient paintings, the foremost concern must be to grasp the ancient master's spirit and life. . . . If it were done merely for the sake of similarity, you had better roll up the picture and forget it at once." Again, "When copying the ancients, you may at first only worry about a lack of similarity; afterward you ought to worry about too much similarity."* One can see how bewildered the less gifted painter might be by such injunctions. Fang urges him to "forget both style and self," and so to lose himself in the creative act.

How this dialectic, or pattern of dialectics, worked itself out in art is nowhere better seen than in the landscapes of Wang Yüan-ch'i (1642–1715). A forceful artistic personality, his work is highly original even when he claims to be painting in the manner of the Yüan masters—generally Ni Tsan. Wang Yüan-ch'i was an establishment figure, a senior official, magistrate, cataloger of the imperial collection, and protégé of the K'ang-hsi emperor, who would often visit him in his studio in the Forbidden City, chatting long hours with him, leaning across his desk as he painted. Wang Yüan-ch'i's compositions (Plate 87) may be inspired by Ni Tsan, but his forms are worked over, pulled apart, and reassembled by a laborious process more reminiscent of Western than of Chinese painting. His paintings obey neither nature nor Ni Tsan but an inner necessity—that passion for pure form that Wilhelm Worringer spoke of as being at the root of the artistic nature. Here is a creative reinterpretation of the past such as Tung Ch'i-ch'ang would have understood and applauded.

Chinese art historians like to categorise painters, a process that does at least help to keep the vast number of names in some sort of order. Stylistically, Wang Yüan-ch'i should be numbered not among the other, lesser Wangs, but among the great Individualists—despite the fact that he was a "court painter," a category he does not fit at all. Far more typical of courtly taste were the skilled professionals who revived, and cleverly manipulated, the classic styles of Li Ch'eng, Fan K'uan, and Kuo Hsi—not, as Wu Pin had revived them, in the service of a twisted form of self-expression but purely for their decorative possibilities. A prominent member of this group was Yüan Chiang (active about 1690–1720). Compositions such as his huge vision of *The Fairy Island P'eng-lai* (Plate 88), which he painted again and again, may be totally lacking in poetic sensibility but are full of interesting detail, brilliantly executed, and effective as decoration. They fulfill their purpose admirably.

**Shan-ching-chü hua-lan* I. Translated by Max Loehr, "Art-Historical Art: One Aspect of Ch'ing Painting," *Oriental Art* (n.s.), 16, no. 1 (Spring 1970), p. 36.

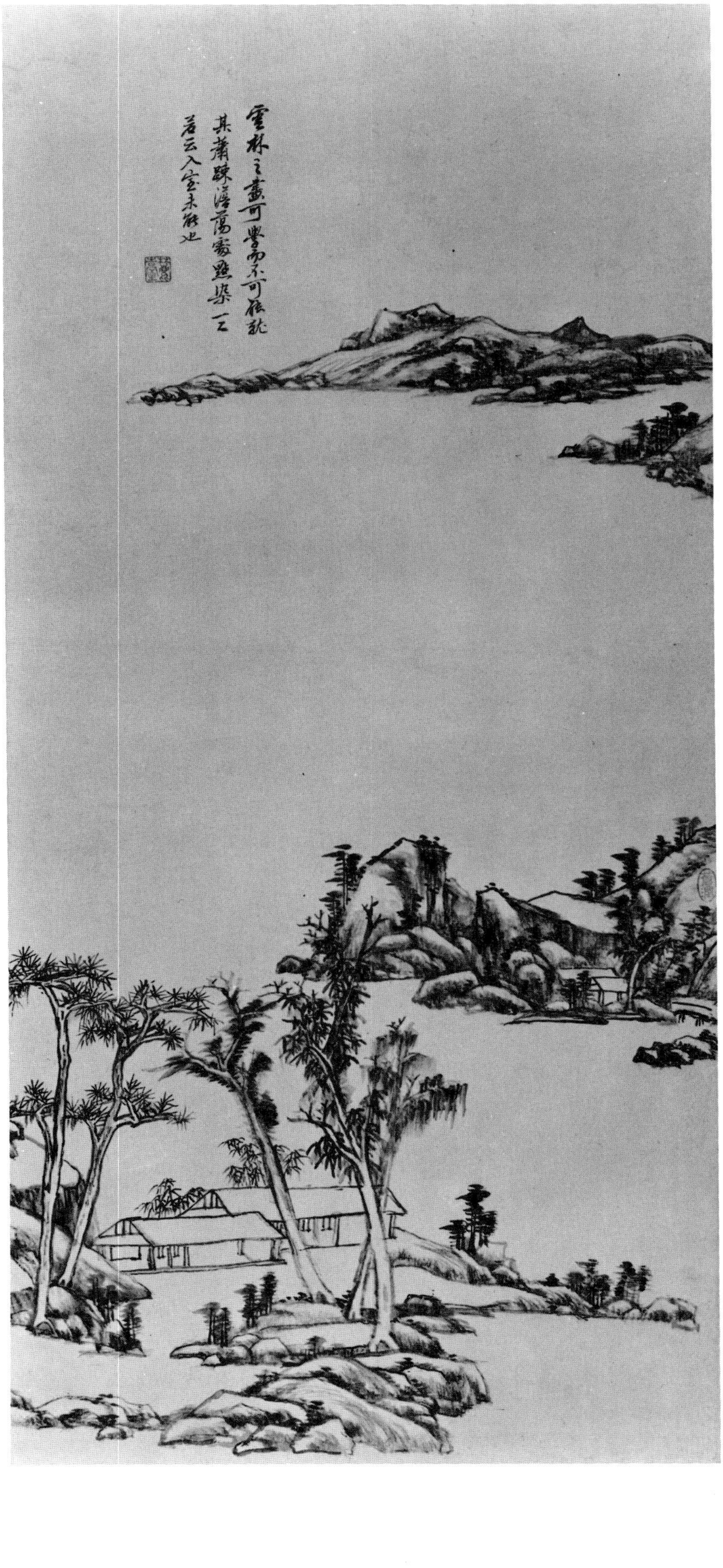

87. Wang Yüan-ch'i 1642–1715): Landscape in the manner of Ni Tsan. Hanging scroll; ink and slight colour on paper. Ht. 103 cm. Ch'ing Dynasty. Kyoto National Museum, Japan.

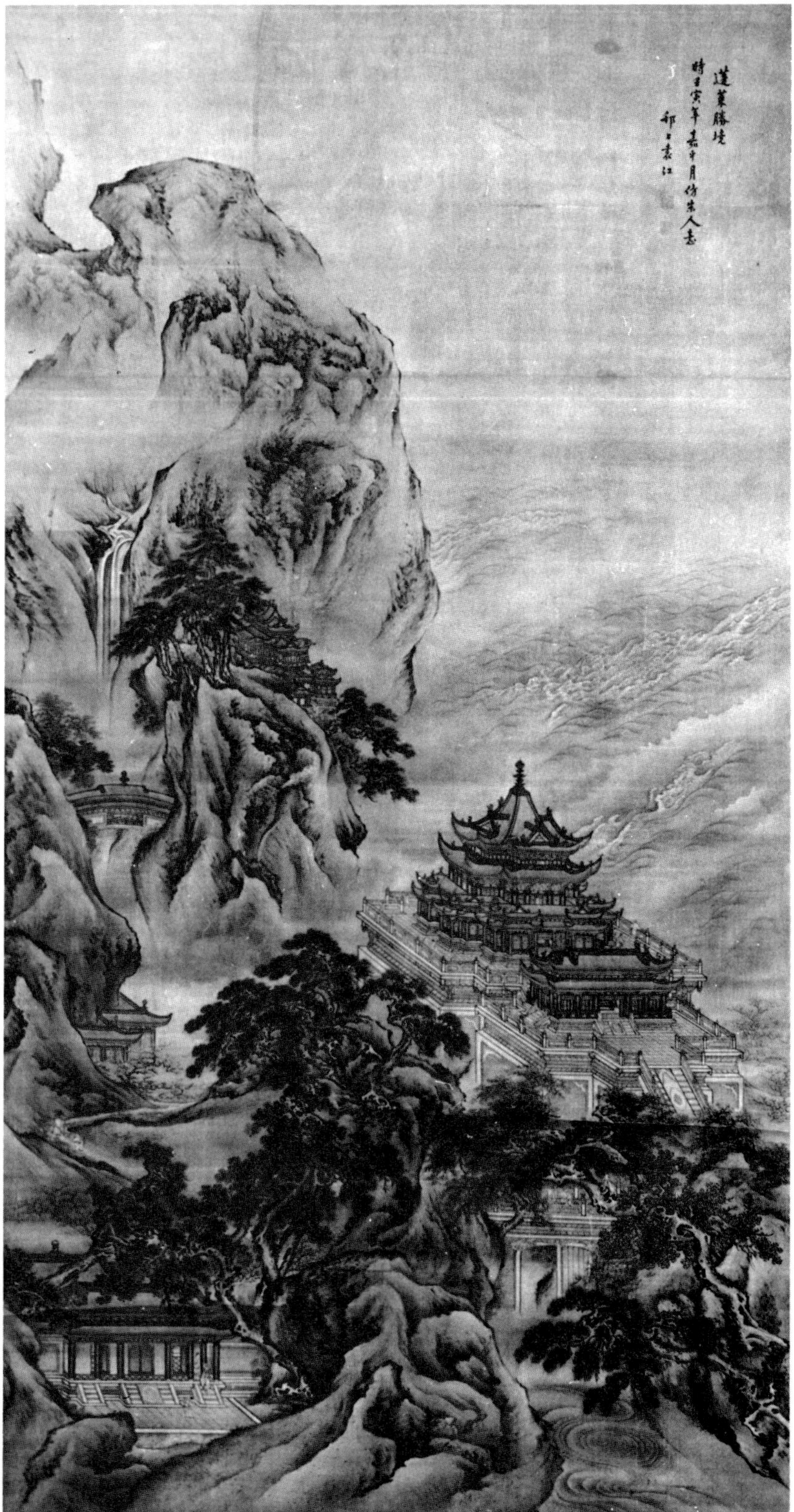

88. Yüan Chiang (active ca. 1690–1725): "The Fairy Island P'eng-lai." Hanging scroll dated 1722; ink and slight colour on silk. Ht. 248 cm. Stanford University Museum of Art. Gift of the Committee for Art.

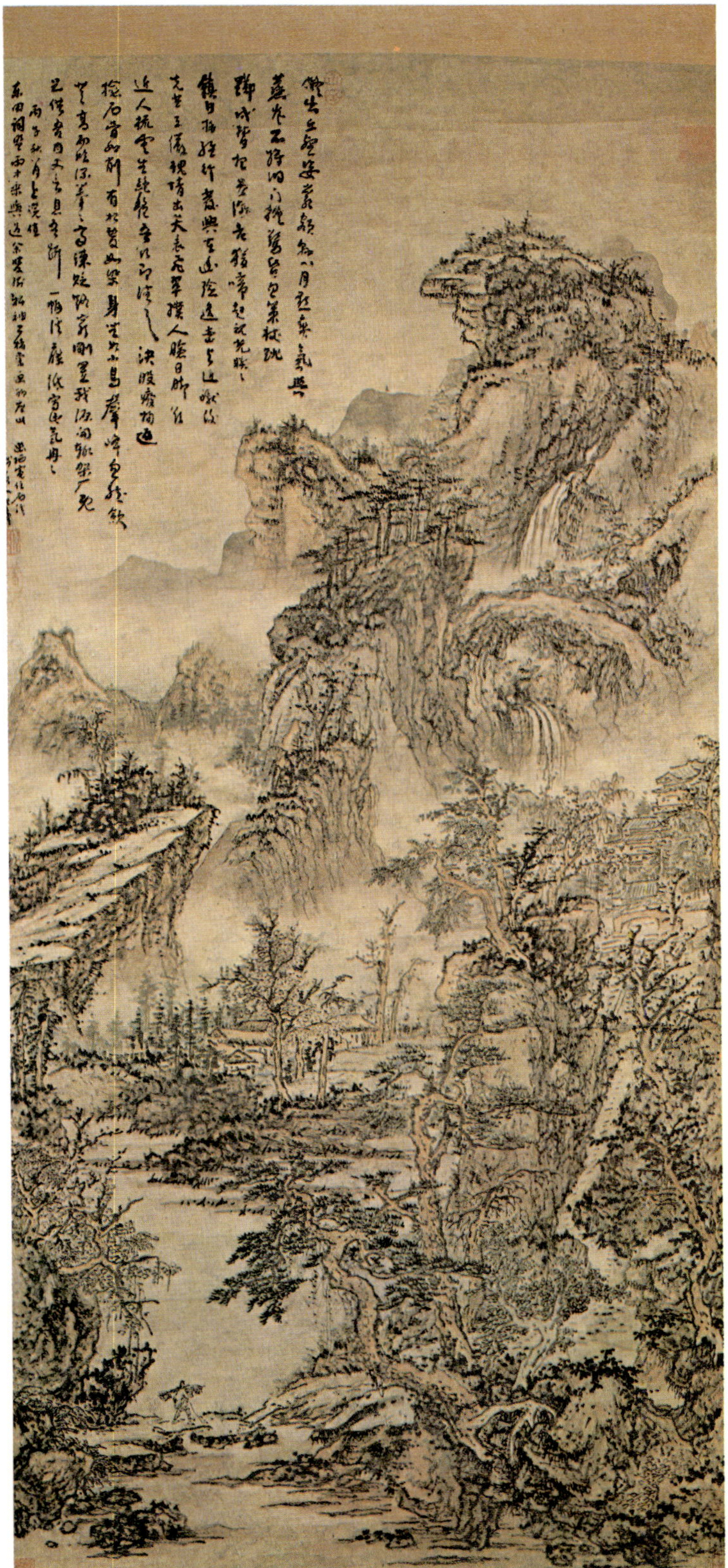

89. *Shih-ch'i (K'un-ts'an, ca. 1610–93): "Climbing Wooded Mountains at Dusk." Hanging scroll dated 1666; ink and colour on paper. Ht. 120 cm. Ch'ing Dynasty. John M. Crawford Collection, New York.*

As we move away from court, outward and downward among the literati, country gentlemen, monks, recluses, and eccentrics, the range of responses to the challenge of the past becomes ever wider and more varied. Look, for instance, at the landscape *Climbing Wooded Mountains at Dusk* (Plate 89), painted by Shih-ch'i in 1666. Shih-ch'i, also known as K'un-ts'an, was a descendant of the Ming imperial house who spent much of his life as a monk, ending as abbot of a Buddhist monastery near Nanking. He was a formidable eccentric who retired to a cottage on a hill above the monastery and lived, it was said, silent and alone on the wild grasses and herbs that he collected and cooked for himself and the occasional visitor. His brushwork in this wonderful painting is marked by a worrying of the surface that ought to be distracting; but such is the delicacy of his touch, the warmth of his colour, that it is in fact beautiful. And for all its restless movement, for all its rapid feathery strokes that make one think of Chopin at his most elegant and lyrical, the painting is profoundly tranquil.

The long inscription that Shih-ch'i wrote at the top describing how he climbed the mountain reads like the record of a spiritual pilgrimage, in which his attainment of the summit to catch the rays of the setting sun has deep religious meaning. "Where the road comes to an end," he writes, "that is where I stand." But, being an educated Chinese, he does not want to embarrass us by being too solemn about it, so he adds, "Since it serves to feast my eyes, it is also fit to rest my blisters." How different from Petrarch!—both in the ecstatic sense of being at one with nature (no higher religious experience can one desire) and in the very human note of that last remark. Here is no conflict between the claims of the soul and of the senses such as Petrarch experienced. Man and nature are in perfect harmony.

Shih-ch'i found peace in a Buddhist monastery. His contemporary Chu Ta (or Pa-ta Shan-jen, 1626–ca.1705), another scion of the Ming imperial house, was for a time a Buddhist teacher, too, but religion seems to have offered no refuge for his tortured spirit. The story goes that when his dumb father died he pasted the character for "dumb" (*ya*) on his door; thereafter he spoke to no one, and would only laugh or cry. He became a wanderer. "One evening," we read, "he tore up his monk's robe, burnt it and ran back to the provincial capital, where he behaved like a madman among the stalls in the market. . . . He ran about the market waving his sleeves and spinning round in circles, so that the boys ran after him gaping and yelling with laughter."* Perhaps his madness was to some extent

*From his biography by Shao Ch'ang-heng, translated by Victoria Contag, *Chinese Masters of the Seventeenth Century* (Rutland, Vt., and Tokyo, Japan, 1969), p. 17.

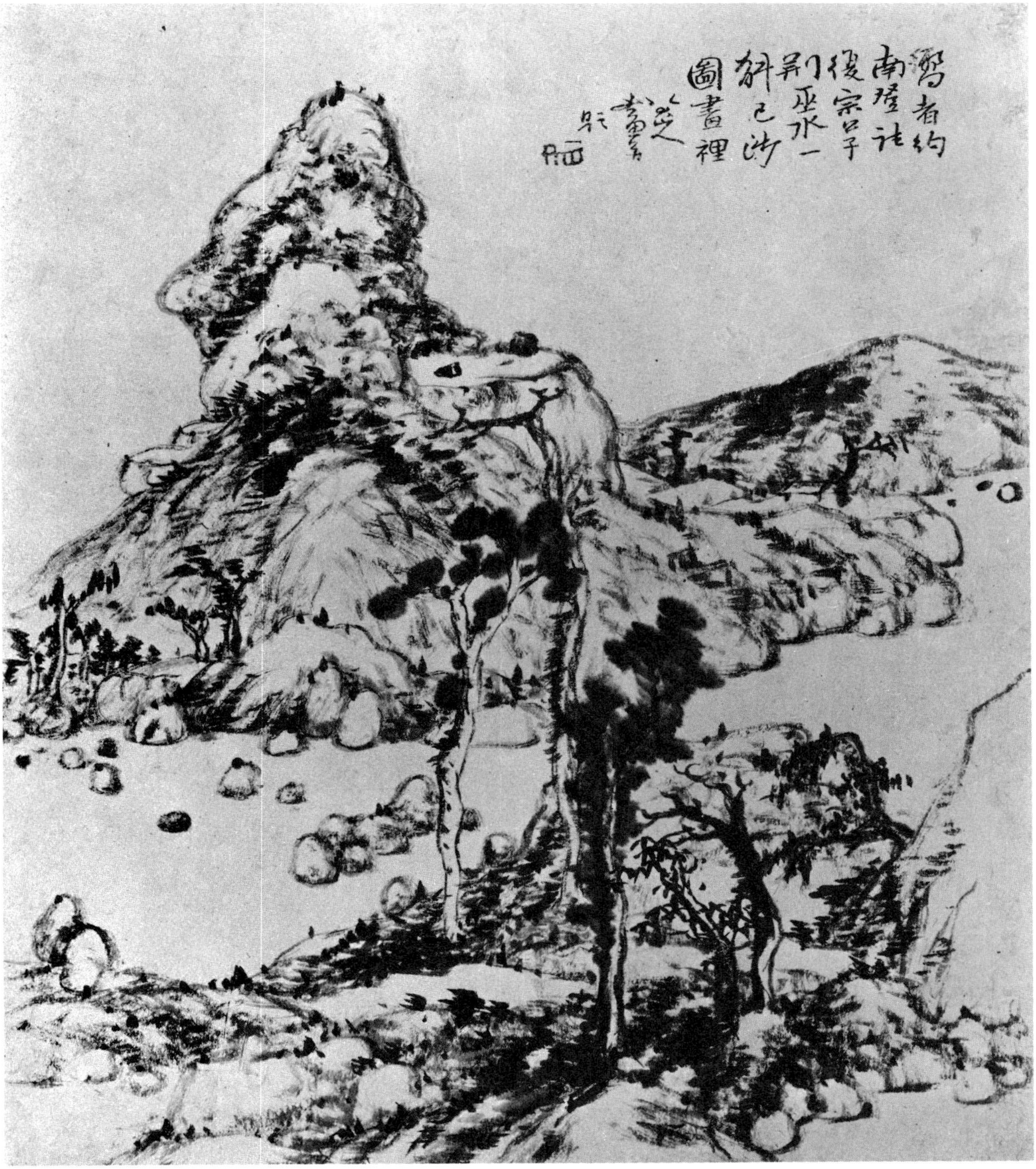

90. Chu Ta (Pa-ta Shan-jen, 1626–ca. 1705): Landscape sketch. Album-leaf; ink on paper. Ht. 31.7 cm. Ch'ing Dynasty. Sumitomo Collection, Kyoto, Japan.

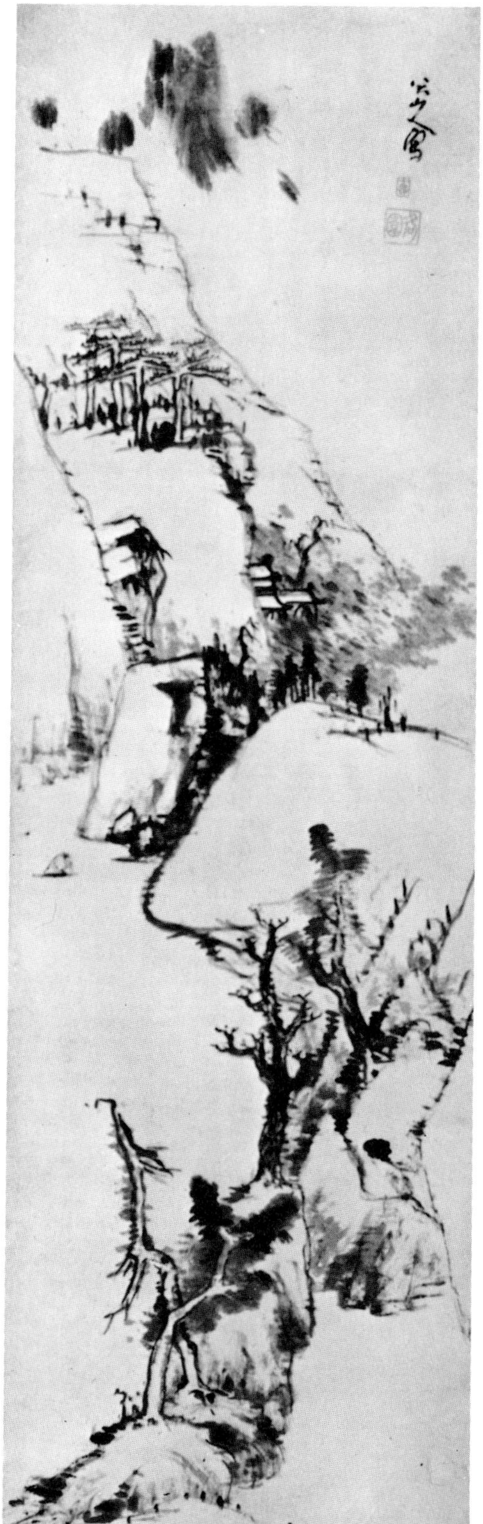

91. *Chu Ta (Pa-ta Shan-jen, 1616–ca. 1705): Landscape. Hanging scroll; ink on paper. Ht. 159 cm. Ch'ing Dynasty. Shōkokuji, Kyoto, Japan.*

assumed, for he may have felt that only extreme eccentricity would convince the authorities that he was no threat to the Manchus. He was actually confined by a district magistrate for about five years from 1678, but it seems that in his later life he stepped back from the brink—or perhaps ceased to play that strenuous part, or both—for he became a prolific painter, who boasted in a colophon of the number of album paintings he could dash off in a single day. A Ch'ing writer said that "the colophons he wrote on his paintings were so strange that no one could understand them. His brushwork was impulsively reckless; he did not stick to any established method, but worked in a firm and thorough and often unrestrained manner."

Wild as he was, Pa-ta Shan-jen never quite turned his back on tradition, and in his most impetuous landscapes he still draws inspiration, which he generally acknowledges in his brief inscriptions, from Tung Yüan and Chü-jan (Plate 90). One would think it impossible to go beyond this and still not snap the last link with tradition. But Pa-ta achieved it in his extraordinary landscape in the Shōkokuji temple in Kyoto (Plate 91), a work that approaches pure form. Pa-ta was steeped in both Taoism and Ch'an (Zen). Perhaps if we could have asked him what this picture meant, he might (if he were sober) have spoken of the Tao, or of the Void out of which form is manifest and into which it dissolves again. This picture, executed with no preconceived composition in a kind of aesthetic ecstasy, carries us to the outer limits of pictorial art, to the edge of Void, stopping just short of the point of pure abstraction. It reveals an extreme sophistication of spirit, style, and technique that is utterly remote from the academic precision of, say, Yüan Chiang (Plate 88)—which brings home the point I made in the Introduction that there is a far greater range at this period between the extremes of Chinese painting than we could possibly find, before modern times, in any comparable period in European landscape painting.

Sometime around the year 1699, Pa-ta Shan-jen is thought to have received a letter from a younger painter to whom he had already sent a landscape. The writer says that the landscape sent was too large for his house; could he have a smaller hanging scroll, three feet by one foot, with an old modest house in it on a flat river bank, a few ancient trees, and, in an upper room, just one old man to represent the writer himself. "If there is any space left," he goes on, "I shall beg you to do a few lines of your exemplary handwriting above the painting. This will then become my most precious treasure."

This letter, if indeed it is genuine, is the only known link between

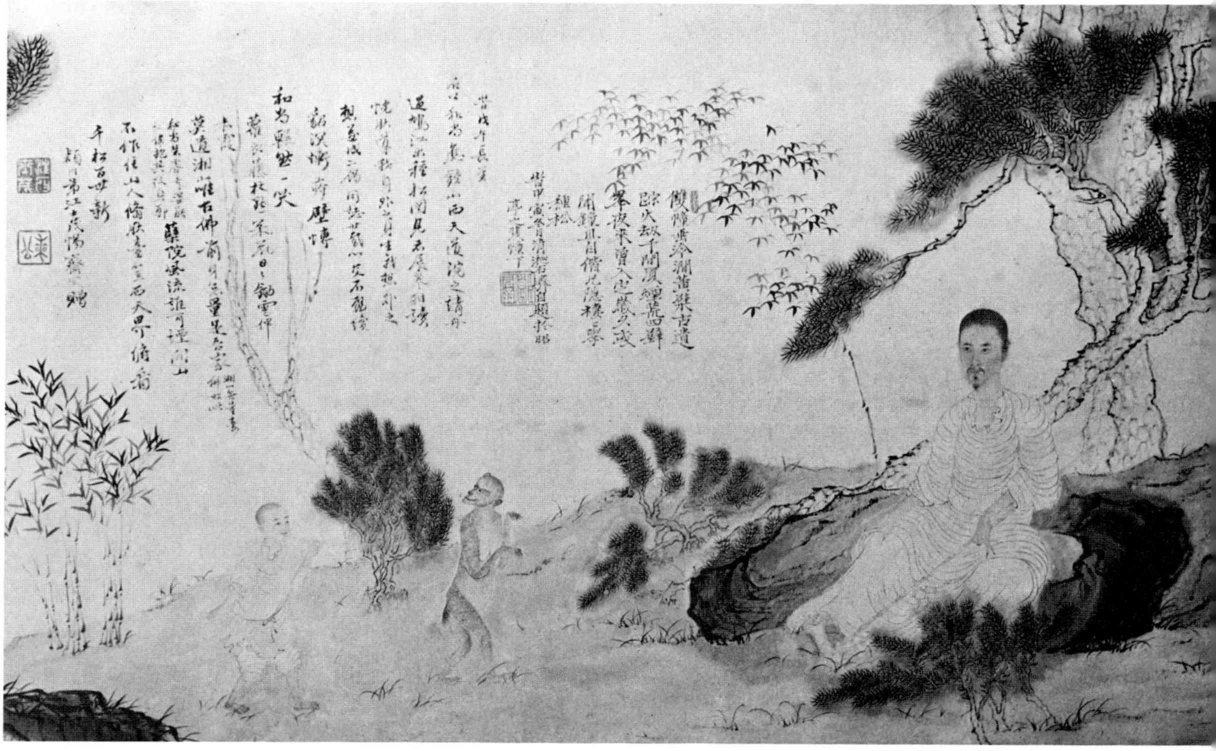

92. Attributed to Shih-t'ao (Tao-chi, 1641–ca. 1710): "Self-Portrait in a Garden Supervising the Planting of Pine Trees." Handscroll dated 1674; ink and slight colour on paper. Ch'ing Dynasty. Lo Chia-lun Collection, Taipei.

Pa-ta and the other great individualist of the late seventeenth century, Shih-t'ao, or Tao-chi, who was born in 1641 and probably died in 1710. He, too, was a distant relative of the Ming royal house, but was only three when the dynasty fell. On one of the K'ang-hsi emperor's progresses to the South, Shih-t'ao was presented, and as a result spent two years in Peking, where he and Wang Yüan-ch'i did a painting of bamboo and rocks together. But that life, not surprisingly, did not suit him. He returned home and spent the rest of his life travelling all over South China, wandering with his friends in the mountains, painting, writing, and designing gardens for the rich merchants of Yangchow. From his style of painting and of living, Shih-t'ao would seem to be the purest type of amateur and individualist; yet we read of him spending three years in copying, for a rich Manchu patron, scrolls by the Ming academic painter Ch'iu Ying, for which he must have been paid in cash or hospitality or both. Like many a gentleman painter of his day, he probably started as an amateur but found before long that with no official career open to him there was no other way to earn his living than with his brush, a fact that may help to account for his huge output.

There could be no better introduction to Shih-t'ao than his self-portrait (Plate 92), sitting in his garden under a pine tree in summer, like a meditating Śākyamuni, while a gardener and a monkey transplant a bush.* The face is refined and alert, the eyes meditative and piercingly intelligent; he has the air of a supremely self-confident young man. Shih-t'ao wrote an essay on painting, *Hua yü lu* (literally, "Record of Sayings About Painting"), which is the manifesto not only of a practitioner of the art—some of the chapters are full of solid technical advice—but of a philosopher steeped in Buddhist and Taoist metaphysics. These lines will give something of its flavour:

> In great antiquity there were no methods; the great state of natural simplicity had not been broken up.
>
> Once this state of natural simplicity had disintegrated, methods (or "rules," *fa*) were established. Upon what were these methods based? They were based on the unifying one-stroke (*i-hua*). This is the origin of all that exists, the root of the innumerable phenomena. Its operations lie open to the gods but have been hidden from men; and seeing that the people of the world do not know it, I have established it. The establishment of this method of the one-stroke means to give birth to a method from no methods and to make it pervade all methods. . . .
>
> Thus one-stroke painting includes everything, extending even beyond the sphere of phenomena, and of the works beyond number of brush and ink there is none which does not find its beginning and end in it. It is there awaiting the man who can grasp it.†

Shih-t'ao speaks of an "all pervading unity," and goes on: "By one spontaneous movement of the hand, mountains, rivers, human beings, birds, animals, plants . . . will assume form according to their characteristics; they will be drawn as if alive, and their meaning will be revealed." "Drawn as if alive"—perhaps after all, for all its air of being a new discovery, this is just a restatement, in more philosophical terms, of Hsieh Ho's age-old *ch'i-yün sheng-tung*, "spirit consonance and life movement," amplified and enriched by Shih-t'ao's reading of later works on aesthetics such as the *Twenty-four Poems on Poetry* by the T'ang critic Ssu-k'ung T'u, with which Shih-t'ao's ideas have much in common.

Whether or not Shih-t'ao's aesthetics are as original as he claimed hardly matters, however, for his art itself expresses these ideas with a controlled spontaneity, a lyrical delicacy that is unique in the whole his-

*Just what Shih-t'ao meant by the monkey is not certain, but on a copy of this painting the scholar and antiquarian Weng Fang-kang (1733–1813) adds a verse beginning, "The monkey tags along to learn to plant pine trees." See Marilyn and Shen Fu, *Studies in Connoisseurship: Chinese Paintings from the Arthur M. Sackler Collection in New York and Princeton* (Princeton, N.J., 1973), p. 241.

†Translated by Osvald Sirén, *Chinese Painting*, vol. 5, p. 171.

tory of Chinese landscape painting. A sense of some mysterious animating force shimmers through his dreamlike vision (Plate 93) of the same Mount Lu that had inspired Shen Chou (Plate 7). That force seems to overawe and envelop the painter standing in the foreground, and yet in some inexplicable way to be a projection of his own consciousness (see the detail reproduced as Plate 94). How far he was inspired by Shen Chou or by the monumental landscapes of the Northern Sung is a nice question: there is a hint of arrogance in his remark that "the beards and eyebrows of the ancients don't grow on my face"; and certainly of all the Ch'ing masters he least of all acknowledges his debt to tradition, or, when he does refer to it, he seems to suggest that there is no obligation on his part.

Does he perhaps protest too much? Is not his defiance of tradition a form of attachment to it? On an album-leaf of 1682 he remarks, "It may look like Tung Yüan, but it is not Tung; it may seem like Mi, but it isn't Mi." He wrote this on a painting now in the Soochow Museum:*

> Ten thousand ugly dots to scare Mi Fu to death!
> Some fibres of soft traces to make Tung Yüan roll over
> laughing!
> From afar the perspective doesn't work—it lacks a
> landscape's winding ways.
> Close up the details are all confused—you can barely
> make out a few simple cottages.

Yet lest we should think he is apologising for his incompetence, he ends:

> Once and for all cut off the "heart's eye" from conventional
> molds,
> Just as the immortal who rides the wind has freed his
> divine spirit from the bounds of flesh and bones!

Thus does the dialectic between the claims of tradition and the genius of the individual animate Chinese painting at its best. For Shih-t'ao, even more than for Shih-ch'i or Pa-ta, the catalyst was nature itself, chiefly the experiences he stored up during his years of wandering on the sacred mountains Lu-shan and Huang-shan with his friend Mei Ch'ing. He scorned the artists "who have never set their eyes on famous mountains or great rivers . . . or stepped more than a hundred *li* beyond the city gates." Like some sensitive instrument, Shih-t'ao tuned in to the delicate vibrations of nature that lie beyond the normal range of our senses, picked them up, and amplified them into a visual music of extraordinary freshness and charm. The sense of being out there, in nature, is most in-

*Quoted in Marilyn and Shen Fu, *Studies in Connoisseurship*, p. 46.

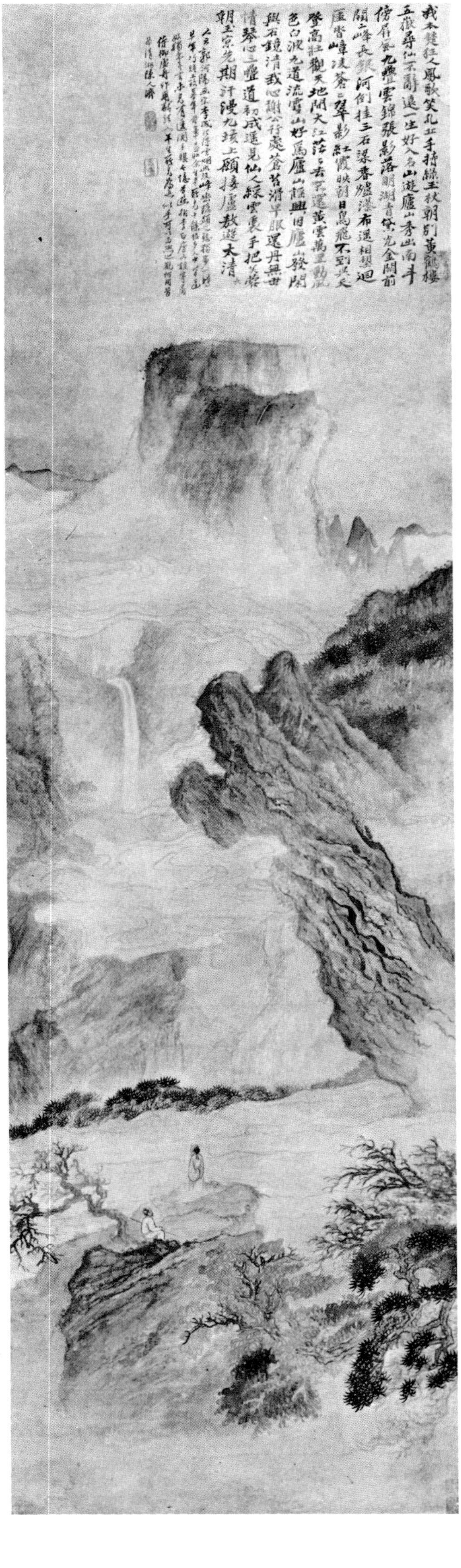

93. *Shih-t'ao (Tao-chi, 1641–ca. 1710): "Mount Lu." Hanging scroll; ink and colour on paper. Ht. 212.2 cm. Ch'ing Dynasty. Sumitomo Collection, Kyoto, Japan.*

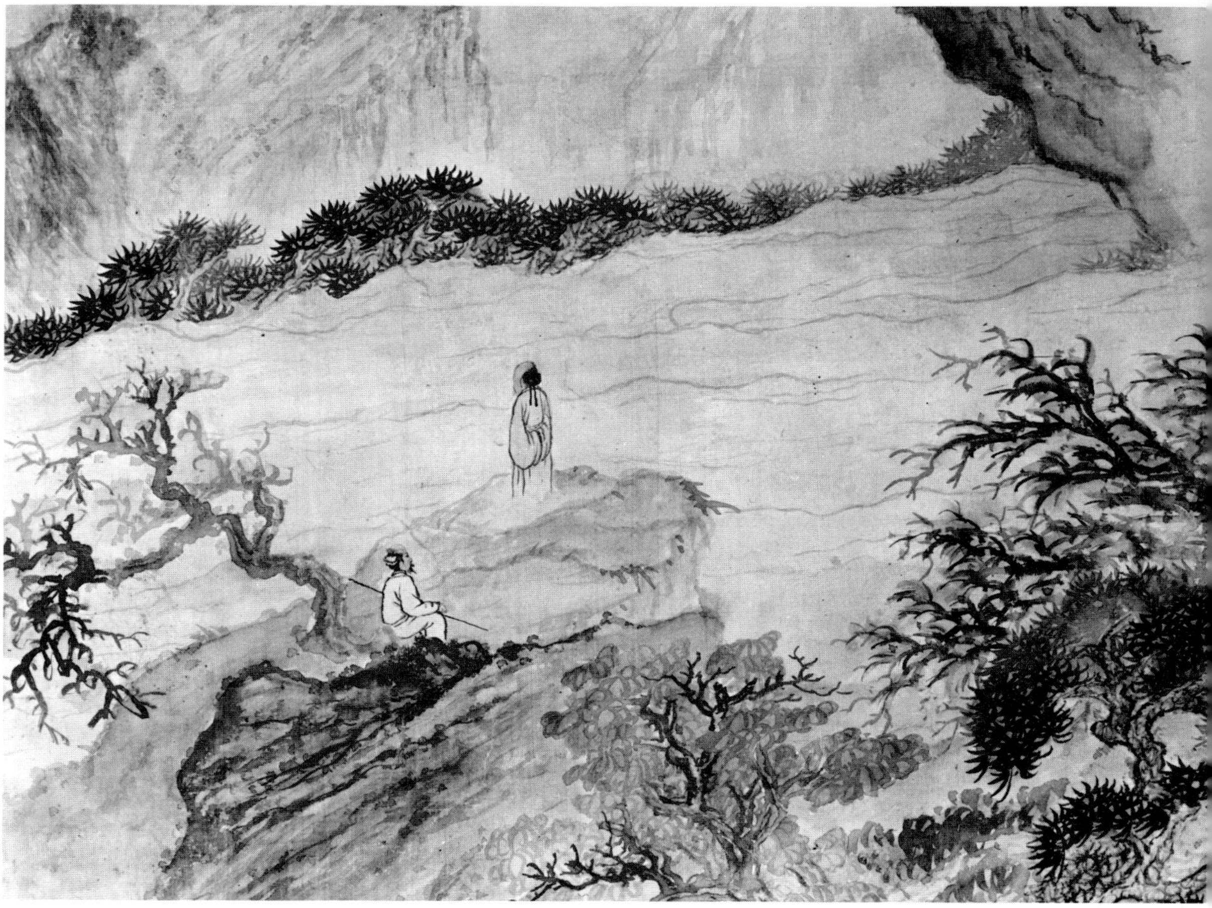

94. Detail of the foreground of Shih-t'ao, "Mount Lu."

tensely felt in his album-leaves, for example the beautiful sketch of a lone boatman on a stream illustrated in Plate 95. The boatman is Shih-t'ao himself (or you, or me), and the picture expresses the longing he must often have felt to get away from patrons, from importunate collectors, and from the bustle of Yangchow. The mood of this picture is unusually serene. Shih-t'ao's personality comes out more forcefully in the leaf from the album in the Nü-wa-chai Collection illustrated in Plate 96. It would be hard to find a statement so passionate as this little sketch, so direct, so concentrated, so complete. The life in it would be easier to understand if it had been painted as a direct response, *sur le motif*. But it was done in the studio and represents no real place; it is purely imaginary, created by the synthesis of Shih-t'ao's experience of nature and remarkable gift of expressing feeling with his brush.

How splendid it would be if we could leave Ch'ing landscape painting with Shih-t'ao, on the heights! But when he died the dynasty was less than 80 years old. The descent is not a headlong one, however, for the settled condition of China through most of the eighteenth century, the

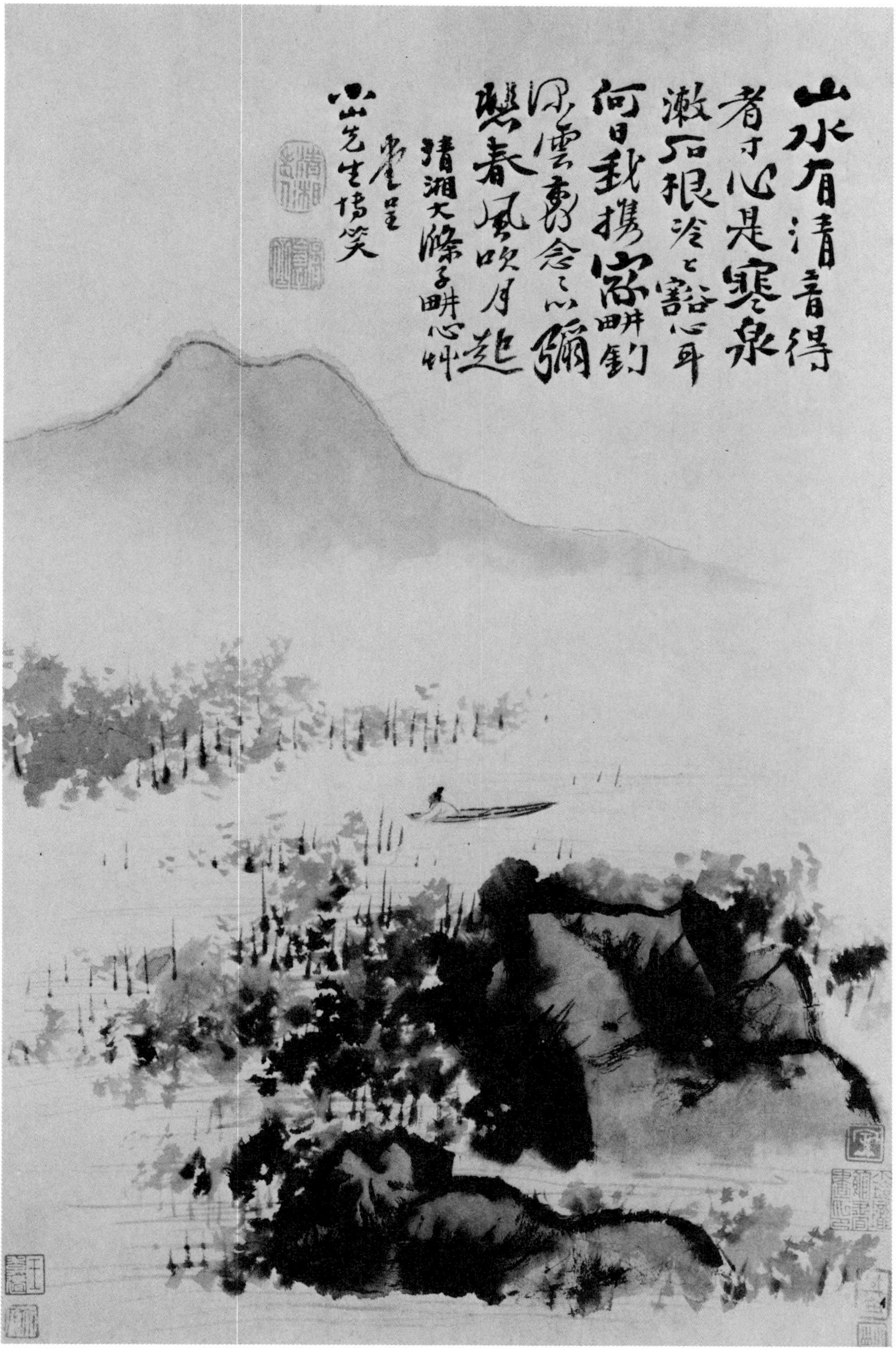

95. Shih-t'ao (Tao-chi, 1641–ca. 1710): "A Lone Boat on a Stream." Album-leaf dated 1703; ink and colour on paper. Ht. 37 cm. Ch'ing Dynasty. Museum of Fine Arts, Boston.

prevalence of wealthy patrons, and the example of the great Individualists provided an ideal climate in which the arts could flourish. The focus of patronage had now shifted from Soochow to the prosperous city of Yangchow, at the point where the Grand Canal meets the Yangtze. Now the patrons were less often high officials than traders and enormously rich salt merchants operating under government license. The social code was free and easy, the distinctions between the scholars and the merchant class more blurred even than they had been in Soochow.

Among the painters who flocked to this thriving city in the footsteps of Shih-t'ao were a number of professionals who quickly saw that what was wanted was not grave classicism or scholarly allusiveness, but pictures that were easy to understand and perhaps gave a pleasurable little shock of surprise as well. One can imagine the salt merchant and connoisseur An I-chou saying to one of these little masters, like Diaghilev, "Etonne-moi, Monsieur Kao!," and Kao Ch'i-p'ei, who had suffered agonies of worry and sleeplessness because he was afraid he would not be able to create an original style of his own, suddenly in a dream, it is said, coming up with the idea of painting with his fingernail, splitting the long nail of his fourth finger and using the back of it like a quill pen. The results were quite sufficiently astonishing to please An I-chou, as we can see from the leaf from Kao's marvelous album in Amsterdam, illustrated in Plate 97.

Huang Shen, a conservative and professional, came all the way from Fukien to Yangchow, where his style broke down, as it were, under the pressure to be original at all costs. At his worst he is mannered and fussy, at his best witty and daring, as in his vision of the chiseled rocks and twisted pines of Huang-shan in the album-leaf in Plate 98. For all its feeling of airy light and space this landscape, as the artist must have known perfectly well, bears not the remotest resemblance to the towering peaks of Huang-shan. Why then refer in his poem to Huang-shan at all? Perhaps because in this decadent age—or decadent art movement, perhaps—such a poem on a painting did not really *mean* anything. One had to write something, however conventional, simply to complete the picture. All that mattered to the struggling eccentric was that he should be able to evoke in the viewer, by his style, a little gasp of surprised delight.

Huang Shen's contemporary Chin Nung (1687–1763) settled, after his hopes of an official career were blighted, to paint in the free and easy atmosphere of Yangchow. He had a hard time getting a living, and for a while had to support himself by painting lanterns. Most of his pictures are of birds and flowers, quickly done. Among his odder works, one of the most uncomfortable is the album of landscapes in which he copied out in his quaint archaic hand twelve famous poems on the theme of escape and seclusion. He must have done this from memory, for he makes many mistakes and when there is no more room on the sheet he just stops (Plate 99). There is an air of slight desperation about the brushwork, suggesting tensions beneath the surface perhaps connected with the strain of the doctoral examinations that Chin Nung sat, and failed, at about this time. The paintings no longer illuminate the text, or the text the paintings: they simply coexist. The relationship has become sterile and conventional. It is hard not to see in such paintings an air of contrivance and a hint of decay. If a tradition can die by feeding upon itself, here we can see that process taking place before our eyes.

All these individualists were of course professionals. One of the few who did become an official was Li Fang-ying (1695–1754). But his fortune did not last, and he too was finally reduced to selling his paintings. Cheng Hsieh (1693–1765) was no eccentric. He was a distinguished calligrapher, and his studies of bamboo and orchids were in the great tradition of scholarly ink painting going back to Su Tung-p'o (see Plate 100). Yet his professionalism cut deep into him. He compensated for it by daring his patrons to despise him. He posted a list of prices on his door, adding, "If you present cold, hard cash, then my heart swells with joy and everything I write or paint is excellent. . . . Honeyed talk of old friendships and past company is only the autumn wind blowing past my ear." Thus by a kind of fiercely inverted intellectual snobbery did he maintain his self-respect. That it was not easy for him is plain from these bitter lines:

> I studied verse to no avail,
> So I quit and studied writing.
> I studied writing to no avail,
> So I quit and studied art.
> Now if I sell enough for a hundred cash a day
> It will be considered making a living,
> And keep one from abject poverty
> In the elegant name of art.
> Now I've escaped all appointments and meetings,
> And begging for official favour.
> The clean fresh air blows through my house,
> And no horses and carriages crowd my gate.

And in a letter to his younger brother he asks, "Is it not a vulgar thing for a man who cannot do some service to the country and improve the lot of

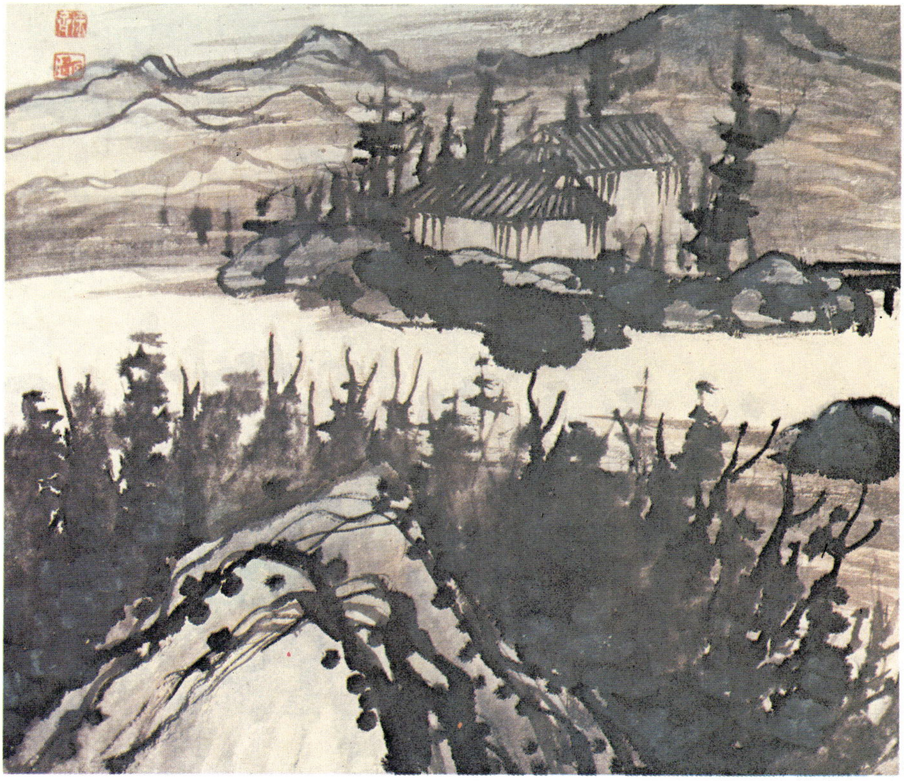

96. *Shih-t'ao (Tao-chi, 1641–ca. 1710): "The Waterside Hut." Album-leaf; ink and colour on paper. Ht. 24.1 cm. Ch'ing Dynasty. Nü-wa-chai Collection, New York.*

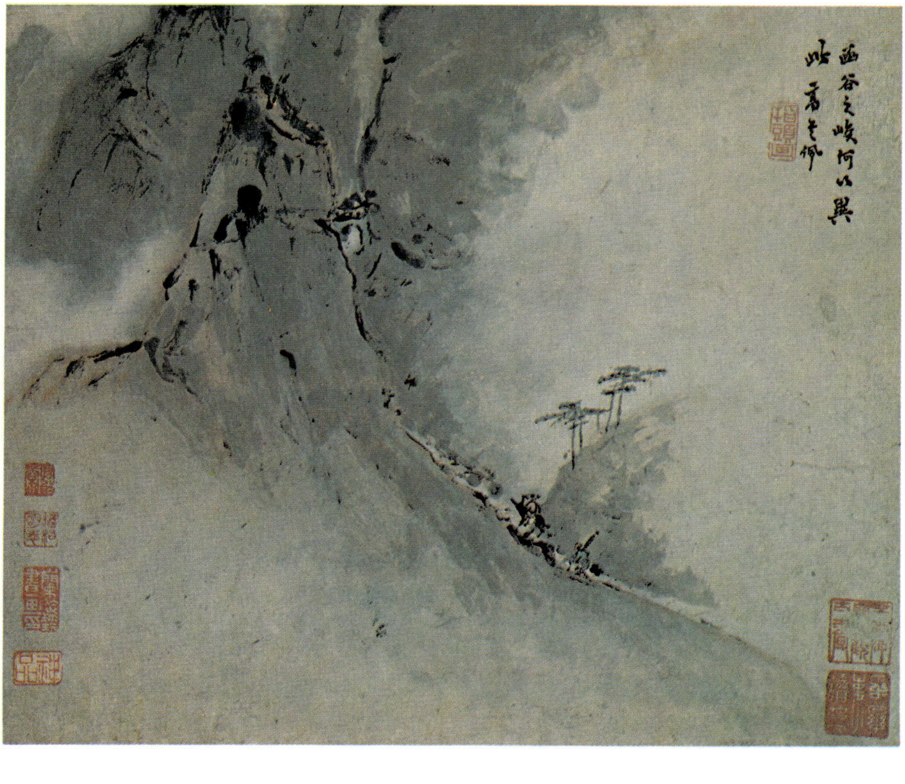

97. *Kao Ch'i-p'ei (ca. 1672–1734). "Travelling in the Mountains." Album-leaf; ink and colour on paper. Ht. 27 cm. Muzeum van Aziatische Kunst, Rijksmuseum, Amsterdam.*

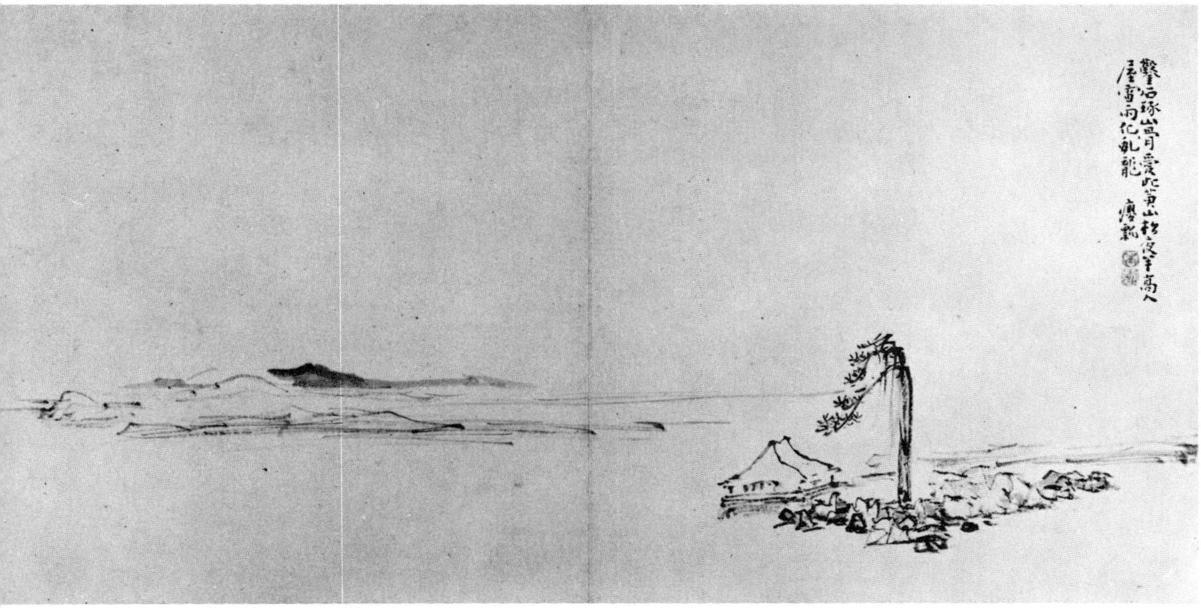

98. Huang Shen (1687–1768): Landscape. Album-leaf; ink on paper. Ht. 23.1 cm. Ch'ing Dynasty. Sumitomo Collection, Kyoto, Japan.

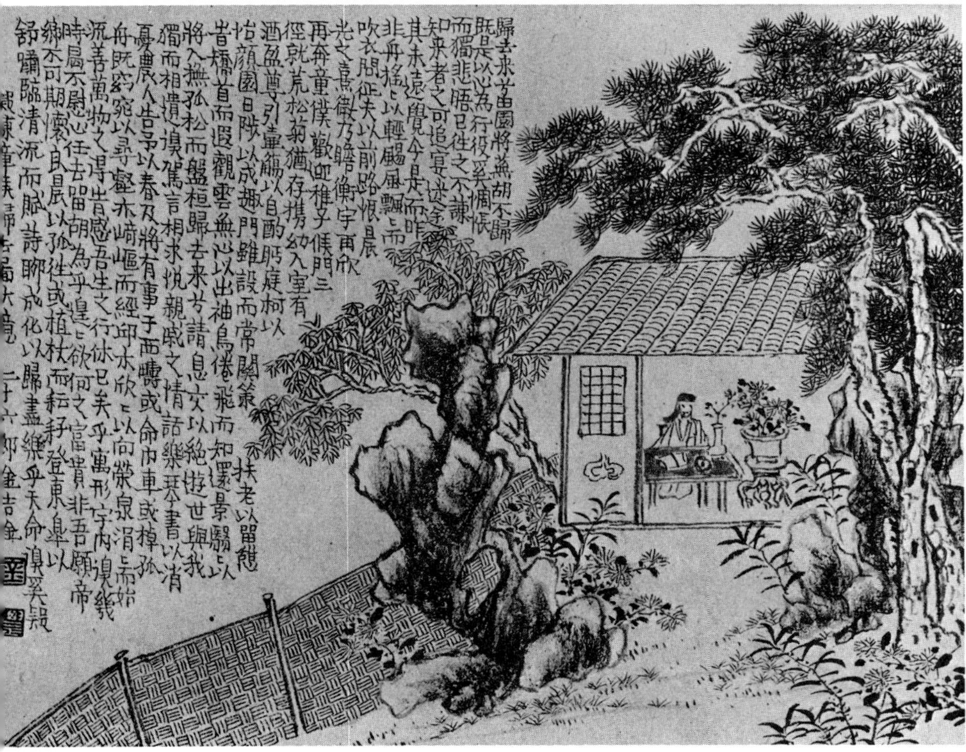

99. Chin Nung (1687–1763): Illustration to T'ao Ch'ien's "Homecoming," after a version by the Ming artist Ch'en Hung-shou. Leaf from an album dated 1736; ink on paper. Ht. 17 cm. Ch'ing Dynasty. Charles A. Drenowatz Collection, Museum Rietberg, Zürich, Switzerland.

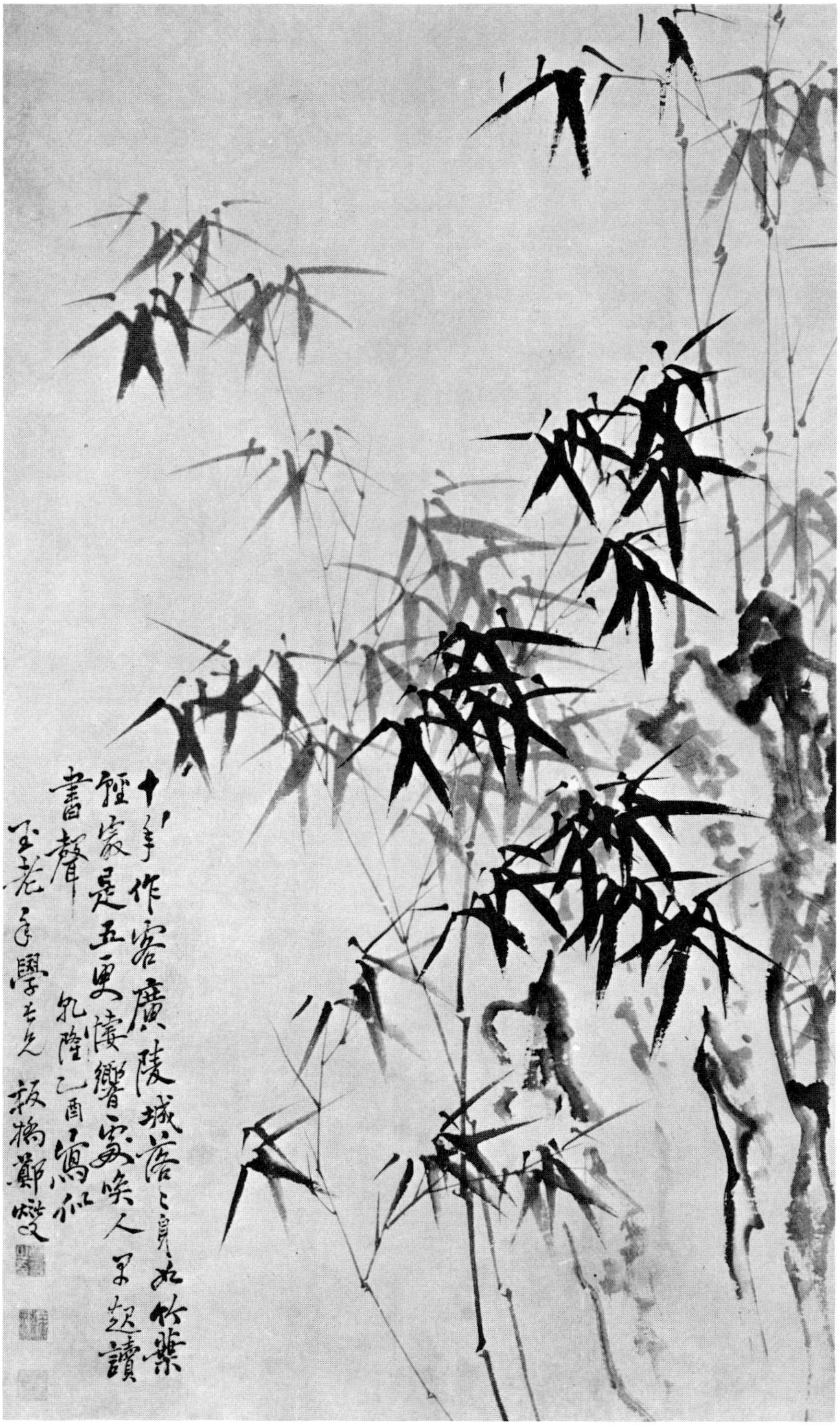

100. Cheng Hsieh (1693–1765): "Bamboo in Mist," dated 1729. Hanging scroll; ink on paper. Ch'ing Dynasty. Huang Pao-hsi Collection, Hong Kong.

the people to occupy himself with pen and ink for the amusement of other people?"* Yet Chang Hsieh's lovely painting of bamboo and orchids give no hint of the bitterness he felt. As for vulgarity, that was harder to avoid. Cheng Hsieh himself avoids it, but others among the Yangchow eccentrics are to be forgiven if in the pursuit of originality they sometimes overstepped the bounds of good taste, for competition for attention was severe. A touch of vulgarity may even be taken as a sign of the vitality of Yangchow, where the chord struck by Shih-t'ao continued to reverberate, though with diminishing intensity, through the eighteenth century.

The Ch'ien-lung emperor abdicated in 1796; Lo P'ing, the last of the Yangchow eccentrics, died in 1799. But the life had gone out of the Yangchow "movement" long before that, and from these last years of the eighteenth century until the dynasty fell in 1912 a creeping paralysis settled over the educated class. It was only with the help of the Europeans that the Manchus were able to crush the Taiping Rebellion of 1850–66, the one great surge of national vitality that interrupted the long, slow process of decline. The literati, meanwhile, having sold out to the Manchus, had lost their credentials as custodians of what was most worth preserving in Chinese culture, while as painters their cautious good manners are reflected in the landscapes of minor masters such as Tai Hsi. A sad reflection on the state of painting in the nineteenth century is the fact that almost the only artists with any vigour at all were the professionals and shop-painters of Shanghai, whose pictures express with a new boldness the vigorous commercial flavour of that rising city.

By now, European culture and art, which the courts of the K'ang-hsi and Ch'ien-lung emperors had flirted with and the scholars had dismissed, were once more hammering at the gates. But this time they were backed by arms and technology that China badly needed if she was to survive in the modern world, and they could not be ignored. In the final chapter we will see how China has dealt with this latest, and greatest, challenge to her traditional civilisation.

*William Scott, "Yangchow and Its Eight Eccentrics," *Asiatische Studien* 1–2 (1964).

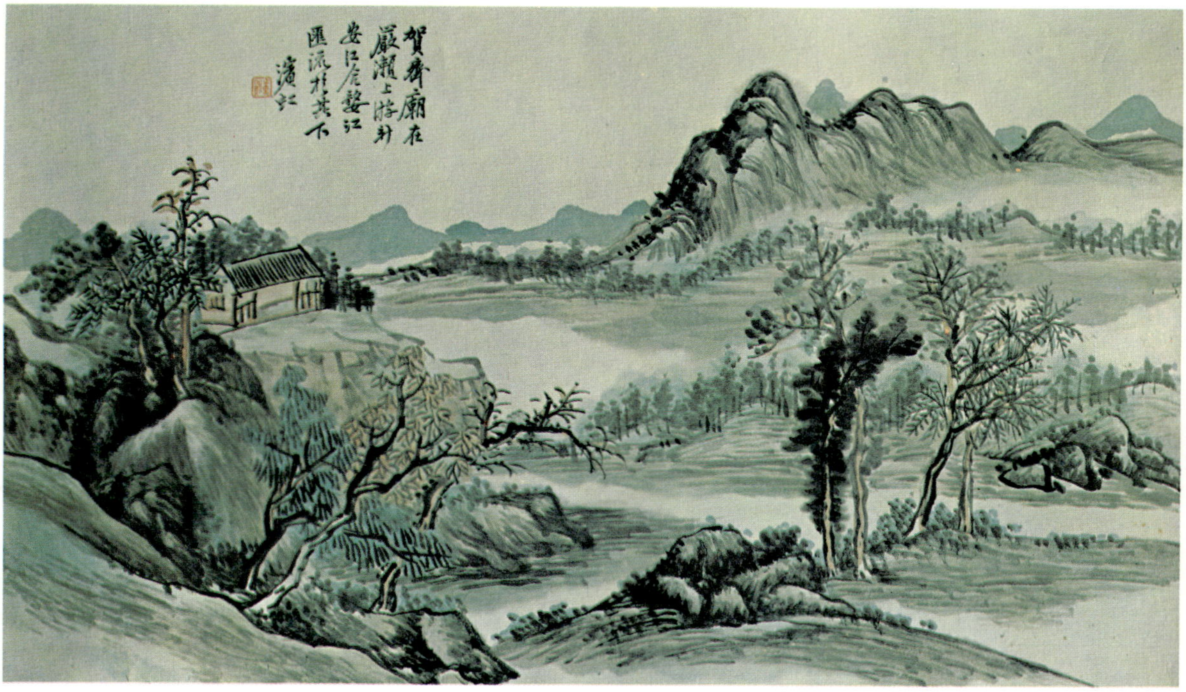

VII The Twentieth Century

101. Huang Pin-hung (1864–1955): Landscape. Album-leaf; ink and colour on paper. Ht. 27.3 cm. Private collection.

To the tensions that enlivened painting in the Ming and Ch'ing dynasties the twentieth century has added far greater tensions of its own. These are not the product of the Communist victory of 1949. They have been present, in some form, since soon after the turn of the century. They were present, for instance, after the Revolution of 1911 when the first private academies of art opened in Shanghai and Canton and young students laid down their brushes and began obediently to learn to draw from casts in the Beaux Arts manner; they were present when in the 1920's the use of nude models in Shanghai caused a public scandal; they were present in the minds of the artists who returned from Paris to find that the oil painting of the *salons* was meaningless to all but the small cosmopolitan set in the French Concession of Shanghai, and that beyond its confines they were strangers among their own people. In fact, these tensions affected all the artists who came into contact with Western culture and were faced with the choice of being "foreign," and progressive, or Chinese, and reactionary.

I have told this story elsewhere, and we need not chronicle these events again.* For us, citizens of the culture-exporting West, it needs an effort of imaginative sympathy to put ourselves in the place of the modern Chinese artist, to try to imagine what it must be like to have our social values, our attitude to the world and to nature, our very ways of expressing ourselves shaken to their roots until we are no longer sure of who we are, or of whether our traditional culture still has any validity at all. When we speak of the influence of Monet on a modern Chinese painter such as Hsü Pei-hung, or of Paul Klee on Zao Wouki, we are speaking not of a stimulus that the artist can accept or reject in the pursuit of his aims (as Monet could accept or reject that of Hokusai), but of a challenge to him to declare himself on fundamental issues that affect his culture as a whole. For Western art reached China in the twentieth century no longer in isolation, but as just one element in a package that included social and economic theory, philosophy and literature, science and technology. However deeply rooted the tradition of Chinese landscape painting, it was not possible that it could escape involvement in this titanic confrontation.

The feebler spirits managed to ignore the problem altogether and went on painting landscapes in the timid, well-mannered fashion of the nineteenth century, feeling, no doubt, that the tradition must at all costs be preserved from change, if not from decay. But some were not so timid. Rather were they stimulated, or provoked perhaps, to reassert all that was best in their traditional styles in the face of the same challenge that had robbed the Japanese after the Meiji Restoration of their self-confidence and led them for two decades to neglect, sometimes even to destroy, their traditional art. For inspiration these spirited Chinese painters turned not to the great Northern Sung masters or to the Yüan literati—for this was not the time for the monumental composition, or for a fastidious withdrawal from the world—but to the early Ch'ing Individualists, above all to Shih-t'ao, whose spontaneous self-expression had once before brought an excessively academic tradition to life. Huang Pin-hung (1864–1955) lived very much in the present, commuting as a teacher and art expert between Peking and Shanghai; yet when he took up his brush he was back in the world of the early Ch'ing masters, as if to proclaim that theirs was, and always would be, a valid way of seeing the world. In his beautiful landscapes (Plate 101) one finds no hint that the artist is living in the twentieth century at all.

Nor did the great individualist Ch'i Pai-shih (1863–1957) make

*See my *Chinese Art in the Twentieth Century* (London and Berkeley, Calif., 1959).

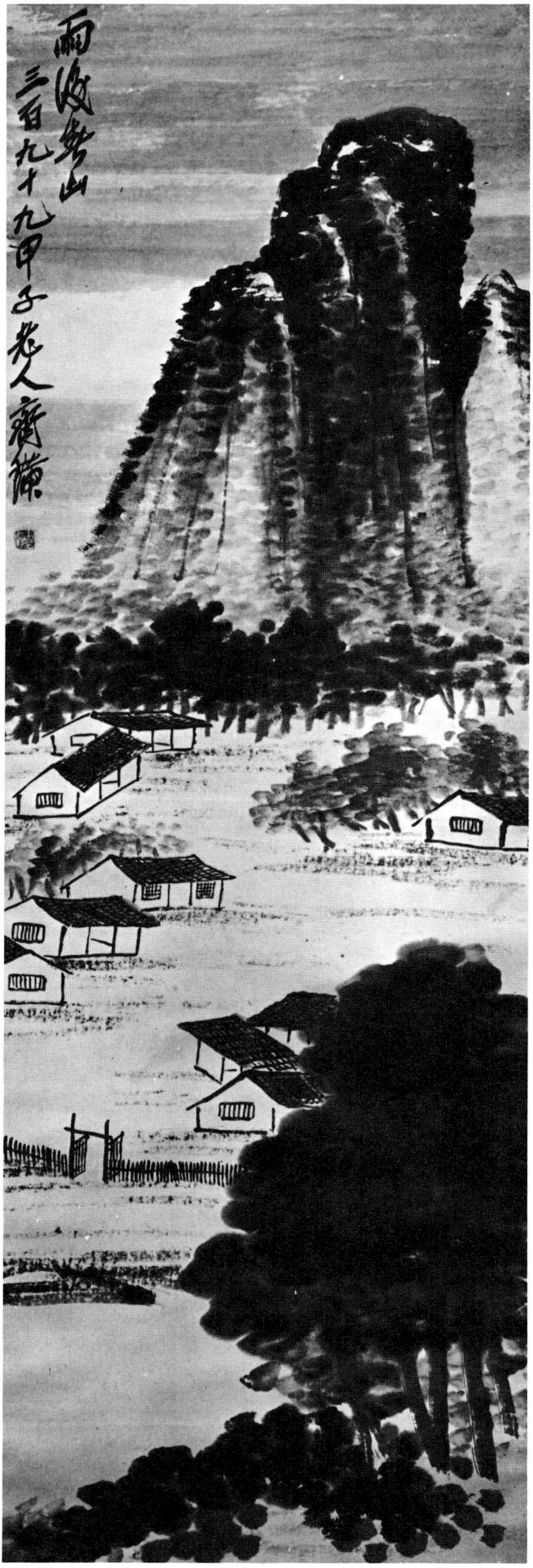

102. Ch'i Pai-shih (1863–1957): "After Spring Rain" (1929). Ink and colour on paper. Private collection.

any concessions to Western art, while his daring use of colour—a new feature of Chinese painting first seen in the late nineteenth century—proclaims his utter self-confidence. He is best noted for his crabs and shrimps, winepots and chrysanthemums, but for a few years he painted landscapes, too (Plate 102). No scholar but a country boy from Hunan, he rose by sheer determination and talent to a dominating position in the art world of Peking. Because he was not nurtured in the scholarly tradition, his work is cruder, more vigorous than that of Huang Pin-hung; yet he, too, was influenced by Shih-t'ao and Pa-ta Shan-jen, and in time he became something of a poet as well.

Our third traditionalist is very different. Fu Pao-shih (1904–65) studied in Japan, where he absorbed a touch of the Japanese feeling for surface and texture, a little of Tessai's restless brushwork, and the faintest hint of Western realism (Plate 103). But he did not make the mistake of deliberately creating a synthetic Sino-Western art as his Japanese teachers had done. A far stronger influence on him was that of Shih-t'ao and the Yangchow eccentrics, while even in his smallest landscapes he captures, chiefly through the tiny scale of his exquisitely drawn figures, something of the monumentality of the Northern Sung. Clearly, with such artists as these at work, the tradition was in safe hands.

They could have argued that there was no need for them to change their landscape painting because the landscape itself did not change. But could they continue to people it with white-robed scholars and poets gazing at waterfalls? Today's scholars were likely to be trousered schoolteachers, travelling by bus. And if one had to look at the figures afresh, should one not also look afresh at the buildings in the landscape, and at the very landscape itself? As early as 1930 the painter Feng Tzu-k'ai was telling his students, "If anyone is found still painting a hermit playing a lute under a pine tree by a waterfall, I shall expel him." It was precisely at this point that the student's problems began. Tradition had not taught him to draw from life, and there were no models for trousered schoolteachers and diesel buses in the painting manuals. Students set to draw such subjects would sometimes ask their teachers for photographs of street scenes that they could copy; that way the camera would have already done the work of transforming the object into a two-dimensional image, so that the student did not have to perform this miracle himself. An equally pressing problem was that of the medium. Running through the whole history of Chinese pictorial art is the idea that form is brought to life through the calligraphic vitality of the brushstroke. How could this quality of inner life be conveyed by the laborious process of painting

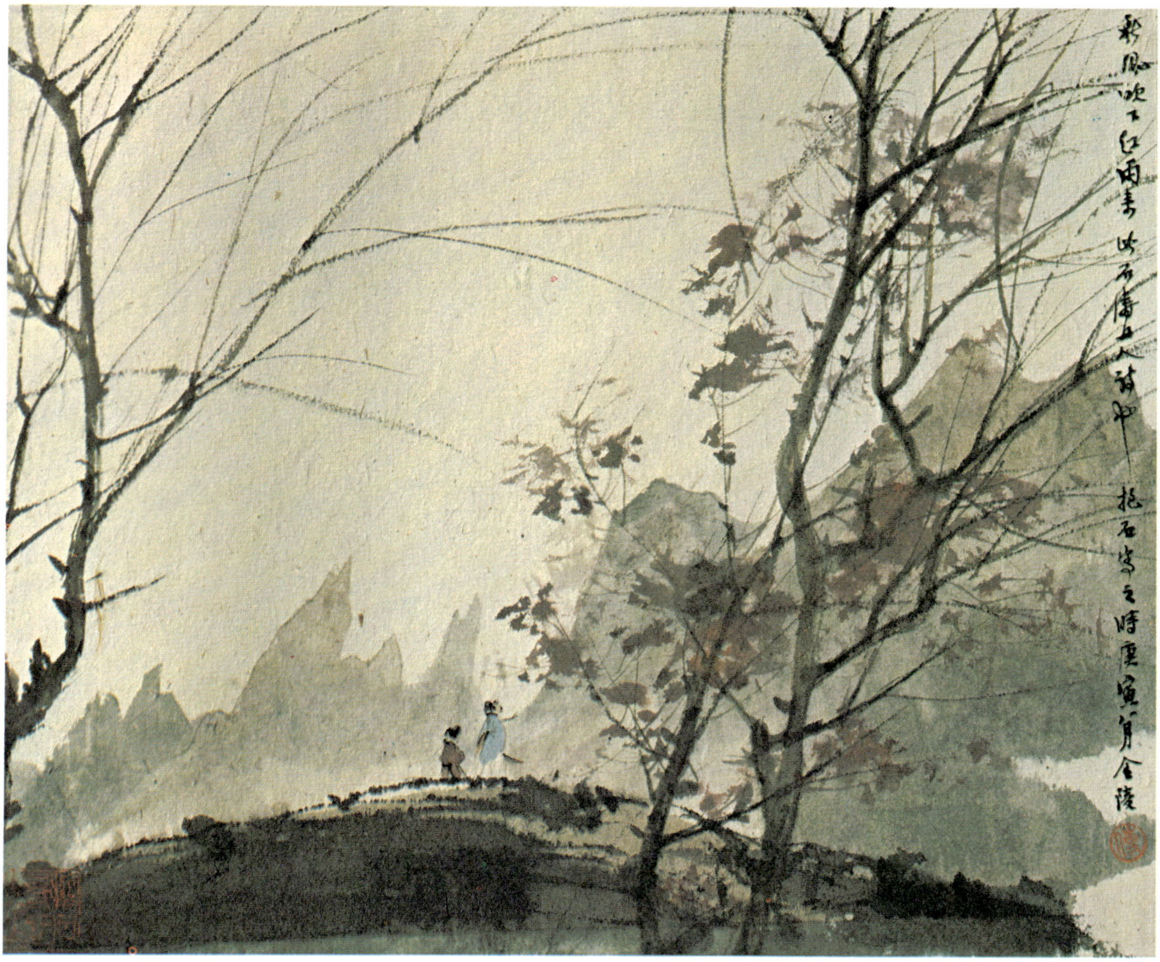

103. Fu Pao-shih (1904–65): "Autumn." Leaf from an album of the "Four Seasons" dated 1950; ink and colour on paper. Ht. 28.1 cm. Private collection.

in oils or shading with a pencil? It was when they found this impossible that many painters returned to the traditional brush and ink.

Problems of artistic technique were of course merely a part of the great debate that raged through the 1920's and early 1930's between those who, like K'ang Yu-wei, believed that traditional culture could still be preserved as the "kernel" of the new Chinese nut, with Westernism merely the "shell," and those who, like the great writer Lu Hsün, denounced decadent Confucianism as a code of man-eaters and held that China could only be saved by a total spiritual and moral regeneration. To Lu Hsün it was not Confucianism that was "moral" but Western science and technology, which promised a better life for the masses. A veneer of Westernisation over a core of Confucianism was nonsense. It was all or nothing. In the same way, the champions of Western art claimed, with much truth, that the traditional landscape conventions had grown stale and empty through repetition, and had become not an aid but a barrier to the expression of the artist's experience. The only logical solution was to abandon them, as the Japanese had done, and start again with Western realism. But those who took this extreme step were few; it was one thing to paint like Courbet in Paris, quite another to do so in Shanghai.

Some artists tried a compromise, a deliberate synthesis. Shortly after the Revolution of 1911, two Cantonese painters trained in Japan, Kao Chien-fu and Kao Ch'i-feng, set out to show how the traditional medium could depict contemporary themes using Western techniques of perspective, shading, and chiaroscuro; Kao Chien-fu even painted a vertical scroll showing a tank, some misty trees, and an airplane hovering in the sky like a butterfly to prove that it could be done. But their work, like that of their Japanese models, was too contrived to convey any real feeling (Plate 104). It was for a later generation, beginning with Hsü Pei-hung, to discover that the synthesis had to take place, if it was to take place at all, not in the head but in the heart of the painter. It was a question not of a conscious blending of styles but of what the artist felt about the world around him—and, even more, of what he felt himself to be. In the intensity of feeling they put into their work, the best of the modern Chinese artists discovered not only a new path for landscape painting but their identity as Chinese in an age of confusion and change, just as once their ancestors had when the Ming Dynasty was collapsing. The late Ming artists had at least known where they stood, for their own art revealed it to them. But for the Chinese artist of the twentieth century to forge a new art that was both Chinese and contemporary was no easy matter. Most refused to take the shortcut, taken by so many Japanese

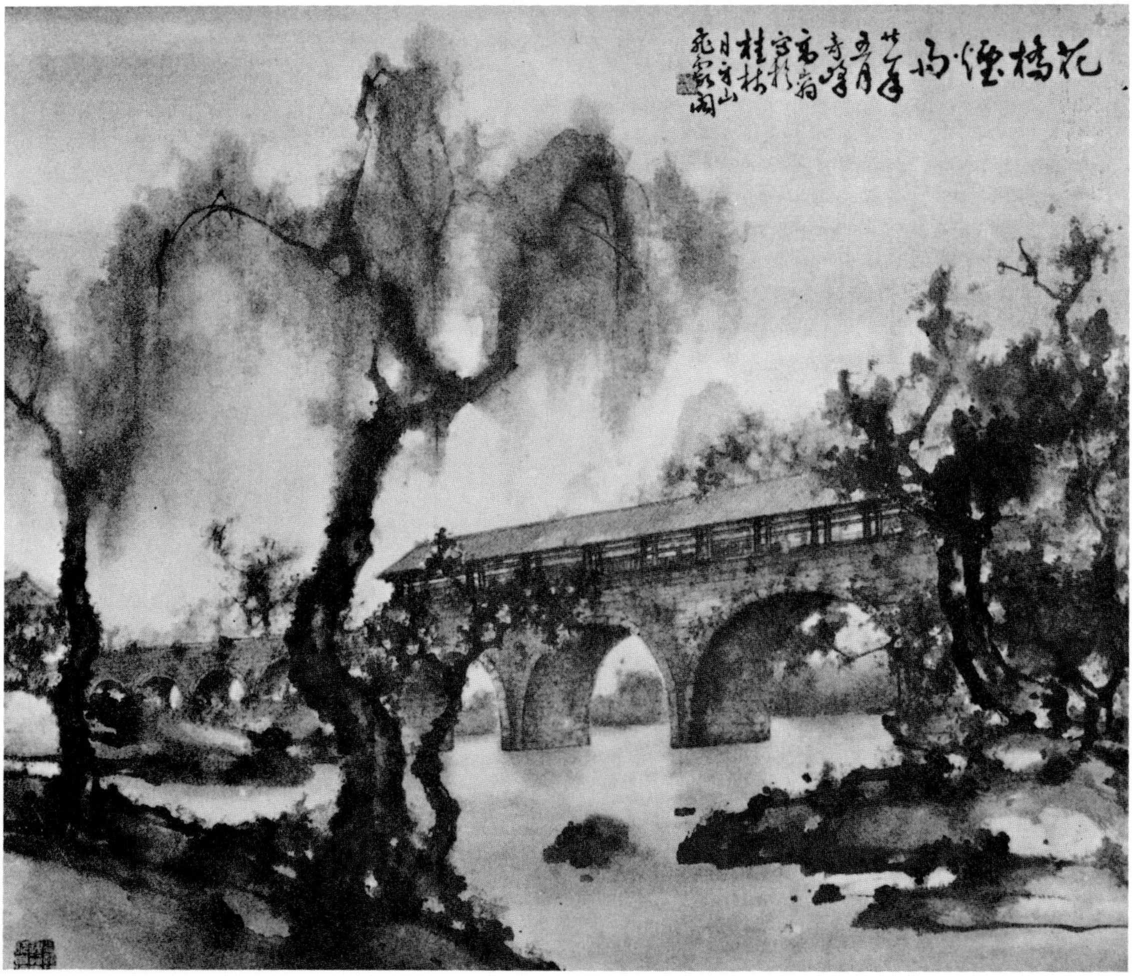

104. Kao Ch'i-feng (1889–1933): "Bridge at Kweilin in the Rain." Hanging scroll dated 1932; ink and slight colour on paper. Present whereabouts unknown.

painters, of immediately and skillfully imitating the latest art movement to arrive from the West. They had to see each movement in Chinese terms before it had any meaning for them, and that could come only after deep reflection.

While Hsü Pei-hung's handling of the Chinese medium was extremely skilful (Plate 105), it was hardly adventurous. It was Lin Fengmien, returning from Paris in 1923 inspired not by the art of the salons but by that of Matisse and Vlaminck, who rediscovered the expressive use of the brush, the spontaneous gesture (Plate 106). He worked rapidly, the floor of his studio piled inches deep in sketches as if his vision were too fresh, his need to express himself too urgent to survive translation

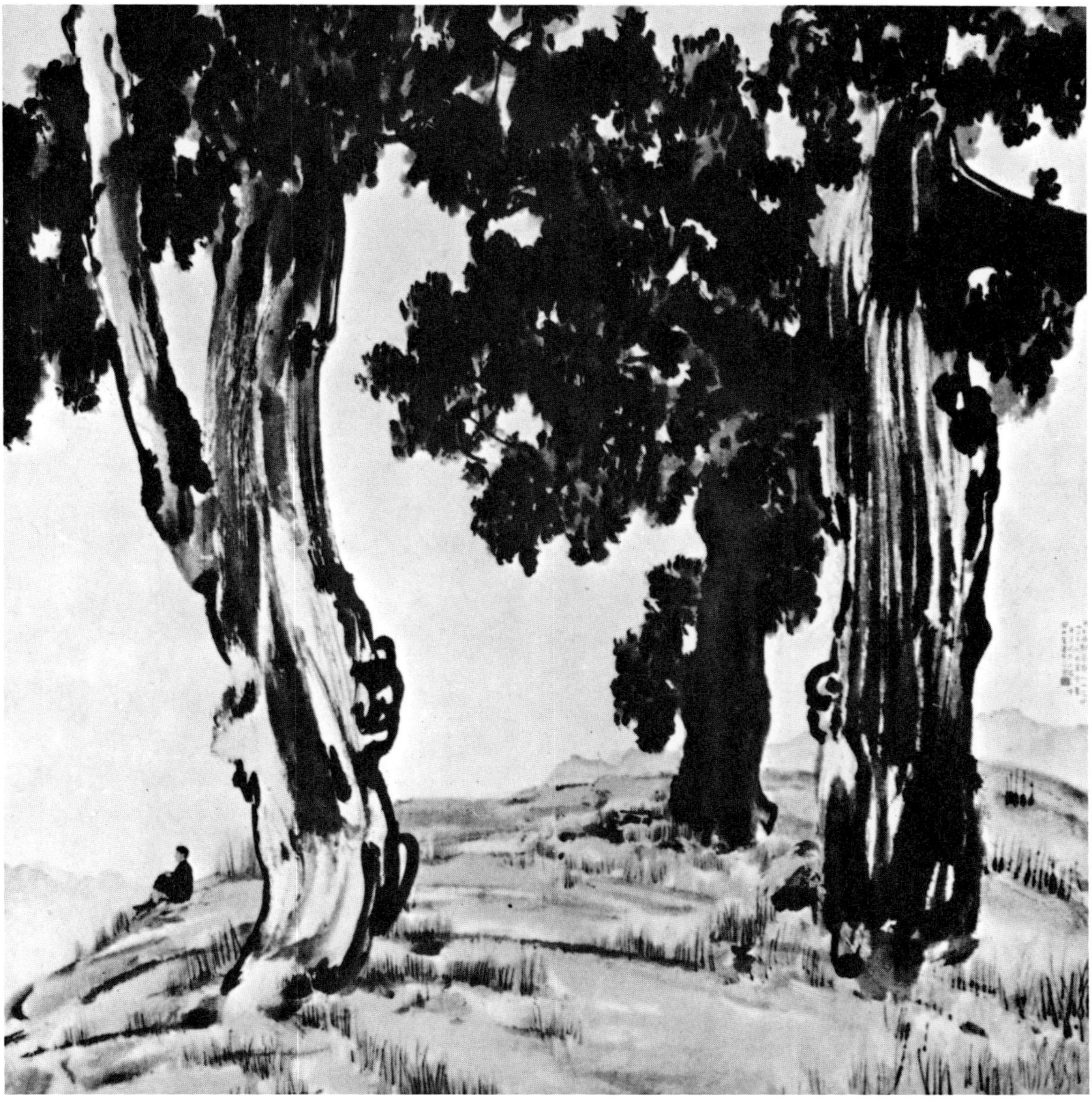

105. Hsü Pei-hung (1895–1953): "Under the Cypress Trees." Ink and colour on paper.

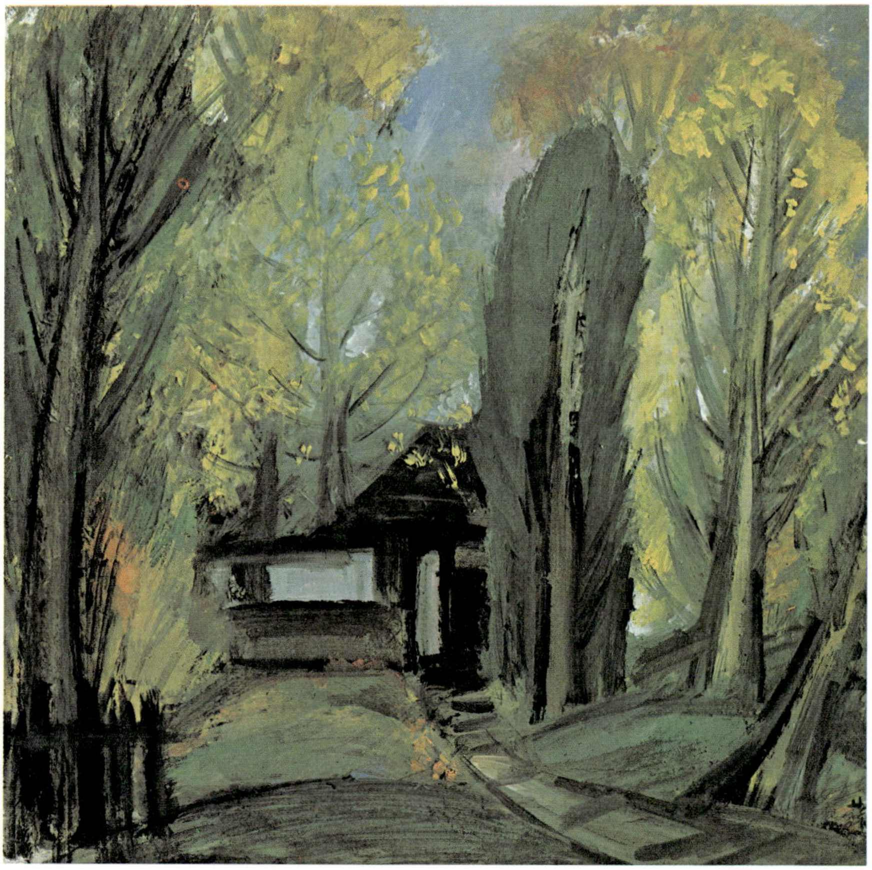

106. Lin Feng-mien (1901 or 1906–): "A Village in the South." Gouache on paper. Ht. 67 cm. Private collection.

into a long-considered work. If he seems no longer buoyed up by tradition, he is not shackled by it either; and indeed the best of his work, and of his pupil Chao Wu-chi, has an air of spontaneous, unreflecting discovery (so different from the expert synthesis of the Cantonese) that proclaims a new dawn for Chinese landscape painting.

By the mid-1930's it seemed that a new kind of painting was coming into being that was Chinese in technique and contemporary in feeling. But the war with Japan brought these exciting experiments to an end, turning Chinese painting in quite another direction. With the coastal cities in Japanese hands, painters and students turned their steps westward toward the mountains. In remote Szechwan and Kwangsi there were no foreign Concessions, no little *salons,* no oil paints. Uprooted artists discovered their own land and their own medium as they never could in the cosmopolitan atmosphere of the Treaty Ports. Their public, moreover, had changed, and if their art during the war years (1937–45) was less "modern" than it had been on the coast, it was also more Chinese. That meant a return to the Chinese way of painting landscapes, and inevitably—although this was not fully apparent at that time—the almost imperceptible development of a new pictorial vocabularly based not on *The Mustard Seed Garden* but on the pioneers' own observation of the spectacular scenery of West China, Tibet, and Central Asia.

At the same time the painter's attitude to his art was changing. The social revolution was gathering speed. With the country torn apart by war and civil war it was no longer possible to paint scholars gazing at waterfalls. Lu Hsün, in launching the Woodcut Movement in 1928, had shown how art could, and indeed must, be used for the betterment of society. As the war dragged on and China sank deeper and deeper into chaos and confusion, almost the only art that spoke with conviction was the art of protest. In such a crisis landscape painting seemed to many artists to serve no useful purpose.

Peace came in 1945, and for a brief moment China's doors were open once more. A few painters managed to get to Europe. Among them was Chao Wu-chi, who in Paris gallicised his name to Zao Wouki. There he soon became a master of the oil medium, creating large calligraphic abstractions that have atmosphere and depth; they suggest mountains and valleys, mist and clouds, demanding to be seen as landscapes. Because these large and splendid oils are now well known, I have chosen to illustrate instead (Plate 107) one of the small watercolours he made in his first years in Paris. Touched, like many modern Far Eastern artists, by the influence of Paul Klee, he goes beyond Klee, for his feeling for the landscape is expressed in typically Chinese fashion in the sensitive language of the brush. These sketches, made when the impact of modern Western art on the young painter was still fresh, have a delightful tentative quality, as though he were reaching out, a little shyly, to the West from his secure place in the Chinese tradition.

The spontaneity of Zao Wouki, like that of the Zen painters, is antihistorical. He meets the challenge of the past not by ignoring it but by so completely sublimating it that it is no longer a recognisable source of his inspiration. Rather different is the art of Tseng Yu-ho. As a young girl in Peking she had been a pupil of a Manchu prince, an accomplished if academic scholar-painter. Yet the effect of her first sight of the Hawaiian Islands in 1948, and of her meeting with Max Ernst, was not to leave her pictorially speechless but to stimulate her to create a series of landscapes, using traditional techniques, that express a fresh visual experience for

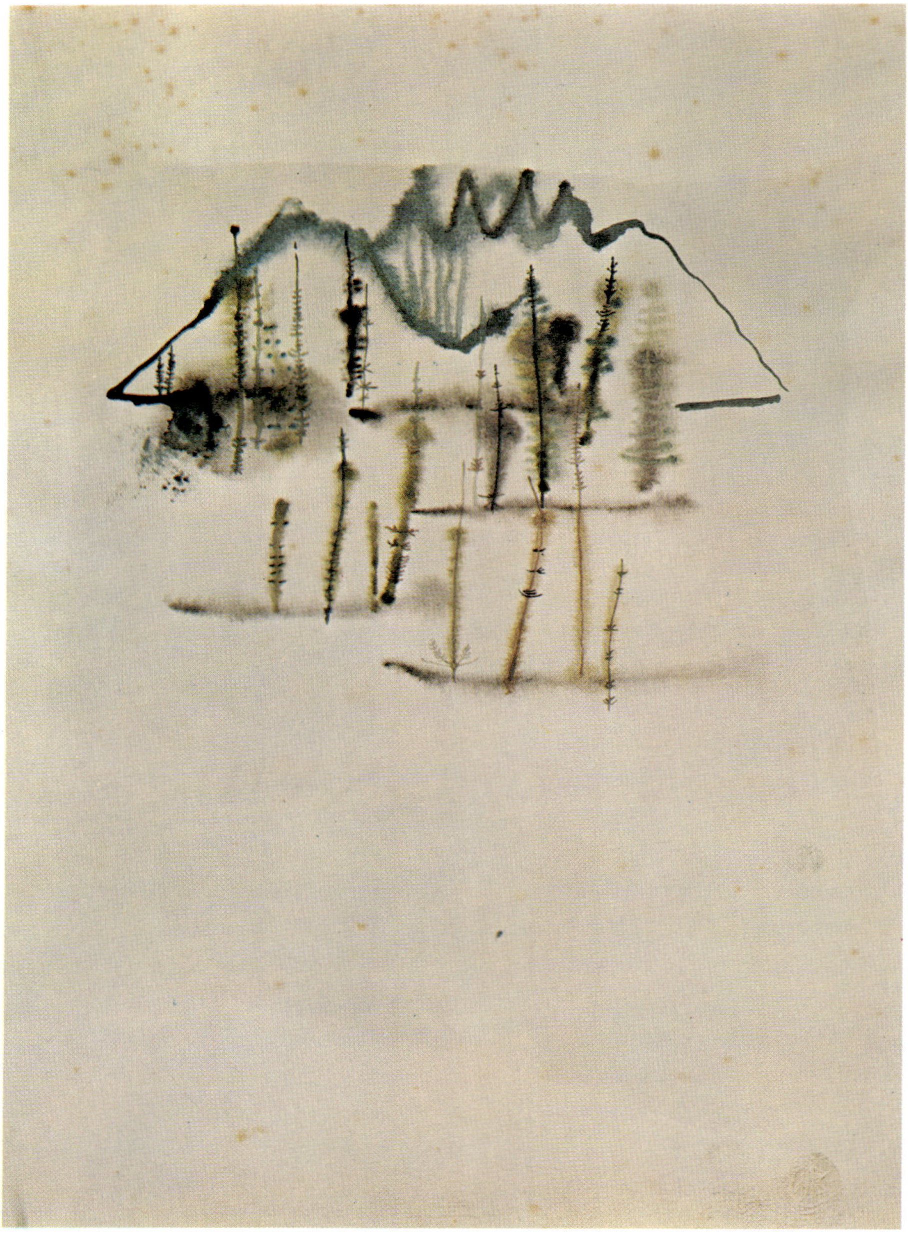

107. Chao Wu-chi (Zao Wouki, 1921–   ): Landscape sketch, 1950. Watercolour on paper. Ht. 30 cm. Collection of the artist.

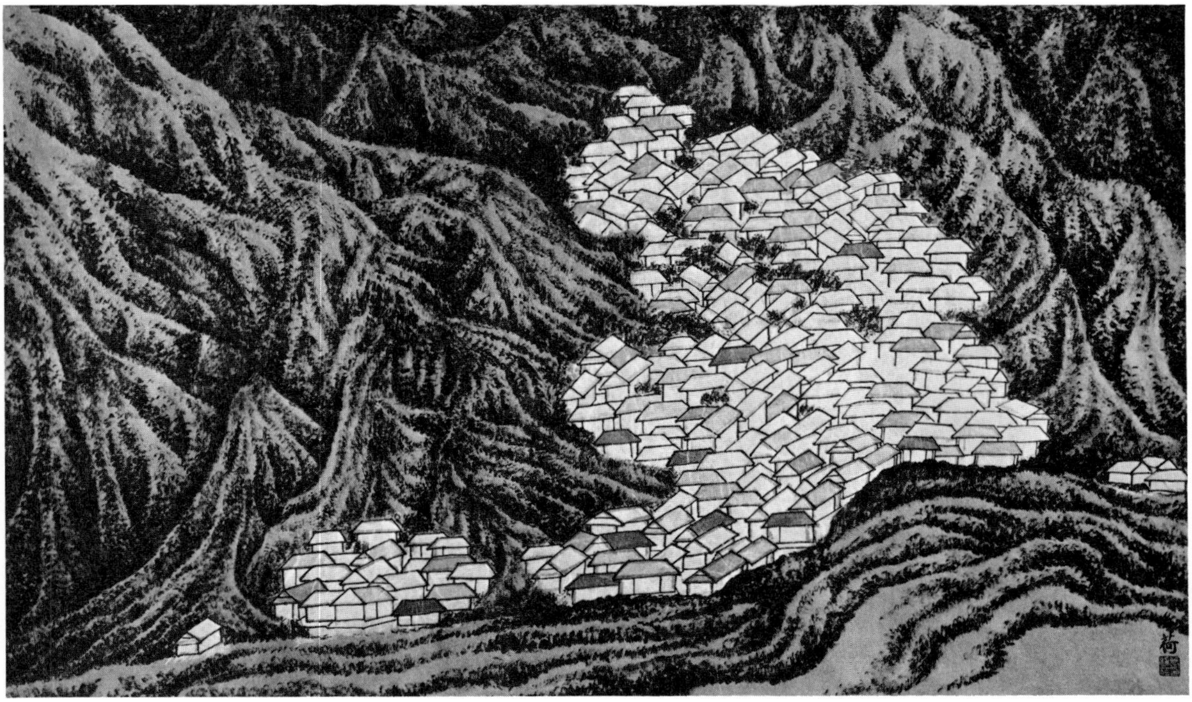

108. Tseng Yu-ho (1923–): "Hawaiian Landscape." Hanging scroll; ink on paper.

which there were no models in *The Mustard Seed Garden*. To anyone who knows the volcanic hills of Hawaii, her reference to the style of Kung Hsien is brilliantly apt (Plate 108); while being both inventive and scholarly, she could don the mask of the great seventeenth-century painter-monk Hung-jen to create a landscape (Plate 109) that captures something of his spirit and yet is entirely personal and contemporary. Thus, in the spirit of Tung Ch'i-ch'ang, does she bring the great tradition to life once more.

These are but two of many responses made by modern Chinese artists to the crisis of the twentieth century. If the People's Republic had not come to power in 1949, these artists would be painting today in Hangchow, Shanghai, and Canton, perhaps even in conservative Peking, and making there, instead of abroad, their uniquely Chinese contribution to the international movement in modern art. But the choice was not theirs to make. The new China repudiated their kind of painting and set out to reform those who returned, filled with patriotic enthusiasm, after Liberation. Modern art in the international styles has been rejected in the People's Republic for many reasons: it is individualistic and subjective; it is associated with bourgeois culture; it is hard for the masses to under-

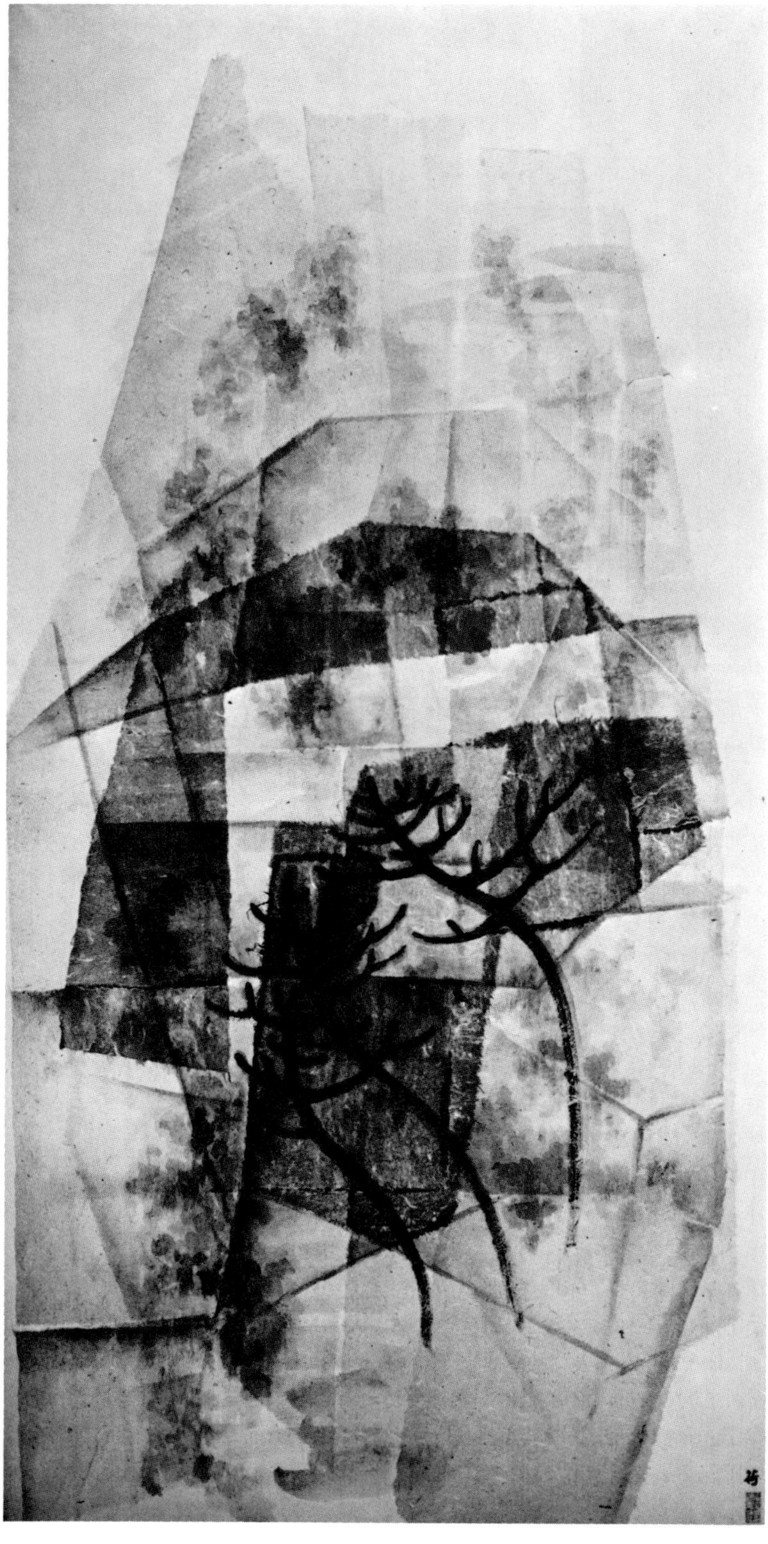

109. Tseng Yu-ho (1923–): "Landscape II: in the Spirit of Hung-jen," 1958. Collage; ink and colour on paper.

stand; its content is often objectionable; and, most fundamentally, it can only be appreciated by applying to it an order of values that obeys no laws but those of art itself, which, in a Communist state, is heresy. In the China of Mao Tse-tung there could be no hidden corners of human thought and action where an independent set of values operated—or, to put it more precisely, where aesthetic values were not subservient to political ones. For Mao Tse-tung did not deny the existence of aesthetic values: "Naturally," he wrote, "in judging the validity of scientific theories or assessing the aesthetic value of works of art, additional pertinent criteria are needed."* But the political criteria are overriding. Blown this way and that by changes in the political climate, creative artists, and particularly the more sophisticated ones, were in a constant state of uncertainty. What was a blooming flower in one year might be a poisonous weed in the next, so all but the boldest played safe. The result was that, for nearly three decades the spectrum of officially approved painting was a great deal narrower than it had been 300 years earlier. Did the painters not long to spread their wings?

The "correct" Chinese reply to the charge of lack of artistic freedom would be that far more important than the self-fulfillment of any individual is the cultural good of the people as a whole; and even China's severest critics must acknowledge how much has been achieved since 1949. Before 1949 the suggestion that Chinese peasants might take up painting, and hold an exhibition that attracted wide attention abroad, would have been greeted with derision. But that has happened, for the masses now have art and music, drama and literature, who before had none. If the range of acceptable styles has narrowed, the social base from which art springs has broadened immeasurably, and this, in the long run, must lead to the enrichment of Chinese art as a whole. Moreover, the Chinese peasant, until recently illiterate, has become proud of his cultural heritage, which he is told was produced by his ancestors and has now been consigned to his care. Does it matter, at this stage, if awkward questions about patronage and the art of the literati are ignored, so long as this attitude produces the remarkable results in archaeology, conservation, and popular education that one sees everywhere in China today?

Yet it is still legitimate to ask how the art of the past is interpreted: how, for instance, a good Communist can enjoy with a clear political conscience paintings that were produced by and for the now discredited class of the Confucian scholar-gentry. Ought such paintings not be con-

*"On the Correct Handling of Contradictions Among the People," in *Four Essays on Philosophy* (Peking, 1968), p. 120.

demned, or hidden from sight as a corrupting influence? But it is one thing to reject the Confucian system to which these painters wholeheartedly subscribed, and quite another to reject the pictures they painted. The scholar-painter Wu Li (1632–1718) was not only a Confucian but a Catholic missionary as well, yet his pictures are on view in the museum in his native Nanking. Ni Tsan was a rich landowner and a poet, but his paintings are exhibited in Peking—although his style is described on the label as "decadent." Only Tung Ch'i-ch'ang is condemned; but official Chinese attitudes in cultural matters have a way of changing suddenly, and even that rapacious landlord may not be beyond redemption.

The clue to this apparent inconsistency is to be found in Mao Tse-tung's famous slogans "Make the past serve the present" and "Make foreign things serve China." Long before 1942, when Mao Tse-tung enunciated these principles in the *Yenan Talks on Art and Literature*, Lu Hsün, who had a considerable influence on Mao's thinking about art, had said that the aim of the modern Chinese artist should be "By selection to accept the historical legacy of Chinese traditional art; to absorb the best in style and technique from foreign art; and thus to establish a new national art in accordance with the demands and needs of the masses." To this Mao Tse-tung added his gloss: "To study the development of this old culture, to reject its feudal dross and assimilate its democratic essence, is a necessary condition of our new national culture." What matters, in other words, is not the object but one's attitude to it.

How does one reject the "feudal dross" of a landscape by a Ming scholar-painter and assimilate its "democratic essence"? Clearly such statements are not meant to be taken too literally, and if one attempts to challenge them, one can be made to look rather foolish. A few years ago I visited an exhibition of paintings by the Ch'ing literati in the Palace Museum in Peking. A notice at the entrance exhorted visitors, most of whom were workers and peasants up for the day, to take the good from these paintings and reject the bad. What is bad about them? I asked my guide. She wasn't very sure, although she could have spoken of the artists' bad class role. "What is good about them, then?" I asked her. "They realistically portray," she said, "the daily life of the common people in those times." I pointed out to her that most were conventional "scholars in landscapes," and that some were just landscapes without any people in them at all. "The common people," she replied, looking me straight in the eye, "loved the landscape, too." While this was, unless one wanted to be tiresome, unanswerable, it was not very important in itself. What

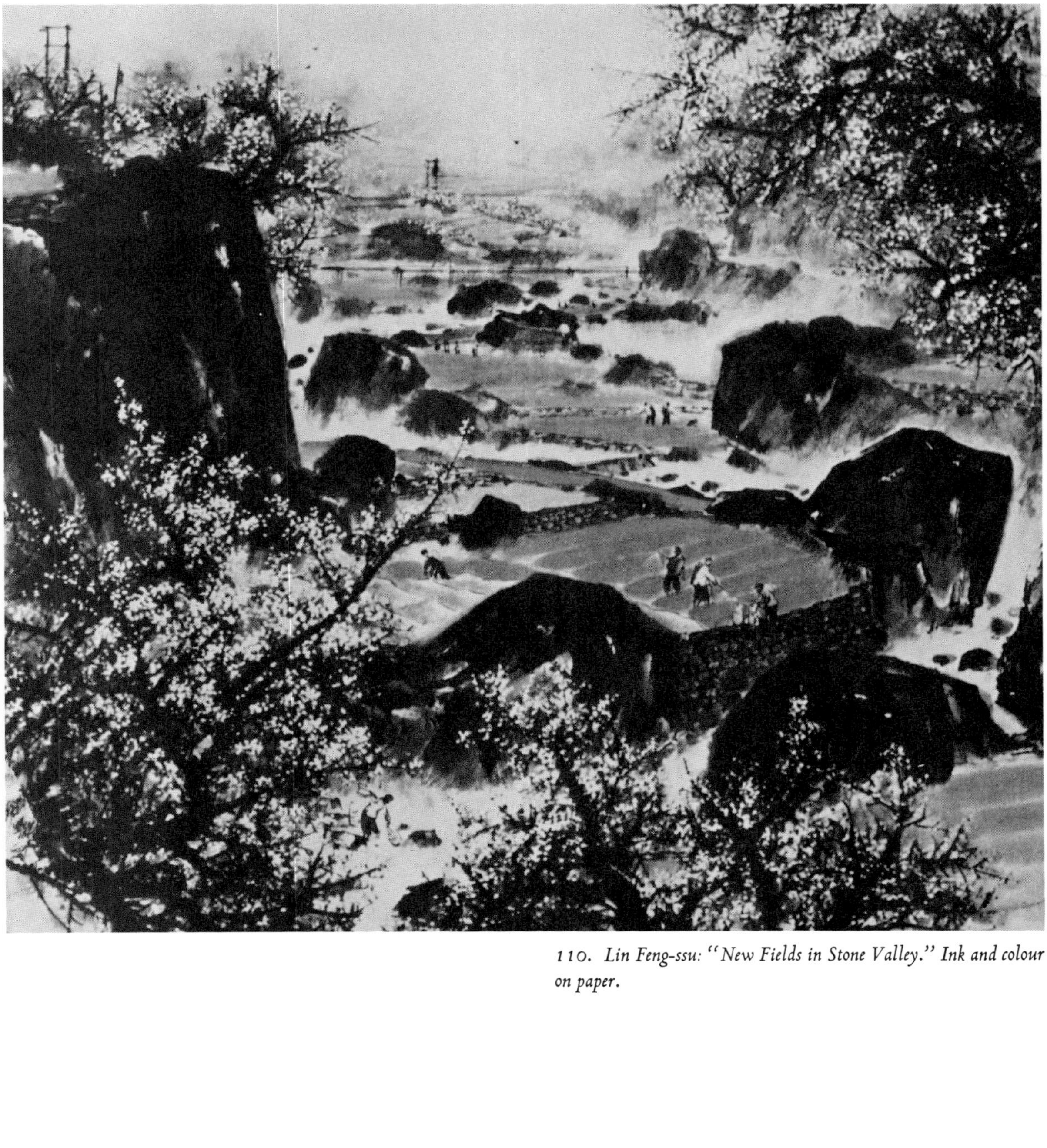

110. Lin Feng-ssu: "New Fields in Stone Valley." Ink and colour on paper.

was important was that in 1973, five years after the Cultural Revolution, paintings by the Ch'ing literati were being seen and enjoyed by peasants and workers, who a generation ago would have felt that such things were only for their betters.

But while the old masterpieces are still exhibited, people's attitudes to the landscape itself have changed profoundly. The mountains and streams are no longer an object of contemplation, in which the viewer must lose himself and forget the "dusty world." They have become for most artists the visible symbol of resurgent China. "Such is the beauty of our mountains and streams," a line from one of Mao Tse-tung's poems, is written in his hand on a huge painting by Fu Pao-shih and Kuan Shan-yüeh depicting the red sun at dawn rising to flood the landscape with the radiance of a new day. The life in the mountains and rivers is regarded today not as the cosmic *ch'i* of the Taoists, but as the source of China's new strength. Images of spring, of the greening of the countryside (Plate 110), of plum blossoms, like the blood of revolutionary martyrs red against the snow, are familiar subjects to which everyone can respond. Thus in making use of traditional symbolism, landscape painting comes once more to embody the most deeply felt ideals of the Chinese people. Besides, faith is literally moving mountains; and painters who record such feats as the construction of the Red Flag Canal (Plate 111) must understand how nature works no less than do the masses who perform them. It is claimed that revolutionary fervour has transformed the artists' style (Plate 112). "These artists," we read, "have . . . introduced innovations in the painting of trees. Laying emphasis on the whole tree, they often use straight lines to depict the boughs; and the resultant sense of vigor suggests the prosperity of our socialist countryside." Art criticism at this level is not to be taken seriously—and has indeed since been ridiculed as typical of the doctrinal excesses of the "Gang of Four." Moreover, these artists' works are in fact no more vigorous than those of Ch'i Pai-shih or Huang Pin-hung. Yet anyone who has seen China transformed—with its millions upon millions of young trees, its irrigation schemes, and its electric light in every peasant's cottage—will not deny that the very positive tone of these paintings reflects an optimism that, on the whole, has characterised Chinese life since 1949.

Such pictures as Li K'o-jan's *Fishing Boats in the Willows* (Plate 113) represent both a deep, age-old Chinese response to the eternal in nature and a sincere celebration of the new. They cannot simply be labelled Socialist Realism, a kind of painting reserved chiefly for depicting the bad old days; scarcely even can they be called Revolutionary Romanticism,

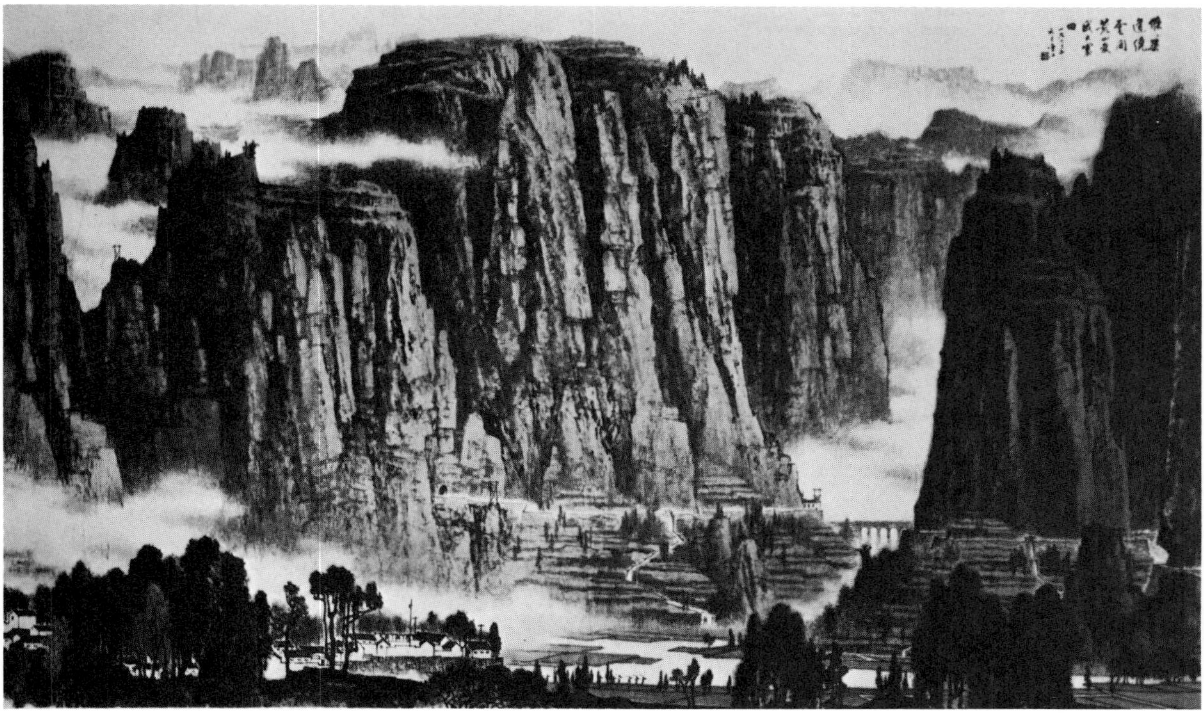

111. Pai Hsüeh-shih: "The Red Flag Canal," 1973. Ink and colour on paper.

the art that evokes a state of prosperity and bliss yet to be achieved. The technique of these paintings is much closer to that of the early Ch'ing Individualists than to that of revolutionary art as generally understood. Whatever officially inspired criticism may say about them, they speak for themselves, and show that the threads of past and present are so subtly interwoven that a crude political interpretation of the art of China today would leave a great deal unexplained. Moreover, Maoist dialectics would seem to support the idea that different kinds of art may coexist in a revolutionary society. "No contradictory aspect," Mao Tse-tung wrote in his famous tract *On Contradictions Among the People*, "can exist in isolation. . . . Without the bourgeoisie there would be no proletariat, without the proletariat there would be no bourgeoisie." Without bourgeois art, therefore, there will be no proletarian art. So we may expect the "bourgeois" tendencies in modern Chinese art—above all individualism, subjectivity, and formalism—to be continually present and to offer their constant challenge to the proletarian virtue of commitment to ongoing revolution.

In the early days of the People's Republic, problems of style were frequently aired in the art journals. Socialist art, it was agreed, should be

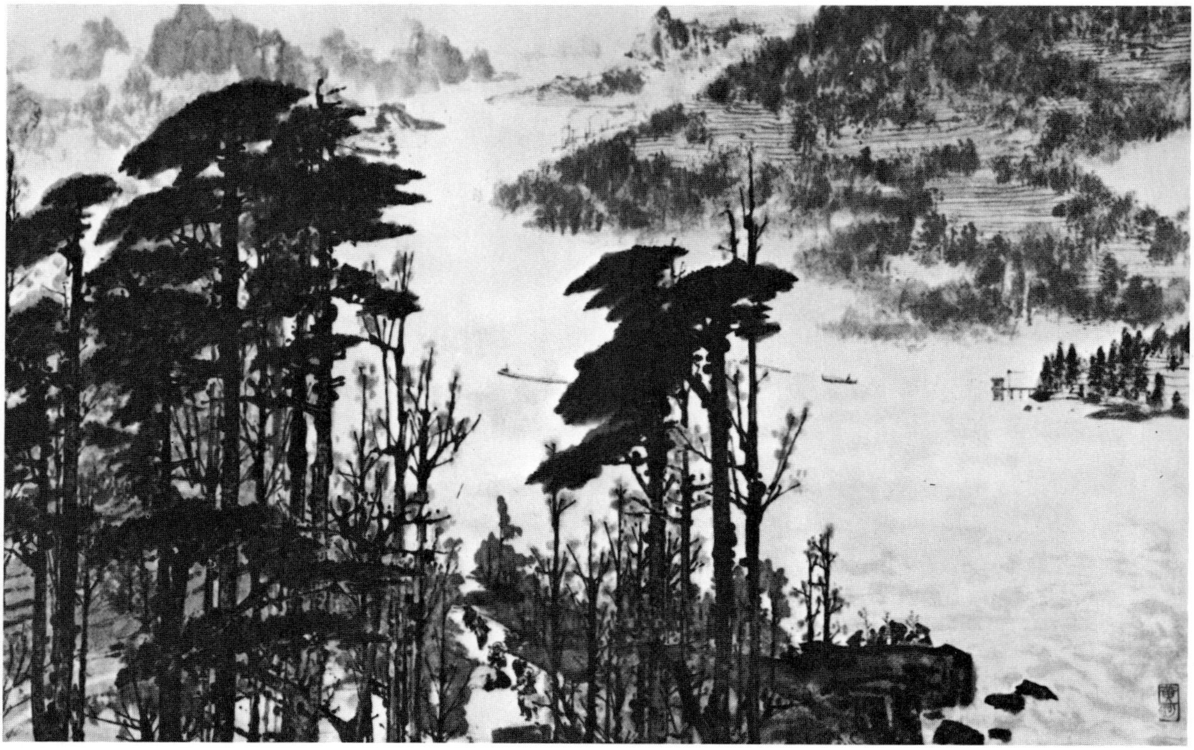

112. Unknown artist. "Clothe the Hills in Green,' 1971–72. Ink and colour on paper.

realistic; yet if we ask what the critics of the 1950's and early 1960's meant by realism we get some surprising answers. When we see that Chang An-chih could write in 1964 that classical landscapes were highly realistic in that they were "a synthesis of nature and the artist's feelings and ideas,"* and that another critic could claim that Pa-ta Shan-jen was a realist because "in a few strokes he captured the very essence of the subject he portrayed," we realize we are in the presence of a very philosophical notion of realism indeed, and one that could equally well embrace Zen painting. Discussions of art at this level were, not surprisingly, killed by the Cultural Revolution, for it is easy to see where they might lead. This does not mean, however, that they are not a major concern of the artists themselves.

We saw in the last chapter how, in the nineteenth century, the language of landscape painting hardened, or decayed, into a set of pictorial formulae that too often became a substitute for the artist's own vision. After the chaos and uncertainty of the 1930's and 1940's, one might have expected that artists in the People's Republic would be told: "Abandon your conventions, and go out and paint what you see." But though the Revolution has inspired much dreary, realistic, and propagandistic figure

*Chang An-chih, "The Painter Ch'ien Sung-yen" *Chinese Literature* (1964, no. 9), p. 103.

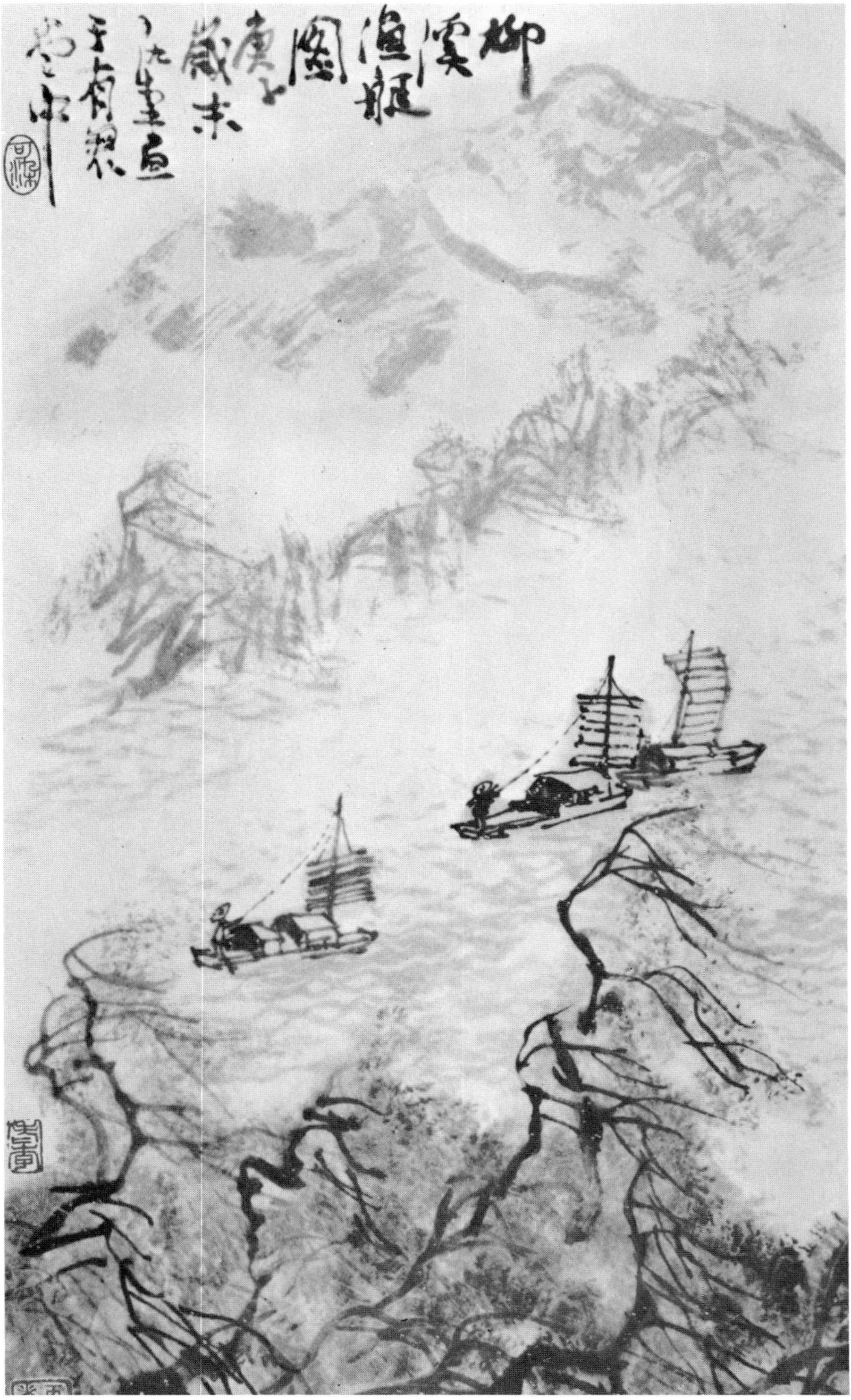

113. *Li K'o-jan (1907–   ): "Fishing Boats in the Willows."*
Ink and slight colour on paper.

painting on the Russian model, this doctrine has been applied much less consistently to landscape painting. Instead of being required to discard their conventional language of texture strokes (*ts'un*)—learned from manuals such as *The Mustard Seed Garden*—artists are encouraged to go into the mountains to *check* their *ts'un* against nature itself. Here is Ch'ien Sung-yen, who painted the delightful *Tavern in North Shansi* (Plate 114) describing the kind of experience that led him to reform his technique: "It was on Mount Hua-shan that I saw for the first time a real specimen of 'lotus-leaf wrinkes' (*ts'un*). The ancients did not concoct these 'wrinkles' out of their imagination, but from the need to represent what they saw in real life. Later artists, however, copied these 'wrinkles' slavishly and did not look around them to study nature, so that gradually these 'wrinkles' no longer represented the real thing. It is correct to carry on tradition, but this should be linked with close observation of reality around us. As soon as I saw Mount Hua-shan I realised that the 'lotus-leaf wrinkles' as shown in painting manuals have lost their authenticity; they should be refashioned by checking against the rocks of Hua-shan."*

By revising their conventional language rather than abandoning it, this generation of artists has ensured that the time-honored way of going about painting landscapes has not been sacrificed to Western, still less to socialist, realism. In doing so, these painters have provided their followers with a new, ready-made vocabulary, so that they need never, in theory, bother to look at the rocks and trees again. But those who decide these matters, including presumably some of the artists themselves, are aware of this danger, and painters are encouraged to spend as much time as they can away from the studio, out in the countryside, integrating with the masses and "checking their *ts'un*," as they put it.

Do they in fact have any choice at all? Is there no protest against what often appears to the Western observer to be an iron regimentation of the arts? What if they want to do something quite different? Since the Hundred Flowers Movement of 1957–58 came down so hard on dissenters, there has been little dissent. But a more subtle and irresistible controlling force than official disapproval or China's cultural chauvinism is an appeal to the artist's conscience. If he demands freedom to follow wherever his creative urge may lead him, claiming that only thus can he fulfill himself and so best serve his country, the answer comes back: "Who are you to demand things for yourself? Every child in China is taught to put others first; why should you artists be any different? There are no specially gifted people: all can fulfill themselves and serve society

**Ibid.*, p. 107.

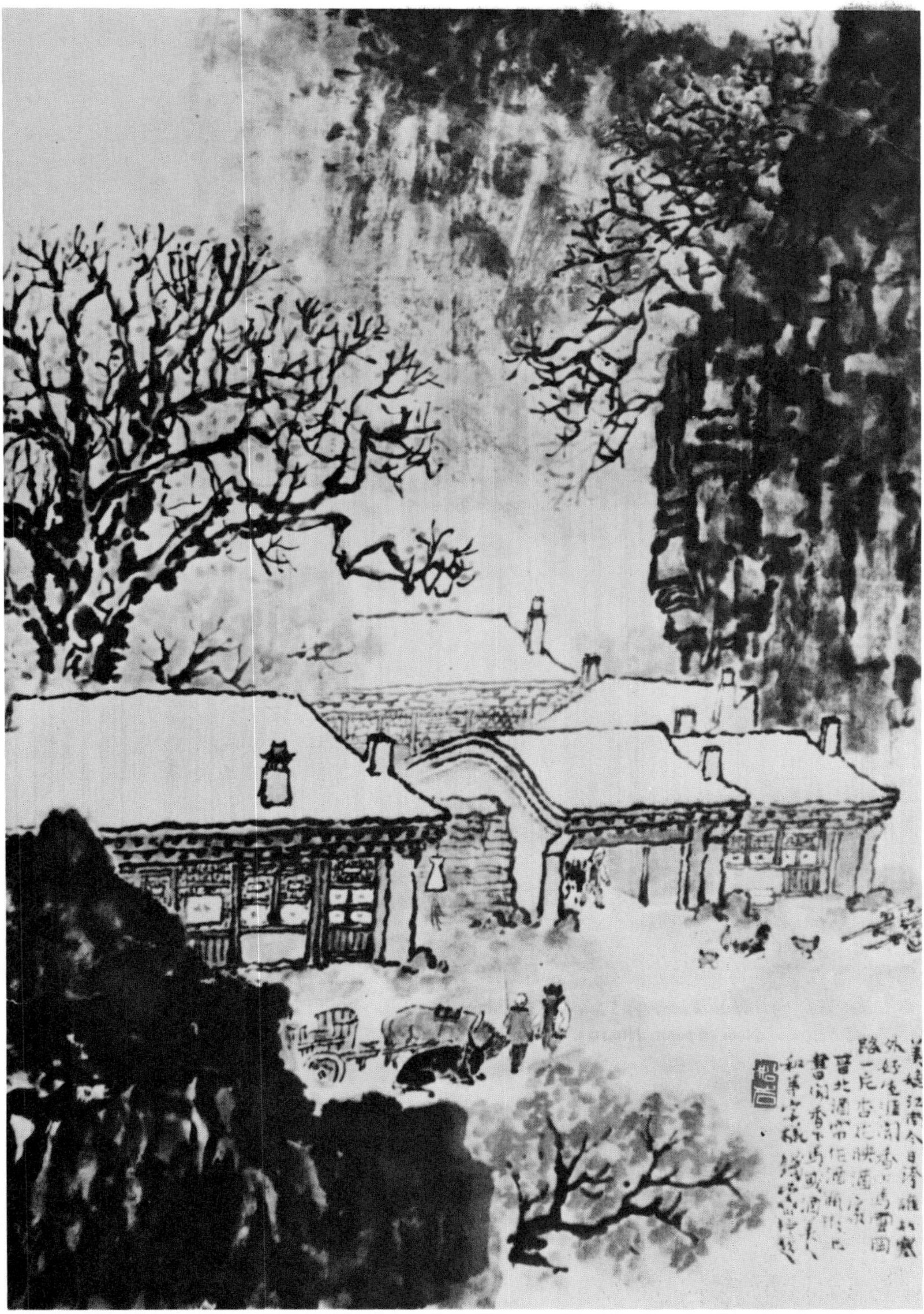

114. Ch'ien Sung-yen (1898–   ): "Tavern in North Shansi, on the road to Yunkang." Ink and colour on paper.

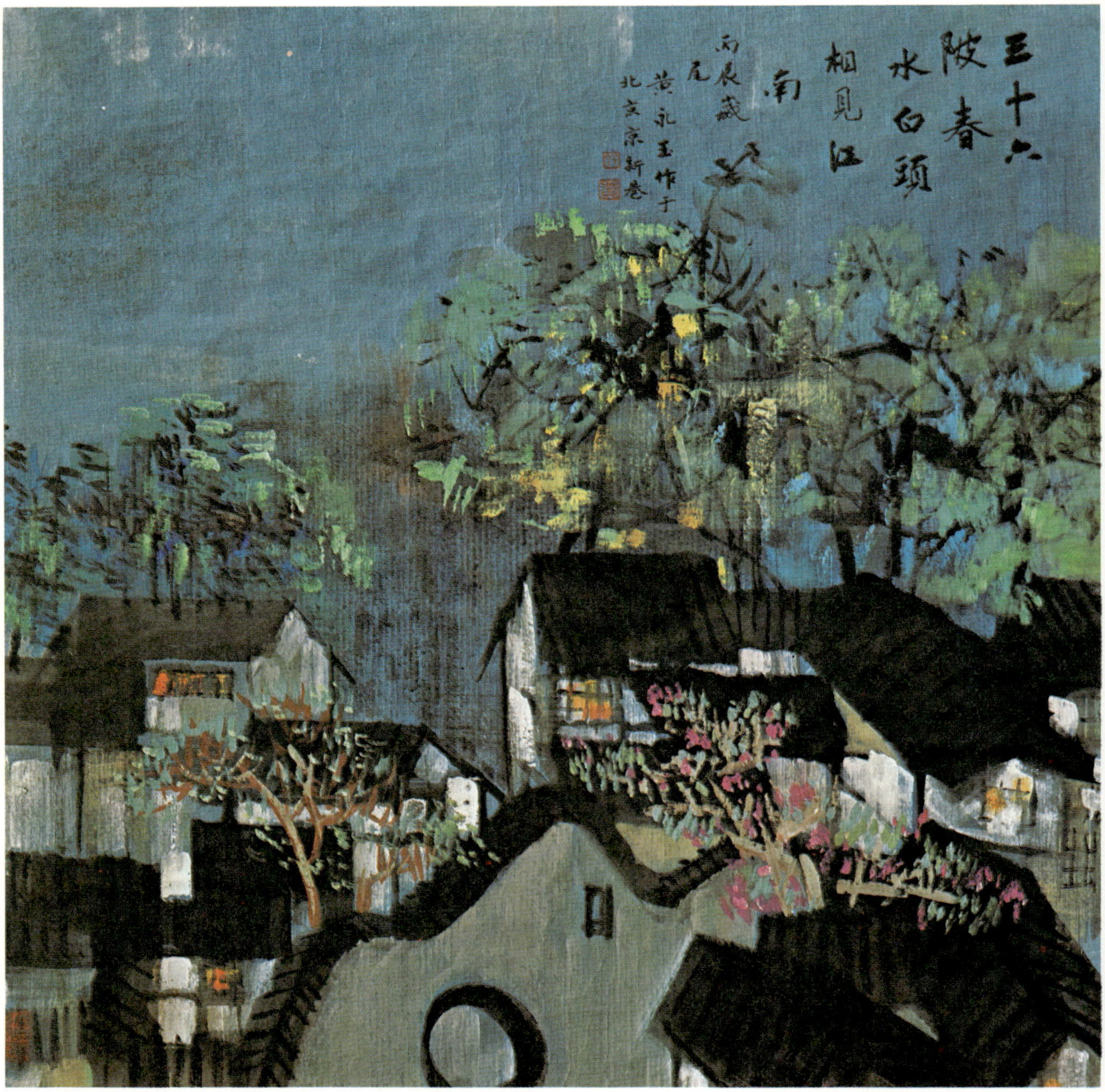

115. Huang Yung-yü (twentieth century): "Southern Landscape," 1976. Ink and mineral colour on paper. Ht. 103.5 cm. Private collection.

if they only have the will. To carry manure is just as good a way as to paint pictures."

Who, faced with this choice, could refuse?—especially since the vast majority of the Chinese people, including many of the artists themselves, appear to believe that the achievements of the Communist regime justify the demands that the government and the party make on every citizen equally. I do not want to paint too rosy a picture. In spite of what I have said, there have been many frustrated artists and writers, particularly during the Great Leap Forward and the Cultural Revolution. The pressure on the artists reached its peak in the mid-1970's, when Chou En-lai was dying of cancer and no longer able to protect them from the fanatical Chiang Ch'ing and her "Gang of Four". In visits to China in 1973 and 1975 I saw no art that was not propagandistic or didactic in purpose, saw no traditional drama, heard no foreign music; if the arts were experimental at all, it was in a strictly technical sense. Held to the level that the masses could understand—and Chiang Ch'ing, it is said, despised the masses—the arts took no effort of the imagination to grasp, presented no challenge to the mind.

In October 1976 Chiang Ch'ing fell from power and the Gang of Four fell with her. At once the clouds began to lift. Artists who had been hounded, disgraced, even imprisoned at her command emerged from obscurity, and soon the works of Lin Feng-mien, Wu Tso-jen, Li K'o-jan, Ch'ien Sung-yen—often quite free of any discernible ideological content—were being exhibited and published once more. One of the outstanding younger artists was Huang Yung-yü, who during his period of disgrace and confinement had continued, in defiance of Chiang Ch'ing's agents, to paint in his own highly original style. Within a short time of Chiang Ch'ing's eclipse, he was loaded with commissions, from mosaics and wall paintings to an official woodcut portrait of Chou En-lai. Meanwhile, in a burst of joy and freedom he produced, for his own pleasure and that of his friends, a series of paintings more free and original than any that have been seen in China since 1949. One of these, illustrated in Plate 115, is a southern landscape that Huang Yung-yü sent to us, since my wife is from South China. The strong line, the freedom of design, the vibrant colour splashed onto the coarse paper—all reveal a man painting in a sudden surge of exhilaration such as had inspired the great Individualists of the past.

When, after the death of Mao Tse-tung in 1976, a mausoleum was constructed in T'ien-an-men Square in Peking, it was Huang Yung-yü who designed the vast tapestry that covers the wall behind the marble figure of the Founder of the People's Republic. Unlike the obviously symbolic landscapes that decorate most public buildings, Huang Yung-yü's work contains no figures, no red flags, no electric pylons, no evidence of the transformation of the land under socialism. It is not a propaganda painting at all, but a panorama of mountains and valleys, forests and streams open to the sky—vast, quietly breathing, profoundly peaceful. Thus, when it comes to the expression of their deepest and most universal feelings, do the Chinese turn, now as always, to nature as the repository not only of beauty and truth but of meaning and value.

It was for this reason that, at the beginning of this book, I suggested that of all the great Western critics, it was Ruskin who would have best responded to Chinese landscape painting. He would have understood the rival claims in Chinese cultural history of ethics and aesthetics, of society and art, for this is precisely the conflict that Ruskin himself wrestled with and in the end found it beyond his power to resolve. "The pity is," Kenneth Clark said of his last Slade lectures, "that Ruskin did not content himself with those realms of mental achievement in which sensibility is supreme. But this he was prevented from doing by his conscience. And this leads me to a more honourable reason for the incoherence of his Oxford lectures on art, that by this time he did not really want to talk about art at all."* In our society, it seems, we have to make this choice: to talk about art, or to talk about ethics. We could once speak of both in the same breath; but that time, when beauty was truth, truth beauty, is long forgotten. Does this not point to a fragmentation, a sickness even, in our society? To Ruskin, as to the Chinese, this question could have but one possible answer.

Although it often wears a Maoist dress, China's present insistence on the ethical function of landscape painting is not the result of the Communist victory of 1949. When Tsung Ping in the fourth century wrote of landscape painting as a spiritually cleansing activity; when the great landscape masters of T'ang and Sung showed that it was a path to wisdom and understanding: when the poet Su Tung-p'o said that a man's painting was a witness to his moral worth; when Tung Ch'i-ch'ang revived and reinterpreted the ancient styles as a form of protest against political decay and moral corruption—each was expressing a view of the function of art in society that Ruskin himself put very directly when he said to one of his lecture audiences: "There is nothing I can tell you with more earnest desire that you should believe than this—that you will never love art well till you love what she mirrors better."

**Ruskin at Oxford: An Inaugural Lecture* (Oxford, 1947), p. 7.

The old Ruskin who wrote these words, and the young Ruskin who wrote the words that I shall end with, would perfectly have understood the aims of the Chinese landscape painters, from their first gropings toward expression nearly 2,000 years ago up to the landscapes of the last 25 years, so it is right that we should end, as we began, with him.

"Then came the question," he wrote to his old tutor Maurice Osborn in 1844 after completing the first volume of *Modern Painters*, "what is the real end of landscape art? And then the conviction that it had been entirely degraded and mistaken, that it might become an instrument of gigantic moral power, and that the demonstration of this high function, and the elevation of the careless sketch or conventional composition into the studied sermon and inspired poem, was an end worthy of my utmost labour—and no short expenditure of life."* The words might have come from the lips of any of the great Chinese painters and critics whose work has been the theme of this book.

*E. T. Cook and A. Wedderburn, eds., *The Works of John Ruskin* III (London, 1903), pp. 665–66.

A Chronological Chart of Chinese History

DYNASTY & CAPITAL		PAINTINGS & PAINTERS	
CH'IN AND HAN DYNASTIES (*221 B.C. to A.D. 220*) Capitals Ch'ang-an (Sian) and Loyang THREE KINGDOMS ERA (*220-280*) Capitals Loyang, Nanking, and Chengtu NORTHERN AND SOUTHERN DYNASTIES (*to 589*)	A.D. 200	Wall paintings in palaces, ancestral shrines, and tombs	
	300	Wang Hsi-chih (calligrapher) (*303-379*) Ku K'ai-chih (*ca. 344-406*)	
	400	Wang Wei (*d. 443*)	Earliest Caves at Tunhuang
	500	Chang Seng-yu (*ca. 500-550*) Chan Tzu-ch'ien (*active ca. 580-620*)	
SUI AND T'ANG DYNASTIES (*581-906*) Capital Ch'ang-an	600	Li Ssu-hsün (*651-719?*)	
	700	Li Chao-tao (*active ca. 700-750*) Wang Wei (*699-761?*)	Tunhuang Cave 217
	800	Late T'ang Expressionists and Ink-flingers Beginning of Ch'an (Zen) Painting	
FIVE DYNASTIES ERA AND NORTHERN SUNG DYNASTY (*906-1127*) Capital Kaifeng	900	Ching Hao (*ca. 900-950*) Li Ch'eng (*d. 967*)	
	1000	Fan K'uan (*late 10th-early 11th cent.*)	
SOUTHERN SUNG DYNASTY (*1127-1279*) Capital Hangchow	1100	Kuo Hsi (*11th cent.*) Chang Tse-tuan (*late 11th-early 12th cent.*) Li T'ang (*ca. 1050-ca. 1130*)	
YÜAN DYNASTY (MONGOL) (*1264-1368*)	1200	Ma Yüan (*active 1190-1225*) Hsia Kuei (*active 1200-1230*) Mu-ch'i (*active mid-13th cent.*) Ch'ien Hsüan (*ca. 1235-after 1301*)	
MING DYNASTY (*1368-1644*) Capital Nanking, then Peking	1300	Chao Meng-fu (*1254-1322*) Huang Kung-wang (*1269-1354*) Wu Chen (*1280-1354*) Ni Tsan (*1301-1374*) Wang Meng (*ca. 1308-1385*)	
	1400	Tai Chin (*1388-1462*) Shen Chou (*1427-1509*) Wen Cheng-ming (*1470-1559*)	
	1500	Tung Ch'i-ch'ang (*1555-1636*)	
CH'ING DYNASTY (MANCHU) (*1644-1912*) Capital Peking	1600	Wang Shih-min (*1592-1680*) Hung-jen (*1610-1664*) Kung Hsien (*1620-1689*)	
	1700	Shih-t'ao (*1641-1710?*) Pa-ta Shan-jen (*1626-1705?*) Lang Shih-ning (Castiglione) (*1688-1766*) Hua Yen (*1682-1755?*) Chin Nung (*1687-1764*)	
	1800	Jen Po-nien (*1840-1896*)	
REPUBLIC (*1912-1949*) PEOPLE'S REPUBLIC (*1949-*)	1900	Ch'i Pai-shih (*1863-1957*) Hsü Pei-hung (*1895-1953*) Li K'o-jan (*b. 1907*)	

EVENTS IN CHINESE CIVILIZATION	SOME COMPARATIVE WESTERN DATES
Rise of Buddhism and Taoism	Pompeii (*buried 79*)
Period of North-South Division	Emperor Constantine (*d. 337*)
	Fall of Rome (*476*)
	Santa Sophia, Constantinople (*532-537*)
Court of Ming-huang Li Po Tu Fu An Lu-shan Rebellion (*755-763*)	
Proscription of Buddhism	Charlemagne (*d. 814*)
	Norman Conquest of Britain (*1066*)
Su Tung-p'o (poet and bamboo painter)	
Chu Hsi (Neo-Confucian philosopher)	Thomas Aquinas (*d. 1274*)
	Giotto (*d. 1337*)
Wang Yang-ming (philosopher)	Fall of Constantinople (*1453*)
Matteo Ricci arrives in Peking	Leonardo da Vinci (*d. 1519*) Michaelangelo (*d. 1564*)
	Rubens (*d. 1640*) N. Poussin (*d. 1665*)
	Gainsborough (*d. 1788*)
Taiping Rebellion	
	Cézanne (*d. 1906*)

Suggestions for Further Reading

Some long-superseded books are still worth reading for their historic interest, insight, or literary value. Among these are Ernest Fenollosa, *Epochs of Chinese and Japanese Art* (2 volumes, London, 1912); Laurence Binyon, *Painting in the Far East* (London, 1923); and Arthur Waley, *An Introduction to the Study of Chinese Painting* (London, 1923), based on Chinese and Japanese literary sources, and written with grace, economy, and wit.

The standard work of reference is Osvald Sirén, *Chinese Painting: Leading Masters and Principles* (7 volumes, London, 1956 and 1958). James Cahill, *Chinese Painting* (Lausanne, 1960), and Sherman E. Lee, *Chinese Landscape Painting* (Cleveland, Ohio, 1962), are both useful surveys. Laurence Sickman and A. C. Soper, *The Art and Architecture of China* (revised ed., London, 1968), and Michael Sullivan, *The Arts of China* (revised ed., Berkeley, Calif., 1977), both contain material on landscape painting.

Among books dealing with particular periods or artists are Richard Edwards, *The Field of Stones: A Study of the Art of Shen Chou* (Washington, D.C., 1962); Michael Sullivan, *The Birth of Landscape Painting in China* (London and Berkeley, Calif., 1962), *Chinese Landscape Painting, Volume II: The Sui and T'ang Dynasties* (forthcoming), and *Chinese Art in the Twentieth Century* (London and Berkeley, Calif., 1959); James Cahill, *Hills Beyond a River: Chinese Painting of the Yüan Dynasty, 1279–1368* (New York and Tokyo, 1976), and *Parting at the Shore: Chinese Painting of the Early and Middle Ming Dynasty, 1368–1580* (New York and Tokyo, 1978).

Books on Chinese aesthetics and connoisseurship include Robert van Gulik, *Chinese Pictorial Art as Viewed by the Connoisseur* (Rome, 1958); Osvald Sirén, *The Chinese on the Art of Painting* (Peking, 1937); Lin Yü-t'ang, *The Chinese Theory of Art: Translations from the Masters of Chinese Art* (London, 1967); Susan Bush, *The Chinese Literati on Painting: Su Shih (1037–1101) to Tung Ch'i-ch'ang (1555–1636)* (Cambridge, Mass., 1971); Michael Sullivan, *The Three Perfections: Chinese Painting, Poetry and Calligraphy* (London, 1974); and Christian F. Murck, ed., *Artists and Traditions: Uses of the Past in Chinese Culture* (Princeton, N.J., 1976).

Catalogues of important collections sometimes have introductions that sum up the results of recent scholarship or present the subject in a particularly illuminating way. Among these are Laurence Sickman, ed., *Chinese Calligraphy and Painting in the Collection of John M. Crawford, Jr.* (New York, 1962); Roderick Whitfield, *In Pursuit of Antiquity: Chinese Paintings of the Ming and Ch'ing Dynasties from the Collection of Mr. and Mrs. Earl Morse* (Princeton, N.J., 1969); Marilyn and Shen Fu, *Studies in Connoisseurship: Chinese Paintings from the Arthur M. Sackler Collection in New York and Princeton* (Princeton, N.J., 1973); and Chu-tsing Li, *A Thousand Peaks and Myriad Ravines: Chinese Paintings in the Charles A. Drenowatz Collection* (2 volumes, Ascona, Switzerland, 1974).

Index

Index

A Note About the Production of This Book

Symbols of Eternity *was typeset in Monotype Centaur and Arrighi by Mackenzie-Harris Corp. in San Francisco. Negatives for the black-and-white plates were supplied by Dharma Press in Emeryville, California, and Thomson Lithograph, Inc. in Palo Alto, California. The color separations were made by Southern Graphics, Inc. in Winston-Salem, North Carolina. The book was printed on Warren's 70-pound Patina and bound in Holliston Roxite cloth by Kingsport Press in Kingsport, Tennessee.*